METROPOLITAN MUSEUM
JOURNAL 50

METROPOLITAN MUSEUM
JOURNAL 50

VOLUME 50 / 2015

The Metropolitan Museum of Art
NEW YORK

Charles Antoine Coypel (French, 1694–1752). *François de Jullienne and His Wife*, 1743. Pastel, 39⅜ x 31½ in. (100 x 80 cm). The Metropolitan Museum of Art, Purchase, Mrs. Charles Wrightsman Gift, in honor of Annette de la Renta, 2011 (2011.84)

for Katharine Baetjer

WHO DEVOTED HERSELF TO THIS PUBLICATION

AND MADE COUNTLESS CONTRIBUTIONS

TO ITS SUCCESS

This publication is made possible by Marica and Jan Vilcek and by a gift from Assunta Sommella Peluso, Ada Peluso, and Romano I. Peluso, in memory of Ignazio Peluso.

The *Metropolitan Museum Journal* is published annually by The Metropolitan Museum of Art.

Mark Polizzotti, *Publisher and Editor in Chief*
Elizabeth L. Block, *Managing Editor*
Lucinda Hitchcock, *Designer*
Paul Booth, *Production Manager*
Ling Hu and Crystal Dombrow, *Image Acquisitions Associates*

The Editorial Board is especially grateful to Sarah McFadden for her work on several manuscripts.

Manuscripts submitted for the *Journal* and all correspondence concerning them should be sent to journalsubmissions@metmuseum.org. Guidelines for contributors are given on p. 8.

Published in association with the University of Chicago Press. Individual and institutional subscriptions are available worldwide. Please direct all subscription inquiries, back issue requests, and address changes to: University of Chicago Press, Journals Division, P. O. Box 37005, Chicago, IL 60637-0005, USA. Phone: (877) 705-1878 (U.S. and Canada) or (773) 753-3347 (international), fax: (877) 705-1879 (U.S. and Canada) or (773) 753-0811 (international), email: subscriptions@press.uchicago.edu, website: www.journals.uchicago.edu

ISBN 978-0-226-32950-5
(University of Chicago Press)
ISSN 0077-8958 (print)
ISSN 2169-3072 (online)

Library of Congress
Catalog Card Number: 68-28799

Typefaces: Calibre, Lyon, and Harriet
Printed on Creator Silk, 100 lb.
Separations by Professional Graphics, Inc., Rockford, Illinois
Printed and bound by Puritan Capital, Hollis, New Hampshire

Front cover illustration: Detail of El Greco (Domenikos Theotokopoulos; Greek, 1540/41–1614), *The Vision of Saint John (The Opening of the Fifth Seal)*, 1608–14. See fig. 15, p. 26.
Back cover illustration: Detail of El Greco, *A View of Toledo*, ca. 1599–1600. See fig. 1, p. 12.

Illustration on p. 2: Detail of *Mercury Changes Aglauros to Stone* from the *Story of Mercury and Herse*. Design, Italian, ca. 1540. Tapestry, Netherlandish, ca. 1570. See fig. 1, p. 148.

Contents

MANUSCRIPT GUIDELINES
FOR THE METROPOLITAN MUSEUM **JOURNAL**

The *Metropolitan Museum Journal* is issued annually by The Metropolitan Museum of Art. Its purpose is to publish original research on works in the Museum's collection. Articles are contributed by members of the Museum staff and other art historians and specialists. Submissions should be emailed to: journalsubmissions@metmuseum.org.

Manuscripts are peer-reviewed by the *Journal* Editorial Board, composed of members of the curatorial, conservation, and scientific departments.

To be considered for the following year's volume, an article must be submitted, complete including illustrations, by October 15.

Once an article is accepted for publication, the author will have the opportunity to review it after it has been edited and again after it has been laid out in pages. The honorarium for image costs is $300, and each author receives a copy of the *Journal* volume in which his or her article appears.

Manuscripts should be submitted as double-spaced Word files. In addition to the text, the manuscript must include endnotes, captions for illustrations, photograph credits, and a 200-word abstract. Each part of

the article should be in a separate file except the endnotes, which should be linked to and appear at the end of the text file.

For the style of captions and bibliographic references in endnotes, authors are referred to *The Metropolitan Museum of Art Guide to Editorial Procedures and Style*, which is available from the Museum's Editorial Department upon request, and to *The Chicago Manual of Style*. Please provide a list of all bibliographic citations that includes, for each title: full name(s) of author or authors; title and subtitle of book or article and periodical; place and date of publication; volume number, if any; and page, plate, and/or figure number(s). For citations in notes, please use only the last name(s) of the author or authors and the date of publication (e.g., Jones 1953, p. 65; Smith and Harding 2006, pp. 7–10, fig. 23).

When submitting manuscripts, authors should include a PDF of all illustrations. Please do not embed images within text documents. If the manuscript is accepted, the author is expected to provide publication-quality images as well as copyright permissions to reproduce them in both the print and electronic editions of the *Journal*. We require either digital scans of at least 300 dpi at 3,000 pixels wide,

color transparencies (preferably 8 x 10 in. but 4 x 6 in. is also acceptable), or glossy black-and-white photographs (preferably 8 x 10 in. with white borders) of good quality and in good condition.

In a separate Word file, please indicate the figure number, the picture's orientation, and any instructions for cropping. Reproductions of photographs or other illustrations in books should be accompanied by captions that include full bibliographic information.

The author of each article is responsible for obtaining all photographic material and reproduction rights.

ABBREVIATIONS
MMA The Metropolitan Museum of Art
MMAB *The Metropolitan Museum of Art Bulletin*
MMJ *Metropolitan Museum Journal*

Height precedes width and then depth in dimensions cited.

METROPOLITAN
MUSEUM
JOURNAL 50

That Walter's first love was seventeenth-century Dutch painting is well known. Not only was it his chosen field of study, but he felt a genuine affinity for the people and culture of the Netherlands and he wrote about the works of art of its golden age with extraordinary eloquence and passion. What distinguishes his 2007 catalogue *Dutch Paintings in The Metropolitan Museum of Art* from the 1984 collection catalogue devoted to Flemish painting is not so much the twenty-five years he devoted to its writing, but the quality of familiarity and personal engagement he brought to the individual works of art. Walter knew the topography of the Low Countries as well as he knew his native northeastern United States, and his writing about the land- and seascapes of Jan van Goyen and Salomon van Ruysdael is informed by personal memories. As he worked on the catalogue, the individual entries began to assume the form of mini-monographs that take the reader into the mind of the artist and the nature of his achievement. The catalogue is a landmark of its kind, its literary ambition taking it far beyond what one normally finds in a collection catalogue.

Walter's work on El Greco—the partial results of which are published here—is of a different character. Who would have thought that Walter harbored a fascination for Spain and its art, let alone that of the most visionary of the artists who worked there? The defining event in the history of the Dutch Republic was the Peace of Münster in 1648, whereby Philip IV acknowledged the independence of the seven northwestern provinces. From that point on, the two cultures—one a Catholic monarchy with a vast colonial empire, the other a small but enormously prosperous Protestant mercantile republic—diverged in every way. Dutch art was not collected by the Spanish: to this day the weakest part of the collections at the Prado is Dutch art. So how did Walter become fascinated with seventeenth-century Spanish

art, which in so many ways is the antithesis of Dutch art? He had, of course, been assigned responsibility at the Metropolitan for the exhibition of Francisco de Zurbarán, held in New York, Paris, and Madrid in 1987–88, and he had followed up this involvement with an article reconstructing the enormous multitiered altarpiece for the Carthusian monastery of Nuestra Señora de la Defensión, outside the city of Jerez de la Frontera. The main canvas from the altarpiece belongs to the Metropolitan, so in a way, that article marks his first incursion into the project he was working on at the time of his death. In any case, after completing the Dutch catalogue, it was suggested to him by Everett Fahy, then chairman of the Department of European Paintings, who knew of Walter's interest in Spanish art, that he consider working on a catalogue of the Spanish paintings. Walter launched himself into the project with his accustomed enthusiasm and zeal and set about learning Spanish, reading about Spanish history, and establishing contacts with the leading scholars. He never did anything by half measure.

When I succeeded Everett Fahy as chairman of the department, Walter and I discussed the project and how it might best be pursued, given the complexity of issues relating to some of the paintings in the collection and the command of the material that would be necessary. He agreed that it would, for example, be foolhardy to undertake the cataloguing of the Museum's holdings of Goya, as Goya scholarship has raised questions that will require years of study and reflection and discussion before consensus is reached. One might have thought that he would have wanted to focus on Velázquez, since he had already written about the equestrian portrait of Don Gaspar de Guzmán (1587–1645), count-duke of Olivares, in an article he coauthored in 1981 and in his book *The Royal Horse and Rider: Painting, Sculpture, and Horsemanship 1500–1800*, published in 1990. To my surprise, he wished to begin with El Greco. As it happens, I had written entries for the Metropolitan's paintings on the occasion of the El Greco exhibition that was held in New York and London in 2003–4, and I mistakenly thought there was little left to be done. What I did not grasp was that Walter's detailed interpretation of contracts (in the case of the *The Vision of Saint John*), his reading of topography (in the case of the *View of Toledo*), and his persistent pursuit of issues of ownership and his analysis of a key inventory (in the case of *Cardinal Fernando Niño de Guevara*) would result in fundamentally new insights.

During the years Walter worked on his El Greco entries, emphasis in the department (and, indeed, the Museum) shifted from published to online cataloguing. Scholarship is a constantly evolving enterprise. The discovery of a new document, the appearance of a new piece of information or work of art, or the asking of a question no one had bothered with earlier—all these things can fundamentally change our analysis and understanding of a work of art. Online cataloguing—rather than an online publication—allows entries to be updated and thus to evolve with scholarship and reflect new information and ideas. By contrast, a published catalogue represents the view of the author at the point of time when the catalogue goes to press, taking its fixed place in the historiography of scholarship until the appearance of a revised edition.

Walter was a book person, and he very much saw his own work as situated in a specific moment of time. Moreover, he loved the form of the scholarly catalogue, with the opportunity it provided to argue at length his point of view or refute the position of another scholar without worrying about the interests of the reader, the assumption of the scholarly catalogue being that it is for fellow scholars rather than the potentially broader audience of an online catalogue. He was, moreover, a master of the extended footnote, which gave him the possibility to digress on matters he thought germane to his subject. So while he was content that the efforts of his research should be incorporated into the online cataloguing effort of the Department of European Paintings, he always hoped his work would be published as he had initially intended. We do so here, *arti et amicitiae*.

KEITH CHRISTIANSEN
John Pope-Hennessy Chairman,
Department of European Paintings,
The Metropolitan Museum of Art

The manuscripts were edited by Katharine Baetjer, Curator, Department of European Paintings, with research assistance by Jennifer Meagher.

fig. 1 El Greco (Domenikos Theotokopoulos; Greek, 1540/41–1614).
A View of Toledo, ca. 1599–1600.
Oil on canvas, 47¾ × 42¾ in. (121.3 ×
108.6 cm). Signed (lower right):

δομήνικος θεοτοκόπουλος ἐποίει
(*Domenikos Theotokopoulos made*).
The Metropolitan Museum of Art, H. O.
Havemeyer Collection, Bequest of Mrs.
H. O. Havemeyer, 1929 (29.100.6)

WALTER LIEDTKE

Three Paintings by El Greco

A View of Toledo, ca. 1599–1600

This most famous of all Spanish landscapes and cityscapes was probably painted shortly before 1600, by which time El Greco had been working in Toledo for more than twenty years (fig. 1). The subject is exceptional in his oeuvre, so that the interests of a patron or other special circumstances might be expected to account for his diversion from a steady production of religious pictures and portraits. The possibility of a commission must be weighed against that of the canvas having remained in the artist's studio: "two landscapes of Toledo" are listed both in the 1614 inventory of the artist's estate and in the 1621 inventory of his son, Jorge Manuel.[1] The painting could also be the "landscape of Toledo [seen] toward the Alcántara Bridge" in the 1629 inventory of the estate of El Greco's important patron Pedro Salazar de Mendoza (ca. 1550–1629).[2]

fig. 2 El Greco, *View and Plan of Toledo*, ca. 1600–1610. Oil on canvas, 52 × 89¾ in. (132 × 228 cm). Museo del Greco, Toledo (CE00014)

Another work listed in the Salazar inventory is a "picture of the city of Toledo with its plan," which most likely refers to the well-known *View and Plan of Toledo* (fig. 2).[3] That painting is probably not identical with the one called "a Toledo" in the 1614 and 1621 inventories, since the measurements given in 1621, "dos baras de largo y bara 1 cuarto de alto," or about 41 × 66⅛ inches (104 × 168 cm), fall nearly 11 inches (28 cm) short in height and nearly 24 inches (60 cm) short in width, compared with a canvas that now measures 52 × 89¾ inches (132 × 228 cm). Furthermore, the composition and several motifs of the *View and Plan* are so uncommon that one would expect it to have been commissioned and, additionally, not to have been described simply as "a Toledo."

In the early literature of El Greco the *View of Toledo* was usually considered to date from after 1600 or from the last ten years of the artist's life, 1604 to 1614, evidently on stylistic grounds. Harold Wethey, by contrast, places the picture about 1595–1600, mainly because a "similar panorama" is included in the background of El Greco's *Saint Joseph and the Christ Child*, one of three canvases executed between late 1597 and 1599 for the Capilla de San José in Toledo (where the painting of the name saint remains).[4] The divided cityscape in the *Saint Joseph* is similar to the *View of Toledo* in that major landmarks, such as the cathedral's tower, the Alcázar (royal palace), a tall Renaissance palace in front of the Alcázar, and other motifs are (as described below) arranged in

ways that depart conspicuously from the actual cityscape as it would have appeared from a vantage point looking south. This strongly supports the hypothesis that the *View of Toledo* or a version of it served as a model for the views of Toledo (or motifs reminiscent of Toledo) in the altarpiece for the Capilla de San José, and in later works.[5]

The *View and Plan of Toledo* is dated by Wethey and most later scholars to the last four or five years of El Greco's life. Wethey associates the wide canvas with the artist's work from 1608 to 1614 on three altarpieces (including *The Vision of Saint John*; see fig. 15) for the Hospital de Tavera in Toledo (Hospital of Saint John the Baptist Outside the Walls). Salazar de Mendoza, who was the institution's administrator, apparently owned the picture, in which the hospital itself is shown floating on a cloud in the center foreground.[6] However, El Greco's work for Salazar dates back to 1595, when he commissioned from the artist a wooden tabernacle with carved figures for the hospital's chapel.[7] The costume of the young man holding the plan in the painting is consistent with a date of about 1600.[8]

In any case, Salazar's interest in the historical importance of Toledo, as well as in maps, landscapes, and city views (as revealed by the inventory of his estate), may have inspired El Greco to paint both cityscapes, as Jonathan Brown and Richard Kagan have proposed.[9] Whatever their chronology, the two pictures

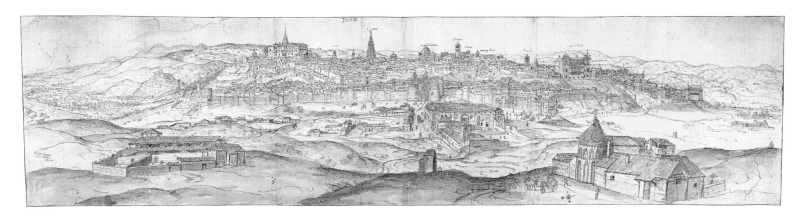

fig. 3 Anton van den Wyngaerde (Flemish, 1525–1571). *View of Toledo Looking South*, 1563. Pen and brown ink and brown wash on paper, 16½ × 42⅜ in. (42 × 107.5 cm). Österreichische Nationalbibliothek, Vienna (MS Min. 41, fol. 19)

have been considered to represent rather different approaches to the subject, the one topographical (except for obvious embellishments) and the other emblematic.[10]

Comparing El Greco's *View and Plan* with the large topographical drawing of Toledo made in 1563 by Anton van den Wyngaerde (1525–1571) as part of a grand project for Philip II (fig. 3), it is clear that not only the painting's symbolic elements—the river god to the lower left, the Hospital de Tavera on a cloud, and the Virgin with angels and Saint Ildefonso's chasuble floating in the sky—but also its sweeping panorama of Toledo represent an interpretive approach.[11] The *View of Toledo*, however, goes much further in reducing and modifying the cityscape: no more than a third of the city is shown high on a verdant hill, with the cathedral tower (now resembling a French Gothic spire) placed not to the right but to the left of the Alcázar, at the top of a precipitous cascade of buildings descending to the Alcántara Bridge over the Tagus River. The outer walls and lower neighborhoods of the city have been eliminated, and one of the inner walls has been reduced to a brown band that curves like a ribbon to the right of the bridge.

Just below the Alcázar, El Greco includes a four-story palace with an arcade on the top floor.[12] The location and the building's height on the north side recall the Hospital de Santa Cruz, but otherwise there is little resemblance to that complex of the early 1500s. In style El Greco's structure is consistent with his remodeling of the Alcázar, and with the north facade of the most modern palace in Toledo, the Casa de Vargas, as seen to the far right in Van den Wyngaerde's view. In the *View and Plan* the Casa de Vargas (center right in fig. 2) is revised in the same manner, as if the taste for the Italian Mannerist architect Sebastiano Serlio (1475–1554) that the artist shared with Diego de Vargas's architect, Francisco de Villalpando (ca. 1510–ca. 1561), gave him license to suggest that new construction in Toledo was au courant with that in Italy.[13]

While these monuments testify to Toledo's modernity, others remind one of the city's importance in the past. The Roman bridge of Alcántara (*al-Qantara* in Arabic) was built between A.D. 104 and 106 by order of Emperor Trajan. The Castillo de San Servando, on the hill to the left, was founded as a monastery a few years after Alfonso VI of Castile and León, in 1085, took Toledo from the Moors; in the late 1300s it was transformed into a castle to protect the bridge from attack. The late medieval Alcázar, which had been built on the site of an Islamic castle, was remodeled beginning in 1543 by the Serlio-inspired architect Alonso de Covarrubias (1488–1570), for Charles V and Philip II.

The building or complex on the cloudlike mound to the left has been variously interpreted. Brown and Kagan suggest that this seemingly imaginary or misplaced motif may have been inserted because of its historical significance, and that the most likely identification would be with the long-lost Agaliense monastery to which the patron saint of Toledo, Ildefonso (607–667), went on a retreat as a youth.[14] However, the presence of figures on the mound and on the nearby pathway to the bridge, as well as the structure's open doorways, could indicate that this site outside the city walls actually existed about 1600 and was accessible to lay Toledans. If so, El Greco may have had in mind the Shrine of San Ildefonso or the neighboring Abbey of Santa Leocadia, which are seen just above the Monastery of San Bartolomé de la Vega to the far right in Van den Wyngaerde's drawing. These two famous saints of Toledo (Leocadia died there about 304) were intensely venerated in the late sixteenth century.[15] Perhaps, like the Hospital de Tavera in the *View and Plan*, the shrine or, more likely, the abbey is depicted here "in the form of a model and moved from its place," to quote the painter's explanation of the floating structure in the panoramic view.[16] As recorded by Van den Wyngaerde, there was no such cluster of buildings on the plain, where the Huerta del Rey

(King's Garden) flourished, partly with the help of large irrigation wheels.

To the lower right in the *View of Toledo*, what appears to be a raised sluiceway recedes into the trees. Some scholars have speculated that this motif refers to the Artificio de Juanelo, the huge mechanical system for bringing water from the Tagus River up to the Alcázar built in the 1560s by the Italian-Spanish engineer, mathematician, and clockmaker Gianello Torriano (Juanelo Turriano).[17] El Greco would have known Torriano's second device, which was completed in 1581 and operated for the next half century. However, the complicated apparatus was housed in a sequence of masonry chambers on the other side of the Alcántara Bridge, and it seems highly improbable that a contemporary viewer of the picture would have taken El Greco's rudimentary contraption as a reminder of the scientific marvel. Brown and Kagan, by contrast, wonder if such a sluiceway might have been connected with a cloth or "fulling" mill.[18] Some support for this view could be found in the group of figures with what are most likely bolts of white cloth laid on the ground near the retaining wall beneath the sluiceway.[19] A reference to cloth manufacture would be appropriate since this was Toledo's leading industry. At the same time, these figures, others near the water's edge—apparently fishing—and the sluiceway could also be taken together as signs of the river's importance to daily life in the city. A related question is whether the sky promises rain, as some writers have assumed.[20] Rain would have been regarded during this period as a gift from God, but it is also possible that the dark background to the skyline and the dramatic play of clouds were intended solely as expressive elements in the overall design.[21]

It is obvious from Van den Wyngaerde's drawing that El Greco exaggerated the city's ascent above the surrounding landscape, especially as seen from the north. Precedents for this kind of enhancement and the exaggeration of key motifs are fairly common in Byzantine and late medieval cityscapes.[22] The painter's artistic origins (unlike Van den Wyngaerde's) predisposed him to the "emblematic" approach, but for an actual model he may have turned to a plate in Georg Braun and Franz Hogenberg's new *Civitates Orbis Terrarum* (Cologne, 1572–1618), several volumes of which were owned by Salazar.[23]

In this famous atlas the fidelity of the cityscapes to their actual topography varies greatly, depending on their sources. The view of Toledo in volume 1 (1572; fig. 4) is based on a drawing recorded at the site in the mid-1560s by the meticulous Fleming Joris Hoefnagel (1542–1601).[24] It provides a detailed record of the major monuments and many houses of Toledo, and the topography is close to that which one would see standing on high ground looking north. (El Greco's view is taken from the opposite side.) When Hogenberg engraved the same view (with a new border inscribed "Depingebat Georgius Hoefnaglius Ao 1566") for publication in volume 5 (ca. 1598), he considerably raised the profile of the city in both a literal and a figurative sense (fig. 5).[25] The proportions of the city proper are now (height to width) one to three rather than one to four; the major buildings have been enlarged; the lesser public buildings (including several churches) and all the houses have been simplified; and the cathedral and the Alcázar are reproduced in large, more detailed images in the lower corners of the plate.

In terms of topography, the circa 1598 Hogenberg view of Toledo looking north could have been of little use to El Greco. There are, however, some surprising similarities in composition between the Museum's painting and the print. The fact that the cathedral (top center in the engraving) is seen left of the Alcázar (on the upper right) is of interest. But perhaps more intriguing is the jagged descent of towers and buildings to the left in the circa 1598 Hogenberg view (fig. 5; compare fig. 1), below which broad grassy areas are embraced by the Tagus (which wraps around the city on the south side but not on the north). A spillway with a pair of small buildings (presumably mills) spans the river to the lower left, where bolts of cloth are being laid out at the water's edge (fig. 6). These motifs (which do not go back to the plate of 1572) were apparently inserted by Hogenberg, and adopted by El Greco.

The second view of Toledo in Braun and Hogenberg's atlas (which El Greco could not have seen before 1598) may have given the painter a point of departure for basic elements of his design and a few motifs, but the publication would have been more important to him (and to Salazar) for the idea of celebrating great cities in pictorial terms. This view, with its inset views labeled *Templum Archiepiscopat* and *Palatium Regium*, is symbolic of princely or noble accomplishment. El Greco perhaps recalled the two large views of the town of Caprarola, seen in profile against hilly landscapes and sky, that Federico Zuccaro painted in 1567 as part of the fresco decorations in the Villa Farnese at Caprarola, where other city views and the grand Sala dei Mappamondi (Hall of World Maps) surveyed Farnese territories and victories.[26] Contemporary accounts record that in two of Philip II's

palaces, El Pardo in Madrid (burned in 1604) and the Alcázar in Madrid (burned in 1734), views of cities by Van den Wyngaerde or a close associate were on display. At the royal palace in Madrid these paintings included prospects of Toledo and at least a dozen other Spanish cities.[27]

As an independent painting and in almost every other respect, the *View of Toledo* remains an exceptional work in the history of Spanish art and in the long history of cityscapes. El Greco's style, employed to spiritual and visionary effect in his religious pictures, seems not merely dramatic but spectacular when applied to a nominally topographical subject like this one.[28] The artist places the essential and most significant monuments of Toledo on a summit between heaven and earth. A knowledgeable viewer of the time would have immediately recognized the cathedral and the Alcázar not only as paired signs of church and crown but also as reminders that the archbishop was primate of Spain and that Toledo was still considered the "Imperial City." The few other identifiable structures suffice to suggest fifteen hundred years of history, while the more modern buildings, the activity of minute figures, and the surprisingly lush landscape (with a repoussoir of urgent vegetation in the foreground) proclaim the city's vitality. The picture is less a "view" of Toledo than a vision, a dream, a revelation—like that of the New Jerusalem:

I saw a new heaven and a new earth.... And I John saw the holy city, new Jerusalem, coming down from God out of heaven (Rev. 21:1–2).

fig. 4 *View of Toledo Looking North*, in Georg Braun and Franz Hogenberg, *Civitates Orbis Terrarum* (1572–1618), vol. 1 (1572), pl. 4. Engraving

fig. 5 *View of Toledo Looking North*, in Georg Braun and Franz Hogenberg, *Civitates Orbis Terrarum* (1572–1618), vol. 5 (ca. 1598), pl. 15. Engraving

fig. 6 Detail of fig. 5; compare with the foreground in El Greco's *View of Toledo* (fig. 1)

fig. 7 El Greco. *Cardinal Fernando Niño de Guevara*, ca. 1600. Oil on canvas, 67¼ × 42½ in. (170.8 × 108 cm). Signed lower center: δομη-νϊκος θεοτοκόπουλος ἐποίει (*Domenikos Theotokopoulus made*). The Metropolitan Museum of Art, H. O. Havemeyer Collection, Bequest of Mrs. H. O. Havemeyer, 1929 (29.100.5)

Cardinal Fernando Niño de Guevara, ca. 1600

This intense portrait, one of the finest and most ambitious painted by El Greco, was purchased by Henry and Louisine Havemeyer in Paris on June 1, 1904 (fig. 7). Best known for their pioneering role in bringing French Impressionist paintings to America, with the encouragement of their adviser and friend the painter Mary Cassatt, the Havemeyers would become important benefactors of The Metropolitan Museum of Art. Their growing interest, beginning in the mid-1880s, in old master paintings (portraits by Bronzino, Rembrandt, and Goya were already in their collection before they bought this one) certainly influenced their appreciation of El Greco, especially his portraits. On their first trip to Spain, in 1901, they met with the El Greco scholar Manuel Cossío, went to Toledo to see paintings by the artist in their original settings, and visited private collections to see and possibly purchase works by El Greco, as well as by Velázquez and Goya. In April 1901 the dealer Joseph Wicht showed Cassatt the present picture, then in the Oñate Palace, Madrid, which effectively began a three-year campaign by the Havemeyers to acquire it. This was achieved by their favorite dealer, Paul Durand-Ruel, who was based in Paris, on trips to Madrid in 1903 and 1904.[1]

THE SUBJECT

The sitter is Fernando Niño de Guevara (1541–1609), a Toledo nobleman whose important ecclesiastical offices in Spain were gained through the favor of Philip II and Philip III.[2] He was the third child of Rodrigo Niño Zapata, Señor (Lord) de Añover y de Lorqui (d. 1558), and Teresa de Guevara.[3] Niño de Guevara studied canon law at the University of Alcalá de Henares, and between 1567 and 1571 earned a doctorate in both canon and civil law at the University of Salamanca.

In the 1570s he served as *oidor* (judge or auditor) in the Chancellery of Valladolid and as archdeacon of the Cathedral of Cuenca. From 1580 he was a member of the Royal Council of Castile and served also on the Council of the Inquisition, most prominently, from 1584, as president of the Chancellery of Granada. In 1596, with the support of Philip II, Niño de Guevara was created cardinal and went to Rome for about three years.[4] In El Greco's portrait the sitter wears a cardinal's biretta, mozzetta, and lace-trimmed rochet.

Niño de Guevara was nominated as inquisitor general of Spain in April 1599; he returned from Rome in November and assumed the office on December 23. His service to the young Philip III (r. 1598–1621) lasted only about two years, since the king's favorite, the duke of Lerma, was determined to place his own uncle in the cardinal's position. To that end, evidently, Niño de Guevara was named archbishop of Seville, on April 30, 1601. The appointment required residence in the diocese, which began officially with a public entry into Seville on December 31, 1601. Niño de Guevara resigned as inquisitor general early in 1602; he remained archbishop of Seville until his death on January 8, 1609.[5]

Most scholars date the Metropolitan's picture either to 1600, when Niño de Guevara (then aged about fifty-nine) was in Toledo as inquisitor general, or to 1601, when he stopped at Toledo en route to Seville. The sitting more likely occurred in 1600, considering that the cardinal was in Toledo for several weeks during March and April, together with the king and queen and members of the court. Philip III and Margarita of Austria entered the city on March 2, 1600, and a few days later attended an *auto public general* (auto-da-fé), at which the king vowed to protect the Holy Office and forty-six transgressors were condemned to death.

fig. 8 Artist unknown. *Cardinal Bernardo de Sandoval y Rojas*, 1599. Engraving. Biblioteca Nacional, Madrid

fig. 9 Luis Tristán (Spanish, 1586–1624). *Cardinal-Archbishop Bernardo de Sandoval y Rojas*, 1618–19. Oil on canvas, 31½ × 21¼ in. (80 × 54 cm). Toledo Cathedral

Niño de Guevara's notoriety as a persecutor has been related by many critics to the vulturine pose and stare of the sitter in El Greco's portrait. Jonathan Brown and Dawson Carr, however, have suggested that he is instead Lerma's mild-mannered uncle Bernardo de Sandoval y Rojas (1546–1618), who was created cardinal-priest on March 3, 1599, and appointed archbishop of Toledo on April 19 of the same year.[6] This hypothesis, based on various conjectures and assumptions, may be discounted mainly because the resemblance between El Greco's sitter and Sandoval, as he appears in an engraving (1599) and in a posthumous portrait by Luis Tristán (1618–19), is not nearly as close as has been claimed, and because further provenance research strongly supports the identification with Niño de Guevara.[7]

In the engraving (fig. 8), which was probably made in Rome in 1599, the fifty-three-year-old Sandoval appears younger and fuller in the face than El Greco's figure.[8] His glance is direct and his expression congenial; this seems to be the Sandoval known for his charity, liberal reforms, and literary interests. His dark beard extends from thick sideburns and follows his jawline (the face below the cheekbones is shaded but bare) down to the squared-off beard. The mustache is rounded downward, rather as the eyebrows are arched. All these features reappear in Tristán's much later

portrait of Sandoval as archbishop (fig. 9), where parts of the beard are now gray and the face has become thinner. But there is still little resemblance to the face that El Greco painted, with its straight brows, thin gray hair at the temples, a heavier beard covering half the cheeks as well as the jawline, a narrower nose, a mustache angled past the corners of a wider mouth, and a nearly white goatee neatly tapered to a point.[9] The apparently thick eyeglasses are secured by strings hooked behind the ears, which suggests that the sitter depended on these "cord-spectacles" not only for reading but for vision in general.[10] The type was modern and fashionable in Spain, suggesting erudition, although glasses would not have been included in a such a portrait unless they were distinctive of the sitter's actual appearance. Glasses are not worn by Sandoval in the two conventional portraits of him, or in Tristán's painting of 1618, *Cardinal-Archbishop Bernardo de Sandoval y Rojas with Saint Bernardo* (Convento de San Clemente, Toledo), where the bareheaded patron reveals very little resemblance to the cardinal painted by El Greco.[11]

EARLY HISTORY

The provenance of the Museum's picture, as revealed by recent research, also supports the identification of the sitter with Niño de Guevara. As noted by Keith Christiansen in 2003, the portrait may be traced back from the Oñate collection through the Condes de Añover to Pedro Lasso de la Vega Niño y Guzmán (1559–1637), 1st Conde de los Arcos, and Señor de Cuerva, Batres y Añover de Tormes. Pedro Lasso (often called Arcos in the literature) had been a supporter of El Greco since at least 1596, when he served as one of the *fiadores* (bondsmen) for the artist in his contract for the great altarpiece he made for the Colegio de Doña Maria de Aragon in Madrid.[12]

The Conde de los Arcos was Niño de Guevara's nephew and "the one titled nobleman known to have belonged to El Greco's circle in Toledo."[13] At the time of his death, in 1637, he owned about seven or eight paintings by El Greco, probably including the *View of Toledo* (see fig. 1), and the *Allegory of the Camaldolese Order* (Instituto Valencia de Don Juan, Madrid), which he must have commissioned about 1599.[14] Richard Kagan suggests that the Conde de los Arcos may have recommended El Greco to his uncle when he was visiting his native city.[15]

The presumption that Niño de Guevara commissioned his own portrait would appear plausible, but it deserves closer examination. There is no known record of the picture having been in his possession or anywhere in Seville (for example, in the Archiepiscopal Palace or the cathedral). Pedro Lasso, one of his uncle's executors, acquired from the estate a "small picture of the Nativity . . . by the hand of Federico Zuccaro," but no work by El Greco appears to have come from the same source.[16] It seems likely that Niño de Guevara owned some devotional images and religious objects but did not collect works of art per se. Of course, portraits were a special case, often marking a new distinction, such as a noble title or ecclesiastical office. Nevertheless, portraits commissioned by the sitters themselves (except at court) were still a novelty in most Spanish cities; Kagan describes those by El Greco as a kind of social climbing on the part of his Toledo patrons.[17] That no other portrait, painted or engraved, dates from his lifetime could indicate that the inquisitor general saw no need to enhance his reputation through portraiture.[18]

A substantial body of circumstantial evidence suggests that Pedro Lasso not only owned the portrait in his later years but commissioned it in the first place. By 1600 he had been El Greco's patron for several years. His position at court, including his creation as Conde de los Arcos in 1599, must have been connected with Niño de Guevara's naming as inquisitor general in April of that year (nephews of Spanish churchmen were often strongly favored by their uncles, since they usually had no sons of their own). The display of such a grand portrait, which asserts the sitter's rank and power, may be regarded as a public gesture, assuming that the painting could have been seen in one of the count's residences, a family chapel, or an institution such as a church that he was known to support. In design and presentation the picture resembles a royal or papal portrait rather than the routine likenesses that were made to record (often in a standardized format) members of a family or a long line of clergymen.

Among the many works of art that Pedro Lasso collected and commissioned were family portraits and portraits of public figures, including famous churchmen and Spanish royalty. According to the inventory of pictures that the count had compiled (by the painter and appraiser Juan Bautista Maíno) from 1632 onward, most of the portraits were installed in the seigneurial castle at Batres, southwest of Madrid. In the *sala grande* could be found, in addition to "two medium-size [pictures] by Domenico Greco," the *Allegory of the Camaldolese Order* (mentioned above) and "a portrait of part of Toledo" (most likely the *View of Toledo*), and many other works of art, "forty-six half-length portraits of famous men of letters and arms, and some kinsmen of the lords of this house."[19]

The numerous religious works on display in the oratory included twelve paintings of the Apostles, an altarpiece depicting the Nativity "made in Venice," a painting of "Nuestra Señora de la Leche [i.e., nursing the Christ Child] de mano del griego" (possibly El Greco's *Holy Family* in the Hispanic Society, New York), and a *Saint Luke* by El Greco, as well as portraits of Saint Teresa of Avila (1515–1582), of Aldonza Niño (Pedro Lasso's mother, who was devoted to Saint Teresa), and of Francisco de Cogolludo (d. 1630), a revered Franciscan monk in the Royal Convent of San Gil in Madrid.[20]

Other rooms in the "casa y forteleza de Batres" featured portraits of the recent popes (and Spanish allies) Pius V (r. 1566–72) and Sixtus V (r. 1585–90), of Cardinal Diego de Espinosa (inquisitor general from 1566 until his death in 1572), and of Bishop Cornelio Musso (1511–1574), a prominent figure at the Council of Trent, known in Spain for his sermons condemning Muslims and Jews. Portraits of much earlier churchmen included those of Saint Gregory the Great (ca. 540–604), Saint Dominic (either Domingo de Silos [1000–1073] or Domingo Félix de Guzmán [1170–1221]), Saint Catherine of Siena (1347–1380), and the Catholic martyr Sir Thomas More (1478–1535). The many portraits of Spanish royalty at Batres are less relevant here, but they included sixteen of Spanish kings and queens.[21] A similar but less extensive group of royal portraits hung in Pedro Lasso's house in Madrid. Family portraits were also displayed in Madrid as well as at Batres.[22]

It is among a group of a dozen family portraits listed (probably by location) in Pedro Lasso's Madrid residence that we come across the first known record of the present portrait by El Greco:

> Un retrato del Cardl D. Ferdo Niño arcobispo de Sevilla. Inquisidor genl sentado en silla. en cien ducos (A portrait of Cardinal Don Fernando Niño archbishop of Seville [and] inquisitor general seated in a chair. [Valued] at 100 *ducados*)

No other portrait of a churchman is listed as in Madrid, whereas a good number were gathered at Batres and a few of those pictures represented prelates comparable to Niño de Guevara. However, Niño de Guevara was not only a prominent member of Pedro Lasso's family but also, like every other family member included in the count's portrait collection, a devoted servant of the crown. The family portraits in Madrid were listed immediately after all the royal portraits, perhaps because they were displayed in the same room. In any case, it appears that Pedro Lasso considered the proper place for the cardinal's portrait to have been at his residence in Madrid rather than at Batres, Cuerva, or Toledo.[23]

NIÑO DE GUEVARA'S FAMILY AS PATRONS OF THE CATHOLIC CHURCH

It is difficult to distinguish supporters of the church from supporters of the crown during this period of Spanish history, since the two institutions were so enmeshed at the social levels under discussion.[24] However, a few words on Niño de Guevara's family, specifically as supporters of convents and churches, may help to explain why they would have valued the portrait by El Greco and to address the question of the work's most likely whereabouts between its creation and its first known mention in 1632.

Two religious institutions were of particular interest to Niño de Guevara's siblings and their successors: the Hieronymite convent of San Pablo in Toledo and the parish church of Santiago Apóstol in Cuerva, near Toledo to the southwest. Niño de Guevara himself, his parents, and other forebears were buried in San Pablo's *capilla mayor*, which the convent sold to the family in 1583. Aldonza Niño de Guevara, the cardinal's sister and Pedro Lasso's mother, lived in the convent after her husband died in 1562, and three of her sisters were also secluded there: the nuns Isabel and Ana Niño and the widowed Costanza (from 1579). A portrait of Niño de Guevara, installed near his tomb monument, is recorded in the 1908 monograph on El Greco by Cossío, who considered it a copy of the present painting. But no such picture is mentioned in the various descriptions of the chapel that date from 1800 to 1890, and there is no evidence of any other family portrait ever having hung there.[25]

In 1585 Aldonza Niño, inspired by Teresa of Avila (who had died three years earlier), founded a convent of Discalced Carmelites (Nuestra Señora de la Encarnación) using family property at Cuerva. She served there as prioress until her death in 1604 and was buried in the adjoining church of Santiago Apóstol, the construction and renovation of which had been supported by her family throughout the 1500s, and by Aldonza herself in a remodeling of 1565–72.[26] In his will of 1615 Aldonza's son Rodrigo, in Flanders, declared that he and his brother, Pedro Lasso, had together resolved to "adorn our burial places in the main chapel in the parish church of Señor Santiago in the town of Cuerva, where our parents and [some of] our forebears are buried," and had ordered that "a chapel be made on the Epistle [right-hand] side of the high altar of the said main chapel, in which [will be] placed and arranged numerous relics . . . acquired from diverse parts outside these realms at much cost and effort and have had adorned [or enshrined] in the best, most decent and richest manner [possible].[27] The will also refers to paintings and other works of art that were to embellish the chapel, but the only picture specified is Luis Tristán's large *Last Supper* (still in situ).[28] The Capilla de Reliquias was constructed between 1616 and 1620, the year of Rodrigo's death, after which Pedro Lasso was the chapel's generous supporter.

Neither Pedro Lasso's mother nor his brother Rodrigo are likely to have commissioned the cardinal's portrait, however highly they might have regarded him. By the time El Greco met the sitter, Aldonza Niño had lived apart for decades, and appears to have concerned herself mainly with monastic affairs.[29] Her removal, in Cuerva, from Pedro Lasso's world in Toledo nonetheless seems slight compared with that of her second son, Rodrigo Niño y Lasso de la Vega (ca. 1560–1620), who was granted the title of 2nd Conde de Añover in 1609. Although deeply pious, he signed on with the Spanish Armada in 1588, and after many trials and severe hardships—sinking off the Irish coast, capture by English troops, and imprisonment in Flanders for more than a year—joined the Spanish army in the Netherlands. By 1595 he had returned to Spain, but in that year he became *gentilhombre de la Cámara* to Cardinal-Archduke Albert (succeeding his uncle Gabriel Niño) and departed with him to Brussels. During the next twenty-five years Rodrigo Niño was

fig. 10 Juan Pantoja de la Cruz (Spanish, 1553–1608). *Philip III*, 1605. Oil on canvas, 74 × 40⅛ in. (188 × 102 cm). El Escorial, San Lorenzo de El Escorial (10034481)

almost always in the Spanish Netherlands, returning to Madrid only on rare occasions (as in 1601 and 1604) to consult with Philip III on Albert's behalf. He rose through the ranks of Albert's household, and by 1615 he held all three of the highest offices at Albert and Isabella's court and had amassed a considerable fortune.[30] Rodrigo also inherited the lucrative office of treasurer of the mint in Toledo, which Pedro Lasso supervised in his brother's absence, together with his properties in Spain.[31] Rodrigo died a childless bachelor in 1620, so that his entitlements and various possessions went to Pedro Lasso, who ceded them to his son, Luis. Rodrigo's brother did not receive from him any portraits of their uncle, Niño de Guevara, nor was such a picture recorded among Rodrigo's possessions in the Netherlands.[32]

Pedro Lasso's son, Luis Lasso de la Vega y Mendoza (1597–1632), 3rd Conde de Añover, served as *gentil-hombre de la Cámara* to the king's younger brother Don Carlos.[33] The prospect of a great career vanished with a sudden illness and his death on March 11, 1632, five years before that of his father (whose wife had died in 1627). Luis Lasso left behind a young widow, María Magdalena Pacheco (b. 1605), and six children. Their birth dates are mostly unknown, but the eldest son and future 2nd Conde de los Arcos, Pedro Lasso de la Vega (1622–1699), was not yet ten years old at the time.[34]

Luis's death, leaving the seventy-three-year-old Conde de los Arcos without an immediate heir, necessitated the inventory of 1632.[35] Much that could have been left to Luis in a few lines of his father's will now needed to be described and appraised before its distribution could be considered. A first draft of the inventory was completed by April 15, a month after Luis's burial in Cuerva. Additions to and drafts of the inventory were made as late as 1639.[36]

As noted above, Maíno valued the portrait of Niño de Guevara at 100 *ducados*. In a column headed "Vendieronse" (They [the following works] were sold), the portrait is marked down "en 880," meaning "for 880 *reales*" (80 *ducados*; one *ducado* equals eleven *reales*). One might take these different numbers as estimates and actual results of a public auction. Brown and Carr, for example, concede that the portrait "was perhaps bought by another member of the family," but they stress the alternative, of "someone outside the family," offering the winning bid.[37] However, the numbers tell a different story. The amount for which a painting or a pair of pictures was "sold" is almost always smaller than Maíno's estimate (a few are the same), and in the great majority of cases the amounts differ by a simple fraction (⅗ being the most common).[38] Such a consistent scheme of reducing Maíno's values by fifths, or, in fewer cases, by quarters, thirds, or half, could not result from competitive bidding.[39] The values clearly record a distribution of pictures among family members, probably with Pedro Lasso, his in-laws, and members of his daughter-in-law's family as the sole or main recipients. Nothing would have been "sold" in the usual sense: the values at which pictures went to individuals would have been totaled in order to ensure a fair or proportional disposition of goods.[40]

Support for this hypothesis comes from a marginal notation on the first page: the *Nativity* by Zuccaro (once owned by Niño de Guevara) was "sent to Cuerva." It was probably Pedro Lasso who set aside the small

devotional picture for the church or family chapel at Cuerva, since he was their main patron during the 1630s. Of course, the shorthand "Cuerva" would not have been used to record a buyer at a public sale.

In their attempt to identify El Greco's sitter with Cardinal Sandoval rather than Niño de Guevara, Brown and Carr point out that "the author of the picture is not named" in the inventory, something that Maíno could have easily done since he "was sufficiently familiar with the style of El Greco," and the painting is signed.[41] However, the great majority of works in the inventory are not attributed, and the value that Maíno assigned to the cardinal's portrait is quite high.[42] The purpose of estate inventories in this period was appraisal, not connoisseurship: objects were described sufficiently to be identified by the interested parties (the description of the cardinal's portrait is almost effusive in this regard). On April 28, 1632 (two weeks after appraising all the paintings in Pedro Lasso's care), Maíno appraised twenty-eight paintings in Luis Lasso's personal collection, and while most were thought to be worth 200 to 440 *reales*, none is attributed.[43] About one-fifth of the approximately 132 pictures in the Duke of Alcalá's collection (Seville) were given artists' names in an inventory made during the 1630s, and less than 10 percent in the 1637 inventory of the duke's estate.[44] Velázquez is known to have appraised five collections between 1625 and 1636, and in only one instance, in 1627, did

fig. 11 Titian (Italian, ca. 1485/90?–1576). *Pope Paul III*, 1543. Oil on canvas, 44¾ × 35 in. (113.7 × 88.8 cm). Museo di Capodimonte, Naples (Q 130)

fig. 12 Workshop of Bartolomeo Passerotti (Italian, 1529–1592). *Pope Pius V*, 1566. Oil on canvas, 55⅞ × 44½ in. (142 × 113 cm). Musée des Arts Décoratifs, Paris (Pe 327)

he record an artist's name—his own—as the painter of *The Waterseller* (1620–22; Apsley House, London), in the collection of his friend Juan de Fonseca y Figueroa.[45]

STYLE AND EXPRESSION

In style and expression, El Greco's painting is one of the most remarkable portraits ever painted in Spain, especially when it is compared with contemporary formal portraits by artists such as Juan Pantoja de la Cruz (fig. 10). The most convincing comparisons with earlier works have been with portraits by Titian, in particular his three-quarter-length seated portrait of Pope Paul III, of 1543 (fig. 11), and the famous full-length portrait *Pope Paul III with His Grandsons Alessandro and Ottavio Farnese*, of 1545–46 (Museo di Capodimonte, Naples). Christiansen emphasizes the latter as important both for "El Greco's understanding of portraiture as characterisation" and for his freedom of execution in the astonishing display of highlights on the cardinal's costume and in other passages.[46]

El Greco would have seen more recent portraits of popes and cardinals when he was in Rome, and probably in Spain as well. As mentioned above, the artist's patron Pedro Lasso had at Batres portraits of Pius V and Sixtus V. Pius was pope during most of the years El Greco worked in Italy, and his principal portraitist, Bartolomeo Passerotti, was himself inspired by Titian in works such as the *Portrait of Pope Pius V*, of 1566 (Walters Art Museum, Baltimore).[47] A portrait of Pius V, probably from Passerotti's workshop (fig. 12), may be compared with El Greco's painting with respect to pose and expression.[48]

But it is Titian's portraits of Paul III that more closely anticipate the present picture in terms of animation and psychological intensity. One also finds in portraits by Titian the use, as here, of a setting or background to expressive effect. Perhaps the best example is *Charles V Seated*, of 1548 (fig. 13), where the chair sits insecurely on a seemingly tilted floor and the background is split between a brocade wall hanging and a generic landscape view (an insubstantial column divides the two).[49] Titian's type of setting, when translated into the stylized manner of Spanish court portraiture, was reduced to abstract patterns pressing toward the picture plane. Thus the door, silk brocade wall covering (not gilt leather, as has been claimed), and tiled floor in the portrait of Niño de Guevara are also anticipated in Alonso Sánchez Coello's large canvas *Isabella Clara Eugenia and Magdalena Ruiz*, of about 1585–88 (fig. 14), where brocade panels, a nearly featureless plane, and a Persian-style carpet contrast in color with the Infanta's elaborately patterned gown.

If Sánchez Coello's approach is essentially decorative, suggesting luxury, El Greco's version of the court convention is restless and unbalanced, implying a forceful personality. The cardinal sits still but tensely, his drapery swept to the right, which together with the dense shadow beneath the chair suggests slight levitation. The difference between his hands (which evoke Van Dyck and Grünewald) is complemented by the forms around them, with the rectilinear section suggesting stability and the brocade agitation, as if the cardinal held within himself a holy rage. The looping pattern on the wall amplifies the thrust of his glance and the impulsive movement sensed in his left arm.[50] He looks to his left, with lips slightly parted, as if reacting to some intrusion (like a Saint Anthony, who has dealt with demons before), or to impart orders, perhaps in response to the unfolded letter on the floor. At least one scholar has seen the hands as suggesting rigid implacability as opposed to the possibility of pardon.[51] The accuracy of these speculations is immaterial compared to the fact that El Greco's characterization of the sitter gives rise to them. Cardinal Niño de Guevara seems to embody the Last Judgment or the Inquisition, if not in action then in resolve.

fig. 13 Titian. *Charles V Seated*, 1548. Oil on canvas, 80¾ × 48 in. (205 × 122 cm). Alte Pinakothek, Munich (632)

fig. 14 Alonso Sánchez Coello (Spanish, 1531–1588). *Isabella Clara Eugenia and Magdalena Ruiz*, ca. 1585–88. Oil on canvas, 81½ × 50¾ in. (207 × 129 cm). Museo del Prado, Madrid (P861)

fig. 15 El Greco. *The Vision of Saint John (The Opening of the Fifth Seal)*, 1608–14. Oil on canvas, 87½ × 76 in. (222.3 × 193 cm). The Metropolitan Museum of Art, Rogers Fund, 1956 (56.48)

The Vision of Saint John (The Opening of the Fifth Seal), 1608–14

In conception and execution, this painting is one of
El Greco's most extraordinary works and a quintessential example of his late expressionist style (fig. 15). In the
twentieth century the picture preoccupied several major
artists, most memorably Picasso in *Les Demoiselles
d'Avignon*, of 1907 (Museum of Modern Art, New York).[1]

The *Vision of Saint John* was painted between 1608
and El Greco's death in 1614 as part of his last major
project for a religious institution. As suggested by the
Evangelist's gesture and glance, a significant part of the
composition has been lost at the top: the painting was
originally almost twice as high (by about 76 in., or
193 cm) and slightly wider to the left (by perhaps 6½ in.,
or 16.5 cm).[2] The work is also unfinished to some extent,
but the painter would not have taken the surviving part
of the picture much further.[3] Fortunately, neither his
son, Jorge Manuel, nor any other assistant had a hand in
the execution.[4]

THE COMMISSION

Three altarpiece ensembles, or retables, were ordered
from the artist in November 1608 for the church of the
new Hospital of Saint John the Baptist Outside the
Walls, on the north side of Toledo. Since the period of
its construction, between the 1540s and 1603, the complex has also been known as the Hospital de Afuera
("outside," in contrast to the older Hospital de Santa
Cruz, within the walls of Toledo) and, more commonly,
as the Hospital de Tavera, named for its founder,
Cardinal Juan Pardo de Tavera (1472–1545), archbishop
of Toledo (1534–45) and inquisitor general of Spain
(1539–45).[5]

The commission for the altarpieces was awarded
by the hospital's administrator and El Greco's patron of
many years, Pedro Salazar de Mendoza (ca. 1550–1629).[6]

In 1595 Salazar had the artist make a wooden tabernacle
(*custodia*) with sculpted figures for the high altar of the
hospital's church, and he had since acquired several
paintings by El Greco for his own collection, including,
most likely, the *View and Plan of Toledo*, where the
Tavera Hospital floats on a cloud in the middle ground
(see fig. 2).

Tavera's magnificent marble tomb monument
stands in the expansive crossing of the church. Carved
by Alonso Berruguete (1486–1561) between 1557 and
1561, it makes the building not only a place of worship
but also an exceptionally grand burial chapel. As seen
from the nave, the monument stands before the high
altar and the main retable and is flanked by tall altarpieces at either side (fig. 16).[7]

Certainly intended for the central location, above
the high altar, was El Greco's *Baptism of Christ* (fig. 17),
infelicitously finished by Jorge Manuel in the early
1620s: the church is dedicated to the Baptist, and the
1621 inventory of Jorge Manuel's possessions refers to
"el bautismo prinzipal del ospital."[8] Furthermore, after
Jorge's failure to finish the project in his lifetime (he
died in 1631), the court painter Félix Castello (1595–
1651) signed a contract (dated April 23, 1635) with the
hospital for "el quadro grande de el Altar mayor, el bautismo de San Juan," and for "dos quadros grandes para
los dos colaterales [side altars], el uno de la encarnación
[Annunciation] y el otro de una visión de apocalipssi."[9]
These details are consistent with the earlier evidence,
and there is no reason to suppose (with Richard Mann)
that Salazar's carefully conceived arrangement might
have been revised.[10]

That *The Baptism* and not *The Vision of Saint John*
was intended for placement above the high altar is indicated not only on the grounds of iconography and docu-

fig. 16 Interior of the church of the Hospital of Saint John the Baptist Outside the Walls (Hospital de Tavera), Toledo

mentation but also by the paintings' dimensions. The matter is complicated, since two of the canvases—*The Vision* and *The Annunciation* (fig. 18b)—have been substantially cut down, and the gilded wood frames designed by El Greco were unfinished at his death and were not installed until after the death of Jorge Manuel.[11] Nonetheless, *The Baptism* (129⅞ × 83⅛ in.; 330 × 211 cm), which remains nearly intact, could never have been intended as a "pendant" to *The Annunciation*, which has the same width (usually given as 209 cm), but, when taken together with its original upper part, the *Concert of Angels*, now in Athens (fig. 18a), was between 161⅝ and 163¾ inches (410/415 cm) high, or about 31½ inches (80 cm) taller than *The Baptism*.[12] The central painting was shorter because it was not framed separately but fit into a much larger scheme, that of the main retable with three levels of architecture and sculpture designed by El Greco, along with his tabernacle of 1595 (64 in. [162.6 cm] high) and, on top of it, his polychrome statue of the Risen Christ (17¾ in. [45 cm] high) placed before the central bay.[13] Thus, *The Baptism* would have been raised higher above the base of the architectural ensemble than were the lateral altarpieces, and it would have been somewhat overlapped at bottom center by *The Risen Christ*.

Of El Greco's three altarpieces, only *The Baptism* was delivered to the church, where it remains (if not in the location for which it was intended).[14] The whereabouts of *The Vision of Saint John* between Jorge Manuel's death and the late nineteenth century has so far remained untraced. *The Annunciation* (fig. 18b), completed by Jorge Manuel, was presumably in different collections than *The Vision* during the eighteenth and nineteenth centuries, before it belonged to the 2nd Marqués de Urquijo (in 1908; d. 1914).[15] The upper part of *The Annunciation*, depicting a concert of angels (fig. 18a), was reportedly cut off in the late nineteenth century and is first recorded in 1908 as owned by the heirs of the Marqués de Castro-Serna (d. 1905).[16]

THE SUBJECT

One of the many paintings listed in the 1614 inventory of El Greco's studio is described as "A small Saint John the Evangelist, who sees the mysteries of the Apocalypse" ("Un S. Juo abangelista q[ue] be [ve] los misterios del apocalipsi pequeño").[17] The work must have been either a *modello* for or a copy (*ricordo*) after *The Vision of Saint John*, and its description suggests a more comprehensive title for the present picture (such as *Saint John the Evangelist Witnessing the Mysteries of the Apocalypse*).[18] The subject itself had become a mystery even before nearly half the composition was cut from the top in 1880, and evidently discarded (perhaps because it was less finished or damaged).

fig. 17 El Greco and Jorge Manuel Theotokopoulos (Greek, 1578–1631). *The Baptism of Christ*, ca. 1608–14 and early 1620s. Oil on canvas, 129⅞ × 83⅛ in. (330 × 211 cm). Hospital de Tavera, Toledo

According to information provided to Cossío in the late nineteenth century, the "religious character" of the upper section led to the notion that it depicted Divine Love, and that the lower part, with its sinuous ensemble of male and female nudes, represented Profane Love.[19] (Perhaps this is why the Córdoban doctor from whom the Basque painter Ignacio Zuloaga bought the canvas in 1905 kept it behind a velvet curtain.)[20]

In proposing, correctly, that El Greco based the subject on the Book of Revelation, chapter 6, verse 9, Cossío supposed that the lost upper part of the canvas would have represented "the Lamb and other Apocalyptic symbols."[21] If so, the Lamb of God must have played a comparatively inconspicuous role, since the misreading of the picture's upper part as an illustration of Divine Love suggests a figural scene. The combination of figure groups in earthly and heavenly spheres had appeared frequently in El Greco's compositions since his first years in Spain, and one need only consider *The Baptism* and especially the reconstructed *Annunciation* to imagine the kind of angelic ensemble that may have crowned *The Vision of Saint John*. It seems plausible that, as in the other two altarpieces, angels in flowing robes consorted with a bevy of cherubs, some of whom descend with heavenly garments in the surviving part of the composition.

Support for this supposition comes from the biblical text and from the images El Greco could have known. In John's vision the Lamb of God, representing the Risen Christ (or Christ as "Saviour of the world"; John 4:42), answers an angel's challenge to open the book, "sealed with seven seals," that has been received from the right hand of God (Rev. 5:1). It is interesting for the Tavera altarpieces that the term "Lamb of God" (Agnus Dei) comes from John 1:29, where John the Baptist, seeing Jesus with his first disciples, declares, "Behold the Lamb of God, which taketh away the sin of the world." According to El Greco's contract, a sculptural group of angels adoring the Lamb of God was intended for the tympanum of the main retable, below which *The Baptism of Christ* was displayed.[22]

Six of the seven seals are opened in chapter 6 of the Book of Revelation, and the seventh in chapter 8. The first four seals reveal the future events—conquest, war, famine, and death—that are perhaps most familiar from Albrecht Dürer's synthesis in *The Four Horsemen of the Apocalypse*, of 1498. The print, illustrated here, from Dürer's Apocalypse series of woodcuts, represents the opening of the fifth and sixth seals (fig. 19), with the latter revealing "the great day of his wrath" (Rev. 6:17),

fig. 18a El Greco and workshop. *A Concert of Angels*, ca. 1608–14 and later. Oil on canvas, 43½ × 80½ in. (110.5 × 204.5 cm). National Gallery and Alexandros Soutzos Museum, Athens (Π.152)

fig. 18b El Greco (and Jorge Manuel Theotokopoulos?). *The Annunciation*, ca. 1608–14 and later. Oil on canvas, 115¾ × 82¼ in. (294 × 209 cm). Fundación Santander, Madrid

shown in the bottom two-thirds of the composition. The figures framed by clouds at the top of the print are the Christian martyrs of the past who are revealed to John with the opening of the fifth seal. Naked souls rise and receive robes from angels at an altar, as described by John:

> I saw under the altar the souls of them that were slain for the word of God, and for the testimony which they held: And they cried with a loud voice, saying, How long, O Lord, holy and true, dost thou not judge and avenge our blood on them that dwell on the earth? And white robes were given unto every one of them; and it was said unto them, that they should rest yet for a little season, until their fellowservants also and their brethren [future martyrs], that should be killed as they were, should be fulfilled. (Rev. 6:9–11)

In El Greco's interpretation, five male and (in the center) two lighter-skinned female nudes receive garments from descending cherubs.[23] The heavenly raiment is rendered as great sheets of cloth, arbitrarily colored yellow and green as well as white.[24] As in other late paintings by El Greco, the drapery functions simultaneously as a backdrop to the figures, as a substitute for space between them, and as a sign of

fig. 19 Albrecht Dürer (German, 1471–1528). *The Opening of the Fifth and Sixth Seals, from the Apocalypse*, ca. 1497–98. Woodcut, sheet 15½ × 11⅛ in. (39.4 × 28.4 cm). The Metropolitan Museum of Art, Gift of Mrs. Felix M. Warburg, 1940 (40.139.6 [6])

spiritual excitement, amplifying the rapturous poses and gestures. This is especially evident in the green drapery, with its electric highlights, that unites the male trio to the right.

Across the middle ground of the composition there is a sense of progress through time. The figures given yellow drapery are just beginning to cover themselves; an elegant male assists the woman beside him. Farther to the right, and closer to the viewer, two men on their knees (as is Saint John himself) reach up to receive the green drapery held by two downward tumbling cherubs. And at the far right, a rather Venetian-looking cherub offers white drapery to an athletic male, who, like other figures in El Greco's late oeuvre, recalls but goes beyond the balletic sculptures of Benvenuto Cellini (1500–1571) in his impossibly extended pose.[25]

While the narrative of receiving garments was carefully conceived, it is visually overwhelmed by the effect of forms fanning away from Saint John, with figures increasing in size and movement and claiming more space. The impression of souls swept by a shared state of ecstasy is underscored by the arc of red drapery and the reddish brown ground (perhaps with the suggestion of an abyss in the foreground), and enhanced by the clouds, which swirl away from the Evangelist's uplifted face and arms. The image of salvation is thus transformed into an experience of high emotional charge. The effect would have been considerably intensified when John's vision of heaven was shown above, probably to a degree not usually seen in El Greco's juxtapositions of terrestrial and celestial realms.[26]

As Christiansen succinctly notes, the three altarpieces for the Hospital de Tavera "offered a synopsis of God's plan of salvation by showing the incarnation of Christ, the manifestion of his divine mission [which begins with the Baptism], and a vision of the elect at the end of time."[27] Formal similarities in the overall design of the altarpieces and between their main figures would have invited the contemporary viewer's contemplation of their related meanings. The main figure in *The Vision of Saint John* (when installed over the left side altar) would have been seen as a counterpart to the oversize angel in *The Annunciation* (fig. 18b) over the right side altar, and these two figures would in turn have been echoed by the tall figures to either side of Christ in the central *Baptism* (fig. 17), that is, the tall angel at left who gestures heavenward and at right the towering figure of John the Baptist.[28] However, the most obvious connection between the three subjects would have been that between baptism, symbolizing the remission of sins, and salvation, as envisioned by Saint John. The saving of souls, as well as care for the sick, the dispossessed, and the dying, was central to the mission of the hospital, where patients were required to confess before seeing a doctor and were expected to receive Holy Communion at least once a week.[29]

THE ARTIST'S SOURCES

Various sources of inspiration for *The Vision of Saint John* have been cited, although late in life El Greco was inclined to revisit his own earlier motifs. In this case, the subject encouraged new invention and the expressive manipulation of borrowed ideas.

Above all, the artist would have recalled (probably with the help of prints) Michelangelo's *Last Judgment* fresco in the Sistine Chapel, the subject of which (like Signorelli's *Resurrection of the Elect*, in Orvieto Cathedral) is closely related to El Greco's (and his patron's) interpretation of the Vision of Saint John. Several of Michelangelo's nudes anticipate the poses, if not the anatomy, of El Greco's male figures. In particular, the figure of Haman in the pendentive above *The Last Judgment* has been compared with El Greco's Saint John, in a pose that also recalls Titian's *Saint John the Evangelist on Patmos*, of 1544–47 (National Gallery of Art, Washington, D.C.), which El Greco would have seen in the Scuola Grande di San Giovanni Evangelista during his years in Venice.[30]

It is, however, important to emphasize again that Michelangelo's twisting, straining figures were emulated by the mature El Greco for their powerful expression of spiritual feeling rather than as models for individual poses or figure groups.[31] This approach reflects long experience and purposeful intention, so that Martin Soria's suggestion, to the effect that the nudes in El Greco's picture were derived from prints after Hendrick Goltzius (1558–1617), fails to acknowledge that El Greco, while himself a master of Mannerist learning, nearly erased any trace of academic exercise in his late work.[32] If there is a hint of anatomical study in *The Vision of Saint John*, it is found only in the female nudes, which bring to mind El Greco's own wood sculpture *Pandora*, of 1600–1610 (Museo del Prado, Madrid), and his practice (following that of Tintoretto) of using small clay, wax, or plaster models for figures in paintings.[33] The male figures, by contrast, relate to the astonished soldiers in El Greco's *Resurrection*, of 1597–1600 (Museo del Prado, Madrid), and to a number of other figure groups, such as the *Laocoön*, of the early 1610s (National Gallery of Art, Washington, D.C.), dating from the artist's last years.[34] Thus, the figures in the present picture are not borrowed from anywhere, but are among the most remarkable examples of a continuous creative process.

The composition as a whole and the painting's iconography are inseparable considerations, given the subject's comparative rarity.[35] El Greco must have known Dürer's print (fig. 19) and perhaps also a woodcut of 1546 by Matthias Gerung (ca. 1500–1570), either of which could have informed motifs if not the style of *The Vision of Saint John* (especially in its lost upper part).[36] The Gerung print features a kneeling Saint John in the foreground; a similar figure occurs also in three of the eight magnificent Apocalypse tapestries made in Brussels about 1556–61 for Philip II. In one of these, *The Adoration of the Mystic Lamb* (now in the Palacio Real de La Granja de San Ildefonso, Segovia), the kneeling Evangelist gestures and looks upward to a vision of angels, martyrs, elders, and the Lamb of God in a ring of clouds.[37]

In the end, however, any such comparison is unsatisfactory because of El Greco's exceptional style and the unusual circumstances of this commission. Most earlier images of the Apocalypse are found in manuscripts (meant for privileged individuals) and in prints (which were addressed to a large public, with a didactic purpose). The *Vision of Saint John* is a devotional picture, one of three altarpieces addressed to a congregation concerned with their last days on earth and the prospect of life after death. With Archbishop Tavera's tomb monument nearby, the viewer intended by Salazar de Mendoza would have seen El Greco's painting (had it been installed) as a call to an exemplary life, an inspiration to repentence, and an offer of eternal peace.

WALTER LIEDTKE
Curator, Department of European Paintings,
The Metropolitan Museum of Art
(1980–2015)

NOTES

Complete documentation may be found at www.metmuseum.org/collection/the-collection-online.

A View of Toledo

1 See San Román y Fernández 1910, p. 194, under doc. no. 52, and San Román y Fernández 1927, p. 300, under doc. no. XXXV, nos. 137, 138 (reprinted in San Román y Fernández 1982, p. 371). The second inventory of El Greco's possessions was made on August 7, 1621, on the occasion of Jorge Manuel's marriage to Doña Gregoria de Guzmán. Both inventories are also published in Marías 1997, pp. 312–15.

2 Kagan 1984, p. 91, no. 240 ("un pais de toledo [h]acia la puente de alcantara"). On Salazar as a patron of El Greco, see Kagan 1984 and Mann 1986, pp. 112–22.

3 Kagan 1984, p. 90, no. 4 ("otro quadro de la cuidad de toledo con su planta").

4 Wethey 1962, vol. 2, p. 85, under no. 129. On the Capilla de San José, see ibid., pp. 11–13, and Xavier Bray in Davies and Elliott 2003, pp. 160–67. The two lateral canvases that El Greco painted for the chapel, *Saint Martin and the Beggar* and *Madonna and Child with Saint Martina and Saint Agnes*, were sold in 1906 to a Parisian dealer and in the same year to Peter Widener; in 1942 they became part of the Widener Collection in the National Gallery of Art, Washington, D.C. (see Brown and Mann 1990, pp. 47–56). The background of *Saint Martin and the Beggar* (which refers to the chapel's patron, Martín Ramírez) also includes, in more fragmentary form, a few Toledo motifs. Jonathan Brown and Richard Mann (ibid., p. 50) suggest that the two vistas of Toledo would have invited local citizens to emulate Joseph's humility and Saint Martin as defender of the faith. The image of Saint Martin cutting his cloak in two, with a vista of Toledo in the background, might also be taken to refer to the city's best-known products of the period, cloth and swords (see Brown and Kagan 1982, p. 22, on these industries).

5 For example, *The Virgin of the Immaculate Conception*, 1608–13 (Museo de Santa Cruz, Toledo). See Davies and Elliott 2003, pp. 200–201, no. 55; see also p. 234.

6 Wethey 1962, vol. 2, p. 85, under no. 128. See also Brown and Kagan 1982, p. 24. The cloud, of course, suggests a vision, as in Alonso Cano's *Saint John the Evangelist's Vision of Jerusalem*, of about 1636 (Wallace Collection, London).

7 See Kagan 1984, p. 86; Mann 1986, pp. 121–25; Keith Christiansen in Davies and Elliott 2003, p. 210; and Marías 2014, pp. 86, 291, no. 107, fig. 86.

8 Fernando Marías (in Marías 2014, p. 102) describes the *View and Plan* as "generally dated to the last years of the artist's life (1600–14)," but in the caption on page 119 dates the pictures to about 1600.

9 Brown and Kagan 1982, p. 25. The authors extend their "admittedly speculative" argument by relating the *View of Toledo* to the city council's efforts in 1595 to encourage Philip II to reside again in Toledo. On Salazar's interest in maps and topographical images, see Kagan 1984, p. 89, and the inventory on pp. 90–91. On the *View and Plan*, see also Calduch Pedralba 2012, pp. 54–57.

10 This distinction is advanced in Brown 1981, p. 37, where, however, the term "cartographic" is used in opposition to "emblematic." Most of that article's content is repeated in Brown and Kagan 1982. In Kagan 1986, pp. 122–23, Juergen Schulz (in Schulz 1978) is credited with the distinction between the older "encomiastic or emblematic view" and the "scientific or topographical tradition." Marías (in Marías 2014, pp. 117–23) finds these distinctions simplistic. See also Links 1972, pp. 12–20, on early city views in Italy.

11 The figure group in the sky of the *View and Plan* was anticipated by El Greco's polychromed sculpture *The Virgin Presenting the Chasuble to Saint Ildefonso*, commissioned about 1581–85 as part of the altar ensemble (it is mounted immediately under El Greco's *Disrobing of Christ*, of 1577–79) in the sacristy of Toledo Cathedral; see Davies and Elliott 2003, p. 124, fig. 37. Van den Wyngaerde's drawing is mislabeled a "print" in ibid., p. 29, fig. 10.

12 As noted by Christiansen in Davies and Elliott 2003, pp. 233–34, the identification of this palace "remains something of a puzzle, though . . . there can be no question but that the artist intended it to be recognisable." Richard Kagan (2000, p. 203) and Marías (2001, p. 10) describe the building as the Hospital de Santa Cruz, but that structure has one of the most distinctive facades in Spain and bears no resemblance to that in the painting. Their identification may go back to Lafuente Ferrari 1969, p. 75, who finds "the monastery of Santa Fe and perhaps, too, the Hospital de Santa Cruz."

13 See Marías on Villalpando (1996, vol. 32, pp. 559–60) and, on the Casa de Vargas, Marías 1983–86, vol. 1, pp. 320–24.

14 Brown and Kagan 1982, p. 26. The authors cite Salazar de Mendoza's *El glorioso Doctor San Ilefonso, Arcobispo de Toledo* (1618) on the subject of the Agaliense monastery (see also Moraleda y Esteban 1928). While this identification is for Brown and Kagan only tentative, in Kagan 2000, p. 203, it is maintained that "these buildings, perched on what appears to be a cloud, undoubtedly refer to the Agaliense Monastery."

15 On the shrine and abbey, see Marías in Kagan 1989, p. 130; see also Mann 1986, p. 8, on the special interest of El Greco's early patron, Diego de Castilla, in the remains of Saint Leocadia.

16 For the original inscription on the *View and Plan of Toledo*, see Wethey 1962, vol. 2, pp. 84–85.

17 For example, Kubler and Soria 1959 and Brown 1981, p. 37. What appears to be a large waterwheel and sluiceway is seen in the lower right corner of *Saint Martin and the Beggar* (National Gallery of Art, Washington, D.C.), which Bray (in Davies and Elliott 2003, p. 164) suggests may refer to Torriano's invention. The background is thought to derive from the *View of Toledo*, but there is no waterwheel in the Museum's painting.

18 Brown and Kagan 1982, pp. 26–27, where (in contrast to Brown 1981) there is no reference to the Artificio.

19 The fulling of woolen cloth (cleansing it of oils, dirt, etc.) was usually done inside water or fulling mills. The detail here is reminiscent of Jacob van Ruisdael's views of bleaching fields outside Haarlem.

20 In Guinard 1956, p. 109, the sky is said to indicate "a raging thunderstorm." See also Mayer 1926, pp. xxxii, 50, no. 315, pl. 68.

21 During El Greco's decades in Toledo serious droughts were common, to judge from the frequency of ceremonies held in the cathedral to pray for rain (Domínguez-Castro et al. 2008, pp. 230, 237–38). John Elliott (1989, p. 269) mentions especially bad harvests in Toledo during 1577 and 1578 (El Greco's first two years in the city) and notes that the progressive weakening of the local economy during the next forty years happened "for reasons not yet fully clear" (although the court's move to Madrid and competition in the textile industry are noted as factors). Toledo had 60,000 inhabitants in about 1550 and a mere 25,000 in the 1640s.

22 Frank Rutter (1930, p. 65) wonders if El Greco "got his idea from one of those Byzantine topographical woodprints of holy places."

23 As noted in Kagan 1984, p. 89. The degrees of fidelity found in Van den Wyngaerde's drawings of cityscapes, in Braun and Hogenberg's plates, and in El Greco's *View of Toledo* are discussed in Kagan 1998, pp. 80–84, 93. Even Van den Wyngaerde would exaggerate the scale of major buildings and move them for pictorial effect, as he did in his drawing of Valencia in 1563 (ibid., p. 83, fig. 3.5).

24 Braun and Hogenberg 2008, p. 53 (1572–1618, vol. 1, pl. 4).

25 Hogenberg also modified a few details, perhaps based on other sources.

26 See Partridge 1969, figs. 196, 197; Faldi 1981, p. 265 (for the more comparable view of Caprarola); Robertson 1992, fig. 99 (discussed p. 110); and Acidini Luchinat 1998–99, vol. 2, p. 23, fig. 40. Italian precedents for Van den Wyngaerde's work in Spain are discussed in Kagan 1986, pp. 131–35.

27 See Kagan 1986, pp. 118–19. Many of the city views were in the *sala grande* of the Alcázar when recorded by Diego de Cuelbis in 1599, but elsewhere in the palace when it was inventoried in 1686. See also Kagan in Kagan 1989, pp. 52–53, on the city views (by Italians) that decorated the late sixteenth-century palace of the Marqués de Santa Cruz at Viso de Marqués (southeast of Ciudad Real).

28 The most similar pictures of the period are Flemish paintings of ancient cities being destroyed by God, or landscapes in which forces of nature are emphasized (as in the Metropolitan's *Mountainous Landscape with a Waterfall*, by Kerstiaen de Keuninck, of about 1600 [1983.452]).

Cardinal Fernando Niño de Guevara

1 See Frelinghuysen et al. 1993, pp. 10–18 (on the Havemeyers' interest in Spanish paintings), 58 (on the present picture), 229 (on the visit to Spain), 233, 236–37, under February 2 and December 29, 1903, and April 12–15 and May 6, 1904 (on Durand-Ruel's role in obtaining the portrait). According to Louisine Havemeyer (1961, pp. 157–58), the purchase extended over a period of four years.

2 Members of his father's family, the Zapatas, had served the church and the crown since the 1300s, and during Niño de Guevara's lifetime several other Zapatas held high church office and served Philip II or Philip III. His father, Rodrigo Niño Zapata, held several important offices, including chamberlain to Charles V, treasurer of the royal mint in Toledo, and ambassador to Venice (see Martz 2003, pp. 180–84).

3 In Brown and Carr 1982, p. 33, Teresa de Guevara is described imprecisely as "a daughter of the Count of Oñate." She was in fact the daughter of Pedro Vélez de Guevara, Señor de Salinillas, and Constanza de Ayala (as shown in Martínez Caviró 1990, p. 313). Teresa's brother Iñigo married Catalina Vélez de Guevara, 5th Condesa de Oñate, whose father, Pedro Vélez de Guevara (not the same person as the Señor de Salinillas), was 4th Conde de Oñate.

4 Niño de Guevara was created cardinal-priest in the consistory of June 5, 1596, and received the red hat on June 8.

5 See Brown and Carr 1982, pp. 33, 41n2. Other sources are cited in the notes below.

6 Brown and Carr 1982 and 1984. The identification with Sandoval is still maintained in Brown 1998, pp. 87–88, fig. 114. Fernando Marías (1986) discusses Sandoval's interests in the arts, including his relationship with El Greco, and rejects the hypothesis that El Greco painted his portrait (see ibid., p. 15).

7 Both questions are reviewed by Keith Christiansen in Davies and Elliott 2003, pp. 282–84, and are here further elaborated. In recent years there has been a strong scholarly consensus that the sitter is in fact Niño de Guevara and not Sandoval. The latter's portrait by Tristán is catalogued in Pérez Sánchez and Navarrete Prieto 2001, no. 123 (see also no. 124, a portrait of Sandoval as cardinal, in Tristán's style).

8 The inscription on the print begins with a reference to the cardinal's titular church in Rome (Santa Anastasia) and, after describing him as archbishop of Toledo, points out helpfully that Sandoval is from Spain. The date ("3 Martij 1599"), the crest, and the inscription at the upper right ("Cr. a Clem. 8") all refer to Sandoval's creation as cardinal-priest by Clement VIII. (Sandoval did not receive his red hat until the consistory of February 26, 1601.) Finally, the print's technical quality suggests an Italian, not a Spanish, engraver.

9 As noted by Christiansen (in Davies and Elliott 2003, pp. 282–84), later damage to the cardinal's face required reconstruction of the nose; this would be based partly on Tristán's "free copy" of the painting in the Museo del Greco, Toledo (Pérez Sánchez and Navarrete Prieto 2001, p. 245, under no. 122).

10 On the cardinal's glasses and their type (seen in Spanish portraits from about 1580 onward), see Scholz-Hänsel 1995.

11 See Brown and Carr 1984, p. 65, fig. 16; Pérez Sánchez and Navarrete Prieto 2001, no. 81. A different, unattributed painting of Saint Bernardo with Cardinal Sandoval is published in Martínez Caviró 1990, p. 89 (ill.).

12 Christiansen in Davies and Elliott 2003, p. 284. On the commission, see ibid., pp. 169–75; Ruiz Gómez et al. 2001. Richard Kagan (1995, pp. 326–27) describes Arcos's role in this contract, and his great library of books and prints.

13 Kagan 1995, p. 325.

14 On the *Allegory*, see Davies and Elliott 2003, no. 44, and Marías 2014, pp. 204–6. On Arcos's possible ownership of the *Laocoön*, of about 1610–14 (National Gallery of Art, Washington, D.C.), see Brown and Mann 1990, p. 64n1.

15 Kagan 2010a, p. 38. The count must have attended the king and queen when they entered Toledo in March 1600. Philip III had granted Pedro Lasso the title of Conde de los Arcos in 1599, and in the same year sent him as one of four *mayordomos* to receive the fourteen-year-old future queen of Spain, Margarita of Austria, into her new country (at Viñaroz, March 21, 1599; see Kagan 1995, p. 327, where the date is mistakenly given as 1600). Arcos remained in the queen's service as *mayordomo*. In 1614 he became *mayordomo* to the Infante Philip, who as king (from 1621) retained him in that office. In his will dated May 7, 1631, Arcos notes his service to three kings and four queens, and the fortune he had spent in their service (ibid., p. 329).

16 See Kagan 1995, p. 331, on the painting by Zuccaro (probably a version of the canvas painted for Philip II about 1588; Nuevo Museo, El Escorial). On the cardinal's estate (of which no inventory is known), see Martínez Caviró 1985, pp. 222–23. Three other members of the family were also executors of the estate: Pedro Lasso's brother, Rodrigo Niño (discussed below); Don Lope de Guzmán, 1st Conde de Villaverde, husband of the cardinal's sister Francisca; and their son-in-law, the Conde de Mora.

17 Kagan 2010b, p. 65. El Greco's later portrait (ca. 1609?) of Fray Hortensio Félix Paravicino (Museum of Fine Arts, Boston; first recorded in 1724) could have been commissioned by the sitter or a member of his family, or initiated by El Greco himself. Any comparison with El Greco's portrait of Niño de Guevara must take into account the fact that Paravicino was famous as an orator and poet (see Brown et al. 1982, no. 63, and Davies and Elliott 2003, no. 81).

18 Brown and Carr (1982, pp. 33, 35, fig. 2) discuss a weak bust-length portrait of Niño de Guevara in the Palacio Arzobispal, Seville, part of a series painted about 1675–1700. The anonymous work was obviously made without the benefit of seeing the portrait by El Greco.

19 Kagan 1995, p. 336, under "sala grande del cierço."

20 See Martínez Caviró 1985, p. 220, and Kagan 1995, p. 337. Portraits of other contemporary Spanish churchmen were inventoried in June 1636 (Kagan 1995, pp. 338–39), including one of "Padre Rojas" (Cardinal-Archbishop Bernardo de Sandoval).

21 Kagan 1995, pp. 337–39. Copies of the inventories of the Arcos collection dating from 1632 to 1639 were kindly made available to the author by the Instituto Valencia de Don Juan in Madrid.

22 Ibid., pp. 335 (Madrid), 337 (Batres).

23 For paintings recorded as in Cuerva and Toledo, see ibid., p. 335. Marías (2013, p. 248) states simply that Pedro Lasso "commissioned a portrait of his uncle," without explaining this conclusion.

24 Readers may recall that Philip IV's brother, Cardinal-Infante Ferdinand, archduke of Austria, was not only a military commander and governor but also (from 1619 until his death in 1641) archbishop of Toledo. Between 1595 and 1598 the same office had been held by Philip II's nephew Cardinal-Archduke Albert of Austria, but in his absence (discussed below) his brief successor as archbishop (1598–99), Garcia de Loaysa, served as governor of the archdiocese (see Kagan 1982, p. 58). The president of the king's Consejo de Castilla was often a cardinal, as preference was given to noblemen with their own agendas (Elliott 1986). For interesting remarks on the royal patronage of monasteries and "Spanish piety as political action," see Rotmil 2010, especially pp. 269–71.

25 See Brown and Carr 1982, pp. 33, 36 (citing Cossío 1908, vol. 1, pp. 423–24), and Martínez Caviró 1990, pp. 291–93, 305–6. The cardinal's parents do appear as donors, on the wings of a triptych by Juan Correa de Vivar, dated 1568, which is now in the cloister of the convent (Martínez Caviró 1990, p. 297, ill.). The version of the cardinal's portrait seen by Cossío was very probably Luis Tristán's "free copy" after the Museum's painting (Museo del Greco, Toledo); see Pérez Sánchez and Navarrete Prieto 2001, pp. 245–46, no. 122, and the full discussion by José Redondo Cuesta in Lavín Berdonces et al. 2007, pp. 149–50, colorpl. There is also a bust-length portrait in the Oskar Reinhart Collection "Am Römerholz," in Winterthur, which is at best a workshop copy; see Wethey 1962, vol. 2, p. 205, no. X-187. An unconvincing effort to defend an attribution to El Greco is made by Mayte García Julliard in Reinhard-Felice 2005, pp. 154–56.

26 Marías 1983–86, vol. 4, pp. 162–64. See also Ainsworth and Sánchez-Lassa 2012, pp. 90–91, where Aldonza's date of death is given as 1603, not 1604. However, the inscription on Aldonza's tomb monument (commissioned by "rodricvs nino et lasso comes d anover") records that she died at the age of seventy on October 15, 1604. The writer is grateful to Ana Sánchez-Lassa for her assistance (May 2013) and for a photograph of Aldonza's tomb inscription.

27 See Ainsworth and Sánchez-Lassa 2012, pp. 92–94, where the document is quoted in Spanish and translated similarly. Lisa Rotmil (2010, p. 272) mentions Philip II's donation of 7,500 relics to the Escorial.

28 Ríos de Balmaseda 1991; Pérez Sánchez and Navarrete Prieto 2001, pp. 66–67, 215, no. 52; Ainsworth and Sánchez-Lassa 2012, p. 95.

29 In the 1580s, Aldonza Niño was named *guardamayor de las damas* to Anne of Austria, wife of Philip II. But one doubts that she was therefore "also a courtier" (Kagan 1995, p. 326), as her husband had been on behalf of Charles V and Philip II. Such titles were often honorary. Kagan (1995, p. 330) also creates the impression that Pedro Lasso may have inherited the cardinal's portrait from Aldonza Niño (an idea repeated in Davies and Elliott 2003, p. 284), but this is most unlikely.

30 On Rodrigo Niño's spectacular career, see Raeymaekers 2011 and Duerloo 2012, pp. 89–90, 96–97 (also index, p. 564, under Añover).

31 Raeymaekers 2011, p. 146. Kagan (1995, p. 327) records that in 1606 Pedro Lasso turned down the king's offer to be ambassador to the imperial court in Vienna, "partly because he had previously agreed to serve as guardian for the children of his absent brother Rodrigo." But there is no evidence that Rodrigo ever married or had children: see the family tree in Martínez Caviró 1985, p. 226, and the one in Martínez Caviró 1990, p. 313, which may be placed below that given in Martz 2003, p. 181. According to Raeymaekers (2011, p. 145), Rodrigo Niño "never got married and remained childless, [so that] his entire legacy went to his relatives in Spain, with his brother Pedro and his nephew Luis as the main heirs."

32 As noted in a private communication from Dries Raeymaekers dated December 6, 2012. If, against all appearances, the portrait was in Niño de Guevara's estate, it could have been left to or acquired by Rodrigo in 1609. But the heir to the entailed estates of the family, Pedro Lasso, would have been a much more likely recipient. At the cardinal's death in 1609 his widowed sister, Aldonza, had been dead for several years and their two brothers were no longer alive: Gabriel Niño (d. 1603?; recorded as deceased in 1607) and the childless Juan Niño de Guevara (1539–1607), 1st Conde de Añover (from 1602). Little is known about Gabriel's life, including his date of birth, or whether he ever married. On Gabriel's service to Archduke Albert, see Raeymaekers 2011, p. 133 and sources cited there.

33 Pedro Lasso had the superior title of Conde de los Arcos and, upon the king's assent, would have passed the countship of Añover to his son, Luis, without taking the title himself. Any such transfer of title was subject to the king's approval and took some time (as in the case of Rodrigo's title, 2nd Conde de Añover, which was granted in 1609, although his uncle, Juan Niño, 1st Conde de Añover, had died in 1607).

34 Pedro Lasso de la Vega was born on June 27, 1622. The date of his death has occasionally been given as 1674, but he died in September 1699 (Charles II made him a grandee of Spain in 1697).

35 The inventory of 1632 appears in Kagan 1995.

36 The date of 1639 is occasionally given, erroneously, as the date of the inventory of Pedro Lasso's estate (for example, in Davies and Elliott 2003, p. 178; the same inventory is dated 1632 on p. 282). But the inventory mostly dates from 1632 and does not represent the "estate" of anyone, in particular not that of Rodrigo Niño (d. 1620), as claimed in Brown and Carr 1984, p. 62, where the list of pictures in Pedro Lasso's house is called "el inventario de los bienes heredados por Luis de su tío." There is no reason to think that Luis's uncle Rodrigo ever owned any of the paintings in question, not even in some technical sense.

37 Brown and Carr 1984, p. 62. See also the previous note.

38 Some variations in the system suggest quick calculation. For example, *ducados* were usually converted to eleven *reales*

apiece, but in some entries tenths appear to have been used arbitrarily. Fifths were probably favored because doubling both numbers (integers and denominators) allows for immediate conversion to decimals. For example, the cardinal's portrait was appraised by Maíno at "D100." In this case a reduction of 20 percent, not the more common 40 percent or more, was applied. The value of 100 *ducados* was multiplied by 11 to give 1100 *reales*. To calculate $^4/_5$ of this amount the fraction $^8/_{10}$ would have been employed, or rather: 1100 was multiplied by 8 (to equal 8800) and a zero was dropped to divide by 10. The result is 880 *reales*, the figure in the left column.

39 The math may be that of Francisco Suárez de Rivera, a known public notary of Madrid (see Burke and Cherry 1997, p. 1669), since the name "franCo suarez" occurs in the left margin of the inventory's first page (but its meaning is unclear). Lower values may have resulted in lower inheritance taxes or some other financial advantage.

40 The modern idea that the paintings might have been sold to family members in order to benefit Luis Lasso's widow may be dismissed. She came from a very wealthy family, and Luis himself left her many valuable things. In his will he notes that the king had been asked to transfer his office as mint master of Toledo to his young son (Barrio Moya 1990, p. 348). In the inventory of his household goods, quantities of gold and silver objects, fine furniture, over 86,000 *reales'* worth of jewelry, and (a mere) 4,646 *reales'* (422 *ducados'*) worth of paintings are listed (ibid., pp. 349–51).

41 Brown and Carr 1984, pp. 62–63. The authors describe the cardinal's portrait as inherited by Luis from Rodrigo (see note 36 above), but the inventory of April 15, 1632, lists all the paintings in Pedro Lasso's possession (which he either owned or held as family property). Luis's own paintings, twenty-eight mostly religious (and evidently minor) works, were appraised by Maíno thirteen days later (April 28), as detailed in Barrio Moya 1990, pp. 348–52. As for pictures inherited from Rodrigo, there is an entry in the inventory of April 15 (Pedro Lasso), under "Pinturas en Cuerva," which lists in one room nine religious paintings and several secular works as "residuos del a[l]moneda del conde de Añover" ("remains from the auction of the Conde de Añover," meaning Rodrigo; Kagan 1995, p. 335).

42 As noted also in Davies and Elliott 2003, p. 284. A rare case of attribution is the "infanta dona Isabel [made by] Bartolome Gonzalez, pintor del rey Felipe III," which is valued at 300 *reales* (Kagan 1995, p. 337, in the list of pictures at Batres). The cardinal's portrait is valued about four times higher (1100 *reales*). Around 1627, Velázquez received 600 *reales* for his portrait of Gaspar de Guzmán, Conde-Duque de Olivares, ordered by the Marqués de Montesclaros (Cherry 1991, pp. 108–11).

43 Barrio Moya 1990, pp. 350–51. See also Barrio Moya 2002, p. 41, noting that none of the many paintings at Batres castle were attributed in the inventory of 1709.

44 Brown and Kagan 1987, p. 237, where it is noted that "the inventory appears to have been made simply as a record of transactions." See also Kagan 1984, pp. 90–91, for the inventory of Pedro Salazar de Mendoza's estate (Toledo, 1629), in which none of the paintings (including what must be El Greco's two views of Toledo) is attributed; and Cherry 1991, pp. 112–13, on Vicente Carducho and another artist's appraisal of the 3rd Marqués de Montesclaros's estate (1628), in which no artists are named apart from a set of four canvases assigned to the Bassanos.

45 Cherry 1991, pp. 113–14, and 113nn43–44. The author observes that "artists usually received small fees for valuations and exercised a minimum of connoisseurship" (p. 113n42). Another important example of an inventory of paintings with very few attributions (although works by Titian, Veronese, Tintoretto, Ribera, and Rubens are listed, and given values by Claudio Coello) is that of the 1691 estate inventory of the 10th Admiral of Castile (Burke and Cherry 1997, no. 117; kindly brought to my attention by Leticia Ruiz).

46 Christiansen in Davies and Elliott 2003, p. 284. See also Kagan 2010b, p. 60, on the question of character (El Greco's *vida* and Pliny's *anima*).

47 Zeri 1976, vol. 2, pp. 382–83, no. 258.

48 Monique Blanc (personal communication, July 2013) kindly provided information about the portrait of Pius V, dated 1566, in the Musée des Arts Décoratifs, Paris, inv. no. Pe 327, legs Emile Peyre, 1905.

49 Harold Wethey (1969–75, vol. 2, p. 90, under no. 22) mentions the present portrait as related to Titian's *Charles V Seated*.

50 Compare the use of a curtain in the background of El Greco's *Portrait of Vincenzo Anastagi*, of about 1575 (Frick Collection, New York), which suggests the "energetic charge" of a man of action (discerned in both portraits by José Alvarez Lopera in Portús et al. 2004, p. 123).

51 Richard Kagan, in conversation, June 25, 2013. See also the remark about Niño de Guevara's questioning of the laws governing racial and religious purity, in Davies and Elliott 2003, p. 284.

The Vision of Saint John (The Opening of the Fifth Seal)

1 On modern responses to *The Vision of Saint John*, see Keith Christiansen in Davies and Elliott 2003, pp. 212–13, and the literature cited there; Wismer and Scholz-Hänsel 2012, especially pp. 142–43, 158, 174, 216, 222, 331; and Birgit Thiemann's essay "Zuloaga as Collector and Intermediary," in ibid., pp. 374–81.

2 See Cossío 1908, vol. 1, pp. 355–57, 359, 603, no. 327, vol. 2, pl. 66.

3 There are many losses of the paint layer and ground distributed throughout. The only significant features that have required reconstruction are the proper right side of the face of the male nude at far right, the head and proper right hand of the female nude at center, and the fingers of the proper left hand of Saint John.

4 José Alvarez Lopera (2005, vol. 2, p. 230) suggests that the red, yellow, and green draperies were finished by Jorge Manuel. One might gain this impression from reproductions, but when one stands before the canvas itself, the folds, highlights, rhythms, and spatial effect of these sheets of cloth seem too careful, expressive, and consistent with El Greco's own handling in late works not to be by him.

5 On the hospital and Cardinal Tavera, see Wilkinson 1977; Marías 1983–86, vol. 2, pp. 231–43; and Marías 2007. Tavera and the hospital are discussed from a sociological viewpoint in Martz 1983, pp. 16–19, 168–88.

6 On Salazar de Mendoza and El Greco, see Kagan 1984 and Mann 1986, chap. 3.

7 See the plan in Marías 2007, p. 151. The placement of Tavera's tomb monument (decided by his heirs, not the cardinal himself) is discussed in Wilkinson 1977, chap. 6 ("The Commemorative Church"), especially pp. 103–7. See also Castán Lanaspa 1993, pp. 366–68, and Marías 2007, pp. 159–62.

8 San Román y Fernández 1982, p. 374, no. 184. The phrase is generally taken to mean "the Baptism main [altarpiece] of the hospital." Mann (1986, p. 121) translates the entry as "the principal Baptism for the hospital." The preceding entry in the 1621 inventory refers to "two large unfinished paintings for the side altars of the hospital" (San Román y Fernández 1982, p. 373, no. 183),

making it clear that *The Baptism* was not intended for one of the side altars. John the Baptist is also the subject of three reliefs on one side of Tavera's tomb monument: a central medallion representing the saint full-length and figure groups at either side representing the Baptism of Christ and the Beheading of John the Baptist. The other side of the monument has three similar reliefs devoted to the patron saint of Spain, Santiago el Mayor. See Arias Martínez 2011, pp. 199, 280 (ills.).

9 San Román y Fernández 1982, pp. 408–9, doc. XLI. Mann (1986, pp. 141–46) advances the "admittedly controversial" hypothesis that *The Vision of Saint John* was the central altarpiece, mainly on iconographic grounds. Later authors have convincingly dismissed the idea, for example, Christiansen in Davies and Elliott 2003, p. 212; Alvarez Lopera 2005, vol. 2, pp. 217–24; and Marías 2007, pp. 168–70.

10 See note 9 above on Mann 1986. Alvarez Lopera (2005, vol. 2, p. 221) maintains that the placement of *The Baptism* on the main retable is "the one certainty" that may be deduced from the inventories of 1614 and 1621 (see also p. 229).

11 See Wethey 1962, vol. 2, pp. 20–22, on the architecture of the high altar and p. 22 on that of the lateral altars. See also Alvarez Lopera 2005, vol. 2, pp. 217–31. The main retable was modified in 1625 and again in the early 1630s. The lateral altarpiece frames survive largely as El Greco designed them, except for the white paint covering the original gilding.

12 Mann (1986, p. 142) suggests, unconvincingly, that *The Baptism* may also have been cut down, without offering any technical or otherwise objective evidence. A crude scene of the river Jordan was added by Jorge Manuel or another artist to the bottom of *The Baptism*, presumably to make up the difference in height when it was installed not on the main retable but above the proper left side altar (see Alvarez Lopera 2005, vol. 2, pp. 221–22, under no. 75, referring to the description and photograph of this addition in Cossío 1908, where the dimensions with the addition are given as 412 × 195 cm).

13 See Wethey 1962, vol. 2, pp. 19–20, and Mann 1986, pp. 122–25, 145.

14 *The Baptism* was never installed above the high altar, probably because the main retable was not completed until after Jorge Manuel's death (see Marías 2007, p. 168). The delivery (in April 1623) of *The Baptism*, its installation on the left side altar, and its later locations are reported incorrectly in Mann 1986, p. 143; somewhat vaguely in Wethey 1962, vol. 2, p. 23; and accurately in Alvarez Lopera 2005, vol. 2, pp. 221–22, under no. 75.

15 On the debated question of Jorge Manuel's intervention in *The Annunciation*, see the summary of opinions in Alvarez Lopera 1999, pp. 437–38, no. 89a.

16 See Cossío 1908, p. 575, no. 136 (the Urquijo *Annunciation*), and p. 617, no. 387, under "references and citations," where the "upper half" of *The Apocalypse* is recorded as owned by the heirs of the Marqués de Castro-Serna (and thus mistakenly identified with the *Concert of Angels*). Cossío (ibid., p. 340) did not think that the Urquijo *Annunciation* was from the Tavera Hospital, but was a much earlier work ("1576 to 1584?"). The proper connection was made in San Román y Fernández 1927, as noted in Wethey 1962, vol. 2, p. 34, no. 44a.

Rousseau 1959, p. 254, shows the *Concert of Angels* reproduced above *The Annunciation*, with a plausible gap (lost or folded-over canvas) in between. This reconstruction is also illustrated in Brown et al. 1982, p. 174; in Alvarez Lopera 1999, p. 328; and in Alvarez Lopera 2005, vol. 2, fig. 132. José M. Pita Andrade erroneously reports (in Brown et al. 1982, p. 160) that

The Annunciation "remained on the high altar of the hospital until the nineteenth century," whereas Alvarez Lopera (2005, vol. 1, p. 437) states correctly that the canvas was "never delivered to the Hospital." It is curious that *The Annunciation* and *The Vision of Saint John* were both cut down, but there is no apparent reason to think that the pictures might have been together about 1880–1900; the common fate may simply reflect the difficulty of installing paintings at least four meters high (plus their frames) in private residences.

The Banco Urquijo, often cited in the literature as owning *The Annunciation*, was established in 1918 by the sons of the 2nd Marqués de Urquijo, and in the late 1900s was one of the financial institutions merged into the Banco Santander Central Hispano (renamed Banco Santander in 2007).

17 San Román y Fernández 1910, p. 191, under doc. no. 52.

18 As observed by Christiansen in Davies and Elliott 2003, p. 210. El Greco's practice of keeping *ricordi* in his studio is well known, but Alvarez Lopera (2005, vol. 2, pp. 225–26) considers it "practically certain" that the small canvases in the artist's estate which correspond with the Tavera altarpieces were *modelli* for that project.

19 Cossío 1908, p. 356.

20 As reported in Milward 1926, p. 24, where the painting (based on Zuloaga's information) is still called *Sacred and Profane Love*.

21 Cossío 1908, p. 356. The suggestion is taken up in Camón Aznar 1950, vol. 2, pp. 948–57, 1371, no. 266. See also Alvarez Lopera 2005, vol. 2, p. 229.

22 As noted by Christiansen in Davies and Elliott 2003, p. 212. For this line in the contract, see Cossío 1908, p. 680 (item no. 3 in the description of the main retable).

23 Alvarez Lopera (2005, vol. 2, p. 229) remarks that there are seven nudes, a "magic number repeated numerous times in the Apocalipsis and which was used also by Dürer and other artists in representing the same passage."

24 See Christiansen in Davies and Elliott 2003, p. 212, quoting Meyer Shapiro (notes in the departmental files of the Department of European Paintings, MMA) on an "old French gloss on the Apocalypse," according to which white stoles signify that the souls and bodies of martyred saints are in the earth, and they will receive other (presumably colored) garments after their resurrection. By contrast, Anna Reuter (in Giménez and Calvo Serraller 2006, p. 136) suggests that the green and yellow drapes "are possibly the funerary shrouds being discarded during the figures' passage to eternal life." It is, however, totally implausible to read the action of El Greco's nude figures as a casting off rather than receiving of garments. When it comes to heavenly raiment, throughout his oeuvre El Greco is much less consistent than the Book of Revelation. Furthermore, he was less likely to have been familiar with a thirteenth-century French manuscript than with Veronese's defense of artistic license before the Holy Office in 1573 (see Klein and Zerner 1989, pp. 129–32).

25 Compare, for example, Cellini's marble *Ganymede*, of about 1549–50 (Museo Nazionale del Bargello, Florence).

26 By comparison, the angel to the far left in *The Baptism of Christ* (fig. 17), although posed like Saint John, seems to gesture heavenward as a guide to the viewer.

27 Christiansen in Davies and Elliott 2003, p. 212.

28 It may be added that both saints named John may be taken as references to Juan (John) de Tavera, although his patron was the Baptist. Ronda Kasl observed, in conversation (2013), that it was not unusual at the time for someone named Juan to have John the Baptist as his patron saint. She also mentioned earlier

retables on which both Johns appear prominently. Fernando Marías (personal communication, July 2013) cited as an example the main retable (1520–22) by the sculptor Felipe Bigarny, in the Capilla Real, Granada.

29 Mann 1986, p. 118, citing Salazar's biography of Cardinal Tavera (Salazar de Mendoza 1603, pp. 287–90, 294–97).

30 On *The Last Judgment* and Michelangelo's Haman as a source for *The Vision of Saint John*, see Christiansen in Davies and Elliott 2003, p. 212 (where Signorelli's fresco is also mentioned). Titian's ceiling painting is discussed in Mann 1986, pp. 134–35.

31 As observed in Joannides 1995, p. 214, quoted by Christiansen in Davies and Elliott 2003, p. 212.

32 Soria 1948, p. 249. The reference is to Jan Muller's engravings after Goltzius's series The Creation of the World, of 1589–98, which offers no more than superficial parallels.

33 The comparison with El Greco's sculpture of Pandora (thought at the time to represent Eve) was made by its then owner, the Conde de las Infantas (Infantas 1945, p. 198); see Gabriele Finaldi in Davies and Elliott 2003, p. 236, on El Greco's *Epimetheus* and *Pandora*, and for Francisco Pacheco's report of seeing clay models by El Greco in 1611.

34 See Davies and Elliott 2003, pp. 174, 245.

35 See Carey 1999, especially Peter Parshall's essay "The Vision of the Apocalypse in the Sixteenth and Seventeenth Centuries," pp. 99–124.

36 The Dürer print is often mentioned, for example in Mann 1982, p. 67. On Gerung, see Christiansen in Davies and Elliott 2003, pp. 210–12, citing Nicos Hadjinicolaou in the Greek edition of Alvarez Lopera 1999, suppl. entry no. 90. The comparison appears to be original with Kehrer 1960, p. 72.

37 See Valencia de Don Juan 1903, vol. 2, pl. 84 (pls. 82–89 for the entire set), or the much less adequate reproduction in Junquera de Vega and Herrero Carretero 1986, vol. 1, p. 57. The central vision in this tapestry illustrates Rev. 7:9–13. On the complicated history of the Apocalypse tapestries, see Iain Buchanan in Campbell 2002, pp. 435–40, no. 51.

REFERENCES

Acidini Luchinat, Cristina
1998–99 *Taddeo e Federico Zuccari: Fratelli pittori del Cinquecento*. 2 vols. Milan: Jandi Sapi.

Ainsworth, Maryan W., and Ana Sánchez-Lassa
2012 "La Sagrada Familia de Jan Gossart." *Boletín del Museo de Bellas Artes de Bilbao* 6, pp. 73–112.

Alvarez Lopera, José
1999 as editor. *El Greco: Identidad y transformación. Creta, Italia, España.* Essays by José Alvarez Lopera, Nicos Hadjinicolaou, Maria Constantoudaki-Kitromilides, Lionello Puppi, Claudio Strinati, José Manuel Pita Andrade, Fernando Marías, and David Davies; catalogue entries by José Alvarez Lopera et al. Exh. cat., Museo Thyssen-Bornemisza, Madrid; Palazzo delle Esposizioni, Rome; National Gallery and Museum Alexandros Soutzos, Athens. Madrid: Museo Thyssen-Bornemisza; Milan: Skira. Also published in English, Greek, and Italian editions.
2005 *El Greco: Estudio y catálogo.* 2 vols. Madrid: Fundación de Apoyo a la Historia del Arte Hispánico.

Arias Martínez, Manuel
2011 *Alonso Berruguete: Prometeo de la escultura.* Palencia: Diputación de Palencia.

Barrio Moya, José Luis
1990 "El pintor alcarreño Juan Bautista Maíno tasador de la colección pictórica del Conde de Añover (1632)." *Wad-al-Hayara* 17, pp. 345–52.
2002 "El madrileño Castillo de Batres, según un inventario de 1709." *Castillos de España*, no. 126 (July), pp. 38–46.

Braun, Georg, and Franz Hogenberg
1572–1618 *Civitates Orbis Terrarum.* 6 vols. Cologne: Petrum à Brachel.
1966 *Civitates Orbis Terrarum, "The Towns of the World," 1572–1618.* Facsimile ed. 3 vols. Cleveland: World Publishing Co.
2008 *Städte der Welt: 363 Kupferstiche revolutionieren das Weltbild; Gesamtausgabe der kolorierten Tafeln, 1572–1617, nach dem Original des Historischen Museums Frankfurt. Civitates Orbis Terrarum.* Edited by Stephan Füssel. Cologne: Taschen.

Brown, Jonathan
1981 "In Detail: El Greco's View of Toledo." *Portfolio* 3, no. 1 (January–February), pp. 34–39.
1982 as editor. *Figures of Thought: El Greco as Interpreter of History, Tradition, and Ideas.* Studies in the History of Art 11. Washington, D.C.: National Gallery of Art.
1998 *Painting in Spain, 1500–1700.* New Haven and London: Yale University Press.

Brown, Jonathan, et al.
1982 *El Greco of Toledo.* Contributions by Jonathan Brown, William B. Jordan, Richard L. Kagan, and Alfonso E. Pérez Sánchez. Exh. cat., Museo Nacional del Prado, Madrid; National Gallery of Art, Washington, D.C.; Toledo Museum of Art, Toledo, Ohio; Dallas Museum of Fine Arts. Boston: Little, Brown and Company.

Brown, Jonathan, and Dawson A. Carr
1982 "*Portrait of a Cardinal*: Niño de Guevara or Sandoval y Rojas?" In Brown 1982, pp. 33–42.
1984 "El 'Retrato de un cardenal': Símbolo o simulacro?" In *Visiones del pensamiento: El Greco come intérprete de la historia, la tradición y las ideas*, edited by Jonathan Brown, pp. 55–73. Madrid: Alianza.

Brown, Jonathan, and Richard L. Kagan
    1982 "View of Toledo." In Brown 1982, pp. 19–30.
    1987 "The Duke of Alcalá: His Collection and Its Evolution." *Art Bulletin* 69 (June), pp. 231–55.

Brown, Jonathan, and Richard G. Mann
    1990 *Spanish Paintings of the Fifteenth through Nineteenth Centuries.* The Collections of the National Gallery of Art: Systematic Catalogue. Washington, D.C.: National Gallery of Art.

Burke, Marcus B., and Peter Cherry
    1997 *Collections of Paintings in Madrid, 1601–1755.* Edited by Maria L. Gilbert. 2 vols. Documents for the History of Collecting: Spanish Inventories 1. Los Angeles: Provenance Index of the Getty Information Institute.

Calduch Pedralba, Juan
    2012 "Dibujar, escribir, pintar: El Greco pintor de mapas." *EGE: Revista de expresión gráfica en la edificación*, no. 7 (October), pp. 44–59.

Camón Aznar, José
    1950 *Dominico Greco.* 2 vols. Madrid: Espasa-Calpe.

Campbell, Thomas P.
    2002 *Tapestry in the Renaissance: Art and Magnificence.* Contributions by Maryan W. Ainsworth et al. Exh. cat. New York: MMA.

Carey, Frances, ed.
    1999 *The Apocalypse and the Shape of Things to Come.* Contributions by Jonathan Alexander et al. Exh. cat. London: British Museum; Toronto and Buffalo: University of Toronto Press.

Castán Lanaspa, Javier
    1993 "A propósito del testamento del Cardenal Tavera." *Boletín del Seminario de Arte y Arqueología* 59, pp. 365–78.

Cherry, Peter
    1991 "New Documents for Velázquez in the 1620s." *Burlington Magazine* 133 (February) pp. 108–15.

Cossío, Manuel B.
    1908 *El Greco.* 2 vols. Madrid: Victoriano Suárez.
    1972 *El Greco.* New ed. Edited by Natalia Cossío de Jimenez. Barcelona: Editorial R. M.

Davies, David, and John H. Elliott
    2003 *El Greco.* Catalogue entries by Xavier Bray, Keith Christiansen, and Gabriele Finaldi; contributions by Marcus Burke and Lois Oliver; edited by David Davies. Exh. cat., MMA and The National Gallery, London. London: National Gallery Company.

Domínguez-Castro, Fernando, Juan I. Santisteban, Mariano Barriendos, and Rosa Mediavilla
    2008 "Reconstruction of Drought Episodes for Central Spain from Rogation Ceremonies Recorded at the Toledo Cathedral from 1506 to 1900: A Methodological Approach." *Global and Planetary Change* 63, nos. 2–3 (September), pp. 230–42.

Duerloo, Luc
    2012 *Dynasty and Piety: Archduke Albert (1598–1621) and Habsburg Political Culture in an Age of Religious Wars.* Burlington, Vt.: Ashgate.

Elliott, John Huxtable
    1986 *The Count-Duke of Olivares: The Statesman in an Age of Decline.* New Haven: Yale University Press.
    1989 *Spain and Its World, 1500–1700.* New Haven: Yale University Press.

Faldi, Italo
    1981 *Il Palazzo Farnese di Caprarola.* Turin: Seat.

Frelinghuysen, Alice Cooney, et al.
    1993 *Splendid Legacy: The Havemeyer Collection.* Contributions by Alice Cooney Frelinghuysen, Gary Tinterow, Susan Alyson Stein, Gretchen Wold, Julia Meech et al. Exh. cat. New York: MMA.

Giménez, Carmen, and Francisco Calvo Serraller, eds.
    2006 *Spanish Painting from El Greco to Picasso: Time, Truth, and History.* Exh. cat. New York: Solomon R. Guggenheim Museum.

Guinard, Paul
    1956 *El Greco: Biographical and Critical Study.* Translated by James Emmons. Lausanne: Skira.

Hadjinicolaou, Nicos, ed.
    1995 *El Greco of Crete: Proceedings of the International Symposium Held on the Occasion of the 450th Anniversary of the Artist's Birth; Iraklion, Crete, 1–5 September 1990.* Iraklion: Municipality of Iraklion.

Havemeyer, Louisine Waldron
    1961 *Sixteen to Sixty: Memoirs of a Collector.* New York: privately printed.

Infantas, Conde de las
    1945 "¿Dos esculturas del Greco?" *Archivo español de arte* 18, no. 70, pp. 193–200.

Joannides, Paul
    1995 "El Greco and Michelangelo." In Hadjinicolaou 1995, pp. 199–214.

Junquera de Vega, Paulina, and Concha Herrero Carretero
    1986 *Catálogo de tapices del Patrimonio Nacional.* Vol. 1, *Siglo XVI.* Madrid: Patrimonio Nacional.

Kagan, Richard L.
    1982 "The Toledo of El Greco." In Brown et al. 1982, pp. 35–73.
    1984 "Pedro de Salazar de Mendoza as Collector, Scholar, and Patron of El Greco." In *Symposium Papers II: El Greco: Italy and Spain*, edited by Jonathan Brown and José Manuel Pita Andrade, pp. 85–93. Studies in the History of Art 13. Washington, D.C.: National Gallery of Art.
    1986 "Philip II and the Art of the Cityscape." In *Art and History: Images and Their Meaning*, edited by Robert I. Rotberg and Theodore K. Rabb, pp. 115–35. Cambridge: Cambridge University Press.
    1989 as editor. *Spanish Cities of the Golden Age: The Views of Anton van den Wyngaerde.* Berkeley: University of California Press.
    1995 "The Count of Los Arcos as Collector and Patron of El Greco." In Hadjinicolaou 1995, pp. 325–39. Originally published in *Anuario del Departamento de Historia y Teoría del Arte* 4 (1992), pp. 151–59.
    1998 "*Urbs* and *Civitas* in Sixteenth- and Seventeenth-Century Spain." In *Envisioning the City: Six Studies in Urban Cartography*, edited by David Buisseret, pp. 75–108. Chicago and London: University of Chicago Press.
    2000 *Urban Images of the Hispanic World, 1493–1793.* New Haven and London: Yale University Press.
    2010a "El Greco in Toledo: The Artist's Clientele." In *El Greco's Pentecost in a New Context*, pp. 19–41. Dallas: Meadows Museum, Southern Methodist University.
    2010b "El Greco's Portraits Reconsidered." In Schroth 2010, pp. 58–68.

Kehrer, Hugo
    1960 *Greco in Toledo: Höhe und Vollendung, 1577–1614.* Stuttgart: W. Kohlhammer.

Klein, Robert, and Henri Zerner, eds.
  1989 *Italian Art, 1500–1600: Sources and Documents.* Evanston, Ill.: Northwestern University Press.

Kubler, George, and Martin Soria
  1959 *Art and Architecture in Spain and Portugal and Their American Dominions, 1500 to 1800.* Baltimore: Penguin Books.

Lafuente Ferrari, Enrique
  1969 *El Greco: The Expressionism of His Final Years.* Translated by Robert Erich Wolf. New York: Harry N. Abrams.

Lavín Berdonces, Ana Carmen, et al.
  2007 *Tesoros Ocultos: Fondos selectos del Museo del Greco y del Archivo de la Nobleza.* Exh. cat., Hospital Tavera, Toledo. Madrid: Ministerio de Cultura.

Links, J. G.
  1972 *Townscape Painting and Drawing.* New York: Harper and Row.

Mann, Richard G.
  1982 "The Altarpieces for the Hospital of Saint John the Baptist, Outside the Walls, Toledo." In Brown 1982, pp. 57–76.
  1986 *El Greco and His Patrons: Three Major Projects.* Cambridge: Cambridge University Press.

Marías, Fernando
  1983–86 *La arquitectura del Renacimiento en Toledo (1541–1631).* 4 vols. Toledo: Instituto Provincial de Investigaciones y Estudios Toledanos; Madrid: C.S.I.C.
  1986 "La obra artística y arquitectónica del Cardenal Sandoval y Rojas." In *El Toledo de Felipe II y El Greco,* edited by Fernando Marías, F. J. Portela Sandoval, M. Casamar, and M. Estella, pp. 9–23. Toledo: Consejería de Educación y Cultura, Museo de Santa Cruz.
  1996 "Villalpando, Francisco de." In *Dictionary of Art,* edited by Jane Turner, vol. 32, pp. 559–60. New York: Grove's Dictionaries.
  1997 *El Greco: Biografía de un pintor extravagante.* Madrid: Nerea. French ed.: *El Greco: Biographie d'un peintre extravagant.* Translated by Marie-Hélène Collinot. Paris: Cohen & Cohen.
  2001 *El Greco in Toledo.* Edited by Moira Johnston; translated by Gilla Evans. London: Scala.
  2007 *El Hospital Tavera de Toledo.* [Seville]: Fundación Casa Ducal de Medinaceli.
  2013 *El Greco: Life and Work, a New History.* Translated by Paul Edson and Sander Berg. New York: Thames & Hudson.
  2014 as editor. *El Greco of Toledo: Painter of the Visible and the Invisible.* Translated by Philip Sutton. Exh. cat. Toledo: Fundación El Greco.

Martínez Caviró, Balbina
  1985 "Los Grecos de Don Pedro Laso de la Vega." *Goya* 184 (January–February), pp. 216–26.
  1990 *Conventos de Toledo: Toledo, Castillo Interior.* Madrid: Ediciones El Viso.

Martz, Linda
  1983 *Poverty and Welfare in Habsburg Spain: The Example of Toledo.* Cambridge and New York: Cambridge University Press.
  2003 *A Network of Converso Families in Early Modern Toledo: Assimilating a Minority.* Ann Arbor: University of Michigan Press.

Mayer, August L.
  1926 *Dominico Theotocopuli El Greco: Kritisches und illustriertes Verzeichnis des Gesamtwerkes verfasst und eingeleitet.* Munich: F. Hanfstaengel.

Milward, Jo
  1926 "The Zuloaga Collection of El Grecos." *International Studio* 83 (February), pp. 23–29.

Moraleda y Esteban, Juan de
  1928 "El Monasterio Agaliense de Toledo." *Boletín Real Academia de Toledo,* ser. 1, no. 35 (June), pp. 130–38.

Partridge, Loren W.
  1969 "The Frescoes of the Villa Farnese at Caprarola." PhD diss., Harvard University, Cambridge, Mass.

Pérez Sánchez, Alfonso E., and Benito Navarrete Prieto
  2001 *Luis Tristán, h. 1585–1624.* Madrid: Ediciones del Umbral.

Portús, Javier, et al.
  2004 *The Spanish Portrait from El Greco to Picasso.* Contributions by José Alvarez Lopera et al. Exh. cat., Museo Nacional del Prado, Madrid. London: Scala.

Raeymaekers, Dries
  2011 "The 'Gran Privado' of Archduke Albert. Rodrigo Niño y Lasso, Count of Añover (ca. 1560–1620)." In *Agentes e identidades en movimiento España y los Países Bajos, siglos XVI–XVIII,* edited by René Vermeir, Maurits Ebben, and Raymond Fagel, pp. 129–49. Madrid: Silex Ediciones.

Reinhard-Felice, Mariantonia
  2005 *Oskar Reinhart Collection "Am Römerholz" Winterthur: Complete Catalogue.* Basel: Schwabe.

Ríos de Balmaseda, Antonia
  1991 "La capilla de reliquias de Cuerva y el cuadro de la Sagrada Cena de Tristán." *Toletum* 27, pp. 129–43.

Robertson, Clare
  1992 *"Il Gran Cardinale": Alessandro Farnese, Patron of the Arts.* New Haven and London: Yale University Press.

Rotmil, Lisa A.
  2010 "Understanding Piety and Religious Patronage: The Case of Anne of Austria and the Val-de-Grâce." In Schroth 2010, pp. 266–81.

Rousseau, Theodore, Jr.
  1959 "El Greco's Vision of Saint John." *MMAB,* n.s., 17, no. 10 (June), pp. 241–62.

Ruiz Gómez, Leticia, et al.
  2001 *Actas del Congreso sobre el Retablo del Colegio de Doña María de Aragón del Greco.* Essays by Leticia Ruiz Gómez and eight other contributors. Madrid: Museo Nacional del Prado.

Rutter, Frank
  1930 *El Greco (1541–1614).* New York: E. Weyhe.

Salazar de Mendoza, Pedro
  1603 *Chronico de el Cardenal don Juan Tavera.* Toledo: Pedro Rodriguez.
  1618 *El glorioso Doctor San Ilefonso, Arcobispo de Toledo, Primado de las Españas.* Toledo: Diego Rodriguez.

San Román y Fernández, Francisco de Borja de
  1910 *El Greco en Toledo ó nuevas investigaciónes acerca de la vida y obras de Dominico Theotocópuli.* Madrid: Librería general de Victoriano Suárez.
  1927 "De la vida del Greco (Nueva serie de documentos inéditos)." *Archivo español de arte y arqueología* 3, pp. 139–95, 275–339. Reprinted in San Román y Fernández 1982, pp. 287–410.
  1982 *El Greco en Toledo: Vida y obra de Domenico Theotocópuli.* Toledo: Zocodover. Facsimile reprint of works published 1910–41.

Scholz-Hänsel, Michael
  1995 "The Spectacles of the Grand Inquisitor: Counter-Revolutionary Aspects in the Work of El Greco and Humanistic Ideas in the Thinking of Spanish Inquisitors." In Hadjinicolaou 1995, pp. 295–307.

Schroth, Sarah, ed.

    2010 *Art in Spain and the Hispanic World: Essays in Honor of Jonathan Brown*. London: Paul Holberton Publishing.

Schulz, Juergen

    1978 "Jacopo de' Barbari's View of Venice: Map Making, City Views, and Moralized Geography before the Year 1500." *Art Bulletin* 60 (September), pp. 425–74.

Soria, Martin S.

    1948 "Some Flemish Sources of Baroque Painting in Spain." *Art Bulletin* 30 (December), pp. 249–59.

Valencia de Don Juan, Juan Bautista Crooke y Navarrot, Conde de

    1903 *Tapices de la corona de España*. 2 vols. Madrid: Hauser y Menet.

Wethey, Harold E.

    1962 *El Greco and His School*. 2 vols. Princeton, N.J.: Princeton University Press.

    1969–75 *The Paintings of Titian*. 3 vols. London: Phaidon.

Wilkinson, Catherine

    1977 *The Hospital of Cardinal Tavera in Toledo*. Outstanding Dissertations in the Fine Arts. New York and London: Garland.

Wismer, Beat, and Michael Scholz-Hänsel, eds.

    2012 *El Greco and Modernism*. Contributions by Judith F. Dolkart et al. Exh. cat., Museum Kunstpalast, Düsseldorf. Ostfildern: Hatje Cantz Verlag.

Zeri, Federico

    1976 *Italian Paintings in the Walters Art Gallery*. 2 vols. Baltimore: Walters Art Gallery.

NICHOLAS REEVES

A Rare Mechanical Figure from Ancient Egypt

He saw her charming, but he saw not half
The charms her down-cast modesty conceal'd.[1]
—James Thomson, 1700–1748

One of the more curious pieces to be found among the extensive Egyptian holdings of The Metropolitan Museum of Art is a small and delicately carved statuette in wood representing a woman wearing nothing more than a heavy, shoulder-length wig (fig. 1). Though the figure is unclothed, propriety is maintained by the surviving right hand, which is strategically placed to cover the sex, while a missing left arm appears originally to have shielded the breasts. The modesty is nonetheless feigned, for at the pull of a string the arms are designed to rise and display the subject's feminine charms in full. This is no ordinary Egyptian statuette, but a "proto-automaton," an object type encountered occasionally in the archaeological record of the Nile Valley, though seldom at this level of mechanical sophistication and never with such overtly erotic overtones.[2] First seen by Metropolitan Museum curator William C. Hayes

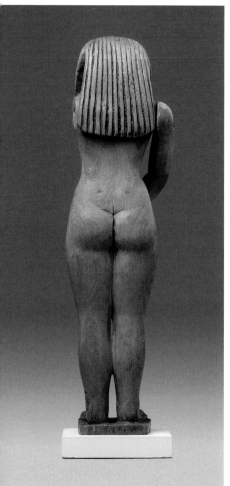

at the gallery of New York art dealer Michel Abemayor (1912?–1975) in January 1958, the object sparked immediate interest.[3] The outcome of a preliminary examination by the Museum's then Technical Laboratory was positive: though the piece displayed what appeared to be a layer of "modern varnish," beneath lay a "carved wood surface" that was evidently "of very ancient date."[4] For Hayes this determination provided sufficient grounds to proceed with the object's acquisition as "a fine example of small figure sculpture of the best period of the Egyptian Middle Kingdom"—that is to say, the Twelfth Dynasty (ca. 1981–1802 B.C.).[5]

Within months of the statuette's first public display, however, this Middle Kingdom dating was quietly dropped as a stylistic improbability, and the figure was reassigned to the end of the Eighteenth Dynasty (ca. 1550–1295 B.C.).[6] Sometime after that—presumably because an Eighteenth Dynasty attribution was itself unconvincing—the pendulum swung back, and a Twelfth Dynasty date was mooted once again.[7] By 1990, the now problematic "toy" had been withdrawn from view, consigned as a possible forgery to the study room of the Department of Egyptian Art.[8] And there for decades—since it is always easier to condemn than to rehabilitate—the piece would languish, unpublished and essentially unknown.

In 2010, the writer's attention was drawn to this statuette during a trawl through the Museum's Egyptian study reserves, prompting a detailed reexamination. The results of this review, detailed in part 1 of the present study, indicate forcefully that the figure is indeed the ancient work Hayes originally perceived it to be, and not the modern piece of gentlemen's whimsy that others subsequently may have come to suspect.[9] The questions raised by this remarkable little object are several, however, and these are addressed in part 2. Who is the intended subject? Why was the figure mechanized, and what was its intended use? Is the piece indeed Egyptian, or merely egyptianizing? The answers ventured point to the exceptional importance of the Metropolitan's statuette not only as a rare specimen of ancient mechanics but also as key to a broader understanding of identity and role within Egypt's minor arts during the first millennium B.C.

fig. 1 Female figure with internal mechanism. Egyptian, ca. 945–664 B.C. Wood, H. 4⅝ in. (11.8 cm). The Metropolitan Museum of Art, Purchase, Funds from Various Donors, 1958 (58.36a–c)

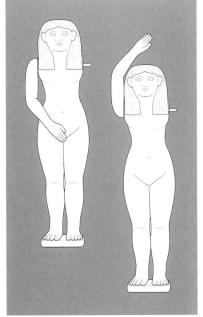

fig. 2 Diagram of fig. 1, showing movement of the surviving right arm

fig. 3 Detail of right side of statuette shown in fig. 1, showing square-cut aperture to receive the axle

fig. 4 Right arm and axle removed from statuette shown in fig. 1

PART I:
ESTABLISHING AUTHENTICITY AND DATE

Physical Description

The sculpture stands just 4⅝ inches tall and is carved from a light, close-grained wood. The female subject's feet are placed side by side on an integral base, and she wears a heavy, striated wig that extends below the shoulders. The figure displays what by ancient Egyptian standards is a relatively full body, that of an adult rather than a young girl, with breasts and genital area summarily defined, the usual dimples above the buttocks, and heavy thighs—a piece modeled both competently and tastefully, albeit in the somewhat bland style that has for years frustrated attempts to assign to the work a precise date.

As already observed, the statuette's physical stance is a curious one: rather than adopting the usual pose of an ancient Egyptian female figure, with arms held straight down on either side, the subject bends a surviving right arm to conceal her sex behind a strategically placed open hand. Stranger still, this arm was designed to lift and expose in tandem with its lost companion (fig. 2).

The motion depended on a true mechanism—a rotating axle introduced into the torso through a square-cut hole in the right shoulder (fig. 3). This aperture gives access to a large, neatly cut void and a small, drilled exit hole. One end of the axle is fashioned as a tenon, and onto this tenon the figure's right arm is firmly mortised. The axle's distal end preserves the remains of a similar tenon—now little more than a rounded stump—that originally carried the left arm. The positioning of this missing arm, and the likely reason for its loss, are considered below.

The axle (fig. 4) was hand-carved from a single piece of dark hardwood, with its middle section fashioned in the form of a spool around which a string could be wound. This string, now missing, was tied in place through a single, transverse piercing in the center. How the axle was made to turn is revealed by an X-radiograph (fig. 5): this shows the precise form of the axle cavity and the string's course through a narrow channel running from the floor of the cavity, down the statuette's left leg, and out through the base (fig. 6).[10] The mode of operation was simple: grasp the figure by the waist, pull the string to turn the axle, and watch as the arms miraculously rise.[11]

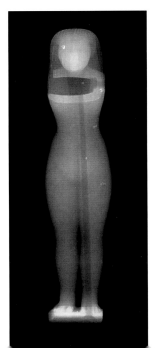
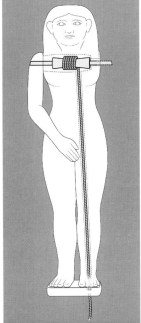

fig. 5 X-radiograph of statuette seen in fig. 1, showing the hollowed-out upper torso and channel drilled through the left leg for the operating string

fig. 6 Diagram of fig. 1, showing the operating mechanism (axle in beige, string in pink)

Sampling and Testing

Since the exceptional character of this object has provoked considerable skepticism over the years, the question of authenticity was revisited in collaboration with the Museum's Sherman Fairchild Center for Objects Conservation. The detailed scientific research upon which the following paragraphs are based was coordinated by conservator Ann Heywood and carried out between 2011 and 2013.

Visual examination of the figure's three surviving elements, together with material sampling of the torso, indicated that both the body and the surviving arm were very probably carved from boxwood (*Buxus* sp.), the material of choice, experience would suggest, for the production in ancient Egypt of high-quality, small-scale sculptures of this type.[12] A macroscopic examination of the axle suggests that it was carved either from a species of ebony (*Diospyros L.*) or from African blackwood (*Dalbergia melanoxylon*).[13] Most interesting of all, radiocarbon (C-14) testing revealed that the tree from which the body was sculpted was felled sometime between 910 B.C. and 800 B.C.—that is, during the Twenty-Second Dynasty (945–712 B.C.).[14]

While the materials from which the figure was constructed were appropriate for an ancient work of art, still the possibility remained that old wood might have been employed to carve a completely modern figure and mechanism. Further examination was therefore necessary.

As the statuette had received little substantive treatment since its arrival at the Museum, a detailed investigation could be undertaken of the underlying surface.[15] The modern coating ("varnish") first noted in 1958 was removed, greatly reducing the darkened, saturated appearance of the wood. The earlier surfaces of the work's three components were then examined using X-radiograph fluorescence spectroscopy (XRF).[16] The results were instructive. Trace elements of calcium,

iron, and chlorides on the body, arm, and axle provided a likely indication of age, while traces of copper on the body and arm possibly reflected the use of copper tools. A sample of the wig's pigment fill (now mostly lost) was examined by polarizing light microscopy and identified as a carbon black mixed with a small amount of Egyptian blue.[17] Elevated levels of copper were also noted. While the trace of Egyptian blue may represent nothing more than an impurity, its presence speaks well for the antiquity of the figure. If the coloring was applied deliberately, then its presence could point to an identification of the subject: with its hair mimicking the appearance of lapis lazuli, clearly the figure would have been intended to be understood as the image of a goddess.[18]

Dating and Likely Origin

The carbon-14 test results provide a reliable point of departure for determining the figure's date of production. Since the tree that supplied the statuette's wood was felled no earlier than the late tenth or ninth century B.C., previous attributions to the Twelfth and Eighteenth Dynasties may obviously be ruled out. If the wood was carved soon after the tree was felled, the work may be assigned to the Third Intermediate Period (ca. 1070–712 B.C.), a dating that in fact correlates with the figure's heavyset femininity. That the statuette appears to have been laid out according to a proportional grid[19] strengthens the presumptions of antiquity and local Egyptian workmanship—or at least of a work designed and realized by a native craftsman rather than by a foreign (Mediterranean) artisan following a vague, egyptianizing aesthetic.[20]

Stylistic Anomalies

While a proposed dating within the first half of the first millennium B.C. seems consistent with both the scientifically established age of the wood and the figure's

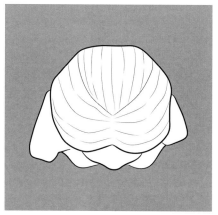

fig. 7a Detail of statuette shown in fig. 1, showing the parting of the wig on the crown

fig. 7b Rendering of the carved wig of a limestone statuette, showing crown parting similar to that in fig. 7a. Egyptian Museum, Cairo (JE 43582)

fig. 7c Rendering of the carved wig of an ebony statuette, showing shoulder parting similar to that in fig. 1. Rijksmuseum van Oudheden, Leiden (AH 167-a)

fig. 8a Wood statuette with pose similar to that seen in fig. 1. H. 10¼ in. (26 cm). Ägyptishes Museum, Berlin (12662)

fig. 8b Wood statuette with pose similar to that seen in fig. 1. H. 9½ in. (24.1 cm). Private collection

overall style and proportions, a number of idiosyncratic features displayed by the piece warrant consideration and comment.

The first peculiarity of note is the modeling of the figure's wig. Although it is of the same tripartite pattern as wigs traditionally worn by Egyptian divinities, the hair is arranged not with the usual central parting but in a decidedly odd manner—with a T-shaped parting that divides side to side and also backward (fig. 7a). A second curious feature is the manner in which the hair falls over each shoulder, leaving a large and deep triangular void through to the level of the neck (see fig. 1). As anomalous as these details at first sight appear, however, neither one is unique: an extensive search through the literature reveals sound Egyptian parallels for both (figs. 7b,c).[21]

A third and more disquieting feature is the form of the statuette's surviving arm: eccentrically angled and positioned, it appears to break every rule of Egyptian sculptural representation. Yet it is clear that the three surviving components of the artwork—torso, arm, and axle—share a long common history, and thus that a crooked right arm was indeed part of the original design. Microscopic examination confirms that the arm is carved from a wood similar to the wood of the torso, while XRF readings for this limb are consistent with those of the main figure. The undue width of the surviving right shoulder, moreover, would seem to rule out any suggestion of modern alteration—i.e., the possibility that the statuette might originally have been a static work that was subsequently "improved" in modern times by sawing off the arms, hollowing out the torso, and adding a winding mechanism.

The most convincing of all the evidence supporting the statuette's proposed age and authenticity is the revelation that the figure's curious pose is not unique. Two direct parallels have now been identified: one in Berlin (fig. 8a), which, like the Metropolitan's sculpture, covers the genital area with its right hand; and a closely similar piece on the website of the Young Museum of Ancient Cultural Arts, Burnet, Texas, which shields with the left (fig. 8b).[22] Albeit with bodies somewhat fuller in form than that of the Metropolitan Museum figure, and wearing wigs of a significantly shorter, more fashionable style, these two images represent obvious variations on the same theme, differing from the Museum's work only in date.[23] With the Metropolitan statuette to be assigned to the earlier part of the Third Intermediate Period on grounds of material analysis and style, the two static images, judged on the basis of style alone, are clearly slightly later.[24]

**PART II:
ESTABLISHING MEANING AND SIGNIFICANCE**

Identity

An important though seldom discussed feature of ancient Egyptian art is the greater compositional freedom accorded the minor arts in comparison with larger, more formal sculptures in stone. This can be explained in part by the fact that the decorative realm is where visual art and popular literature converge: it is here, for example, in a range of casual, two-dimensional contexts, that we find images alluding to the Myth of the Sun's Eye.[25] In three dimensions, other art-text crossovers are evidently to be recognized in a number of recurring, rule-flouting representations: the kitten-holding girl casually brushing back her hair, the dwarf struggling under the weight of an enormous jar, the dancer turning her head to cast a backward glance as she lifts her skirt.[26] Since only the smallest portion of Egyptian folk tales has come down to us, the literary contexts of these images have mostly been lost; to the ancients, however, the allusions would have been obvious, neatly conveyed by a singular pose or meaningful gesture.

Is it possible that the Metropolitan's statuette conceals a similar literary reference? The evidence suggests that it might.

fig. 9 Papyrus Chester Beatty I, ca. 1147–1143 B.C., recto, p. 4. Chester Beatty Library, Dublin

"The Contendings of Horus and Seth" is a coarsely humorous tale about an official hearing, held before Re-Harakhty and the Great Ennead, to assess the respective claims advanced by Horus and Seth to succeed to the throne of the deceased Osiris.[27] At the particular point in the story that interests us (fig. 9), the sun god has retired from the fray offended and has fallen into a deep depression. Alan Gardiner's translation of the relevant passage takes up the narrative:

> (4, 1) And the great god [Re-Harakhty] passed a day / lying upon his back in his arbour, and his heart was very sore, and he was alone.
> (2) And after a long space / Hathor, the lady of the southern sycomore, came and stood before her father, the Master of the Universe, and she uncovered her nakedness before his face.
> (3) And the great god / laughed at her. . . .[28]

This story is of interest on several levels. Beyond its simple amusement value, the episode has an important propagandist aim, which is to affirm the goddess Hathor's pivotal role in the maintenance of the cosmic order (*maat*).[29] Through this narrative, Hathor's unique power is emphasized: she alone possesses the ability to rouse her sun-god father from his lethargy and persuade him to reengage with the world, and she achieves this feat by revealing her "nakedness."

Gardiner's rendering of the text at this point, however, is so imprecise as to be misleading, with the translation "nakedness" concealing a "grosser" but far more illuminating word: *kꜣt*, "vagina."[30] The deliberate exposure of Hathor's sex so forcefully brings to mind the poses of the Berlin and Young Museum figures and the mechanical action of the Metropolitan Museum's statuette that all three are surely to be recognized as referencing this same lewd act.[31] In short, "The Contendings of Horus and Seth" confirms all three works not only as images of a goddess (a possibility already implied by the Egyptian-blue wig inlay of the Metropolitan's piece) but as manifestations of the preeminent divinity Hathor in her guise as "lady of the vulva" (*nb.t ḥtp.t*).[32]

Role

What was the intended function of the Museum's doll-like carving? There are several possibilities for such string-operated figures.

A forthcoming textual study by Alexandra von Lieven identifies comparable objects in a long-known autobiography from the early Eighteenth Dynasty: two goddess figures, Nekhbet and probably Wadjet, with operable arms perhaps not dissimilar from those of the Metropolitan's piece.[33] These figures represent component parts of a seemingly unique "super clock" invented by the owner of Theban tomb C2, Amenemhat, and anticipate by a millennium and more the string-operated automata later devised by Heron of Alexandria (ca. A.D. 10–70).[34]

Less sophisticated in design than the Amenemhat mechanism but perhaps closer to what we see represented in the Metropolitan Museum figure are the independent string-operated images mentioned by Herodotus in his description of the Egyptian "festival of Dionysus," an important text reminding us that ancient Egyptian objects with movable parts are not always to be regarded as childish playthings.[35]

> [2] The rest of the festival of Dionysus is observed by the Egyptians much as it is by the Greeks, except for the dances; but in place of the phallus, they have invented the use of puppets (νευρόσπαστα) two feet high moved by strings, the male member nodding and nearly as big as the rest of the body, which are carried about the villages by women; a flute-player goes ahead, the women follow behind singing of Dionysus. [3] Why the male member is so large and is the only part of the body that moves, there is a sacred legend that explains.[36]

The well-known group of ivory dancing dwarfs found at Lisht (South Pyramid Cemetery) by the Metropolitan Museum's Egyptian Expedition in 1933–34

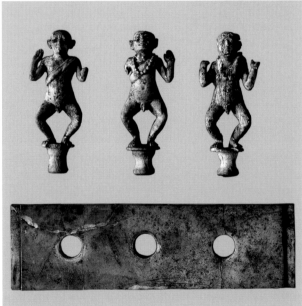

fig. 10 Three views of a dancing dwarfs tableau. Egyptian, ca. 1950–1900 B.C. Ivory, H. of figures 2½ in. (6.4 cm). Separate figure at top left: The Metropolitan Museum of Art, Rogers Fund, 1934 (34.1.130); rest of tableau: Egyptian Museum, Cairo (JE 63858)

falls into a similar category (fig. 10).[37] Discovered on the threshold of a Twelfth Dynasty tomb, this small tableau seems originally to have belonged to a young girl named Hepy, whose other possessions (found alongside the dwarfs) we now see point to an association with the goddess Hathor.[38]

A principal role of Hathor and of dwarfs in general was, of course, to entertain. One aspect of the goddess's entertainment skills has been recounted above in the discussion of "The Contendings of Horus and Seth." For dwarfs, we have a famous inscription in the tomb of Harkhuf at Qubbet el-Hawa, Aswan, which mentions "a dwarf (*dng*) who dances for the god"—a gift for the young Pepi II (ca. 2246–2152 B.C.) from the land of Iam.[39] Another inscription, Pyramid Text spell P465, makes reference to the king himself as "a *dng* of the god's dances, an entertainer before [his] great seat."[40] Both dwarf references point up an interesting fact: that the rituals carried out on behalf of the gods consisted of more than simple censing, the offering of food, and the changing of the divine images' clothes; it is clear that periodically the divine presence required meaningful entertainment also.

The evidence combines to suggest for the Lisht dwarfs a cultic role, and this, by extension, hints at a possible and legitimate function for the Metropolitan's statuette. In whatever manner Hathor's mechanical image was actually employed—whether by a priest in the immediate presence of a cult image (of Re), or before a wider, festal audience—the reenactment of the goddess's sexual exposure went far beyond ordinary amusement.[41] The function of the Metropolitan Museum figure was both serious and profound: to reenergize the supreme deity, and by so doing guarantee the continued functioning of the cosmos.

Pose

To understand the precise nature of the entertainment offered by the Museum's piece, it is essential to consider how the work might have appeared when complete—i.e., how the missing left arm was originally arranged. As described above, for this figure two static parallels may be invoked, one in Berlin and one shown on the website of the Young Museum (see figs. 8a, b). For these parallels, several similarly static variants exist with arms arranged in other ways (see below, "Related Images in Wood").[42] Because the New York figure's arms were both conjoined and movable, however, the options for their original positioning are greatly reduced. In fact, only one reconstruction is both mechanically feasible and physically meaningful,

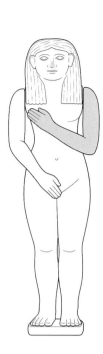

fig. 11 Diagrams of fig. 1, with reconstruction of missing left arm shown in lowered and raised positions

fig. 12 Figure of a goddess (Hathor?). Wood, H. 29⅛ in. (74 cm). Private collection, Rome

fig. 13 Detail of fig. 1, showing damage to the nose and mouth probably resulting from repeated impacts by the missing left arm

a conjoined left arm arranged to cover the breasts would, when lifted, have impacted the nose and chin (fig. 13). It is obvious, moreover, that repeated impacts over time would have placed considerable strain on the tenon, causing it eventually to fail and the limb to become detached.

Significance

What did the ancient craftsman seek to achieve by incorporating a mechanism into this figural type? Recall for a moment the Lisht tableau and the motion it sought to capture—not a single, one-off movement, but the twisting, to-and-fro choreography of a troupe of dancing dwarfs (see fig. 10). Was it perhaps by means of a similar, cheekily comic dance that Hathor first gladdened the sun god's heart? Was this how Hathor's crude physical exposure was in practice reenacted in temples and festivals? Was the intended aim of the Metropolitan Museum's piece to capture, through the repeated operation of its mechanism, the fundamental movements of such a ritual performance?

   An answer to all of these questions is suggested by the pose of the Museum's figure: lowered, the arms not only conceal but also tease; raised, they do not merely reveal but also display. Intriguingly, the form of that display recalls a specific movement in the so-called belly dance of the Ghawazi.[44] Details from romanticized Western representations of the dance, by Jean-Auguste-Dominique Ingres (1780–1867) and David Roberts (1796–1864), here serve to illustrate the resemblance (figs. 14, 15).[45]

   Is this similarity in pose mere coincidence? Perhaps not. It is interesting to note the profound moral disapproval generated in both East and West by the practitioners of Ghawazi dance: banished to Upper Egypt by Muhammad Ali in 1834 as part of his social reforms, the Ghawazi were characterized two years later by Edward William Lane as "the most abandoned of the courtesans of Egypt."[46] Charles Dudley Warner, writing of his own experiences in 1874–75, called the troupe "an aristocracy of vice."[47] If the Ghawazi or similar performers did indeed trace their origins back to Hathor, such dancing not only would have been essentially idolatrous but would have borne associations even more challenging. For in the days of the goddess, the focus was not the gyrating midriff of today's dance but the performer's fully exposed and deliberately proffered sexual parts (figs. 16, 17).[48]

and that is a pose in which the left arm, echoing the function of the right, is artfully arranged first to conceal and then to reveal the breasts (fig. 11).

   Not only is this *pudica* ("modest" or "shameful") pose attested elsewhere in the Egyptian archaeological record—in another, privately owned static image, again conceivably of Hathor (or of one of her priestesses), this time shown clothed and wearing a plain tripartite wig (fig. 12)—but physical proof of the positioning of the Metropolitan statuette's missing left arm may in fact be discerned in the condition of the object itself.[43] It can be no coincidence that the work displays surface damage at precisely the point where

fig. 14 Jean-Auguste-Dominique Ingres (French, 1780–1867). Detail of *The Turkish Bath*, 1832. Oil on canvas, mounted on wood, Diam. 42½ in. (108 cm). Musée du Louvre, Paris (RF 1934)

fig. 15 David Roberts (Scottish, 1796–1864). *The Ghawazee, or Dancing Girls, Cairo.* Hand-colored lithograph, 9⅞ × 14 in. (25 × 35.5 cm). Reproduced in Roberts 1849, pl. 37

fig. 16 Ostracon decorated with an image of a Hathor *khener* dancer. Egyptian, ca. 1503–1482 B.C. Painted limestone, 4⅛ × 6⅝ in. (10.5 × 16.8 cm). Museo Egizio, Turin (7052)

fig. 17 Statuette representing a Hathor *khener* dancer. Egyptian, ca. 1938–1630 B.C. Limestone, L. 6⅞ in. (17.3 cm). Brooklyn Museum, Gift of the Egypt Exploration Fund (13.1024)

fig. 18a Hathor image. Wood,
H. 2⅛ in. (5.5 cm). Highclere
Castle, Newbury, United
Kingdom

fig. 18b Hathor image. Wood,
H. 8¼ in. (20.9 cm). Royal-
Athena Galleries, New York

fig. 18c Hathor image. Wood,
H. 27¼ in. (69 cm). Staatliches
Museum Ägyptischer Kunst,
Munich (ÄS / 2958)

Related Images in Wood

Our discussion turns now to a series of related figures
in wood (and occasionally ivory) that fall within the
same object class as the Hathors of the Berlin and
Young Museums—images consistently heavyset, wearing short, bobbed wigs, and all of uncertain identity.
As already observed, there are several known poses.[49]
The one most commonly encountered is that shown
in figure 18a, with arms positioned straight down
by the sides; the second most frequent is seen in figure 18b, which has the left arm raised to the level of the
breasts—an arrangement reminiscent of the Ishtar/
Astarte figures of the Near East. Less common poses
are seen in figures 8a,b, in which the hand is lowered to
cover the subject's sexual parts, and in figure 18c, in
which an already strong impulse to associate the entire
class with the entertainer-goddess is strengthened by
the inclusion within the composition of a musical
instrument.

Why so many variations? One explanation might
be that each variant is a manifestation of Hathor or her
proxy in one of the various roles enacted by or for the
goddess in the cultic festivities periodically held in her
honor. The relief-carved surface of a Late period steatite
bowl inscribed in Demotic, now in the British Museum,
depicts one such celebration in full swing (fig. 19).[50] It
will be observed how the participants echo in their variety of poses not merely the three-dimensional Hathor
types in wood, but later imagery also. The bowl's fourth
figure from the right—a woman slapping her buttocks
and lifting her skirt—is of particular interest. Her action
not only recalls the exposure seen in the Metropolitan
Museum's mechanical figure but serves directly to associate that work with the *anasyrma* (skirt-lifting) motif
commonly found in a range of variously attributed terracottas of the Greco-Roman period (fig. 20).[51]

The suspicion that Hathor is the goddess univer-
sally represented in this wooden figural type finds ulti-
mate confirmation in an articulated version now in
Edinburgh (fig. 21).[52] The peculiar manner in which this
statuette's legs are designed to move offers indisputable
proof of both role and identity: the hinges at the hips
allow the legs to move not only front to back from the
knees down, in the usual manner, but also sideways—
i.e., not only to walk, but to part and reveal. The reference, again, will be to Hathor's sexual exposure before
her father Re.

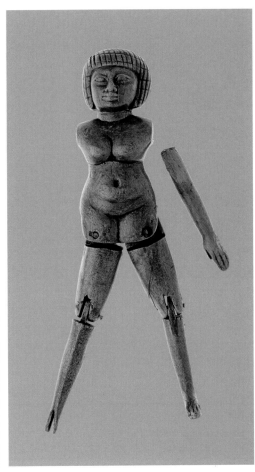

fig. 19 Bowl showing Hathoric festival, 664–404 B.C. Steatite, carved in raised relief. Diam. 6 in. (15.3 cm). British Museum, London (47992)

fig. 20 Figure of a goddess lifting her skirt, 1st century B.C. Terracotta, H. 5¾ in. (14.6 cm). Ägyptisches Museum, Universität Leipzig (3634)

fig. 21 Mobile-limbed statuette in wood with legs hinged laterally at the hips. H. 11½ in. (29.2 cm). National Museums Scotland, Edinburgh (A.1956.132)

fig. 22a Mobile-limbed Hathor figure. Later Intermediate Period. Bronze, H. 9½ in. (24.1 cm). Walters Art Museum, Acquired by Henry Walters (54.2085)

fig. 22b Mobile-limbed Hathor figure. Later Intermediate Period. Bronze, H. 6¾ in. (17 cm). Brooklyn Museum, By exchange (42.410)

fig. 22c Mobile-limbed Hathor figure. Later Intermediate Period. Bronze. Formerly Museum August Kestner, Hannover (B291), now lost

fig. 22d Mobile-limbed Hathor figure. Later Intermediate Period. Bronze, H. 5½ in. (14 cm). British Museum, London (37162)

Related Images in Bronze

If the Edinburgh piece is now to be recognized as an image of Hathor, and if the attribution may indeed be extended to the entire range of poses within this figural class in wood, then it is a priori likely that a series of analogous sculptures in bronze which feature similar pivoting arms (and sometimes mobile legs) are also to be associated with the goddess (figs. 22a,b,c,d). Although these sculptures were the subject of an important discussion by Elizabeth Riefstahl more than half a century ago, few conclusions have in fact ever been reached for this important subset.[53]

Most of the bronzes wear the same bobbed wig as the Hathor figures in Berlin, the Young Museum, and Edinburgh.[54] They also display the same physical nakedness and the same mature proportions that identify them as products of the later Third Intermediate Period. Furthermore, a single example in the British Museum shows evidence of having carried in its right hand a mirror, the Hathoric associations of which are well known.[55]

If a general assignment to Hathor is accepted for this class of bronzes, then they make an interesting contribution to the discussion. It has been put to the present writer that, while the hands of these figures do not actively conceal their sexual parts, the mobility incorporated within both wood and bronze versions of this naked, bob-wigged type may have been intended to accomplish such concealment and revelation by grasping a liftable *lost textile skirt*.[56] A bronze specimen excavated from the Heraion on the island of Samos hints at the validity of this proposition (fig. 23).[57] The upper limbs of the Heraion bronze are frozen in position by corrosion: clearly, the figure was deposited in the temple in antiquity with its arms raised, and thus, one might presume, with its hypothetical skirt lifted in the now familiar Hathoric gesture of revelation and reinvigoration.[58] If this was indeed the case, then the possibility highlighted above of an association between the concealing/revealing hands of the Metropolitan Museum's statuette and the later *anasyrma* terracottas of Greco-Roman times would of course be strengthened.

Proto-automata and Puppetry

The Riefstahl bronzes not only display fully or partially mobile limbs but also loops—either a single large hoop or two small ones—on top of their heads (fig. 22c, fig. 24). Foot loops, too, are occasionally found.[59] These fittings differ markedly from those encountered in ordinary Egyptian bronzes, which seem likely to have been

fig. 23 Hathor figure with
arms corroded in position, as
if to raise a textile skirt. Found
in the Heraion, Samos. Bronze,
H. 5⅝ in. (14.3 cm).
Archaeological Museum of
Vathy, Samos

fig. 24 Bronze Hathor head
fitted with two loops. Ashmolean
Museum, Oxford (1872.85)

supplied for the figures' suspension as votive offerings.[60] The head loops of the Riefstahl images bring
to mind instead a very different function: that of a
bracket—specifically, the bracket found in premodern
overhead-rod puppets. The most familiar examples of
this class are, of course, the "Sicilian marionettes"
of the *opera dei pupi*, which are manipulated by means
of a metal bar attached to the crown (fig. 25).[61]

As a type, the overhead-rod puppet is of some
antiquity, with versions of it attested in Greece as far
back as the third to the second century B.C. (fig. 26).[62] If
the identification now proposed for the mobile-limbed
bronzes of Egypt's Third Intermediate Period is
accepted, then clearly the type's origins go back further
still, and by several centuries. A recognition of the
Riefstahl bronzes as Sicilian-style puppet representations of Hathor would in fact serve to place both those
figures and the Metropolitan Museum's articulated
statuette in precisely the same conceptual class.

As the evidence mounts, the possibility of a related
puppet-performance origin seems increasingly plausible
for the Museum's figure and, by extension, for the
majority of string-operated Egyptian proto-automata
currently known.

CONCLUSIONS

Given the frequency with which wood and bronze
images of Hathor are evidently to be discerned in the
archaeological record of the first millennium B.C., it is
obvious that the goddess and her worship were both
widely spread and frequently celebrated—far more,
perhaps, than has been recognized previously. Represented in a variety of poses, Hathor was clearly a familiar and popular presence, and not only within Egypt
itself: her images are encountered throughout the
Mediterranean world, alongside, for example, and often
indistinguishable from, those of her Near Eastern
equivalent, Astarte.[63]

The Metropolitan Museum's figure represents a
rare and unusual version of this Hathor type, produced between the Twenty-Second and Twenty-Fifth
Dynasties, and most likely during the earlier part of that
range. The piece's mechanical nature renders it particularly significant. Frivolous to us in its string-operated
action, the figure's purpose was in fact deeply meaningful, alluding in both its pose and its motion to Hathor's
crucial, energizing exposure of her sex as documented
in "The Contendings of Horus and Seth." In essence a
puppet, the object was intended to entertain and
appease the supreme deity, Re-Harakhty, and so ensure
the continued functioning of the cosmos. Whether it
was operated in seclusion, by a priest before the sun god
in his shrine, or employed in a more communal religio-
theatrical setting remains uncertain.

The two static parallels here identified as sharing
the unusual pose of the Metropolitan Museum's image
are a figure now in Berlin and a specimen presented on
the website of the Young Museum in Texas (figs. 8a, b).

These permit us to suggest that a majority of associated and previously unidentified figures in wood and bronze are similarly to be understood as images of the goddess Hathor. Given the mobile limbs displayed by a number of the former and the majority of the latter (which, additionally, carry marionette-style brackets), it is likely that the works in this group, too, had a ritualistic function; and while there is no evidence that the Museum's figure was ever clothed, it is very possible that the later bob-wigged versions in wood and bronze were originally equipped with simple linen dresses that their mobile limbs were intended to lift.

Finally, it is obvious that the Metropolitan Museum's Hathor image was mechanized for a reason. The proposal put forward here is that, in common with the tableau of ivory dwarfs from Lisht (fig. 10), the purpose of the Metropolitan's puppet was to capture the movements of a sacred dance. In the simple lifting and lowering of Hathor's upper limbs, the performance would have both framed and softened the graphic nature of the goddess's sexual exposure. Significantly or not, the motion and positioning of the figure's arms bring particularly to mind images of premodern Egyptian dance—especially the belly dancing of the famed nineteenth-century Ghawazi troupe.

ACKNOWLEDGMENTS

My thanks are due to Dorothea Arnold, Caris-Beatrice Arnst, Gustavo Camps, Yassana Croizat-Glazer, Luc Delvaux, Tony Frantz, Daniel Hausdorf, Marsha Hill, Jack Josephson, Nanette Kelekian, Tim Kendall, Alexandra von Lieven, Marijn Manuels, Joan Mertens, Brian Muhs, Diana Craig Patch, Gay Robins, Ann Macy Roth, Magda Saleh, Phyllis Saretta, Friederike Seyfried, Michael Seymour, and Francisco Tiradritti for their advice, information, comments, and practical assistance. To Robyn Gillam, Ann Heywood, and Maya Muratov, I owe a particular debt of gratitude.

NICHOLAS REEVES
University of Arizona Egyptian Expedition

fig. 25 Overhead-rod-operated marionette. Sicily, 19th century. Mixed media, H. 39⅜ in. (100 cm). Location unknown

fig. 26 Three overhead-rod-operated puppets (rods now missing). Probably South Italy (Magna Graecia), 3rd–2nd century B.C. Terracotta. Formerly Campana Collection, Rome. Probably Musée du Louvre, Paris (left to right: CP 4647, CP 4656, CP 4635)

NOTES

1 James Thomson, *The Seasons* (Edinburgh: Alexander Donaldson, 1774), "Autumn" (l. 229).

2 Price 1964, especially p. 10. For a selective list of Egyptian "proto-automata," see note 35 below.

3 For more on Michel Abemayor, see Bierbrier 2012, p. 3. The statuette heads a penciled list, in the handwriting of W. C. Hayes, of eight objects viewed at Abemayor's gallery on January 13, 1958: "1. Wooden Statuette of Nude Girl Thebes (?) H. 4⅞ [in.]," with the price. Department of Egyptian Art, MMA.

4 Typewritten Recommendation for Purchase, January 20, 1958, Department of Egyptian Art.

5 Ibid.

6 The statuette was initially displayed as part of a special exhibition of recent accessions, February 27–October 2, 1958. Its assignment to the end of the Eighteenth Dynasty was recorded in the object accession cards of the Department of Egyptian Art.

7 Penciled note: "probably XII Dyn. – DBS." Object accession cards, Department of Egyptian Art.

8 Again, notes on object accession cards in the Department of Egyptian Art reveal the changing fortunes of the statuette within the Museum. One, seemingly from the 1980s, describes the piece as "Toy, Mechanical: in form of a nude dancing girl"; another, "Forgery?" is penciled in unidentified handwriting thought to predate the early 1970s (verbal communication from curator Marsha Hill); a third card is marked, also in pencil, "1990 Study Room." The statuette had probably been removed from view some years prior to this date.

9 Skeptical curators may have had in mind those erotic automata, often in pocket-watch form, that were popular during the eighteenth century and later; see Landes 1983, p. 269. See also John Joseph Merlin's famous silver dancer as described in Schaffer 1998–99.

10 I owe to Marijn Manuels, Conservator, Sherman Fairchild Center for Objects Conservation, MMA, the observation that sufficient differences in diameter may be observed in the X-radiographs between the bottom and top of the channel to indicate that the piercing was not achieved by means of a modern drill.

11 For the sake of completeness, it should be mentioned that a note in the Supplementary Files of the Department of Egyptian Art mistakenly identifies as functional a piercing to the left side of the throat, adjacent to the left lappet of the wig: "The arms (right [*sic*] arm now missing) were attached at the shoulders to the ends of a spool-shaped bar which passes through a transverse 'tunnel' inside the breast of the figure and was rotated by two [*sic*] threads running down the inside of the left leg of the figure and out through the base. A third [*sic*] thread, also wound round this spool, passed out through a small hole in the breast of the figure and operated the left hand or something in the left hand (sistrum, ceremonial necklace) [*sic*]." This third hole is in fact accidental, the result of an inadvertent thinning of the wood at this point at the time the interior was being hollowed out. It served no practical purpose, and there is no evidence that the object was ever intended to be operated by more than a single string.

12 The wood was initially examined by Marijn Manuels. The sample—a tiny sliver taken from a radial split in the figure's left side, just beneath the piercing for the egress of the axle—was too small for standard processing using microtomy; it was embedded in as-found condition, after which only the largest of cellular structures could be observed under the microscope. Since the majority of such statuettes are female, it seems reasonable to speculate that boxwood owed its popularity as much to its yellow tint—a color associated with ancient Egyptian female representation—as to its fine grain.

13 The wood of the axle was examined by Daniel Haussdorf, Assistant Conservator, Sherman Fairchild Center for Objects Conservation.

14 Beta Analytic Carbon Dating Laboratory, Miami, FL, Lab. No. Beta 306312. Report date October 6, 2011. "Conventional radiocarbon age 2700 ± 30 B.P.; 2 Sigma calibrated result (95% probability) Cal. 2860-2750 B.P. (Cal. 910–800 B.C.). Intercept of radiocarbon age with calibration curve Cal. 2780 B.P. (Cal. 830 B.C.); 1 Sigma calibrated results (68% probability) Cal. 2840-2820 B.P. (Cal. 890–870 B.C.) and Cal. 2800-2760 B.P. (Cal. 850–810 B.C.). Material/Pretreatment: (wood): acid/alkali/acid. Comment: The original sample was too small to provide a 13C/12C ratio on the original material. However, a ratio including both natural and laboratory effects was measured during the 14C detection to calculate the true Conventional Radiocarbon Age." Regrettably, the small size of the arm and the axle precluded sampling and radiocarbon testing of those elements.

15 Little physical work beyond rejoining the figure's detached right hand seems to have been carried out: see Technical Laboratory Request for Treatment, no. 87, January 20, 1958, Department of Objects Conservation. A report from March 20 of that year (Department of Egyptian Art) by the Department of Objects Conservation describes the piece (erroneously numbered 56.36) as still "dirty, with glue stains," and with its single surviving arm held firmly in place with copious amounts of wax dripped into the hollowed-out upper torso. A 1981 treatment consisted of the removal of this wax "fill," the application of fresh wax to fix the arm to the axle, and the application of pigmented wax to make the join of the hand to the arm less visible.

16 Analyses were carried out by Ann Heywood using a Bruker Artax 400 X-radiograph fluorescence spectroscopy unit.

17 For a discussion of Egyptian blue, see Lee and Quirke 2000, especially pp. 108–11.

18 For the association of lapis lazuli with divinity, see the Book of the Divine Cow in reference to the sun god Re: "his bones were of silver, his limbs were of gold, his hair was real lapis lazuli." Translated from the German given in Hornung 1982, pp. 1 and 37, ll. 4–6.

19 Perhaps the eighteen-square grid, which was replaced by the twenty-one-square grid in common use by the time of the Twenty-Fifth Dynasty (ca. 733–664 B.C.). See Robins 1994.

20 See, for example, Hölbl 1979; Institut du Monde Arabe 2007; and Carbillet 2011.

21 T-shaped parting on the crown: Hornemann 1966, pl. 989 (Egyptian Museum, Cairo, JE 43582; limestone; New Kingdom). Dividing of the wig above the shoulders and resultant hollow: ibid., pl. 847 (Rijksmuseum van Oudheden, Leiden, AH 167-a, E VII 245; ebony; 18th Dynasty); and, significantly, since it is a figure of the otherwise exclusively bob-wigged type considered later in this essay (see "Related Images in Bronze"), ibid., pl. 855 (Ägyptisches Museum, Berlin, 9064; bronze, Twenty-Fifth Dynasty), and note 23 below.

22 The Berlin figure is reproduced in Fechheimer 1921, pl. 110. I am grateful to Caris-Beatrice Arnst (emails to author, September 17 and October 4, 2013) for informing me that this piece was pur-

chased by the diplomat Carl August Reinhardt (1856–1903) from an Egyptian dealer in 1895, possibly at Saqqara. The figure in a private collection is displayed on the website of the Young Museum of Ancient Cultural Arts, Burnet, Texas. According to that source, it was offered for sale at Sotheby's, New York at a time not specified; www.youngmuseum.com//new_page_14.htm (accessed April 16, 2015).

23 Besides the commonality of pose, other clear overlaps with the MMA's statuette may be discerned in the differently wigged types. Although most related images in wood have the short, bobbed wig (see "Related Images in Wood" in this article), one ivory figure belonging to the class (Ägyptisches Museum, 17000; Wildung 2000, p. 171, no. 187) displays a wig similar to that worn by MMA 58.36; among the bronze subset (see "Related Images in Bronze" in this article), there is at least one with an "echeloned" version of the MMA figure's wig, and it divides in the same awkward manner over each shoulder (Ägyptisches Museum, 9064; Hornemann 1966, pl. 855). As we shall consider, the subject is in all cases likely to be the same goddess, and the wig distinction probably cultic and/or temporal rather than north-south regional, given the apparent occurrence of both wig types in Upper and Lower Egyptian contexts.

24 Reference should also be made to a similarly posed nude and bob-wigged statuette (Museo Egizio, Turin, Provv. 912 [unprovenanced, Reeves 2015, fig. 12]) somewhat crudely carved in wood, in which the subject similarly conceals her sex behind a flattened right hand; with her left she grasps the right arm at the wrist. While the figure superficially resembles MMA 58.36, Berlin 12662, and the Young Museum piece, the Turin statuette's obvious *contrapposto* of the right leg points to a later, Classical date (see Havelock 1995, pp. 16–18).

25 Two-dimensional examples include a faience bowl in the Myers Collection, Eton College (ECM 1590), into the principal decoration of which are intruded a cat and ducks—Spurr, Reeves, and Quirke 1999, p. 28, no. 27; and several extant figured ostraca. For a discussion of images referencing the Myth of the Sun's Eye, see Hoffmann and Quack 2007, pp. 195–229, with ill. on p. 203. Brian Muhs (email to author, June 5, 2012) points out that the MMA statuette's assignment to the Third Intermediate Period makes it roughly contemporaneous with a relief on a temple wall at Medamud representing, in texts and images, scenes from fables with talking animals linked to the cult of the Dangerous Goddess, and thus, ultimately, to the Myth of the Sun's Eye; see von Lieven 2009. Clearly, the formalization of such folk literature was in progress by the time the MMA's figure was produced.

26 For the girl holding a kitten, see Hornemann 1966, pls. 904, 905 (British Museum, London, EA 32733—wood; Louvre, Paris, N 1603—wood), 964 (Rijksmuseum van Oudheden, E XVIII 132—bronze). For the figure of the dwarf, see Dasen 1993, pls. 35.2 (Museum of Fine Arts, Boston, MFA 48.296—wood), 35.3 (MMA 17.190.1963—Egyptian alabaster); 37.1 (Ashmolean Museum, Oxford, 1911.407—Egyptian alabaster), 37.3 (British Museum, EA 29935—ceramic), 37.4 (Petrie Museum, University College London, 15758—Egyptian alabaster). For the dancer, see Hornemann 1966, pl. 970 (Musées Royaux d'Art et d'Histoire, Brussels, E 5849—wood).

27 The tale is preserved in the Papyrus Chester Beatty I, which has been dated to the reign of Ramesses V (ca. 1147–1143 B.C.); see Gardiner 1931.

28 Ibid., p. 16, pls. III, IV.

29 For a discussion of the humor, see Morris 2007.

30 Gardiner 1931, p. 16n7. For *kꜣt*, see *Wb.* V, 93.12–94.2; *MedWb* 894 f. (*Thesaurus Linguae Aegyptiae*, accessed April 16, 2015, http://aaew.bbaw.de/tla/index.html); Landgráfová and Navrátilová 2009, p. 57; and Hannig and Vomberg 2012, p. 324.

31 The story has interesting parallels in the Japanese tale of the sun goddess Amaterasu cheered by the naked Ame-no-Uzume-no-Mikoto, *kami* (spirit) of merriment, and in the Classical myth of Demeter and Baubo; see Morris 2007.

32 Bonnet 1952, pp. 298–99, s.v. "Hetepet."

33 Von Lieven n.d. (forthcoming). I am grateful to Alexandra von Lieven for an early sight of her paper.

34 *Pneumatika* 1.16–17; Schmidt 1899, pp. 392–97. I owe this reference to Alexandra von Lieven.

35 Examples of such animated objects include: dog pouncing on captive (British Museum, EA 26254—wood; Brooklyn Museum 37.612E [part]—wood); lion with string-operated lower jaw (British Museum, EA 15671—wood); hunting dog with lever-operated lower jaw (MMA 40.2.1—ivory); frog with string-operated lower jaw (Egyptian Museum, CG 68182—ivory); mouse with string-operated lower jaw and tail of wood (National Museums Scotland, Edinburgh, A.1952.178—painted clay); crocodile with string(?)-operated lower jaw (Rijksmuseum van Oudheden—wood); string-operated kneeling figure grinding corn (Rijksmuseum van Oudheden, AH84—wood); and see note 37 below.

36 Herodotus, *Histories* 2.48, translated by A. D. Godley (1920), available online at www.perseus.tufts.edu/hopper/text?doc =Perseus:abo:tlg,0016,001:2:48&lang=original. See also Lloyd 1976, pp. 222–23.

37 On dwarfs versus pygmies, see the discussion in Dasen 1993, pp. 25–33. The Lisht find is now divided between Cairo, which owns the principal tableau (Egyptian Museum, JE 63858), and the Metropolitan Museum, which owns the separate figure shown clapping to keep the three dancers in time (MMA 34.1.130). The grouping is discussed in Lansing 1934, pp. 30–40. More extensive records of the discovery are preserved in the Department of Egyptian Art. The original arrangement of the figures in the tableau may be considered briefly. As with MMA 58.36, the Lisht piece was string-operated, though a recent display in Cairo gives a false impression of how the dwarfs' movement was achieved. The holes from which multiple strings are now seen to protrude (see the photograph reproduced in Rawlings 1999, http://pages.citenet.net/users/ctmw2400 /chapter1.html [accessed April 16, 2015]) were in fact originally for pegs employed to attach the (now decayed) sides and floor of what appears to have been a dark wood, box-like base. The actual manner in which the dwarfs were made to dance is revealed by the box's ivory top-plate, which serves as a platform for the figures. A deep, regular groove cut into the underside of the plate shows distinct parallel scratches consistent with the movement of a sliding rod attached to a cord wound tightly around spools connected to each of the three dwarfs. As the rod was pulled and pushed, the dwarfs would have turned and "danced." The basic arrangement of the mechanism is perhaps similar to that encountered in certain premodern Japanese toys (*Kōbe ningyō*; see an example in the Japan Toy Museum, Himeji, illustrated in Inoue 2002, p. 39, fig. 9). The manner in which the separate dwarf (MMA 34.1.130) was integrated into the principal tableau is uncertain, though a pair of parallel transverse piercings through its base may suggest a bowing motion. Similar piercings—the one at the rear slightly larger in diameter than that to the fore—are seen in two small, separately modeled dogs now held respectively by the British Museum (EA 13596—ivory)

and the Walters Art Museum, Baltimore (WAM 22.2—ebony). These canine figures were obviously components of separate but identical mechanical tableaux whose complete form is suggested by a static, Twelfth Dynasty version in faience in Basel; Wiese 2001, p. 71, no. 37. Interestingly, what may be similar, paired, transverse piercings appear to be visible on the base of the much larger wooden statue in private hands (fig. 12 and note 43 below).

38 Dorothea Arnold will demonstrate Hepy's close relations to the Hathor cult in a forthcoming publication on Lisht South. Dorothea Arnold, email to author, October 8, 2013.

39 Strudwick 2005, p. 332.

40 Allen 2005, p. 159.

41 Gillam 2005, pp. 154–55. Filip Coppens (2009, p. 2) distinguishes in Egyptian ritual passive and active contexts: "passive" encompassing daily ritual within the sanctuary, and "active" comprising festivals and other public occasions. The latter would have included religious performances such as those known from the Ramesseum Dramatic Papyrus, the Triumph of Horus inscribed on the Temple of Edfu, or the Demotic Myth of the Sun's Eye.

42 Both arms straight down by the sides (e.g., Highclere Castle, England—wood; Louvre, E 27429—ivory); the left arm positioned straight down by the side (e.g., Ägyptisches Museum, 12662—wood; see note 22 above); left arm emphasizing or supporting one or both of the breasts (e.g., Royal-Athena Galleries, New York—wood); left arm holding a musical instrument (Staatliches Museum Ägyptischer Kunst, Munich, AS/2958—wood). See figures 16a, 8a, 16b,c.

43 Possible links between the Egyptian pudica pose and Classical forms are considered by the author in a recent article; Reeves 2015. The Rome statue shown in fig. 12 is known to me only from photographs. It was examined at first hand by Francisco Tiradritti, for whose comments and suggestions—even those not followed—I am grateful. The piece was previously seen and reported on by Alessandro Roccati, and by Steffen Wenig, www.bild-art.de/artefact/artifact.htm (accessed April 16, 2015).

44 The resemblance of the pose to a position in premodern Egyptian dance was first pointed out to me by Phyllis Saretta, to whom I am grateful for helpful discussion. On the Ghawazi and their dance form, see Wood and Shay 1976; Van Nieuwkerk 1995; Shay 2005; and Peck 2009. The seemingly casual term "belly dance" might have originated in the Arabic raqs al-balad (dance from the countryside); see Shay 2005. The suggestion that the dance may have its origins in Egypt's ancient past is not new: as long ago as 1927, Alexander Scharff proposed that the raised arms of Naqada IIa "celebrant" figures might possibly identify the subject as a dancer (Scharff 1927, p. 61); G. D. Hornblower (1929, pp. 35–36n3) extrapolated that the pose is "suggestive even of the 'ghâwâzi' with their danse du ventre [belly dance]."

45 For reproductions of the complete paintings and other information, see, for Ingres's The Turkish Bath, Toussaint 1971 and François De Vergnette, www.louvre.fr/en/oeuvre-notices/turkish-bath (accessed April 16, 2015); and for Roberts's The Ghawazee, or Dancing Girls, Cairo, Roberts 1849, pl. 37.

46 Lane 1871, vol. 2, p. 88.

47 Warner 1881, p. 354.

48 Cf. Morris 2011, p. 72, where it is argued that paddle dolls, of which a greatly enlarged pubic triangle is the principal feature, "represent female members of the Theban khener-troupe."

49 See note 42 above.

50 Shore 1964–65.

51 For example, Krauspe 1997, pp. 116–17. These terracottas, both skirt-lifting and non-skirt-lifting versions, are variously identified. Donald Bailey (2001) sees them as representations of Hathor of the West. For possible instances of the anasyrma motif in bronzes directly associated with the MMA 58.36 image, see the following section of this article.

52 Rhind 1862, pp. 161, 162 (ill.). An associated arm and iron peg are numbered A.1956.132A and B respectively. A second specimen of this same specific type, again displaying evidence of outward opening legs (arms and legs missing), though this time wearing a short echeloned wig, was discovered in 1990, again at Thebes and in a "Third Intermediate Period" cemetery context "at the southern side of the road leading to Deir el-Bahari" (a site sacred to Hathor), adjacent to the causeway of the mortuary temple of Hatshepsut. See Nasr 1992, p. 142, pl. XXIX.

53 Riefstahl 1943–44. See Roeder 1956, pp. 320–23, §404–5.

54 See note 42 above.

55 For the British Museum piece (EA 55019), see Roeder 1956, p. 322, fig. 419. For the association of mirrors with Hathor, see Lilyquist 1979.

56 I thank Ann Macy Roth for this suggestion (email to author, December 4, 2011).

57 Jantzen 1972, p. 13, no. B 1517, pl. 15.

58 Note that the figure's right hand is clenched as if to grasp.

59 For example, on the Heraion figure's movable leg; see note 57 above and fig. 22.

60 Perdu 2003, p. 165, though this is questioned by Hill 2007, pp. 87–88.

61 History of Puppetry 1959, pp. 30, 35–36. See further Pasqualino 1980 and Reimann 1982.

62 The three specimens shown in fig. 24, formerly in the collection of Giampietro Campana (1808–1880), marchese di Cavelli, are particularly suggestive. I am grateful to Maya Muratov for information on the present whereabouts of two of these and for much expert advice on the subject of puppetry both in the Classical world and in general; see Muratov 2005 and 2012. While Muratov has suggested (email to author, October 5, 2013) that the rods shown in the illustration may be replacements, the presence of similar rods in antiquity would seem to be assured. I am informed (again by Muratov) that other figures with rods in place are in the Museo Archeologico Nazionale di Napoli.

63 Böhm 1990.

REFERENCES

Allen, James P.
2005 *The Ancient Egyptian Pyramid Texts.* Atlanta: Society of Biblical Literature.

Bailey, Donald M.
2001 "Two Figures of Hathor." In *Cleopatra of Egypt: From History to Myth,* edited by Susan Walker and Peter Higgs, pp. 108–9, no. 346. Exh. cat., Palazzo Ruspoli, Rome; British Museum, London; Field Museum, Chicago. London: British Museum Press.

Bierbrier, Morris L., ed.
2012 *Who Was Who in Egyptology.* 4th ed. London: Egypt Exploration Society.

Böhm, Stephanie
1990 *Die "Nackte Göttin": Zur Ikonographie und Deutung unbekleideter weiblicher Figuren in der frühgriechischen Kunst.* Mainz am Rhein: Philipp von Zabern.

Bonnet, Hans
1952 *Reallexikon der ägyptischen Religionsgeschichte.* Berlin: Walter de Gruyter.

Carbillet, Aurélie
2011 *La Figure hathorique à Chypre (IIᵉ–Iᵉʳ mill. av. J.-C.).* Münster: Ugarit-Verlag.

Coppens, Filip
2009 "Temple Festivals of the Ptolemaic and Roman Periods." In *UCLA Encyclopedia of Egyptology,* edited by Jacco Dieleman and Willeke Wendrich, pp. 1–11. Los Angeles. http://escholarship.org/uc/item/4cd7q9mn.

Dasen, Véronique
1993 *Dwarfs in Ancient Egypt and Greece.* Oxford: Clarendon Press.

Fechheimer, Hedwig
1921 *Kleinplastik der Ägypter.* Berlin: Bruno Cassirer Verlag.

Gardiner, Alan H.
1931 *The Library of A. Chester Beatty: Description of a Hieratic Papyrus with a Mythological Story, Love Songs, and Other Miscellaneous Texts. Chester Beatty Papyri, No. I.* London: Oxford University Press.

Gillam, Robyn
2005 *Performance and Drama in Ancient Egypt.* London: Duckworth.

Godley, A. D., trans.
1920 *Herodotus.* Vol. 1, *Books I and II.* Cambridge, Mass.: Harvard University Press.

Hannig, Rainer, and Petra Vomberg
2012 *Wortschatz der Pharaonen in Sachgruppen: Kulturhandbuch Ägyptens.* 2nd ed. Mainz am Rhein: Philipp von Zabern.

Havelock, Christine Mitchell
1995 *The Aphrodite of Knidos and Her Successors: A Historical Review of the Female Nude in Greek Art.* Ann Arbor: University of Michigan Press.

Hill, Marsha, ed.
2007 *Gifts for the Gods: Images from Egyptian Temples.* New York: MMA.

History of Puppetry
1959 *History of Puppetry.* Exh. cat. Los Angeles: Los Angeles County Museum and Los Angeles County Guild of Puppetry.

Hoffmann, Friedhelm, and Joachim Friedrich Quack
2007 *Anthologie der Demotischen Literatur.* Berlin: Lit Verlag.

Hölbl, Günther
1979 *Beziehungen der Ägyptischen Kultur zu Altitalien.* 2 vols. Leiden: E. J. Brill.

Hornblower, G[eorge] D[avis]
1929 "Predynastic Figures of Women and Their Successors." *Journal of Egyptian Archaeology* 15 (May), pp. 29–47.

Hornemann, Bodil
1966 *Types of Ancient Egyptian Statuary.* Vol. 4. Copenhagen: Munksgaard.

Hornung, Erik
1982 *Der Ägyptische Mythos von der Himmelskuh: Eine Ätiologie des Unvollkommenen.* Freiburg: Universitätsverlag; Göttingen: Vandenhoek & Ruprecht.

Inoue, Shigeyoshi
2002 "Kobe Dolls." *Daruma* 34 (Spring), pp. 37–45.

Institut du Monde Arabe
2007 *La Méditerranée des Phéniciens de Tyr à Carthage.* Exh. cat. Paris: Institut du Monde Arabe/Somogy.

Jantzen, Ulf
1972 *Ägyptische und Orientalische Bronzen aus dem Heraion von Samos. Samos 8.* Bonn: Rudolf Habelt Verlag.

Krauspe, Renate
1997 *Das Ägyptische Museum der Universität Leipzig.* Mainz am Rhein: Philipp von Zabern.

Landes, David S.
1983 *Revolution in Time: Clocks and the Making of the Modern World.* Cambridge, Mass.: Harvard University Press.

Landgráfová, Renata, and Hana Navrátilová
2009 *Sex and the Golden Goddess I: Ancient Egyptian Love Songs in Context.* Prague: N.p. [Czech Institute of Egyptology].

Lane, Edward William
1871 *An Account of the Manners and Customs of the Modern Egyptians: Written in Egypt during the Years 1833, -34, and -35, Partly from Notes Made during a Former Visit to That Country in the Years 1825, -26, -27, and -28.* Edited by Edward Stanley Poole. 5th ed. 2 vols. London: John Murray.

Lansing, Ambrose
1934 "The Excavations at Lisht: The Burial of Hepy." In "The Egyptian Expedition 1933–34," *Bulletin of The Metropolitan Museum of Art* 29, no. 11, part 2 (November), pp. 27–40.

Lee, Lorna, and Stephen Quirke
2000 "Painting Materials." In *Ancient Egyptian Materials and Technology,* edited by Paul T. Nicholson and Ian Shaw, pp. 104–20. Cambridge: Cambridge University Press.

von Lieven, Alexandra
2009 "Fragments of a Monumental Proto-Myth of the Sun's Eye." In *Actes du IXᵉ Congrès International des Etudes Démotiques,* edited by Ghislaine Widmer and Didier Devauchelle, pp. 173–81. Cairo: Institut Français d'Archéologie Orientale.
n.d. "The Movement of Time: News from the 'Clockmaker' Amenemhet." Forthcoming.

Lilyquist, Christine
1979 *Ancient Egyptian Mirrors.* Münchner Ägyptologischer Studien, no. 27. Munich and Berlin: Deutscher Kunstverlag.

Lloyd, Alan B.
1976 *Herodotus Book II.* [Vol. 2], *Commentary 1–98.* Leiden: E. J. Brill.

Loeben, Christian E.

    2011 *Die Ägypten-Sammlung des Museum August Kestner und ihre (Kriegs-)Verluste.* Contributions by Thorsten Henke, Barbara Lüscher, Anne Viola Siebert, and André B. Wiese. Exh. cat., Museum August Kestner, Hannover. Rahden/Westf.: Verlag Marie Leidorf.

Matthews, Brande

    1916 *A Book about the Theater.* New York: Charles Scribner's Sons.

Morris, Ellen F.

    2007 "Sacred and Obscene Laughter in *The Contendings of Horus and Seth,* in Egyptian Inversions of Everyday Life, and in the Context of Cultic Competition." In *Egyptian Stories: A British Egyptological Tribute to Alan B. Lloyd on the Occasion of His Retirement,* edited by Thomas Schneider and Kasia Szpakowska, pp. 197–224. Münster: Ugarit-Verlag.

    2011 "Paddle Dolls and Performance." *Journal of the American Research Center in Egypt* 47, pp. 71–103.

Muratov, Maya B.

    2005 "From the Mediterranean to the Bosporos: Terracotta Figurines with Articulated Limbs." PhD diss., Institute of Fine Arts, New York University.

    2012 "With Strings Attached: Puppet Theater as Popular Entertainment in Antiquity." Lecture delivered at the conference "Locating Popular Culture in the Ancient World," University of Edinburgh, July 5.

Nasr, Mohamed

    1992 "New Discoveries at Thebes-West." *Memnonia: Bulletin édité par l'Association pour la Sauvegarde du Ramesseum* 3, pp. 141–43.

van Nieuwkerk, Karin

    1995 *A Trade Like Any Other: Female Singers and Dancers in Egypt.* Austin: University of Texas Press.

Pasqualino, Fortunato

    1980 *Il teatro con i pupi siciliani.* Palermo: Cavallotto Editore.

Peck, William H.

    2009 "The Dancer of Esna." http://williamhpeck.org/the_dancer_of_esna. Accessed April 16, 2015.

Perdu, Olivier

    2003 "Des Pendentifs en guise d'ex-voto." *Revue d'Egyptologie* 54, pp. 155–66.

Price, Derek J. de Solla

    1964 "Automata and the Origins of Mechanism and Mechanistic Philosophy." *Technology and Culture* 5, no. 1 (Winter), pp. 9–23.

Rawlings, Keith

    1999 *Observations on the Historical Development of Puppetry.* http://pages.citenet.net/users/ctmw2400/index.html. Updated April 2003 and March 2011.

Reeves, Nicholas

    2015 "The Birth of Venus?" In *Joyful in Thebes: Egyptological Studies in Honor of Betsy M. Bryan,* edited by Richard Jasnow and Kathlyn M. Cooney, pp. 373–86. Atlanta: Lockwood Press.

Reimann, Horst

    1982 *Siziliens kleines Volkstheater, opera dei pupi.* Bochum: Deutsches Institut für Puppenspiel.

Rhind, A[lexander] Henry

    1862 *Thebes: Its Tombs and Their Tenants, Ancient and Present, Including a Record of Excavations in the Necropolis.* London: Longman, Green, Longman, and Roberts.

Riefstahl, Elizabeth

    1943–44 "Doll, Queen, or Goddess?" *Brooklyn Museum Journal* 2, pp. 5–23.

Roberts, David

    1849 *The Holy Land, Syria, Idumea, Arabia, Egypt and Nubia.* Vol. 6, *Egypt & Nubia: From Drawings Made on the Spot by David Roberts; with Historical Descriptions by William Brockedon; Lithographed by Louis Haghe.* Part 3. London: F. G. Moon.

Robins, Gay

    1994 *Proportion and Style in Ancient Egyptian Art.* Austin: University of Texas Press.

Roeder, Günther

    1956 *Ägyptische Bronzefiguren.* Mitteilungen aus der ägyptischen Sammlung 6. Berlin: Staatliche Museen zu Berlin.

Schaffer, Simon

    1998–99 "Babbage's Dancer." Hypermedia Research Centre, University of Westminster. www.hrc.wmin.ac.uk/theory-babbagesdancer2.html. Accessed April 16, 2015.

Scharff, Alexander

    1927 *Grundzüge der aegyptischen Vorgeschichte.* Leipzig: J. C. Hinrichs'sche Buchhandlung.

Schmidt, Wilhelm, ed.

    1899 *Heronis Alexandrini opera quae supersunt omnia.* Vol. 1, *Pneumatica et Automata. Herons von Alexandria Druckwerke und Automatentheater, Griechisch und Deutsch.* Leipzig: B. G. Teubner.

Shay, Anthony V.

    2005 "Danse du ventre." In *The International Encyclopedia of Dance,* edited by Selma Jeanne Cohen. London: Oxford University Press. Online edition: www.oxfordreference.com/view/10.1093/acref/9780195173697.001.0001/acref-9780195173697-e-0459.

Shore, A[rthur] F[rank]

    1964–65 "A Rare Example of a Dedicatory Inscription in Early Demotic." *British Museum Quarterly* 29 (Winter), pp. 19–21.

Spurr, Stephen, Nicholas Reeves, and Stephen Quirke

    1999 *Egyptian Art at Eton College: Selections from the Myers Museum.* Exh. cat., Eton College, Myers Museum; MMA. New York: MMA.

Strudwick, Nigel C., trans.

    2005 *Texts from the Pyramid Age.* Atlanta: Society of Biblical Literature.

Toussaint, Hélène

    1971 *Le Bain turc d'Ingres.* Musée du Louvre, Dossiers du Département des Peintures 1. Paris: Éditions de la Réunion des Musées Nationaux.

Warner, Charles Dudley

    1881 *My Winter on the Nile.* Rev. ed. Boston: Houghton, Mifflin.

Wiese, André

    2001 *Antikenmuseum Basel und Sammlung Ludwig: Die Ägyptische Abteilung.* Mainz am Rhein: Verlag Philipp von Zabern.

Wildung, Dietrich, ed.

    2000 *Ägypten 2000 v. Chr.: Die Geburt des Individuums.* Exh. cat., Residenz, Würzburg; Kunstforum in der Grundkreditbank, Berlin. Munich: Hirmer.

Wood, Leona, and Anthony Shay

    1976 "Danse du ventre: A Fresh Appraisal." *Dance Research Journal* 8, no. 2 (Spring–Summer), pp. 18–30.

KEELY ELIZABETH HEUER

Vases with Faces: Isolated Heads in South Italian Vase Painting

Of the ancient vases in the collection of The Metropolitan Museum of Art, more than 430 were produced in southern Italy and Sicily, a region of the Mediterranean often referred to in antiquity as Magna Graecia (Great Greece), owing to its many Greek settlements (fig. 1). The vases were made between about 440 B.C. and the early third century B.C. and were decorated in the red-figure technique. Exactly how the technique was transferred from Athens to the Italian peninsula is as yet unclear, but South Italian red-figure vases were produced and used in five regions—Lucania, Apulia, Campania, Paestum, and Sicily—which share their names with their respective wares.[1] Among the Museum's South Italian vases are diverse examples of the most common and characteristic motif of South Italian vase painting, the isolated head, which appears as a primary or secondary decorative element on more than 7,400 pieces, well over one-third of the published corpus.[2]

MAP OF SOUTHERN ITALY AND SICILY

(*MAGNA GRAECIA*)

fig. 1 Map of southern Italy and Sicily

fig. 2 Apulian red-figure kantharos attributed to the Painter of Bari 5981. Greek, South Italian, ca. 325–300 B.C. Terracotta, H. with handles 11 in. (27.9 cm). The Metropolitan Museum of Art, Rogers Fund, 1906 (06.1021.233). Obverse showing a female head emerging from a flower

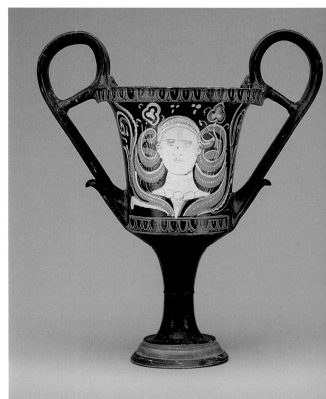

The depiction of isolated heads on vases is not unique to southern Italy and Sicily. Painted heads decorated pottery of the Greek mainland and the Aegean starting in the late eighth century B.C., but they occur erratically and relatively infrequently, often on vases from particular workshops. The motif was one of many iconographic elements that likely traveled with the red-figure technique as it spread from Athens. Given its long history in the Greek heartland, the isolated head provides an ideal case study of a subject that evolved in function and meaning when transplanted to another part of the Mediterranean, one well acquainted with Greek culture through large numbers of settlements, imports, and more than five hundred years of uninterrupted contact. Partly because of the overwhelming quantity of surviving examples on South Italian vases, the motif has not been the subject of a detailed study until now. Close consideration of the vases reveals patterns of use linking

fig. 3a Apulian red-figure volute-krater attributed to the Baltimore Painter. Greek, South Italian, ca. 330–310 B.C. Terracotta, H. with handles 31 in. (78.7 cm), H. to rim 26¾ in. (68 cm). The Metropolitan Museum of Art, Purchase, Mrs. James J. Rorimer Gift, 1969 (69.11.7). Obverse showing, on the neck, a head with Phrygian cap; on the body, the Judgment of Paris above Athena and Pan among Trojans

fig. 3b Reverse of fig. 3a, showing a woman in a naiskos surrounded by women and youths

them to the funerary realm and to the likelihood that the isolated heads served as symbolic representations of beliefs associated with the afterlife.

SOUTH ITALIAN AND ATTIC USE OF ISOLATED HEADS

The earliest appearance of the heads on South Italian vases coincides with the period during which South Italian vase painting began to diverge from Athenian models and adapt to local conventions, about 410–400 B.C.[3] The size of a vase often determined whether the isolated head painted on it would play a primary or secondary role. Until 340 B.C., heads usually occurred as the primary decoration on smaller vases, such as the Metropolitan Museum's kantharos (drinking cup with high handles) attributed to the Painter of Bari 5981 (fig. 2);

after this date, the motif served as the main decoration on larger vases as well. The frontal female head emerging from a flower and surrounded by spiraling tendrils on the Museum's kantharos is similar to heads appearing as secondary decoration on larger vases, exemplified by two works in the Museum's collection: the Apulian volute-krater attributed to the Baltimore Painter (fig. 3a,b) and the Campanian neck-amphora by the Pilos Head Group (figs. 4a,b). The use of the motif as secondary decoration began between about 380 and 370 B.C., when isolated heads appeared nearly simultaneously in all five South Italian wares. Heads were applied to the various shapes within each ware, although not with equal frequency in all wares: they are most common in Apulia and Campania.[4]

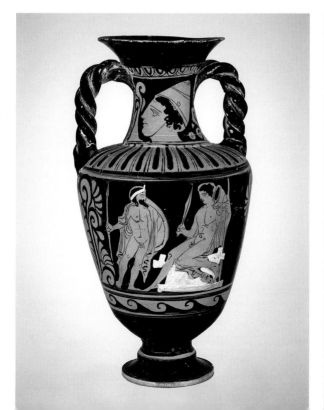

fig. 4a Campanian neck-amphora attributed to the Pilos Head Group. Greek, South Italian, ca. 350–325 B.C. Terracotta, H. 11 in. (27.9 cm). The Metropolitan Museum of Art, Museum Accession (X.21.19). Obverse showing a young warrior seated on an altar facing a bearded warrior; on the neck, the head of a youth wearing a pilos

fig. 4b Reverse of fig. 4a, showing a seated youth holding a spear; on the neck, a female head

figs. 5a,b Attic black-figure lip-cup by the Epitimos Painter. Greek, ca. 550–540 B.C. Terracotta, H. 7⅝ in. (19.4 cm), Diam. 11¾ in. (29.8 cm). National Museum of Denmark, Copenhagen (13966). Obverse showing the head of Athena; reverse showing the head of Enkelados

fig. 6 Attic red-figure squat lekythos attributed to the Achilles Painter or his workshop. Greek, ca. 450–425 B.C. Terracotta, preserved H. 3½ in. (9 cm). Staatliche Antikensammlungen, Munich (7505)

On Athenian vases, isolated heads are often carefully identified by inscription or attribute. For example, on a black-figure lip-cup in Copenhagen attributed to the Epitimos Painter (figs. 5a,b), two isolated heads occur, each one centered between the two handles, on opposite sides.[5] One is the bust of Athena, recognizable by her Attic helmet, upraised spear, and shield decorated with a protruding snake. The reverse shows the bust of a male warrior, his face largely obscured by his Corinthian helmet. He too is poised to release his spear and carries a shield with a three-dimensional ornament, a satyr head. The retrograde inscription on his helmet's crest, *ΕΝΚΕΛΑΔΟΣ*, identifies him as the giant Enkelados, Athena's opponent in the Gigantomachy. The inscription demonstrates the vase painter's concern that the specific subject be clearly recognized. The practice of identifying heads of mythological figures continued into fifth-century Athenian red-figure vase painting, such as on the numerous squat lekythoi (oil flasks) of the Achilles Painter's workshop, about 450–425 B.C., which are contemporary with the earliest South Italian red-figure vases. For example, on a piece in Munich (fig. 6), Hermes is recognized by his kerykeion (herald's staff), his wide-brimmed hat slung behind him, and his cloak pinned at the shoulder, sartorial details associated with travelers in Greek art.

In contrast, few isolated heads on South Italian vases can be readily identified by today's viewers. Just one South Italian head is inscribed: the frontal, polos-crowned female head on the neck of a volute-krater in the British Museum is labeled *Aura* (figs. 7a, b);[6] and few South Italian heads have distinguishing attributes. The only mythological figures recognizable among South Italian heads are Pan and Dionysos, found on a small number of Apulian and Paestan vases, and satyrs of various ages, such as the one on a bell-krater in the Museum's collection (fig. 8), which occur in all South Italian wares except those from Sicily.[7]

The overwhelming majority of heads are female, usually with the hair pulled up and contained in a headdress, and nearly always wearing jewelry—necklaces, earrings, and diadems of various forms. Isolated female heads are indistinguishable from the heads of their full-length counterparts, both mortal and divine, on South Italian vases, making specific identification virtually impossible.[8] Compare, for instance, three examples in the Museum's collection: the typical female head on an Apulian skyphos (deep drinking cup) (fig. 9); the head of Athena on a volute-krater by the Capodimonte Painter (fig. 10); and the heads of the mortal women surrounding the grave monuments on a loutrophoros (ceremonial vase

7b

8

9

7a

fig. 7a Apulian red-figure volute-krater by the Iliupersis Painter. Greek, South Italian, ca. 370–350 B.C. Terracotta, H. 23⅝ in. (59.9 cm). British Museum, London (F 277). The abduction of Persephone by Hades, with Hermes and Hekate

fig. 7b Detail of fig. 7a showing the head of Aura

fig. 8 Campanian red-figure bell-krater attributed to the Painter of Oxford 1945.73. Greek, South Italian, ca. 360–330 B.C. Terracotta, H. 7½ in. (19.1 cm). The Metropolitan Museum of Art, Rogers Fund, 1941 (41.162.263). Obverse showing the head of a satyr in profile

fig. 9 Apulian red-figure skyphos. Greek, South Italian, ca. 325–300 B.C. Terracotta, H. 7½ in. (19.1 cm). The Metropolitan Museum of Art, Gift of L. P. di Cesnola, 1876 (76.12.15). Obverse showing a female head in profile

fig. 10 Detail of Apulian red-figure volute-krater by the Capodimonte Painter. Greek, South Italian, ca. 320–310 B.C. Terracotta, H. without handles 36 in. (91.6 cm). The Metropolitan Museum of Art, Fletcher Fund, 1956 (56.171.63). Seated Athena holding a helmet

10

fig. 11a Apulian red-figure
loutrophoros attributed to the
Metope Painter. Greek, South
Italian, ca. 350–325 B.C.
Terracotta, H. 34¾ in. (88.3 cm).
The Metropolitan Museum
of Art, Purchase, The Bernard
and Audrey Aronson Charitable
Trust Gift, in memory of her
beloved husband, Bernard
Aronson, 1995 (1995.45.1).
Obverse showing statues of a
woman and an attendant in
a naiskos flanked by women and
youths. On the shoulder, Eros
with alabastron and mirror

fig. 11b Reverse of fig. 11a
showing the statue of a woman
in a naiskos flanked by youths
and women. On the shoulder, a
female head emerges from a
flower surrounded by tendrils
and palmettes.

for water) attributed to the Metope Painter (figs. 11a, b). Even when traditional indicators of divine status are present—a nimbus, for example, or the polos crown worn by Aura—they are too indeterminate to afford precise identifications.[9] Furthermore, their rare occurrence does little to illuminate the identity of the attribute-less majority.

Other types of heads, such as those of youths and mature males, likewise lack identifying attributes (see fig. 4a). Heads flanked by outstretched wings or wearing Phrygian caps are usually ambiguous in gender, leading to a variety of interpretations. Particularly popular in Apulia, winged heads, like that on the neck of the Lucanian nestoris (two-handled jar) (fig. 12), often wear the same headdresses and jewelry as female heads. While it would be logical to identify them as Nike, they also resemble Eros, a more frequent full-length figure in South Italian vase painting and often represented in a highly effeminate guise, as seen on the interior of the Apulian patera (libation bowl) (fig. 13).[10] The Phrygian cap is found repeatedly on isolated heads on Apulian vases, such as the one on the obverse shoulder of a second Metope Painter loutrophoros in the Museum's collection (figs. 14a, b).[11] If female, the heads probably represent Amazons, although they may depict Artemis Bendis.[12] If male, they might represent Arimasps, a

mythological race from the far north, or the mythological figures Orpheus, Adonis, or Paris. The identification of heads wearing Phrygian caps flanked by wings, a motif not seen in mainland Greek art, remains elusive.[13]

South Italian vase-painters frequently inscribed the names of full-length figures and provided them with defining attributes in mythological scenes. The seemingly intentional ambiguity of the isolated heads is therefore striking. Most scholars associate the heads with divinities, tentatively identifying various female heads, for example, as Aphrodite, Hera Eileithyia, and Persephone. Others see no religious connection, arguing that the heads functioned purely as decoration or as models of human comeliness.[14] Perhaps the meaning of isolated heads on vases in southern Italy and Sicily was so obvious to their intended users that explicit identification was deemed unnecessary. Unfortunately, no ancient literary or epigraphic sources survive that might explain the widespread significance of these motifs, requiring modern viewers to glean the heads' meaning exclusively from the vases themselves.

Past efforts to identify the heads have focused solely on Greek mythology, ignoring the fact that, while South Italian vases were produced in Greek settlements, most with known provenance come from areas

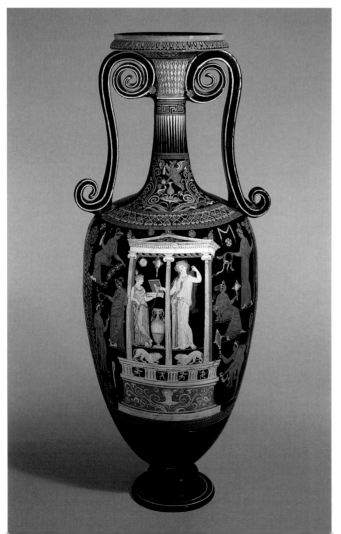

fig. 12 Lucanian red-figure nestoris by the Painter of New York 52.11.2. Greek, South Italian, ca. 360–350 B.C. Terracotta, H. with handles 15 in. (38.1 cm), H. without handles 14 in. (34.6 cm). The Metropolitan Museum of Art, Rogers Fund, 1952 (52.11.2). On the body, a standing youth offering a bird to a seated woman; on the neck, a head in profile flanked by wings

fig. 13 Apulian red-figure knob-handled patera attributed to the Menzies Group. Greek, South Italian, ca. 330–320 B.C. Terracotta, H. 3½ in. (8.7 cm). The Metropolitan Museum of Art, Purchase by subscription, 1896 (96.18.55). Eros, seated, holding up a mirror

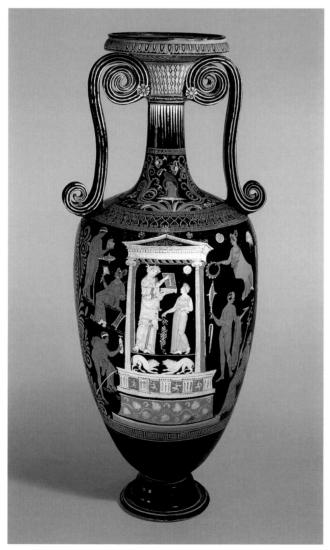

fig. 14a Apulian red-figure loutrophoros attributed to the Metope Painter. Greek, South Italian, ca. 350–325 B.C. Terracotta, H. 32¾ in. (83.2 cm). The Metropolitan Museum of Art, Purchase, The Bernard and Audrey Aronson Charitable Trust Gift, in memory of her beloved husband, Bernard Aronson, 1995 (1995.45.2). Obverse showing, on the shoulder, a head with Phrygian cap; on the body, a woman and attendant in a naiskos

fig. 14b Reverse of fig. 14a. On the shoulder, a female head; on the body, a woman with a fan in a naiskos surrounded by women and youths

fig. 15 Attic red-figure hydria by the Herakles Painter. Greek, ca. 370 B.C. Terracotta, H. (restored) 13⅞ in. (35.3 cm), Diam. 13¾ in. (35.1 cm). Musées Royaux d'Art et d'Histoire, Brussels (R 286). Female head flanked by Erotes and satyrs holding pickaxes

fig. 16 Attic red-figure bell-krater attributed to the Persephone Painter. Greek, ca. 440 B.C. Terracotta, H. 16⅛ in. (41 cm); Diam. of mouth 17⅞ in. (45.4 cm). The Metropolitan Museum of Art, Fletcher Fund, 1928 (28.57.23). Obverse showing Persephone rising from the underworld, with Hekate, in the presence of Hermes and Demeter

fig. 17 Attic red-figure volute-krater attributed to the workshop of Polygnotos. Greek, ca. 450 B.C. Terracotta, H. 19 in. (48.2 cm), Diam. 13⅞ in. (35.2 cm). Ashmolean Museum of Art and Archaeology, Oxford (G 275). The creation of Pandora

fig. 18 Apulian red-figure plate by the Painter of Vatican Z 3. Greek, South Italian, ca. 340–320 B.C. Terracotta, Diam. 8½ in. (21.6 cm). Field Museum of Natural History, Chicago (182636). A hand beside the female head holds up the mirror

that were not under Greek political control during the fourth century B.C.—among them, Cumae, Capua, and Paestum. Despite growing hostilities between Greek settlements and neighboring Italic groups such as the Lucani and Brutii, Hellenic products were in high demand in indigenous settlements and former Greek cities, and Greeks actively sought out these markets.[15] In Apulia, Italic demand for painted vases became so great that by the mid-fourth century B.C., South Italian workshops were established in Daunian and Peucetian communities such as Ruvo, Ceglie del Campo, and Canosa.[16] Given the wide range of cultures commissioning South Italian vases, the heads' vague identity was perhaps intentional, allowing for various interpretations by

viewers with disparate ethnic and religious affiliations. A Greek in Taranto might have read a female head quite differently from a Daunian in Ruvo, but the same image could have had significance to both.

In Attic vase painting, isolated heads are often a key component in anodos scenes, images presenting the rising of a deity from the chthonic realm (underworld). The ascending figure, usually female, is represented either with a truncated body or simply as an oversized head and neck, like the figure of Aphrodite on a hydria (water jar) in Brussels (fig. 15).[17] The anodos of a god is rarely depicted, but when it occurs, the deity involved is usually Dionysos.[18] Full-length figures typically witness these epiphanies and may facilitate the

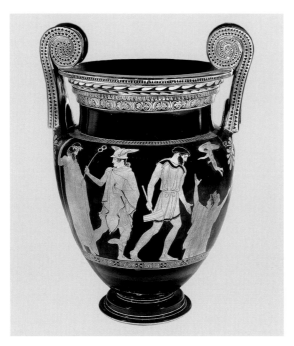

fig. 19 Archaic bronze herm. Greek, Arcadian, ca. 490 B.C. Bronze, H. 3⅝ in. (9.2 cm). The Metropolitan Museum of Art, Gift of Norbert Schimmel Trust, 1989 (1989.281.56)

fig. 20 Statue of a man wearing a toga. Roman, Augustan, 1st century A.D. Marble, H. 72 in. (182.9 cm). The Metropolitan Museum of Art, Gift of John D. Crimmins, 1904 (04.15)

upward movement of the ascending deities by breaking up the soil, as the satyrs do on the Brussels hydria.[19]

Often such images are associated with the return of Persephone to her mother, Demeter, as described in the "Homeric Hymn to Demeter." This narrative is depicted on the Museum's bell-krater by the Persephone Painter; on the obverse, the young goddess emerges from a fissure in the earth in the presence of Demeter, Hekate, and Hermes (fig. 16).[20] Other anodos scenes represent the creation of Pandora. On a volute-krater in the Ashmolean Museum, the rising protagonist is labeled as Pandora, and the bearded male figure reaching out to her is inscribed as Epimetheus (fig. 17).[21]

When inscriptions or clear attributes are lacking, the full-length figures may help to identify the rising individual; the presence of Erotes, winged gods of love, as on the Brussels hydria, implies the appearance of chthonic Aphrodite.[22] In Athenian vase painting of the second and third quarters of the fourth century B.C., anodos scenes containing heads flanked by full-length figures, usually women and youths or Erotes, appear increasingly on vessels of many shapes: pelikai, hydriai, stemless cups, lekanides, pyxides, kylixes, and kraters.[23] The discovery of these vases predominantly around the Black Sea and in modern-day Libya suggests that they had a particular appeal in colonial settings where Greek and native beliefs intermingled.

While isolated heads repeatedly play a narrative role in anodos scenes on Attic vases, parallel iconography in South Italian vase painting is very rare.[24] Fewer than forty isolated heads out of the thousands of extant South Italian examples are accompanied by full-length figures, and these occur only on Apulian vases. Flanked generally by Erotes, the heads emerge from flowers. This composition has no parallel in Attic vase painting, nor is it explained in surviving ancient literature.[25] Thus, Apulian heads in the presence of figures are not part of any known narrative or mimetic ritual associated with a mythological event.

Heads in South Italian vase-painting emerge from blossoms or acanthus leaf calyxes and are typically placed within vegetal frames of varying complexity, ranging from simple, stylized scrolls to lushly spiraling, flowering tendrils, as seen on the shoulders of the Museum's loutrophoroi by the Metope Painter (see figs. 11, 14). Eyes frequently gaze upward, and the head itself may be upturned.[26] Occasionally a hand, either empty or holding an object, appears next to the face, implying a body out of the viewer's sight (fig. 18).[27] Objects were sometimes painted in the field around isolated heads. While certain among them, such as

rosettes, could be decorative fill, most are items carried by women, nude youths, and Eros in funerary scenes, and thus have a cultic function and significance. They include thyrsoi (staffs of fennel and ivy carried by the followers of Dionysos), incense burners, cross-bar torches, ivy, and—most frequently—libation bowls.[28] Even altars appear, usually at the eye level of the head.[29]

ISOLATED HEADS AND THE ITALIC CONCEPTION OF THE BODY

Unlike the Greeks, particularly in the Classical period, who favored a holistic representation of the human body in the visual arts—even herms were typically given genitalia, implying a full-length figure (fig. 19)—the peoples of the Italian peninsula and Sicily seem to have regarded the body as an assemblage of various parts that could function independently. An Italic conceptualization of a "deconstructed" body has been used to explain the curious practice in Roman portrait sculpture of attaching heads to bodies that clearly do not match their subjects' age or physique.[30] Richard Brilliant summarized the principles behind such portraits under the term "appendage aesthetic."[31] Indeed, many surviving Roman statues, particularly of togate males, are headless and have holes between the shoulders for the insertion of separate portrait heads (fig. 20).[32]

fig. 21 Tarentine pediment fragment from a small funerary naiskos. Greek, South Italian, ca. 300 B.C. Limestone, H. 5½ in. (14 cm), L. 13¼ in. (33.7 cm). The Metropolitan Museum of Art, Purchase, Moses Fried Foundation and Dr. and Mrs. Jerome M. Eisenberg Gift, 1992 (1992.11.1)

fig. 22 Apulian red-figure volute-krater by the Iliupersis Painter. Greek, South Italian, ca. 370–355 B.C. Terracotta, H. 27⅛ in. (69 cm). Museo Archeologico, Bari (1394). Obverse showing, on the neck, a female head emerging from a leafy base; on the body, a grave stele surrounded by male and female mourners and offerings, including a red-figure amphora decorated with a funerary stele

Prior to the fourth century B.C., isolated heads were represented in a wide variety of media in the visual culture of native Italic peoples. The heads occurred in terracotta antefixes in Etruria and Campania, in Etruscan and South Italian amber carvings, and in relief decorations on bucchero pesante ceramics produced around Orvieto, Vulci, and Chiusi from the second quarter of the sixth to the early fifth century B.C.[33]

The most convincing explanation for the popularity of isolated heads in the red-figure wares of southern Italy and Sicily is probably, and perhaps quite simply, the Italic peoples' aesthetic predilection for the motif. Most South Italian vases decorated with the heads are found within non-Greek contexts and were produced in areas politically controlled by indigenous peoples. The findspots of Athenian vases decorated with painted and raised-relief heads provide further support for Italic interest in the motif. Rarely found in Attica, nearly half of these vases were exported to various sites in Italy, such as Vulci in Etruria and Spina on the northern Adriatic coast, suggesting that Athenian potters and painters purposely selected the motif for vases intended for export to these areas.[34]

THE FUNERARY SIGNIFICANCE OF ISOLATED HEADS IN SOUTH ITALIAN VASE PAINTING

To ascertain what the isolated heads meant to ancient Greek and Italic peoples in Magna Graecia, one must consider the context in which the vases bearing the motif are found and the imagery with which the heads were regularly paired. South Italian vases decorated with heads have been found overwhelmingly in funerary contexts, either within or above tombs. To the writer's present knowledge, none come from domestic contexts, but a small number have been discovered in civic spaces and in the votive deposits of sanctuaries.[35]

The supposition that vases decorated with heads served mainly funerary functions is supported by the motif's prevalence on monumentalized Apulian volute-kraters, amphorae, and loutrophoroi with intentionally perforated lower bodies that render the vessels

useless as functional containers. In the necropoleis of Taranto, these objects served as grave markers through which libations could be poured, reaching the remains of the deceased below.[36] Such vases were also favored grave goods in central and northern Apulia, where they have been found in significant numbers in the rock-cut chamber tombs of the Italic elite. While regional preferences can be discerned, the three most common types of imagery with painted heads are funerary scenes featuring grave monuments; mythological tableaux; and scenes of women, youths, and Eros.

In funerary scenes, tomb monuments take a variety of forms, often dictated by local predilections, and may be flanked by mourners bearing offerings to the deceased. The depiction of funerary monuments on South Italian vases became common during the second quarter of the fourth century B.C., when the Iliupersis Painter established a funerary vase archetype in Apulia that persisted until the early third century B.C. On the obverse of his monumental volute-kraters, the Iliupersis Painter favored a naiskos, a small, temple-like shrine with Ionic columns supporting an architrave and pediment. Typically, the Iliupersis Painter's naiskos contains a statue of the deceased, who is sometimes shown with family members or attendants, as on the obverse of one of the Metropolitan's loutrophoroi by the

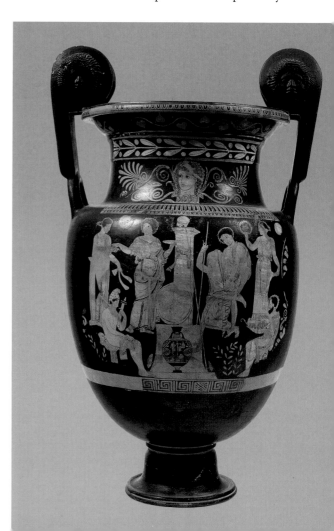

fig. 23a Campanian red-figure hydria attributed to the APZ Painter. Greek, South Italian, ca. 330–300 B.C. Terracotta, H. 27½ in. (69.9 cm). The Metropolitan Museum of Art, Rogers Fund, 1906 (06.1021.227). Obverse showing three women in a naiskos

fig. 23b Side view of fig. 23a: below the handle, a female head in profile faces the primary scene

Metope Painter, which shows an older woman and an attending girl (see figs. 14a, b).[37] The naiskoi and the figures inside them are usually painted in added white, presumably in imitation of stone or stuccoed wood.

The structures bear a resemblance to later monuments that stood in the cemeteries of Taranto. Made of local limestone, they were decorated with reliefs and three-dimensional sculpture (fig. 21).[38] Numerous fragments of these structures survive. On the reverse of his funerary volute-kraters, the Iliupersis Painter usually depicted a tall, narrow stele standing on a rectangular or stepped base. This stele, often tied with black fillets, became the preferred type of funerary monument depicted in other South Italian wares, such as Campanian and Paestan.[39]

The association of isolated heads with funerary scenes began not long after the first appearances of grave monuments on South Italian vases about 380–370 B.C. For example, a volute-krater found at Ceglie del Campo, attributed to the workshop of the Iliupersis Painter, features on the neck a female head with loose, curly hair in three-quarter view to left (fig. 22).[40] Emerging from a leafy base, the head is flanked by roughly symmetrical spiraling tendrils, the upper pair terminating in palmettes. Below, on the body of the vase, women and men of various ages stand, sit, and kneel around a rectangular stele on a tall, flaring base. Grave offerings include the patterned fillet tied around the stele, a spear, a shield, a helmet, and a red-figure amphora that is itself decorated with a funerary stele.

Before ca. 340 B.C., as seen on the volute-krater mentioned above, isolated heads were secondary decorative elements paired with funerary scenes. They were most often placed centrally, above depictions of tomb markers, in lush vegetal settings on the necks of volute-kraters or the necks and shoulders of amphorae and loutrophoroi. Heads were also painted under the horizontal handles of hydriai decorated with grave markers, as on the Metropolitan's vase by the APZ Painter (figs. 23a, b).[41] During the third quarter of the fourth century B.C., isolated heads began to be used as primary decoration on the reverse of vases that featured funerary scenes on the obverse, a pattern that seems to have originated in the work of the Patera and Amphorae Painters.[42]

The connection between isolated heads and South Italian funerary iconography is strengthened further by the presence on several Apulian vases of heads depicted within or as decoration on the naiskoi. For instance, on the obverse of one of the Metropolitan Museum's Metope Painter loutrophoros (see fig. 11a), a typical female head emerges from a flower on the lower part of the base of the naiskos rather than in the canonical position on the vase's shoulder, above the shrine.[43] Isolated heads within naiskoi, in the space usually occupied by statues, are mostly female, but on a volute-krater attributed to the Virginia Exhibition Painter, the naiskos contains a winged head rising from a campanula flower.[44]

Heads accompany a wide variety of mythological scenes relating to death, many of which closely adhere to the texts of Athenian tragedies, especially those of Euripides.[45] From about 380 B.C., isolated heads were frequently painted as secondary decoration on vases decorated with mythological tableaux representing themes such as the demise of one or more characters, the underworld and its inhabitants, the rescue of figures from certain death through heroic or divine intervention, and the granting of immortality, sometimes through forcible abduction by a deity.[46]

The sampling of works described in the remainder of this section provides compelling evidence for the purposeful pairing of isolated heads with mythological themes that possess additional layers of meaning in a funerary context. On the obverse of the Museum's Campanian neck-amphora attributed to the Pilos Head Group (see fig. 4), the young warrior protagonist seated on an altar with his sword drawn appears to be either Orestes, the son of Agamemnon and Klytemnestra of Mycenae, or Neoptolemos, Achilles's son, whose victims during the sack of Troy included Priam and Polyxena. In Euripides's *Andromache*, it is revealed that Hermione, the daughter of Helen and Menelaos of Sparta, was promised to both young men, resulting in Orestes's

murder of Neoptolemos. Perhaps the seated youth on the reverse of the vase is intended to represent the rival of the younger man on the obverse.

Depictions of the meeting of Orestes and his sister Elektra at the tomb of their murdered father are frequently accompanied by isolated heads on Campanian and Paestan vases.[47] These vases, presumably inspired by the *Elektra* plays of Aeschylos and Sophocles, depict the crucial tomb scene during which the siblings plot to kill their mother, Klytemnestra, and her lover, Aegisthus.

A mythological scene involving the sparing of an individual from certain death is paired with an isolated head on the obverse of the Metropolitan's loutrophoros by the Darius Painter (fig. 24). Directly below the somewhat damaged female head on the shoulder of the vase, shown in three-quarter view to left emerging from a flower, Persephone and Aphrodite, both closely linked to the underworld in South Italian cult, appeal to either Zeus or Hades for Adonis, who was fatally gored by a boar.[48] Their pleas were answered: Adonis was made immortal, becoming a minor vegetation deity, and divided his time between the two goddesses.

figs. 26a,b Apulian red-figure situla attributed to the Lycurgus Painter. Greek, South Italian, ca. 360–340 B.C. Terracotta, H. 11 in. (27.9 cm). The Metropolitan Museum of Art, Fletcher Fund, 1956 (56.171.64). Obverse and reverse showing satyrs and maenads with Dionysos

fig. 26c Detail of figs. 26a,b, showing underside with face

Heads are frequently painted in conjunction with representations of the underworld and its inhabitants on Apulian vases.[49] Below the head inscribed *Aura* on the volute-krater in the British Museum, Hades, lord of the dead, abducts his consort, Persephone (see fig. 7). Other vases with an isolated head as secondary decoration depict Hades and Persephone presiding in their underworld palace, surrounded by mythological figures such as Orpheus.[50] He can be seen to the left of the palace, playing his kithara, on an elaborate volute-krater in Munich (fig. 25).[51]

Orpheus was credited in antiquity with composing poetry extolling the religious beliefs and practices that would become the central tenets of Orphism, a mystery cult that enjoyed great popularity in southern Italy and Sicily.[52] The doctrinal core of Orphism focused on the birth, death, and rebirth of Dionysos and on a belief in an immortal soul that experienced multiple reincarnations in its attempt to reunify with the divine.[53]

Dionysiac imagery, used in the context of Orphism as well as in the mystery cult of Dionysos, is the most common mythological iconography to be paired with isolated heads in South Italian vase painting.[54] As a chthonic vegetation deity, Dionysos has numerous connections to the realm of the dead. He not only retrieved his mortal mother, Semele, from Hades but, according to certain variants of his mythology, was himself a resurrected being. The popularity of his cult can probably be explained by the benefits it promised in the afterlife.[55] An unusual pairing of Dionysiac imagery

with an isolated head is found on the Metropolitan's Apulian situla (wine bucket) attributed to the Lycurgus Painter (figs. 26a, b, c).[56] On the obverse, Dionysos arrives in a chariot drawn by two griffins. In the center of the lower foreground, a papposilenos (elderly satyr) dips a jug into a calyx-krater with his right hand, while in his left he holds an offering bowl, which he will use to serve wine to the god. Two seated maenads, one nude above the waist, flank the satyr. To the left of the god's chariot, a second papposilenos plays the aulos (double pipes). On the reverse, Dionysos, seated between a standing satyr and a maenad, holds a thyrsos. Curiously, the isolated head—it is frontal, with a cherubic face, large eyes, slightly parted lips, and short, curly locks of hair—appears as a sketch on the underside of the vase.

Luca Giuliani advances the idea that the mythological scenes portrayed on monumental Apulian vases, roughly 60 percent of which are decorated with one or more isolated heads, not only reflected the somber mood of funerary rites but also served a ritual function.[57] He suggests that at a funerary banquet, the story on the vase would be told as part of a eulogy in which the myth portrayed would be related to the fate of the deceased, thereby heroizing the dead and comforting the mourners. Giuliani's theory is compelling, as it places the function and appropriateness of mythological imagery in the funerary sphere beyond mere appreciation of Greek mythology and tragic theater.[58] Thus, representations of myths involving abduction, such as Oreithyia swept away by Boreas, would have served

fig. 27a Apulian red-figure thymiaterion associated with the Stuttgart Group. Greek, South Italian, ca. 325–300 B.C. Terracotta, H. 12 in. (30.5 cm). The Metropolitan Museum of Art, Rogers Fund, 1906 (06.1021.220). On the base, Eros with a situla and a phiale

fig. 27b Top of the thymiaterion in fig. 27a: female head in profile

fig. 28a Detail of an Apulian red-figure column-krater by the Patera Painter and the Amphorae Painter (reverse). Greek, South Italian, ca. 340–320 B.C. Terracotta, H. ca. 17¾ in. (45 cm). The State Hermitage Museum, Saint Petersburg (553). Obverse showing a woman with a thyrsos, mirror, and wreath following a youth in Oscan dress with cista, tympanon, and situla

fig. 28b Reverse of fig. 28a, with a large female head in profile

as allegories of the death of a young man or woman in his or her prime.[59] As many abduction myths led to the bestowal of immortality upon the chosen victims, the stories would have conveyed hope for a deceased youth's continued and improved existence in the afterlife.

The tableaux most frequently paired with isolated heads feature women, youths, and Erotes. As mentioned above, the figures carry objects that serve ritual functions in funerary observances, such as torches and offering bowls, or that have connections with Dionysiac cult, such as bunches of grapes and thyrsoi.[60] An Apulian thymiaterion (incense burner) in the Metropolitan's collection (figs. 27a, b) provides an example.[61] A female head in profile is depicted on the surface of the shallow receptacle at the top; on the base, Eros, seated on a bundle of drapery, holds a situla—a vase frequently used as a wine vessel and thus with clear connections to Dionysos—and a phiale, an offering bowl for making libations.

When two or more figures are depicted in these tableaux, they often move in the same direction, as if participating in a procession. Ritual activity is further indicated by the presence of altars.[62] On some Apulian and Campanian vases decorated with heads, the women and youths wear non-Greek forms of dress, mainly in the style associated with the Oscans, an Italic people who inhabited parts of Campania, Lucania, and perhaps Apulia. An Apulian column-krater in Saint Petersburg attributed to the Patera and Amphorae Painters (figs. 28a, b) features a procession on the obverse led by a youth wearing a typical Oscan short tunic and wide belt; he carries a situla, a cista (box) with offerings, and a tympanon (hand drum) suspended

below the cista.[63] A woman follows him, carrying a mirror in her upraised left hand, a filleted wreath in her right hand, and a thyrsos in the crook of her right arm. The position of her legs indicates a dance-like movement and recalls depictions of maenads. On the reverse of the vase is a large female head in profile to left. The elements of Dionysiac cult—the situla, tympanon, and thyrsos—on this vase and others depicting non-Greek peoples strongly suggest that the Greeks and their neighbors shared religious practices.[64]

On some vases with isolated heads, the adjoining scenes of women, youths, and Erotes depict bridal preparations or feature a couple embracing in the presence of Eros.[65] These scenes present clear iconographic parallels to images of Greek nuptial and funerary rites, markers of major life transitions.[66] Such scenes on South Italian vases may support H. R. W. Smith's theory that in Magna Graecia, concepts of an afterlife possibly included the reunion of spouses, who together would enjoy the bounties of the hereafter.[67] Nike, sometimes in the company of women and youths, occasionally appears on vases painted with isolated heads and may well represent beliefs in immortality and hopes for an

fig. 29 Tomb slab from Metaponto, tomb 117. Greek, South Italian, late 4th century B.C. Terracotta, H. 13¾ in. (35 cm), Diam. 27¾ in. (70.5 cm). Museo Archeologico Nazionale, Metaponto (319201). The mold-made relief decoration shows a frontal head wearing a Phrygian cap

fig. 30 Bust of a female wearing a polos, from the rock sanctuary below San Biagio, Agrigento. Greek, South Italian, ca. 400–350 B.C. Terracotta, H. 14⅝ in. (37 cm), W. 12⅝ in. (32 cm). Museo Archeologico Regionale Paolo Orsi, Syracuse (16085)

afterlife.[68] It is significant that other genre scenes, with subjects such as symposia and the gymnasium, do not occur in association with isolated heads, nor do representations of comedies, which enjoyed such favor in southern Italy and Sicily.[69] This suggests that the significance of the heads is extraneous to the common or slapstick and supports the idea that the heads belong to the realm of epic and tragedy.

ISOLATED HEADS IN OTHER MEDIA IN SOUTH ITALIAN FUNERARY CONTEXTS

Isolated heads found in other media in funerary and chthonic contexts throughout southern Italy and Sicily corroborate the motif's sepulchral significance in South Italian vase painting. From the late 10th to the 8th century B.C., heads carved from local stone were placed on top of tombs in Daunia, the northern region of Apulia, predominantly at Monte Saraceno but also at Troia and Arpi.[70] Heads also served as decorative elements in South Italian tombs of the Classical period and appeared on semicircular terracotta antefixes used as roofing elements on tomb monuments in Taranto and other Greek settlements.[71] In Tomb 117 at Metaponto, a late fourth-century B.C. burial, a mold-made antefix with a frontal head wearing a Phrygian cap was attached to the large terracotta slab that closed the short end of the tomb, corresponding to the placement of the deceased's head (fig. 29).[72]

Among the famous painted tombs of Paestum, a frontal head with short curly hair was depicted between a panther and a lion in tomb 29 of the Spinazzo necropolis.[73] Female heads, often with vegetal surrounds, occur in the decoration of fourth-century B.C. rock-cut hypogeum tombs (underground burial chambers). Examples of these relief carvings include heads rising from acanthus calyxes on pilaster capitals in the Medusa tomb at Arpi and in a tomb in the Cristallini district of Naples, as well as a female head flanked by floral scrolls in the center of a frieze in the entry passage to the burial ground in the Palazzo Palmieri garden in Lecce.[74]

Through the third century B.C., isolated heads were a recurring motif on terracotta votive gifts offered to chthonic deities at sites in southern Italy and Sicily, among them, the Sanctuary of the Chthonic Deities and San Biagio, in Agrigento; the Malophoros sanctuary at Selinunte; and the Mannella sanctuary at Locri Epizephyrii in Calabria.[75] Most are in the form of shoulder busts, which can stand independently (fig. 30), or protomes, isolated reliefs that were leaned against a support, laid flat, or hung on a wall, probably of a temple or temenos (holy precinct).[76] The votive heads

frequently wear polos crowns, sometimes quite tall, and may be veiled. Over time, the religious significance of the protomes was emphasized by the inclusion of attributes such as lotus flowers, pomegranates, cross-bar torches, and piglets, all items associated with Demeter and Kore-Persephone.[77] Female busts with a small winged figure, presumably Eros, placed in the area of the collarbones are also known, suggesting a connection to Aphrodite, whose chthonic aspect was worshiped in Magna Graecia.[78] Protomes and busts could be included among grave goods, as exemplified by the remarkable janiform bust of a bearded man and a young woman wearing a polos found in a tomb at Locri Epizephyrii.[79] Another funerary role of terracotta busts might have been that of cenotaph, as seen in the so-called pot-burial at Locri, dating to the Classical period.[80]

fig. 31 Arula from Taranto with a frontal female head surrounded by spiraling tendrils. Greek, South Italian, second half of the 4th century B.C. Terracotta. Museo Nazionale Archeologico, Taranto (208342)

Additionally, terracotta appliqués in the form of frontal female heads have been found in two Paestan painted tombs dating to the first half of the fourth century B.C.[81]

Frontal heads rising from an acanthus calyx within a floral surround, very similar to those seen on South Italian vases, decorate a significant number of portable terracotta altars, called arulae (fig. 31).[82] Arulae are mainly discovered in tombs or in chthonic sanctuaries, and the subjects of their reliefs—sphinxes, sirens, and Dionysiac scenes—have funerary associations.[83] Another type of votive gift featuring an isolated head and dedicated to underworld deities is the pinax (terracotta plaque). Made in the mid-fifth century B.C., pinakes of this sort were discovered at Francavilla, in Sicily. Many of the motifs on them are clearly derived from similar plaques produced for the cult of Persephone at Locri Epizephyrii, but those with heads appear to be unique to the Francavilla examples.[84] Pinakes with heads come in three types, two of which feature overlapping, left-facing male and female heads, with the female head in the foreground. The third variety features a female head in profile to left.[85]

THE SYMBOLIC ROLE OF THE ISOLATED HEAD IN SOUTHERN ITALY AND SICILY

Since isolated heads in South Italian vase-painting were paired with, but not integrated into, narrative scenes populated with full-length figures, they are likely symbolic representations of abstract concepts and are probably best regarded as personifications of metaphysical ideas, such as Themis (divine law or order), or a state of being, such as Athanasia (immortality).

One of the challenges in identifying personifications in Greek art is that, unlike divinities or other mythological figures, personifications frequently lack unique attributes.[86] This is certainly true of the overwhelming majority of heads on South Italian vases, excepting only those of satyrs, Pan, and the few possible heads of Dionysos. The identification of a personification usually depends upon the presence of an inscription or the inclusion of the personifying figure within a known mythological context. However, the South Italian heads lack both inscriptions and context.

South Italian vase painting is richly populated with personifications identified by inscriptions.[87] They may be protagonists, such as the Hyades snuffing out the flames, as seen on a bell-krater in London, or simply observers like Astrape, Eniautos, and Eleusis on a volute-krater at the Getty Villa of the J. Paul Getty Museum.[88] Although most often represented as full-length figures, personifications are rendered half-length or as busts on certain Paestan vases.[89] Unlike isolated heads, the personifications always appear in mythological scenes. They provide geographical and temporal context to the unfolding action, embody divine forces at work, or indicate changes in a character's state of being.[90]

The simplest explanation for an isolated head is that it is an abbreviated stand-in for a full-length figure.[91] This idea certainly holds for those few heads on South Italian vases that have a hand, either empty or holding an object, raised to the level of the face, implying the existence of a body that is out of sight. It is doubtful that heads were favored over full-length figures because of space limitations, since the motif appears as the single decorative feature on the sides of large-scale vases such as Apulian amphorae and volute-kraters. Therefore, the representation of a head or bust isolated from the body must have been deliberate, selected for its capacity to convey meaning. That the motif functioned primarily as a funerary emblem is supported by several factors: the discovery of vases with heads almost exclusively in tombs; the consistency in the types of images painted on vessels with isolated heads; and the presence of heads in other media in mortuary and chthonic contexts in southern Italy and Sicily.

The frequent emergence of isolated heads from flowers or leafy calyxes and their surrounds of lush, spiraling floral tendrils link the isolated head motif to the regenerative power of nature, a cornerstone of ancient Greek religious belief and ritual. Especially on those vases on which such imagery was placed directly above funerary scenes, as if springing from the top of the grave monument itself, the combination of elements could thus be a potent visual expression

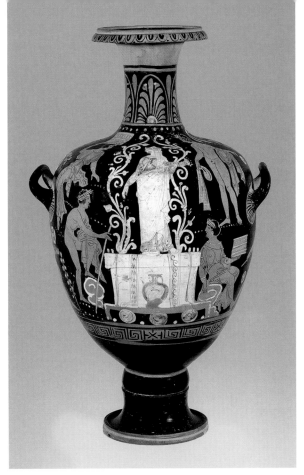

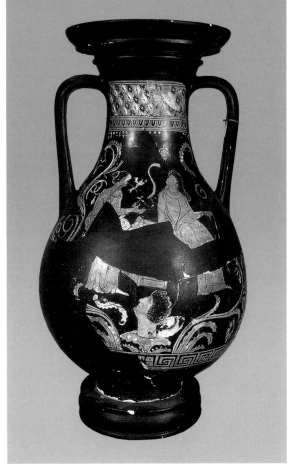

fig. 32 Campanian red-figure hydria attributed to the Olcott Painter. Greek, South Italian, ca. 360–330 B.C. Terracotta, H. 22¼ in. (56.5 cm). The Metropolitan Museum of Art, Rogers Fund, 1906 (06.1021.230). Obverse showing a funerary monument consisting of a tall base surmounted by a statue of a bride surrounded by tendrils and flanked by youths and women

fig. 33 Apulian red-figure pelike by the Darius Painter. Greek, South Italian, ca. 340–320 B.C. Terracotta, H. ca. 19¼ in. (49 cm). Allard Pierson Museum, Amsterdam (2578). Obverse showing an oracular (?) head and two women, one holding a lyre and the other seated beside an open cista

of the yearning for immortality and the belief that life could issue forth from death.

In southern Italy and Sicily during the fourth century B.C., images of lush floral tendrils developed strong associations with the sacral and funerary realms.[92] On Apulian, Lucanian, and Campanian vases, small flowering plants are depicted growing beside funerary monuments and appear within funerary naiskoi in place of a human figure.[93] A leafy vine, floral tendrils, and rosettes are common decoration on the bases of painted naiskoi, and occasionally, tall, flowering spiral tendrils form an arborlike structure around funerary statues, such as on the Metropolitan Museum's Campanian hydria (fig. 32).[94] Leafy branches are sometimes depicted in fields next to grave stelai, and flowers and branches are painted next to figures within naiskoi.[95] The frequent representation on vases of women and youths presenting vegetal and floral offerings at grave monuments corresponds well with literary references to plants and flowers laid in graves.[96] Painted floral garlands and suspended wreaths decorate walls of South Italian tombs, and an epitaph on a child's grave expresses the hope that flowers will grow there as a sign that the deceased is beloved by the gods and lives on as the flowers do.[97] Sometimes the dead were buried wearing gold, bronze, or gilded terracotta wreaths. Many of these objects are so delicate that they were probably intended exclusively for funerary use.[98]

Acanthus, another plant from which heads emerge, has a long tradition in Greek funerary art. It is seen in relief on Attic marble anthemia stelai (grave markers with volute-palmette decoration) starting in the third quarter of the fifth century B.C. and is depicted on funerary monuments painted on Classical Attic white-ground lekythoi.[99] Given the frequent presence of flowers and vegetation in funerary iconography and ritual, perhaps it is not surprising that Pindar described the islands of the blessed—the site where the afterlife awaits the virtuous—as a place where "flowers of gold are ablaze, some from radiant trees on land, while the water nurtures others; with these they weave garlands for their hands and crowns for their heads."[100]

An unusual representation of a head rising from a flower on an Apulian pelike in Amsterdam may offer further evidence of isolated heads as emblems of life after death (fig. 33). The head, with its accompanying flower, acanthus calyx, and floral tendrils, is painted in the lower foreground and gazes up at two full-length female figures, one standing and holding a lyre, the other seated beside an open cista.[101] The scene has parallels in three probable depictions of Orpheus's oracular head in mainland Greek art.[102] In each instance, the head rests on the ground, albeit not emerging from vegetation, and gazes up at two flanking figures. Similar heads resting on the ground in the presence of full-length figures are found on engraved Etruscan bronze mirrors.[103] The heads—of males, satyrs, and wearers of Phrygian caps—have counterparts in South Italian vase painting. Nancy de Grummond proposes that they represent oracular heads, either of chthonic origin or decapitated, and notes that the scenes in which they occur usually represent key points in life—birth, marriage, and death—that were predicted or affected by the heads' divine messages.[104]

Although isolated heads on South Italian vases do not appear to speak, their popularity indicates that they communicated a potent message with mass appeal in the funerary sphere. The heads, in the Greek tradition of embodying abstract concepts in human form, may well represent elpis, the hope or anticipation of a future event. Elpis had both positive and negative associations in Greek literature, but in a sepulchral context, it presumably referred to the hope for a blissful afterlife.[105] The only creature that remained, by the will of Zeus, inside the infamous pithos (jar) given to Pandora, Elpis does not appear in Greek art as a personification identified by inscription.

One of its few possible representations occurs in a tableau on a red-figure amphora produced between 450 and 425 B.C., found in Basilicata, and now in the British Museum (figs. 34a,b).[106] The scene wraps around the vase, beginning at one end with a woman (presumably Pandora) rising from the ground. She reaches to the right, toward a youth wearing a pilos helmet and chlamys (short cloak) and holding a hammer similar to the type carried by satyrs in Attic anodos scenes.[107] Farther to the right stands a bearded man with a walking stick and himation (mantle). Jenifer Neils

persuasively identifies this figure as Zeus, comparing it to the god's depiction on the volute-krater in Oxford, the one certain example of the anodos of Pandora (see fig. 17: the figure of Zeus is on the far left).[108] Zeus gazes toward a vessel—a pithos—standing on a low platform. Remarkably, a tiny female head wearing a headcloth rises from the vessel's mouth, clearly differentiated from the vase by a line across her neck. Given the other elements in the scene, the female in the container must be Elpis. She is not represented as a winged creature (as the evils in the jar were said to have been) but, rather, as a head in isolation. Perhaps the unusual apparition was created by an inventive vase painter to express a concept that had no preexisting visual form.[109]

CONCLUSION

The isolated heads represented on South Italian vases in the Museum's collection illustrate the broad patterns of the use of the motif in the red-figure wares of southern Italy and Sicily. The painting of heads on vases was not a South Italian invention; the motif was present, but never widespread, in the wares of the Greek mainland and Aegean. However, over half a century after the transfer from Athens of the red-figure technique and its associated imagery, heads gradually became the predominant theme of South Italian vase painting, a phenomenon seemingly fueled by native Italic interest in the motif. At the same time, the iconographic association of isolated heads clearly shifted from mythological narrative to the funerary realm. This evolution may document a change in southern Italy and Sicily in concepts of the human soul and its existence after death—a turning away from the gloomy precepts of the Homeric and Hesiodic tradition toward Pythagorean philosophy and the blissful promises of mystic cults, such as those of Dionysos and Orpheus, all practiced in the region.[110] Plato, in his *Gorgias*, written about 380 B.C., describes Magna Graecia as a place where discussions of the human soul abounded amid religious and philosophical speculation.[111] The various types of isolated heads on South Italian vases might well reflect the views of immortality espoused by diverse contemporary belief systems, and the heads' indeterminate identities may have offered viewers of diverse ethnic and religious backgrounds wide flexibility of interpretation.

KEELY ELIZABETH HEUER
*Assistant Professor, State University
of New York at New Paltz*

fig. 34a Owl Pillar Group amphora. Greek, ca. 450–425 B.C. Terracotta, H. 12⅛ in. (30.8 cm). British Museum, London (F 147). Frieze around the body showing the creation of Pandora

fig. 34b Reverse of fig. 34a, probably showing Elpis emerging from Pandora's jar in the presence of a bearded male, perhaps Zeus

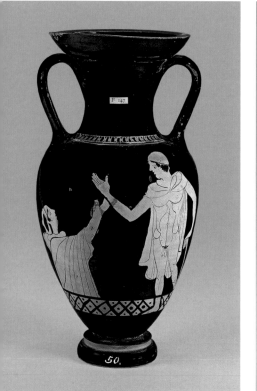

NOTES

1 Theories about the transfer of the red-figure technique range from Athenian participation in the Panhellenic settlement established at Thurii in 443 B.C. (Furtwängler 1893, pp. 149–52) to the return of South Italian vase painters and potters to their homeland after training in Attic workshops (Denoyelle 1997; Giudice and Barresi 2003). Athenian artisans may have been encouraged to emigrate to Magna Graecia by Pericles's designs on the region, as recorded by Thucydides (3.86.115; 4.2.2; 4.59–65; and 7.35.1; see also Meiggs and Lewis 1969, pp. 80–82, no. 37, and pp. 171–76, nos. 63, 64; and Fornara 1977, pp. 137–39, nos. 124, 125). These culminated in the failed Athenian expedition against Syracuse in 415–413 B.C. The Athenian defeat in the Peloponnesian War led to a sig-nificant decline in Attic vase exports to the west in the late fifth century B.C., an important factor in the continued growth of red-figure vase manufacture in southern Italy and Sicily (Giudice and Barresi 2003). The onset of the Peloponnesian War in 431 B.C. might also have encouraged artisans to emi-grate to more lucrative locations to establish workshops (*LCS*, p. 3; MacDonald 1981; *RVAp II*, p. 16; Trendall 1989, p. 17; Schmidt 1996, pp. 444–45).

2 This statistic is based upon those pieces in the catalogues of A. D. Trendall and the volumes of the *CVA* published up to 2013.

3 Trendall 1990.

4 Of the South Italian vases appearing in the works of Trendall and the volumes of the *CVA*, the number of vases decorated with at least one isolated head in each of the five wares is as follows: Apulian: 5,376; Campanian: 1,176; Paestan: 447; Sicilian: 301; and Lucanian: 70.

5 Copenhagen 13966: *Para.* 48; *CVA* Copenhagen (8) III He, pls. 124, 125, pp. 253–54.

6 The British Museum (hereafter B.M.) volute-krater is in *RVAp I* 8/5, p. 193.

7 Ten examples of heads of Pan are found in the publications of Trendall and the volumes of the *CVA*; for example, Vatican AA 2 inv. 18255 (*RVAp I* 8/13, p. 194) and Rizzo collection, Mandelieu, France (*RVAp Suppl. 2* 17/40-B, p. 507). Heads of Dionysos are found on four South Italian vases known to the author, all of which are Paestan: e.g. MMA 65.11.18 (*RVP* 9/834, p. 223); Cleveland 1989.73 (Trendall 1992; and Denoyelle and Iozzo 2009, p. 132).

8 Cambitoglou 1954, pp. 111–21; *RVAp II*, pp. 445, 447–48, 456, 462–63, 473, 486, 601–2, 604–5, 647–49; Schauenburg 1957, pp. 210–12; Smith 1976, pp. 50–51; Lehnert 1978; Kossatz-Deißmann 1985, pp. 229–39; Schauenburg 1989, pp. 36–37.

9 For examples of the nimbus, see Bologna 567 (*RVAp II* 23/19, p. 728; *CVA* Bologna [3] IV Dr, pl. 7.3–4, p. 6) and Saint Petersburg 578 (St. 354) (*RVAp II* 23/21, p. 728).

10 *RVAp II* 26/456, p. 848. For discussions of the ambiguity of winged heads in South Italian vase-painting, refer to Cambitoglou 1954, p. 121; Schauenburg 1957, p. 212; Schauenburg 1962, p. 37; Schauenburg 1974, pp. 169–86; Schauenburg 1981, pp. 467–69; Schauenburg 1982, pp. 250–55; and Schauenburg 1984b, pp. 155–57.

11 Schauenburg 1974, pp. 171–72, 174–85; Schmidt 1975, pp. 130–32; Schauenburg 1981, p. 468; Schauenburg 1982, pp. 253–55; Schauenburg 1984a, p. 364; and Kossatz-Deißmann 1990, pp. 517–20.

12 Heads wearing Phrygian caps and jewelry, suggesting a female subject, are on Taranto 52.389 (*RVAp Suppl. 2* 22/469b,

p. 215); the volute-krater by the Patera Painter once in the Biedermann collection in Bremen (*RVAp II* 23/17, p. 728); and the patera in the Lagioia collection in Bari (*RVAp II* 28/357, p. 954). Nearly all examples of heads wearing Phrygian caps are clean shaven, but a bearded male head wearing the headdress is on a chous once on the California market (Intercontinental Antiquity Corporation 4067: *RVAp Suppl. 1* 22/41a, p. 112).

13 Such as on Ruvo 1372 (*RVAp Suppl. 1* 15/36, p. 402) and Vatican V 64 inv. 18097 (*RVAp II* 28/191, p. 940).

14 Furtwängler 1912, p. 32; *RVAp I*, p. lii.

15 Lewis et al. 1994, pp. 386–402.

16 *RVAp II*, p. 450; Robinson 1990; Carpenter 2003. The traditional interpretation is that vase painters emigrated from Taranto, the only major Greek colony in Apulia, to Italic settlements in the region during the mid-fourth century B.C. However, other scholars have noted the lack of archaeological evidence for early Apulian workshops in Taranto, suggesting that they might have been located elsewhere, such as in Peucetia, the central part of Apulia, where there seem to have been strong trade connections between Italic settlements and Athens throughout the fifth century B.C. (Carpenter 2003, pp. 5–6; Carpenter 2009, pp. 29–31; and Thorn 2009). For Attic vase imports into Apulia, see Mannino 1997; Mannino and Roubis 2000; and Mannino 2004. See also Macchioro 1912, pp. 168–71, and Thucydides 6.44, 7.33.

17 Brussels R 286 (*ARV²*, p. 1472, no. 4; *CVA* Brussels [2] III I c, pl. 2.4a–c, p. 2). A further example is on the skyphos Boston 01.8032, attributed to the Penthesilea Painter, where nearly three-quarters of the female figure rising between the two animated Pans is visible (*ARV²*, p. 888, no. 155; *Para.* 428).

18 Examples include Chartres 94 (Bérard 1974, pl. 5.20); Louvre F 311 (*CVA* Louvre [2] III He, pl. 5.1); and B.M., Hope 163 (Metzger 1951, p. 262, pl. 35). For analysis of these as images of Dionysos, see Bérard 1974, pp. 103–15, 141–51.

19 Frequently the satyrs in these scenes wield tools that resemble a mallet or pickax, objects not otherwise associated with them in Greek art. The source for this iconography may have been a satyr play, particularly the lost work of Sophocles entitled either *Pandora* or *The Hammerers*; see Buschor 1937, p. 10, and Brommer 1959, pp. 52–53, 56. Hammers are ill-suited for plowing and aerating the soil to allow a divinity to ascend, and thus their use may echo a comedic version of a ritual activity in a satyr play. Jane Harrison proposed that the mallets were part of a ritual that prepared the soil for Persephone (Kore) to emerge; her appearance was the mythological parallel to the emergence of wheat shoots in spring. To strengthen her argument, Harrison pointed to the ancient custom of smiting the earth to summon the earth spirits, as Pausanias (8.135) records was done during the great festival of Demeter Kidaria at Pheneus, in Arcadia. Refer to Harrison 1900, pp. 106–7; Harrison 1908, pp. 282–83; and Lehnert 1978, pp. 44–45. The tools in the hands of the satyrs perhaps served to open springs, and the rising female figures were nymphs of the spring that accompanied the rising fresh water, an interpre-tation proposed by Carl Robert (1886, p. 200). Robert later proposed that anodos scenes had to do with a pre-Hesiodic version of the Pandora myth in which Ge (Mother Earth), manifested as Pandora above ground, was trapped during the winter months and freed by the brothers Epimetheus and

Prometheus; Robert 1914, pp. 17–18. Erika Simon (1989) agrees with Robert's suggestion that at least some representations of women rising from the earth might be nymphs and points to the stamnos Louvre C 10754 as a possible example.

20 *ARV²*, p. 1012, no. 1.

21 *ARV²*, p. 601, no. 23; *CVA* Oxford (1), pl. 21.1–2, pp. 18–19.

22 For anodos scenes as evidence of belief in chthonic Aphrodite, see Buschor 1937, p. 17; Rumpf 1950–51, p. 168; Metzger 1951, pp. 72–73; Langlotz 1954, pp. 7–8; and Sgouropoulou 2000.

23 For examples of women and youths, see Cabinet des Médailles 472 (*ARV²*, p. 1489, no. 156) and London F 18 (*ARV²*, p. 1481, no. 1). For examples of Erotes, refer to Louvre MN 746 (*ARV²*, p. 1468, no. 129) and Naples Stg. 287 (*ARV²*, p. 1524, no. 2).

24 The author knows of two fifth-century B.C. pieces painted with truncated figures rising from the earth: the Lucanian bell-krater with lugs at Matera by the Pisticci Painter (*LCS*, p. 14, no. 1) and the fragmentary large Apulian bell-krater attributed to the Hearst Painter in the Cahn collection in Basel (*RVAp I* 1/25a, p. 11; Cambitoglou 1997, pp. 61–64). A third, later example may be represented on Louvre K 51, a Lucanian skyphos attributed to the Primato Painter (*LCS*, p. 178, no. 1062).

25 Such as Bari 872 (*RVAp II* 18/43, p. 497) and Saint Petersburg Inv. 1710 (St. 406) (*RVAp II* 18/21, p. 490).

26 E.g., Como C 60 (*RVAp II* 22/625, p. 700; *CVA* Como [1] IV D, pl. 8.1a–b, p. 6) and Berlin F 3231 (*LCS*, p. 564, no. 947).

27 For example, Taranto 143532 (*CVA* Taranto [4], pl. 37.3, p. 12) and B.M. F 534 (*CVA* British Museum [7] IV E b, pl. 1.5).

28 For thyrsoi, see Bari 1406 (*RVAp II* 22/32, p. 652) and an Ixion Painter bell-krater (*RVAp Suppl. 1*, p. 161, no. 836). For incense burners, refer to once New York market, Hesperia Arts Auction Ltd. (*RVAp Suppl. 2* 29/I, p. 353) and once Woodyat collection, Naples (*RVAp II* 17/74, p. 471). Examples of cross-bar torches occur on Parma C 112 (*RVAp II* 29/441, p. 997; *CVA* Parma [2] IV D, pl. 8.2–3, p. 5) and Bochum S 59 (*RVAp II* 29/393, p. 995; *CVA* Bochum [3], pl. 53.1–2, p. 70), where the object appears on only one side of the head with an X-shaped cross at its top. For ivy, see Copenhagen 35 (*RVAp II* 22/263, p. 669; *CVA* Copenhagen [6], pl. 267.1a–b, p. 208) and Lecce 874 (*RVAp II* 22/206, p. 667; *CVA* Lecce [2], pl. 56.1, p. 34). Libation bowls appear on Göttingen F 40 (*CVA* Göttingen [1], pl. 21.1–2, p. 36) and Foggia 131487 (found in tomb 185 at Salapia; *RVAp II*, p. 658).

29 On Chevron Group bell-kraters Bari 11966 (*RVAp II* 22/83, p. 657) and one once on the Zürich market (*RVAp II* 22/57, p. 655), a wide stele or altar bearing small, round offerings in added white appears next to a female head in profile. An altar supporting a leafing branch appears beside a satyr's head on another bell-krater of the Chevron Group once on the New York market (*RVAp Suppl. 2* 22/42a, p. 202).

30 The Flavian matron's head atop the body of a voluptuous nude Venus found near Lago Albano (Copenhagen, Ny Carlsberg Glyptotek 711, ca. A.D. 90) is but one example. For more on this practice and the head as a separable portrait element, see Stewart 2003, pp. 47–59, and Squire 2011, pp. 148–52.

31 Brilliant 1963, pp. 10, 26–31.

32 For discussions of the symbolic importance of the head in Roman culture and the visual manifestation of this in sculpture, refer to Richlin 1999 and Hallett 2005, pp. 281–95.

33 For terracotta antefixes, refer to Andrén 1940, pp. cxxx–ccxlii; Winter 1974 and 1978; *Enciclopedia dell'arte antica classica e orientale, Secundo Supplemento, 1971–1994*, vol. 1 (Rome, 1994), pp. 242–52, s.v. "Antefissa"

(M. Mertens-Horn); C. Marconi 2005; and Winter 2009, pp. 49–54, 85–88, 147, 157, 169–74, 223–36, 245–50, 311–17, 321–24, 344–50, 395–96, 400, 425–44. For carved amber heads, see Popovic 1975, pp. 91–92; Pontrandolfo 1977; Causey-Frel 1984, pp. 18–19, 32–34, 85–95; Causey 1993; and Losi, Raposso, and Ruggiero 1993, pp. 203–5, 209. For relief decoration on bucchero pesante ceramics, see Donati 1967, 1968, and 1969.

34 Of the 810 Athenian vases featuring a painted or plastic isolated head with known provenance in the Beazley Archive's database as of July 2014, 379 pieces (47 percent) were discovered on the Italian peninsula and Sicily. Examples of the vases found at Vulci include the lip-cup London B 401 (*ABV* 171, 3; *CVA* London [2] III He 6, pl. 14.9, p. 6), the eye-cup Munich 2019 (*ABV* 204, 12; *CVA* Munich, Antikensammlungen [13], pls. 68.6–7, 69.1–5, pp. 107–9), the neck-amphora Munich J396 (*ABV* 121, 9; *CVA* Munich, Museum Antiker Kleinkunst [7], pl. 327.3–4, pp. 29–30), and the plastic female head oinochoe Berlin F 2190 (*ARV²*, p. 1531, no. 3). Attic potters and painters produced a form of stemmed plate particularly for the market at Spina during the last third of the fifth century B.C. and often decorated the interior tondo with a profile head, usually that of a woman or youth. Heads of mythological figures, including Dionysos, satyrs, Apollos, and Athena are less frequent, as are heads of "foreigners," including Africans and those wearing Phrygian caps. Nearly all have been found in tombs at Spina, although a few have been uncovered at Bologna. Refer to *ARV²*, pp. 1305–10. The majority of fourth-century B.C. askoi decorated with heads were also uncovered at Spina, such as Ferrara T. 408 (*ARV²*, p. 1504, no. 1) and Ferrara T. 834 (*ARV²*, p. 1504, no. 6), as well as many Athenian oinochoai (shape 2), e.g., Ferrara T. 378 B VP (*ARV²*, p. 1492, no. 1) and Ferrara T. 631 (*ARV²*, p. 1492, no. 5).

35 Examples found in civic spaces include: Gela 8572, a lekanis (dish) lid with a female head on each side that was found in the Timoleonic level of the acropolis at Gela (*LCS*, p. 610, no. 172). A fragmentary piece, either a bottle or squat lekythos, was discovered at Agrigento in a Greek cistern that was reused in the Christian catacomb (Agrigento AG 1295; *CVA* Agrigento [2], pl. 67.1–2, p. 69). Five pieces—four plates and a lekanis attributed to the Apulianizing Group—were uncovered in the agora of Paestum: Paestum E 65 III (*RVP* 13/705-1, p. 360), Paestum E 65 II (*RVP* 13/705-3, p. 360), Paestum E 59 II (*RVP* 13/705-4, p. 360), Paestum E 58 I (*RVP*, 13/705-5, p. 360), and Paestum (*RVP* 13/705-6, p. 360). Examples deposited in sanctuaries include the twenty-four vases uncovered at the Temple of Hera at Foce del Sele in Paestum. They range in date from the earliest to the latest of Paestan red-figure. Most are lebetes gamikoi and lekanides, but a hydria, a neck-amphora, two squat lekythoi, a skyphoid pyxis, and three bottles decorated with heads were found in the same area. A few of the pieces are: Paestum IV/462 (*RVP* 10/979, p. 246), Paestum 48432 (*RVP* 13/701, p. 359), and Paestum (*RVP* 9/677, p. 210). A skyphoid pyxis (box) close to the Portale Painter with a female head on one side of the body was uncovered in the sanctuary of Demeter and Kore at Morgantina (Morgantina 59.613: *LCS*, p. 650, no. 437), and at Agrigento, two skyphoi and a squat lekythos (oil flask) decorated with heads were found in 1958 in a large pit in the area to the south of the Temple of Olympian Zeus: Agrigento AG 2198bis (*LCS*, p. 587, no. 21; *CVA* Agrigento [2], pl. 58.2–3, p. 62), Agrigento AG 1325 (*CVA* Agrigento [2], pl. 59.1–2, p. 62), and Agrigento AG 2196 (*LCS*, p. 587, no. 22; *CVA* Agrigento [2], pl. 63.3–4, p. 66).

36 Lippolis 1994, pp. 109–28; Fontannaz 2005, p. 126.

37 Some naiskoi contain an object such as a vase, shield, fillet, mirror, or plant rather than a figure. The most exhaustive study of grave monuments represented on South Italian vases is Lohmann 1979.

38 Klumbach 1937; Bernabò Brea 1952, 1970; Carter 1973, and Carter 1976. The dating of the Tarentine limestone naiskos continues to be debated, with the earliest date placed between 330 and 300 B.C. and production continuing possibly as late as the second century B.C.; see Lippolis 1987; 1990, pp. 15–71; and 2007. Based on extant archaeological remains, the earliest naiskoi images on vases do not replicate contemporaneous stone monuments in Apulia, although the sculptural motifs within the naiskoi echo motifs found on Attic grave stelai of the late fifth and fourth centuries B.C. For a broader discussion of the various types of Tarentine funerary markers and the various subject matter seen in funerary sculpture, see Lippolis 1994, pp. 109–28.

39 Other funerary monuments feature Ionic columns on stepped bases. Examples are on Frankfurt 605 (*LCS*, p. 370, no. 63; *CVA* Frankfurt am Main [3], pl. 31, pp. 24–25) and Brussels R 287 (*LCS*, p. 370, no. 62; *CVA* Brussels [3] IV E, pl. 1.8a–c, p. 3). For stelai, refer to Dresden 114 (*LCS*, p. 456, no. 30; *CVA* Dresden [1], pl. 42, pp. 71–72) and Capua, from Caivano (*LCS*, p. 457, no. 39; *CVA* Capua [1], pls. 18.2–3 and 20.3, p. 9). Much more rarely, grave monuments on South Italian vases take the form of a statue of the deceased, found as early as the beginning of the fourth century B.C. in the work of the Gravina Painter. A complete catalogue and discussion are found in Lohmann 1979, pp. 25–51. Some Campanian and Paestan vases produced between ca. 330 and 320 B.C., a period of strong Apulianizing influence in these regions, bear images of naiskoi.

40 Bari 1394: *RVAp I* 8/101, p. 203.

41 *LCS*, p. 507, no. 498.

42 For example, refer to the amphora Lecce 842 (*RVAp II* 23/162, p. 746; *CVA* Lecce [2] IV Dr, pl. 44.2,3,5, p. 26).

43 *RVAp Suppl. 1* 18/16d, p. 72. The artist, active in the third quarter of the fourth century B.C., is named for the figured metopes on the bases of the unusually elaborate naiskoi pictured on his two loutrophoroi in the MMA.

44 For isolated female heads within naskoi, see Milan 227 (*RVAp II* 22/539, p. 692) and Toronto 396 (*RVAp II* 28/144, p. 935). Particularly unusual is a column-krater in the Altrock collection in Munich (*RVAp II* 24/264, p. 785) attributed to the Group of the Temple Hydria, which links the work of the Amphorae and Armidale Groups. This is the only piece known to the author on which a funerary scene is painted on a South Italian column-krater; the fact that it contains a female head in three-quarter view to left on the reverse makes the object all the more remarkable. The White Saccos Painter, active ca. 330–310 B.C., at times placed an adjunct, such as an alabastron or a mirror, beside the female head within the naiskos. Refer to once London market, Sotheby's (*RVAp Suppl. 2* 29/3e–f, p. 356). On the volute-krater attributed to the Virginia Exhibition Painter: once Paris market, *RVAp Suppl. 2* 28/86-25, p. 335.

45 Athenian tragedies as the inspiration for mythological scenes on South Italian vases: Jahn 1839; Watzinger 1899; Séchan 1926; Trendall and Webster 1971; Kossatz-Deißmann 1978; Todisco 2002, pp. 53–54, 73–89; and Todisco 2003. For the South Italian proclivity to represent scenes of Euripides on vases, see Vogel 1886; Allan 2001; and Taplin 2007, pp. 108–219. For the nature of the transference of Attic tragedy to the Greek and Italic populations of southern Italy and Sicily, refer to Giuliani 1995, pp. 18–19; Robinson 2004; Taplin 2007, pp. 6–15; and Carpenter 2009, pp. 31–34.

46 Examples may be found in the early work (ca. 380 B.C.) of the Cassandra Painter, the earliest Campanian vase painter, whose name vase, Capua 7554, depicts Ajax dragging Cassandra from the altar, to the right of which stands Athena (*LCS*, p. 225, no. 1; *CVA* Capua [1], pl. 22, pp. 10–11). Painting isolated heads on vases decorated with mythological scenes began in Apulia, Paestum, and Sicily around 370 B.C. An important example is Edinburgh 1873.21.1, an Apulian volute-krater that is the earliest known example of the isolated head motif serving as secondary decoration on a large-scale Apulian vase (*RVAp I* 7/45, p. 171; *CVA* Edinburgh [1], pls. 41, 42, pp. 37–38).

47 For example, Port Sunlight 5043 (*RVP* 10/1002, p. 253); Kassel T. 646 (*RVP* 7/348, p. 168; *CVA* Kassel [2], pl. 82.1–3, pp. 56–57); Saint Petersburg Inv. 3164 (*LCS*, p. 341, no. 815); and a neck-amphora in the Termer collection in Hamburg attributed to the Danaid Painter (*RVAp Suppl. 1*, p. 208, no. 495a).

48 *RVAp* 18/20, p. 489. This scene also appears on later volute-kraters attributed to the Baltimore Painter: once New York market, Royal-Athena Galleries HNH 46 (*RVAp Suppl. 2* 27/23f, p. 275) and Geneva, Sciclounoff collection (*RVAp Suppl. 2* 27/23g, p. 275).

49 E.g., Naples Stg. 11 (*RVAp Suppl. 1* 16/54, p. 424) and Urbana-Champaign, University of Illinois, World Heritage Museum 82.6.1 (*RVAp Suppl. 1* 27/23a, p. 152; *CVA* Urbana-Champaign [1], pls. 36–38.1–2, 39.1–2, 40.1–2, 41.1–2, 42.1–2, pp. 34–36).

50 For example, a volute-krater by the Perrone Painter now in Bari (Perrone collection no. 14: *RVAp II* 18/225, p. 523) and Saint Petersburg Inv. 1701 (St. 498) (*RVAp II* 23/46, p. 733).

51 Munich 3297: *RVAp II* 18/282, p. 533.

52 A brief bibliography of Orphism: Rohde 1907, pp. 335–61; Mead 1965; *Orfismo in Magna Grecia* 1975; Detienne 1979; and Guthrie 1993. The presence of Orphic worship in Magna Graecia is supported by ancient texts that closely associate the cult with the Pythagorean movement in Magna Graecia (Herodotus 2.81; Diogenes Laertius 8.8). Pythagoras emigrated from Samos to Croton around 520 B.C. and is believed to have died in Metaponto at the end of the sixth century B.C. His followers established so-called clubhouses throughout southern Italy and Sicily until ca. 450–415 B.C., when they were destroyed during an outbreak of civil unrest (Polybius 2.39).

53 The most concrete evidence for the practice of Orphism in Magna Graecia is provided by the famous inscribed gold lamellae, or tablets, found in tombs in Lucania at Hipponium, Thurii, and Petelia; see Kern 1922; Pugliese Carratelli 1988, pp. 162–70; Maddoli 1996, pp. 495–96; Pugliese Carratelli 2003; Graf and Johnston 2007; and Bernabé and Jiménez San Cristóbal 2008. The texts provide the deceased with specific instructions to help the soul successfully navigate the path to a blissful eternal afterlife in the presence of the divine. However, Günther Zuntz (1971, pp. 277–393) rightly points out that at least some of the lamellae are a product not of Orphic beliefs but, rather, of faith in Persephone's ability to guarantee salvation. Giovanni Pugliese Carratelli (1993), who divides the laminae by their geographic findspots, believes that those related to Orphism are from Petelia and Hipponium, while those from Thurii refer to Persephone. The frequent presence of Orpheus in representations of the underworld in Apulian vase painting has been pointed to as evidence of Orphic beliefs (Schmidt 1975 and Pensa 1977).

54 Nearly one-quarter of the published monumental Apulian vases decorated with Dionysiac scenes as part of their primary imagery also feature isolated heads.

55 The most recent discussions of the cult of Dionysos in Magna Graecia, along with much bibliography, may be found in Casadio and Johnston 2009.

56 *RVAp I* 16/17, p. 417.

57 Of the 284 large-scale Apulian vases bearing one or more mythological scenes as primary decoration published in Trendall's catalogues and the volumes of the *CVA*, 171 (60.21 percent) are also decorated with an isolated head.

58 Giuliani 1995, pp. 149–50, 155–56. Luigi Todisco (2006, pp. 20–24) also discusses a possible function for these vases in funerary rites. For the comforting function of mythological imagery, refer to Schefold and Jung 1988, pp. 324–26, and Geyer 1993, pp. 448–50.

59 For an example of this myth paired with isolated heads, see Cracow 834 (*LCS*, p. 341, no. 814; *CVA* Cracow [1] Cracow, Museum Czartoryski, pl. 18.1a–c, p. 21). Another abduction story repeatedly painted on South Italian vases with heads is Europa and the bull, seen on both Naples 3218 (inv. 81952; *RVAp II* 18/46, p. 497) and Bari 872 (*RVAp II* 18/43, p. 497).

60 E.g., Como C 60 (*RVAp II* 22/625, p. 700; *CVA* Como [1] IV D, pl. 8.1a–b, p. 6); Louvre K 424 (*LCS*, p. 276, no. 336); and Paestum 27029 (*RVP* 13/649, pp. 349–50).

61 Associated with the Stuttgart Group: *RVAp II* 29/276, p. 985.

62 On a Chevron Group bell-krater in an Austrian private collection, a standing woman holds a thyrsos in her left hand and a phiale in her right over a flaming altar (*RVAp Suppl. 1* 22/67d, p. 113). A female head in profile to left is on the reverse. Many of the earliest of these scenes in Apulia appear on bell-kraters attributed to the Chevron Group, such as once French market (*RVAp Suppl. 1* 22/67c, p. 113) and once Amsterdam market, J. Schulman (*RVAp Suppl. 1* 22/67b, p. 113). Two examples of Sicilian vases are Biancavilla, Portale collection 6 (*LCS*, p. 631, no. 304) and Catania 4328 (*LCS*, p. 634, no. 320).

63 In Apulia, depictions of non-Greeks are most commonly painted on column-kraters, perhaps because, particularly in Peucetia, vases of that shape were substituted for the traditional ollae placed in Italic graves.

64 Other examples depicting non-Greeks and decorated with heads are Ruvo 529 (*RVAp I* 12/61, p. 324) and B.M. F 297 (*RVAp I* 13/197, p. 357).

65 Depictions of bridal preparations include Paestum 20351 (*RVP* 11/21, pp. 274–75) and Paestum 20296 (*RVP* 10/965, p. 239). A possible courting or marriage preparation scene is found on a lekythos of special shape in a private collection in Turin (*RVP* 10/972, p. 245). For couples embracing in the presence of Eros, refer to Bloomington, Indiana University Museum of Art 75.104 (*RVP* 12/392, p. 311), and Hamburg, Termer collection (*RVP* 12/595, p. 336).

66 Reeder 1995, pp. 287–89.

67 Smith (1976, pp. 4, 140–43, 168–75) argued that for those who died unmarried, ideal unions were arranged, overseen, and blessed by chthonic Aphrodite and Dionysos.

68 See Malibu 78.AE.405 (*LCS Suppl. 2*, p. 260, no. 291a; *CVA* Malibu 4, pl. 230) and Lipari 716A (*LCS*, p. 630, no. 294). A vase decorated with Nike and an isolated head, found in the Sanctuary of Demeter and Kore at Morgantina (Morgantina 59.613: *LCS*, p. 650, no. 437), strengthen the connection between Nike, isolated heads, and the underworld.

69 The author knows of only one vase with a head in conjunction with a comedic performance. It is on an Apulian bell-krater with a large head of Dionysos framed by a grapevine (Cleveland 1989.73). To either side of the head is a figure in comic mask and costume, one of whom offers a cup of wine to the god (Trendall 1992; Denoyelle and Iozzo 2009, p. 132).

On Würzburg H 4540, an Apulian aryballos (short-necked, single-handle flask or bottle) from Taranto dated to the early fourth century B.C., the frieze around the body features a ball player, a discus thrower, two wrestlers with their trainer, and a youth playing with a top. On the underside is a female head in three-quarter view to right (*CVA* Würzburg [4], pl. 26, p. 33).

70 The heads are globular in shape and have noses that protrude slightly from the flattened face; the eyes are drilled and the mouth is an incised line. On some, earrings are carved on the sides of the head below small protruding ears; a few are elongated at the back as if representing a chignon. Such features suggest that the pieces depict women. Most remarkable is an example found at Monte Saraceno that has a circular pattern of small, round holes on top of the head, perhaps for the attachment of a metal wreath or diadem. De Juliis 1984b, pp. 142–45; De Juliis 2009, pp. 61–64.

71 Laviosa 1954, pp. 217–50. Etruscan head antefixes, too, have been found in funerary contexts, such as those belonging to a small building adjacent to the cemetery of Grotta Porcino at Vetralla, near Viterbo (Winter 1974, pp. 151–54).

72 Metaponto 319201: Pugliese Carratelli 1996, pp. 651–52.

73 Rouveret 1990, p. 339; Rouveret and Pontrandolfo 1983, p. 125.

74 For the Medusa tomb at Arpi, see Mazzei 1984, p. 197, and Pontrandolfo 1996, p. 470. For the Naples tomb, refer to ibid. The Lecce tomb, which dates to the fourth century B.C., also contains carved pilasters decorated with isolated heads; see Bendinelli 1915, pp. 10–11, 18–19, 23–24.

75 For isolated heads on terracotta votive gifts found at Agrigento, see P. Marconi 1929, pp. 579–80; P. Marconi 1933, p. 47; Kilmer 1977, pp. 83–84, 101–9; and Uhlenbrock 1988, pp. 125–26. For those from Selinunte, see Kilmer 1977, pp. 73–74, 87–88, 115–16, 133–34. See also Uhlenbrock 1988, pp. 20n8 and 128. For those at Locri Epizephyrii, see Zuntz 1971, pp. 160–61; Kilmer 1977, pp. 74, 89–91, 133–34; Barra Bagnasco 1986; and Lattanzi 1987, pp. 54–59. These offerings were not dedicated to chthonic deities only, as is often implied in scholarship (Zuntz 1971, p. 143; Uhlenbrock 1988, pp. 139–56; and Lippolis 2001). For votive terracotta busts uncovered at Italic sanctuaries, refer to Bottini 1988, pp. 75–81.

76 Zuntz 1971, p. 142; Kilmer 1977, p. 65. A protome from Granmichele still preserves a long piece of corroded iron, perhaps a nail, from the hole at the top (Uhlenbrock 1988, p. 150).

77 Kilmer 1977, p. 98; Otto 1996, pp. 177–78. The connection between Demeter and the terracotta busts is strengthened by Pausanias's description of the cult statue of Demeter Thesmophoros at Thebes as being "visible to the chest," or in the form of a bust (Pausanias 9.16.5).

78 Zuntz 1971, pp. 156–57; Kilmer 1977, pp. 197, 262–63.

79 For protomes and busts among grave goods, see Kilmer 1977, pp. 75–76; Lehnert 1978, p. 135; and Uhlenbrock 1988, pp. 125, 129. For the janiform bust found at Locri Epizephyrii, see Orsi 1911, pp. 68–70. Janiform busts with two female heads are found in southern Italy and Sicily, as exemplified by the one found in Agrigento. Janiform female heads also appear on coins from Syracuse issued under Timoleon (Kilmer 1977, p. 131).

80 Kurtz and Boardman 1971, p. 259.

81 Both burials contained male skeletons. Twelve female heads wearing polos crowns were found in the tomb Contrada Andriuolo 20 (1969), dated to ca. 380 B.C. (Pontrandolfo and Rouveret 1992, pp. 309–11). Four female heads were buried in Contrada Laghetto tomb LXIV (1954), dated to ca. 370–360 B.C. (ibid., pp. 353–55).

82 Wuilleumier 1939, p. 434; Jastrow 1946; van der Meijden 1993, pp. 71, 293–95, 309.

83 Jastrow 1946, p. 74.

84 For general information on the sanctuary at Francavilla and its votive deposits, refer to Spigo 2000a.

85 Pinakes with two overlapping heads include Syracuse 85663 (Spigo 2000b, pp. 33–35) and Syracuse 85664 (ibid., p. 39). On both types, the female head is in the foreground. On some examples, the male head is beardless and wears a wreath with a rosette centered over the forehead, while on others, the male head is bearded and wears an oak wreath. The sole known example of a pinax with a single head is Syracuse 85666 (ibid.).

86 Shapiro 1993, pp. 14–16.

87 Aellen 1994.

88 For the London bell-krater (B.M. F 149), see *RVP* 7/239, pp. 139–41. For the Getty volute-krater (Malibu 86.AE.680), see *RVAp Suppl. 2* 20/278-2, p. 180; *CVA* J. Paul Getty Museum (4), pls. 186–88, 189.3–5, pp. 6–9; and Aellen 1994, pp. 98–101, 104–5, 125–26.

89 Such as Mania on Madrid 11094 (*RVP* 5/127, pp. 84, 89–90); the Erinys on Malibu 80.AE.155 (*RVP* 8/418, pp. 183–84); and Ismenos on Naples 3226 (*RVP* 5/132, pp. 85, 95–96).

90 Aellen 1994, pp. 14–15, 19–20.

91 Buschor 1937, p. 10.

92 Ancient literary sources attest that flower painting originated in the work of Pausias, supposedly inspired by his admiration for the flower girl Glycera in his native town of Sicyon about 370 B.C. (Pliny the Elder, *Naturalis Historia* 21.4 and 35.125; Moreno 1987, pp. 136–40; Harari 1995). None of Pausias's work survives, but his influence is visible in the fourth-century B.C. floral pebble mosaics of the Greek mainland, one of which was discovered in Sicyon, Pausias's native city.

93 Examples of flowering plants next to funerary monuments include Bari 6270 (Lohmann 1979, p. 181, no. A59, pl. 12.1, ca. 350–340 B.C., connected to the Painter of Copenhagen 4223) and Bologna C. 566 (ibid., p. 193, no. A160). Vases depicting flowering plants beside funerary monuments include Bari 6270 (ibid., p. 181, no. A59, pl. 12.1, ca. 350–340 B.C., connected to the Painter of Copenhagen 4223) and Bologna C. 566 (ibid., p. 193, no. A160). For flowering plants within funerary naskoi, Hans Lohmann (ibid., pp. 115, 127–30) records fifty-three Apulian, six Lucanian, and two Campanian examples; see also Schauenburg 1957, pp. 198–200, and Jucker 1961, p. 214. Examples are London F 353 (Lohmann 1979, p. 216, no. A354) and Turin 4142 (ibid., p. 265, no. A750; *CVA* Turin [1], pl. 16.4). Flowering plants are an iconographic motif on later Roman funerary altars (Helbig 1891, vol. 1, nos. 81, 330, 367, 392, 1033; vol. 2, nos. 1214, 1683). Rudolf Pagenstecher (1912, pp. 36–39, 98–99) proposed that the plants might be reproductions of paintings used as temporary decorations on actual grave monuments or represented real plants growing within funerary monuments. Konrad Schauenburg (1957, pp. 200–203) countered both ideas, stating that the depictions of plants are stylized and idealized.

94 Compare the floral decoration on the bases of painted naskoi to the running spiral scrolls with flowers seen on fourth-century B.C. grave stelai in Boeotia (Fraser and Rönne 1957, pp. 52–59). For flowering vinelike structures painted around depictions of funerary statues, see *LCS*, p. 411, no. 342, pl. 165.3; and Lohmann 1979, p. 297, no. K113, pl. 11.1. See also Saint Petersburg 567 (St. 878); Lohman 1979, p. 209, no. A285, pl. 9.1.

95 Lohmann 1979, pp. 125–26.

96 For floral and vegetal grave offerings, see ibid., pp. 123–25. Examples include: Bari 1009 (ibid., p. 178, no. A30, pl. 46.1) and Bari 22153 (ibid., p. 183, no. A75, pl. 24.2). Literary references to such offerings include Sophocles, *Electra* 896, and Euripides, *Trojan Women* 1144 and 1247.

97 Painted tombs include Paestum, Andriuolo necropolis tomb 24; Paestum, Andriuolo necropolis tomb 21; and Taranto, tomb no. 34, now in Taranto, Museo Nazionale (Pontrandolfo 1988, pp. 360, 384). For Paestan tombs, refer to Pontrandolfo and Rouveret 1992, pp. 33–36, and Andreae et al. 2007, pp. 46–47. Spiral tendrils, wreaths, garlands, and palmettes occur in Campanian painted tombs as well (Benassai 2001, pp. 26–29, 45–46, 50–54, 71–79, 137–43, 146–51). Particularly distinctive is the painting on the barrel vault of a tomb in Taranto of a grape arbor with flowering plants that, on one side wall, appear to be lilies and rockroses. See Pontrandolfo 1988, p. 379; Lippolis 1994, p. 135; and Pontrandolfo 1996, p. 470. It is possible that the epitaph on the child's tomb reflects Pythagorean beliefs, although there is no conclusive evidence of this. More likely, it is an expression of a general hope for immortality. Schauenburg 1957, p. 203, and Kaibel 1878, p. 231, Epigr. Gr. 569.5.

98 De Juliis 1984a, pp. 70–108.

99 Classical Attic white-ground lekythoi with acanthus include Berlin 2680 (Oakley 2004, p. 123); Athens, National Museum 1380 (ibid., p. 134); and Athens, National Museum 14517 (ibid., p. 183). An acanthus column marking a grave appears on Athens, Kerameikos 1136 (ibid., p. 199). Hans Jucker postulated the funerary nature of later Roman portrait busts emerging from acanthus calyxes (Jucker 1961). See Kurtz and Boardman 1971, p. 124, and Froning 1985 for acanthus on grave stelai.

100 Pindar, *Olympian* 2.73–75; translation by William Race (1997, p. 71).

101 Amsterdam 2578: *RVAp II* 18/215, p. 521. Similarly, on an Apulian pelike connected in style to the Trieste Owl Group in the Academy of the Arts in Honolulu (Inv. 2164; *RVAp II* 23/224, p. 752), a head wearing a Phrygian cap emerges from a flowering plant consisting primarily of three campanula flowers stacked one above the other in the center. To the left of the plant, a woman holding a wreath gazes up at the head and gestures as if conversing with it. Seated on a bundle of drapery on the right is a nude youth, a white fillet in his hair, holding a fillet.

102 Dunedin, Otago Museum E 48.266 (*ARV²*, p. 1174, no. 1); Cambridge, Fitzwilliam Museum, formerly Corpus Christi College (*ARV²*, p. 1401, no. 1); and Basel, Antikenmuseum BS 481 (*CVA* Basel [3], pls. 18, 19, pp. 37–39). See Guthrie 1993, p. 36; *LIMC*, vol. 7 (1994), p. 88, s.v. "Orpheus" (Maria-Xeni Garezou); and De Grummond 2011, pp. 322–24.

103 De Grummond 2006, p. 33, fig. II.10; De Grummond 2011, p. 318, fig. 10.3.

104 De Grummond 2011, pp. 318–32.

105 According to Hesiod (*Works and Days* 80–105), elpis seems to be one of the pernicious gifts the gods bestowed upon Pandora and stored in her jar, or pithos. This negative aspect of elpis is recorded by Thucydides, who states, "Desire contrives the plan, Hope suggests the facility of fortune; the two passions are most baneful, and being unseen phantoms prevail over seen dangers" (*History of the Peloponnesian War* 3.45.5); translation by C. F. Smith (1920, p. 79). However, Theognis, writing in the mid-sixth century B.C., praises elpis as both a divinity and one of the few positive human resources: "Hope is

the one good god remaining among mankind; the others have left and gone to Olympus. . . . as long as a man lives and sees the light of the sun, let him show piety and count on Hope. Let him pray to the gods and burn splendid thigh bones, sacrificing to Hope first and last" (Thgn. 1135–45); translation by J. M. Edmonds (1931, p. 341). For further bibliography on literary sources and commentary on the function of elpis in Greek thought, see *LIMC*, vol. 3 (1986), pp. 722–25, s.v. "Elpis" (F. W. Hamdorf).

106 B.M. F 147: *LCS*, p. 667, no. 3. An imprecise drawing of the amphora made by Costanzo Angelini in 1798 was published in Patroni 1900, pl. 29. Refer also to Harrison 1908, pp. 279–80; Nilsson 1952, p. 618; and *LIMC*, vol. 3 (1986), pp. 724–25, no. 13, s.v. "Elpis" (Hamdorf). The vase was attributed by J. D. Beazley to the Owl Pillar Group, a Campania workshop that imitated Attic red-figure vases about the middle of the fifth century B.C. (Beazley 1943, p. 66; *LCS*, p. 667, no. 3).

107 This figure is often identified as Epimetheus, based upon the scene on the volute-krater Oxford G 275. However, Jenifer Neils (2005, pp. 38–39), comparing the figure to those on the Foundry Painter's name vase, compellingly argues that the figure is Hephaistos, who, according to the Hesiodic account, was charged by Zeus to create Pandora from earth and water.

108 Neils 2005, p. 40; *CVA* Oxford (1), pl. 21.1–2, pp. 18–19; *ARV²*, p. 601, no. 23.

109 Other possible representations of Elpis are a seventh-century B.C. Boeotian molded aryballos and a head from a fifth-century B.C. high-relief marble frieze, found in the Athenian Agora, depicting the birth of Pandora (Neils 2005, pp. 41–44).

110 According to Homer, souls in Hades could to some extent reenact episodes from their lives: Orion, for instance, drove together the wild beasts he slew during his lifetime (*Odyssey* 11.564–75). Generally, however, souls are characterized as shadowy creatures lacking any life force. During the Nekyia in Book 11 of the *Odyssey*, the souls of the dead are unable to collect their thoughts and speak until they partake of the sacrificial blood. See also Richardson 1985. For definitions of "mystery" and "mystic cults," see Casadio and Johnston 2009, pp. 1–7. Sources with further bibliography of the religious practices of Greeks in Magna Graecia: Pugliese Carratelli 1965; Zuntz 1971; Arias 1977; Torelli 1977; Pugliese Carratelli 1988; Tortorelli Ghidini 1994; Hinz 1998; and Casadio and Johnston 2009. For information on the immigration of Pythagoras to Croton and later Metaponto, his teachings, the establishment of Pythagorean clubhouses in southern Italy and Sicily, and their subsequent destruction, refer to Rohde 1907, pp. 374–77; Long 1948; Burkert 1972, pp. 120–65; Guthrie 1993; Hermann 2004, pp. 34–40; Riedweg 2005, pp. 60–89, 98–105; and Luchte 2009, pp. 28, 33–48.

111 Plato, *Gorgias* 493d.

ABBREVIATIONS

ABV	Beazley 1956
ARV²	Beazley 1963
CVA	*Corpus Vasorum Antiquorum*
LCS	Trendall 1967
LCS Suppl. 2	Trendall 1973
LIMC	*Lexicon Iconographicum Mythologiae Classicae* 1981–99
Para.	Beazley 1971
RVAp I	Trendall and Cambitoglou 1978
RVAp II	Trendall and Cambitoglou 1982
RVAp Suppl. 1	Trendall and Cambitoglou 1983
RVAp Suppl. 2	Trendall and Cambitoglou 1991–92
RVP	Trendall 1987

REFERENCES

Aellen, Christian

1994 *A la recherche de l'ordre cosmique: Forme et fonction des personnifications dans la céramique italiote.* 2 vols. Kilchberg: Akanthus.

Allan, William

2001 "Euripides in Megale Hellas: Some Aspects of the Early Reception of Tragedy." *Greece and Rome*, ser. 2, 48 (April), pp. 67–86.

Andreae, Bernard, Marina Cipriani, Dieter Mertens, Nina Simone Schepkowski, and Giuliana Tocco Sciarelli

2007 *Malerei für die Ewigkeit: Die Gräber von Paestum.* Translated from Italian by Marion Koch and Christa Landwehr von Hees. Exh. cat., Bucerius Kunst Forum, Hamburg. Munich: Hirmer.

Andrén, Arvid

1940 *Architectural Terracottas from Etrusco-Italic Temples.* 2 vols. Lund: C. W. K. Gleerup; Leipzig: Harrassowitz.

Arias, Paolo Enrico

1977 "L'arte locrese nelle sue principali manifestazioni artigianali: Terrecotte, bronzi, vasi, arti minori." In *Locri Epizefirii: Atti del sedicesimo Convegno di Studi sulla Magna Grecia, Taranto, 3–8 Ottobre 1976*, pp. 479–579. Naples: Arte Tipografica.

Barra Bagnasco, Marcella

1986 *Protomi in terracotta da Locri Epizefiri: Contributo allo studio della scultura arcaica in Magna Grecia.* Turin: Il Quadrante.

Beazley, J. D.

1943 "Groups of Campanian Red-Figure." *Journal of Hellenic Studies* 63, pp. 66–111.

1956 *Attic Black-Figure Vase-Painters.* Oxford: Clarendon Press.

1963 *Attic Red-Figure Vase-Painters.* 2nd ed. 3 vols. Oxford: Clarendon Press.

1971 *Paralipomena: Additions to Attic Black-Figure Vase-Painters and to Attic Red-Figure Vase-Painters (Second Edition).* Oxford: Clarendon Press.

Benassai, Rita

2001 *La pittura dei Campani e dei Sanniti.* Rome: "L'Erma" di Bretschneider.

Bendinelli, Goffredo

1915 "Un ipogeo sepolcrale a Lecce con fregi scolpiti." *Ausonia* 8 (1915), pp. 7–26.

Bérard, Claude

1974 *Anodoi: Essai sur l'imagerie des passages chthoniens.* Neuchâtel: P. Attinger.

Bernabé, Alberto, and Ana Isabel Jiménez San Cristóbal
  2008 *Instructions for the Netherworld: The Orphic Gold Tablets*. Leiden: Brill.
Bernabò Brea, Luigi
  1952 "I rilievi tarantini in pietra tenera." *Rivista dell'Istituto Nazionale d'Archeologia e Storia dell'Arte*, n.s., 1, pp. 5–241.
Bottini, Angelo
  1988 "La religione delle genti indigene." In Pugliese Carratelli 1988, pp. 55–90.
Brilliant, Richard
  1963 *Gesture and Rank in Roman Art: The Use of Gestures to Denote Status in Roman Sculpture and Coinage*. Memoirs of the Connecticut Academy of Arts and Sciences 14. New Haven: The Academy.
Brommer, Frank
  1959 *Satyrspiele: Bilder griechischer Vasen*. 2nd ed. Berlin: Walter de Gruyter.
Burkert, Walter
  1972 *Lore and Science in Ancient Pythagoreanism*. Cambridge, Mass.: Harvard University Press.
Buschor, Ernst
  1937 *Feldmäuse*. Munich: Verlag der Bayerischen Akademie der Wissenschaften.
Cambitoglou, Alexander
  1954 "Groups of Apulian Red-Figured Vases Decorated with Heads of Women or of Nike." *Journal of Hellenic Studies* 74, pp. 111–21.
  1997 *Céramique de Grande Grèce: La Collection de fragments Herbert A. Cahn*. Hellas et Roma 8. Exh. cat., Musée d'Art et d'Histoire, Geneva. Zürich: Akanthus.
Carpenter, Thomas H.
  2003 "The Native Market for Red-Figure Vases in Apulia." *Memoirs of the American Academy in Rome* 48, pp. 1–24.
  2009 "Prolegomenon to the Study of Apulian Red-Figure Pottery." *American Journal of Archaeology* 113 (January), pp. 27–38.
Carter, Joseph Coleman
  1970 "Relief Sculptures from the Necropolis of Taranto." *American Journal of Archaeology* 74 (April), pp. 125–37.
  1973 "The Figure in the Naiskos-Marble Sculptures from the Necropolis of Taranto." *Opuscula Romana* 9, pp. 97–107.
  1976 "The Sculpture of Taras." *Transactions of the American Philosophical Society*, n.s., 65, no. 7.
Casadio, Giovanni, and Patricia A. Johnston, eds.
  2009 *Mystic Cults in Magna Graecia*. Austin: University of Texas Press.
Causey, Faya
  1993 "Two Amber Pendants in Malibu: East Greek Craftsmanship?" In *Amber in Archaeology: Proceedings of the Second International Conference on Amber in Archaeology, Liblice 1990*, edited by Curt W. Beck and Jan Bouzek, pp. 212–18. Prague: Institute of Archaeology, Czech Academy of Sciences.
Causey-Frel, Faya
  1984 "Studies on Greek, Etruscan, and Italic Carved Ambers." PhD diss., University of California, Santa Barbara.
Corpus Vasorum Antiquorum
  1922– *Corpus Vasorum Antiquorum*. Online edition (2002–) available at www.cvaonline.org.
De Grummond, Nancy Thomson
  2006 *Etruscan Myth, Sacred History, and Legend*. Philadelphia: University of Pennsylvania Museum of Archaeology and Anthropology.
  2011 "A Barbarian Myth? The Case of the Talking Head." In *The Barbarians of Ancient Europe: Realities and Interactions*, edited by Larissa Bonfante, pp. 313–45. Cambridge: Cambridge University Press.
De Juliis, Ettore M.
  1984a *Gli ori di Taranto in età ellenistica*. Exh. cat., Brera 2, Milan; Museo Archeologico Nazionale, Taranto. Milan: Mondadori.
  1984b "L'età del Ferro." In *La Daunia antica: Dalla preistoria all'altomedioevo*, edited by Marina Mazzei, pp. 137–84. Milan: Electa.
  2009 *La rappresentazione figurata in Daunia*. Bari: Edipuglia.
Denoyelle, Martine
  1997 "Attic or non-Attic? The Case of the Pisticci Painter." In *Athenian Potters and Painters: The Conference Proceedings*, edited by John H. Oakley, William D. E. Coulson, and Olga Palagia, pp. 395–405. Oxford: Oxbow Books.
Denoyelle, Martine, and Mario Iozzo
  2009 *La Céramique grecque d'Italie méridionale et de Sicile: Productions coloniales et apparentées du VIIIᵉ au IIIᵉ siècle av. J.-C.* Paris: Picard.
Detienne, Marcel
  1979 *Dionysos Slain*. Translated from French by Mireille Muellner and Leonard Muellner. Baltimore: Johns Hopkins University Press.
Donati, L.
  1967 "Buccheri decorati con teste plastiche umani: Zona di Vulci." *Studi etruschi* 35, pp. 619–32.
  1968 "Buccheri decorati con teste plastiche umani: Zona di Chiusi." *Studi etruschi* 36, pp. 319–55.
  1969 "Vasi di bucchero decorate con teste umane: Zona di Orvieto." *Studi etruschi* 37, pp. 443–62.
Edmonds, J. M., ed. and trans.
  1931 *Elegy and Iambus*. . . . Cambridge, Mass.: Harvard University Press.
Fontannaz, Didier
  2005 "La Céramique proto-apulienne de Tarente: Problèmes et perspectives d'une 'recontextualisation.'" In *La Céramique apulienne: Bilan et perspectives*, edited by Martine Denoyelle, Enzo Lippolis, Marina Mazzei, and Claude Pouzadoux, pp. 125–42. Naples: Centre Jean Bérard.
Fornara, Charles W., ed. and trans.
  1977 *Archaic Times to the End of the Peloponnesian War*. Baltimore: Johns Hopkins University Press.
Fraser, Peter M., and Tullia Rönne
  1957 *Boeotian and West Greek Tombstones*. Skrifter utgivna av Svenska Institutet i Athen, 4°, 6. Lund: C. W. K. Gleerup.
Froning, Heide
  1985 "Zur Interpretation vegetabilischer Bekrönungen klassischer und spätklassischer Grabstelen." *Archäologischer Anzeiger*, pp. 218–29.
Furtwängler, Adolf
  1893 *Meisterwerke der griechischen Plastik: Kunstgeschichtliche Untersuchungen*. 2 vols. Leipzig and Berlin: Giesecke & Devrient.
  1912 *Kleine Schriften*. Vol. 1. Edited by Johannes Sieveking and Ludwig Curtius. Munich: Oskar Beck.
Geyer, Angelika
  1993 "Geschichte als Mythos: Zu Alexanders 'Perserschlacht' auf apulischen Vasenbildern." *Jahrbuch des Deutschen Archäologischen Instituts* 108, pp. 443–55.
Giudice, Filippo, and Sebastiano Barresi
  2003 "La distribuzione della ceramica attica nell'area mediterranea: Dai dati Beazley alle nuove acquisizioni." In *Griechische Keramik im kulturellen Kontext: Akten des Internationalen Vasen-Symposions in Kiel vom 24.–28.9.2001*, edited by Bernhard Schmaltz and Magdalene Söldner, pp. 280–86. Münster: Scriptorium.

Giuliani, Luca
   1995 *Tragik, Trauer und Trost: Bildervasen für eine apulische Totenfeier*. Berlin: Staatliche Museen zu Berlin, Preussischer Kulturbesitz.
Graf, Fritz, and Sarah Iles Johnston
   2007 *Ritual Texts for the Afterlife: Orpheus and the Bacchic Gold Tablets*. London: Routledge.
Guthrie, Kenneth Sylvan, comp. and trans.
   1993 *The Pythagorean Sourcebook and Library: An Anthology of Ancient Writings Which Relate to Pythagoras and Pythagorean Philosophy*. Grand Rapids, Mich.: Phanes Press.
Hallett, Christopher H.
   2005 *The Roman Nude: Heroic Portrait Statuary, 200 B.C.– A.D. 300*. Oxford and New York: Oxford University Press.
Harari, Maurizio
   1995 "An Etruscan Bowl Decorated with a Woman's Head in Floral Surround." In *Classical Art in the Nicholson Museum, Sydney*, edited by Alexander Cambitoglou, pp. 203–10. Mainz: Philipp von Zabern.
Harrison, Jane Ellen
   1900 "Pandora's Box." *Journal of Hellenic Studies* 20, pp. 99–114.
   1908 *Prolegomena to the Study of Greek Religion*. 2nd ed. Cambridge: The University Press.
Helbig, Wolfgang
   1891 *Führer durch die öffentlichen Sammlungen klassischer Altertümer in Rom*. 2 vols. Leipzig: K. Baedeker.
Hermann, Arnold
   2004 *To Think Like God: Pythagoras and Parmenides; the Origins of Philosophy*. Las Vegas: Parmenides.
Hinz, Valentina
   1998 *Der Kult von Demeter und Kore auf Sizilien und in der Magna Graecia*. Palilia 4. Wiesbaden: Reichert.
Jahn, Otto
   1839 *Vasenbilder*. Part 1, *Orestes in Delphi*. Hamburg: Perthes-Besser & Mauke.
Jastrow, Elisabeth
   1946 "Two Terracotta Reliefs in American Museums." *American Journal of Archaeology* 50 (January–March), pp. 67–80.
Jucker, Hans
   1961 *Das Bildnis in Blätterkelch: Geschichte und Bedeutung einer römischen Porträtform*. 2 vols. Lausanne and Olten: Urs Graf.
Kaibel, Georg, ed.
   1878 *Epigrammata graeca ex lapidibus conlecta*. Berlin: G. Reimer.
Kern, Otto
   1922 *Orphicorum Fragmenta*. Berlin: Weidmannsche Buchhandlung.
Kilmer, Martin F.
   1977 *The Shoulder Bust in Sicily and South and Central Italy: A Catalogue and Materials for Dating*. Göteborg: P. Åström.
Klumbach, Hans
   1937 *Tarentiner Grabkunst*. Reutlingen: Gryphius-Verlag.
Kossatz-Deißmann, Anneliese
   1978 *Dramen des Aischylos auf westgriechischen Vasen*. Mainz: Philipp von Zabern.
   1985 "Nachrichten aus Martin-von-Wagner-Museum Würzburg." *Archäologischer Anzeiger*, pp. 229–39.
   1990 "Nachrichten aus dem Martin-von-Wagner Museum Würzburg: Eine neue Phrygerkopf-Situla des Toledo-Malers." *Archäologischer Anzeiger*, pp. 505–20.
Kurtz, Donna C., and John Boardman
   1971 *Greek Burial Customs*. Ithaca, N.Y.: Cornell University Press.

Langlotz, Ernst
   1954 *Aphrodite in den Gärten*. Heidelberg: C. Winter.
Lattanzi, Elena, ed.
   1987 *Il Museo Nazionale di Reggio Calabria*. Rome: Gangemi.
Laviosa, Clelia
   1954 "Le antefisse fittili di Taranto." *Archeologia classica* 6, pp. 217–50.
Lehnert, Pamela A.
   1978 "Female Heads on Greek, South Italian, and Sicilian Vases from the Sixth to the Third Century B.C. as Representations of Persephone/Kore." MA thesis, Michigan State University, East Lansing.
Lewis, David M., John Boardman, Simon Hornblower, and M. Ostwald, eds.
   1994 *The Cambridge Ancient History*. Vol. 6, *Fourth Century B.C.* 2nd ed. Cambridge: Cambridge University Press.
Lexicon Iconographicum Mythologiae Classicae
   1981–99 *Lexicon Iconographicum Mythologiae Classicae*. Edited by John Boardman et al. 9 vols. in 18 parts. Zürich: Artemis.
Lippolis, Enzo
   1987 "Organizzazione delle necropoli e struttura sociale nell'Apulia ellenistica: Due esempi, Taranto e Canosa." In *Römische Gräberstraßen: Selbstdarstellung, Status, Standard; Kolloquium in Munchen vom 28. bis 30. Oktober 1985*, edited by Henner von Hesberg and Paul Zanker, pp. 139–54. Munich: Verlag der Bayerischen Akademie der Wissenschaften.
   1990 *Emergenze e problemi archeologici: Manduria, Taranto, Heraclea*. Manduria: Regione Puglia Centro Regionale Servizi Educativi e Culturali.
   1994 *Catalogo del Museo Nazionale Archeologico di Taranto*. Vol. 3, part 1, *Taranto, la necropolis: Aspetti e problemi della documentazione archeologica tra VII e I sec. A.C.* Taranto: La Colomba.
   2001 "Culto e iconografie della coroplastica votiva: Problemi interpretative a Taranto e nel mondo greco." *Mélanges de l'École française de Rome, Antiquité* 113, pp. 225–55.
   2007 "Tipologie e significati del monumento funerario nella città ellenistica: Lo sviluppo del naiskos." In *Architetti, architettura e città nel Mediterraneo antico*, edited by Donatella Calabi, Carmelo G. Malacrino, and Emanuela Sorbo, pp. 82–102. Milan: Mondadori.
Lohmann, Hans
   1979 *Grabmäler auf Unteritalischen Vasen*. Berlin: Mann.
Long, Herbert Strainge
   1948 "A Study of the Doctrine of Metempsychosis in Greece, from Pythagoras to Plato." PhD diss., Princeton University.
Losi, Maria, Barbara Raposso, and Giusi Ruggiero
   1993 "The Production of Amber Female Heads in Pre-Roman Italy." In *Amber in Archaeology: Proceedings of the Second International Conference on Amber in Archaeology, Liblice 1990*, edited by Curt W. Beck and Jan Bouzek, pp. 203–11. Prague: Institute of Archaeology, Czech Academy of Sciences.
Luchte, James
   2009 *Pythagoras and the Doctrine of Transmigration: Wandering Souls*. London: Continuum.
Macchioro, Vittorio
   1912 "Per la storia della ceramografia italiota." *Mitteilungen des Deutschen Archäologischen Instituts, Roemische Abteilung* 27, pp. 163–88.
MacDonald, Brian R.
   1981 "The Emigration of Potters from Athens in the Late Fifth Century B.C. and Its Effect on the Attic Pottery Industry." *American Journal of Archaeology* 85 (April), pp. 159–68.
Maddoli, Gianfranco
   1996 "Cults and Religious Doctrines of the Western Greeks." In Pugliese Carratelli 1996, pp. 481–98.

Mannino, Katia

1997 "Le importazioni attiche in Puglia nel V sec. a.C." *Ostraka* 6, pp. 389–99.

2004 "I vasi attici di età classica nulla Puglia anellenica: Osservazioni sui contesti di rinvenimento." In *I Greci in Adriatico 2*, edited by Lorenzo Braccesi and Mario Luni, pp. 333–55. Hesperìa 18. Rome: "L'Erma" di Bretschneider.

Mannino, Katia, and Dimitris Roubis

2000 "Le importazioni attiche del IV secolo nell'Adriatico meridionale." In *La Céramique attique du IVᵉ siécle en Méditerranée occidentale: Actes du colloque international organisé par le Centre Camille Jullian, Arles, 7–9 décembre 1995*, edited by Brigitte Sabattini, pp. 67–76. Naples: Centre Jean Bérard.

Marconi, Clemente

2005 "I Theoroi di Eschilo e le antefisse sileniche siceliote." *Sicilia antiqua* 2, pp. 75–94.

Marconi, Pirro

1929 "Plastica agrigentina." *Dedalo* 3, no. 10 (March), pp. 579–99.

1933 *Agrigento arcaica: Il santuario della divinità chtonie e il tempio detto di Vulcano*. Rome: Società Magna Grecia.

Mazzei, Marina

1984 "Dall'ellenizzazione all'età repubblicana: IV e III sec. a.C., il panorama storico archeologico." In *La Daunia antica: Dalla preistoria all'altomedioevo*, edited by Marina Mazzei, pp. 185–211. Milan: Electa.

Mead, G. R. S.

1965 *Orpheus*. London: Watkins.

Meiggs, Russell, and David M. Lewis

1969 *A Selection of Greek Historical Inscriptions to the End of the Fifth Century B.C.* Oxford: Clarendon Press.

van der Meijden, Hellebora

1993 *Terrakotta-Arulae aus Sizilien und Unteritalien*. Amsterdam: A. M. Hakkert.

Metzger, Henri

1951 *Les Représentations dans la céramique attique du IVᵉ siècle*. Paris: E. de Boccard.

Moreno, Paolo

1987 *Pittura greca: Da Polignoto ad Apelle*. Milan: Mondadori.

Neils, Jenifer

2005 "The Girl in the *Pithos*: Hesiod's *Elpis*." In *Periklean Athens and Its Legacy: Problems and Perspectives*, edited by Judith M. Barringer and Jeffrey M. Hurwit, pp. 37–45. Austin: University of Texas Press.

Nilsson, Martin P.

1952 "Die Anodos der Pherephatta auf den Vasenbildern." In *Opuscula Selecta*, vol. 2, pp. 611–23. Lund: C. W. K. Gleerup.

Oakley, John H.

2004 *Picturing Death in Classical Athens: The Evidence of the White Lekythoi*. Cambridge: Cambridge University Press.

Orfismo in Magna Grecia

1975 *Orfismo in Magna Grecia: Atti del quattordicesimo convegno di studi sulla Magna Grecia, Taranto, 6–10 ottobre 1974*. Naples: Arte Tipografica.

Orsi, Paolo

1911 "Locri Epizephyrii." *Notizie degli savi di antichità*, suppl., pp. 3–76.

Otto, Brinna

1996 "Die Göttin mit der Kreuzfackel." In *Fremde Zeiten: Festschrift für Jürgen Borchhardt zum sechzigsten Geburtstag am 25. Februar 1996*, edited by Fritz Blakolmer, pp. 177–86. Vienna: Phoibos.

Pagenstecher, Rudolf

1912 *Unteritalische Grabdenkmäler*. Strasbourg: J. H. Ed. Heitz.

Patroni, Giovanni

1900 *Vasi dipinti del Museo Vivenzio disegnati da Costanzo Angelini nel 1798*. Rome: Gherardo Rega.

Pensa, Marina

1977 *Rappresentazioni dell'oltretomba nella ceramica apula*. Rome: "L'Erma" di Bretschneider.

Pontrandolfo, Angela

1977 "Su alcune tombe pestane: Proposta di una lettura." *Mélanges de l'École française de Rome, Antiquité* 89, pp. 31–98.

1988 "La pittura funeraria." In Pugliese Carratelli 1988, pp. 351–90.

1996 "Wall-Painting in Magna Graecia." In Pugliese Carratelli 1996, pp. 457–70.

Pontrandolfo, Angela, and Agnès Rouveret

1992 *Le tombe dipinte di Paestum*. Modena: Franco Cosimo Panini.

Popovic, Ljubisa B.

1975 *Arhajska grcka kultura na srednjem Balkanu / Archaic Greek Culture in the Middle Balkans*. Belgrade: Narodni Muzej.

Pugliese Carratelli, Giovanni

1965 "Culti e dottrine religiose in Magna Grecia." In *Santuari di Magna Grecia: Atti del quarto convegno di studi sulla Magna Grecia, Taranto-Reggio Calabria, 11–16 ottobre 1964*, pp. 19–45. Naples: Arte Tipografica.

1988 as editor. *Magna Grecia: Vita religiosa e cultura letteraria, filosofica e scientifica*. Milan: Electa.

1993 as editor. *Le lamine d'oro "orfiche."* Milan: Libri Scheiwiller.

1996 as editor. *The Western Greeks*. Exh. cat., Palazzo Grassi, Venice. Milan: Bompiani.

2003 *Les Lamelles d'or orphiques: Instructions pour le voyage d'outre-tombe des initiés grecs*. Translated by Alain-Philippe Segonds and Concetta Luna. Paris: Les Belles Lettres.

Race, William H., ed. and trans.

1997 *Pindar*. Vol. 1, *Olympian Odes; Pythian Odes*. Cambridge, Mass.: Harvard University Press.

Reeder, Ellen D., ed.

1995 *Pandora: Women in Classical Greece*. Exh. cat., Walters Art Gallery, Baltimore; Dallas Museum of Art; Antikenmuseum Basel und Sammlung Ludwig. Baltimore: Walters Art Gallery.

Richardson, N. J.

1985 "Early Greek Views about Life After Death." In *Greek Religion and Society*, edited by P. E. Easterling and J. V. Muir, pp. 50–66. Cambridge: Cambridge University Press.

Richlin, Amy

1999 "Cicero's Head." In *Constructions of the Classical Body*, edited by James I. Porter, pp. 190–211. Ann Arbor: University of Michigan Press.

Riedweg, Christoph

2005 *Pythagoras: His Life, Teaching, and Influence*. Ithaca, N.Y.: Cornell University Press.

Robert, Carl

1886 *Archaeologische Märchen aus alter und neuer Zeit*. Berlin: Weidmann.

1914 "Pandora." *Hermes* 49 (January), pp. 17–38.

Robinson, E. G. D.

1990 "Workshops of Apulian Red-Figure outside Taranto." In *Eumousia: Ceramic and Iconographic Studies in Honour of Alexander Cambitoglou*, edited by Jean-Paul Descoeudres, pp. 179–93. Sydney: Meditarch.

2004 "Reception of Comic Theatre amongst the Indigenous South Italians." *Mediterranean Archaeology* 17, pp. 193–212.

Rohde, Erwin
  1907 *Psyche: Seelencult und Unsterblichkeitsglaube der Griechen.* 4th ed. Tübingen: Mohr.
Rouveret, Agnès
  1990 "Tradizioni pittorische magnogreche." In *Magna Grecia: Arte e artigianato,* edited by Giovanni Pugliese Carratelli, pp. 317–50. Milan: Electa.
Rouveret, Agnès, and Angela Pontrandolfo
  1983 "Pittura Funeraria in Lucania e Campania puntualizzazioni cronologiche e proposte di lettura." *Dialoghi di archeologia,* ser. 3, anno 1, no. 1, pp. 91–130.
Rumpf, Andreas
  1950–51 "Anadyomene." *Jahrbuch des Deutschen Archäologischen Instituts* 65–66, pp. 166–74.
Schauenburg, Konrad
  1957 "Zur Symbolik unteritalischer Rankenmotive." *Mitteilungen des Deutschen Archaeologischen Intituts, Roemische Abteilung* 64, pp. 198–221.
  1962 "Pan in Unteritalien." *Mitteilungen des Deutschen Archaeologischen Intituts, Roemische Abteilung* 69, pp. 27–42.
  1974 "Bendis in Unteritalien?" *Jahrbuch des Deutschen Archäologischen Instituts* 89, pp. 137–86.
  1981 "Zu unteritalischen Situlen." *Archäologischer Anzeiger,* pp. 462–88.
  1982 "Arimaspen in Unteritalien." *Revue archéologique,* pp. 249–62.
  1984a "Unterweltsbilder aus Grossgriechenland." *Mitteilungen des Deutschen Archaeologischen Intituts, Roemische Abteilung* 91, pp. 359–87.
  1984b "Zudiner Hydria des Baltimoremalers in Kiel." *Jahrbuch des Deutschen Archäologischen Instituts* 99, pp. 127–60.
  1989 "Zur Grabsymbolik apulischer Vasen." *Jahrbuch des Deutschen Archäologischen Instituts* 104, pp. 19–60.
Schefold, Karl, and Franz Jung
  1988 *Die Urkönige, Perseus, Bellerophon, Herakles, and Theseus in der klassischen und hellenistischen Kunst.* Munich: Hirmer.
Schmidt, Margot
  1975 "Orfeo e Orfismo nella pittura vascolare italiota." In *Orfismo in Magna Grecia: Atti del quattordicesimo convegno di studi sulla Magna Grecia, Taranto, 6–10 ottobre 1974,* pp. 105–37. Naples: Arte Tipografica.
  1996 "Southern Italian and Sicilian Vases." In Pugliese Carratelli 1996, pp. 443–56.
Séchan, Louis
  1926 *Etudes sur la tragédie Grecque dans ses rapports avec la céramique.* Paris: Champion.
Sgouropoulou, Chrisi
  2000 "H Eikonographia ton Gynaikeion Kephalon sta Aggeia Kerts" Η Εικονογραφια Τον Γυναικειον Κεφαλον Στα Αγγεια Κερτσ [The iconography of the female head on Kertch Vases]. *Archaiologikon Deltion Αρχαιολογικον Δελτιον* 55, pp. 213–34.
Shapiro, H. Alan
  1993 *Personifications in Greek Art: The Representation of Abstract Concepts, 600–400 B.C.* Zürich: Akanthus.
Simon, Erika
  1989 "Hermeneutisches zur Anodos von Göttinnen." In *Festschrift für Nikolaus Himmelmann: Beiträge zur Ikonographie und Hermeneutik,* edited by Hans-Ulrich Cain, Hanns Gabelmann, and Dieter Salzmann, pp. 197–203. Mainz: Philipp von Zabern.
Smith, C. F., trans.
  1920 *History of the Peloponnesian War.* Vol. 2, *Books 3 and 4.* Loeb Classical Library, no. 109. Cambridge, Mass.: Harvard University Press.

Smith, H. R. W.
  1976 *Funerary Symbolism in Apulian Vase-Painting.* Edited by J. K. Anderson. Berkeley: University of California Press.
Spigo, Umberto
  2000a "I pinakes di Francavilla di Sicilia (parte 1)." *Bollettino d'arte,* ser. 6, 85, no. 1, pp. 1–60.
  2000b "I pinakes di Francavilla di Sicilia (parte 2)." *Bollettino d'arte,* ser. 6, 85, no. 3, pp. 1–78.
Squire, Michael
  2011 *The Art of the Body: Antiquity and Its Legacy.* London: I. B. Tauris.
Stewart, Peter
  2003 *Statues in Roman Society: Representation and Response.* Oxford: Oxford University Press.
Taplin, Oliver
  2007 *Pots and Plays: Interactions between Tragedy and Greek Vase-Painting of the Fourth Century B.C.* Los Angeles: J. Paul Getty Museum.
Thorn, Jed M.
  2009 "The Invention of 'Tarentine' Red-Figure." *Antiquity* 83 (March), pp. 174–83.
Todisco, Luigi
  2002 *Teatro e spettacolo in Magna Grecia e in Sicilia: Testi, immagini, architettura.* Milan: Longanesi.
  2003 *La ceramica figurata a soggetto tragico in Magna Grecia e Sicilia.* Rome: G. Bretschneider.
  2006 *Pittura e ceramica figurata tra Grecia, Magna Grecia e Sicilia.* Bari and Rome: La Biblioteca.
Torelli, Mario
  1977 "I Culti di Locri." In *Locri Epizefirii: Atti del sedicesimo Convegno di Studi sulla Magna Grecia, Taranto, 3–8 Ottobre 1976,* pp. 147–84. Naples: Arte Tipografica.
Tortorelli Ghidini, Marisa
  1994 "Visioni escatologiche in Magna Grecia." *Annali dell' Istituto Universitario Orientale di Napoli, Dipartimento di studi del mondo classico e del Mediterraneo antico, Sezione filologico-letteraria* 16, pp. 208–17.
Trendall, A. D.
  1967 *The Red-Figured Vases of Lucania, Campania, and Sicily.* Oxford: Clarendon Press.
  1973 *The Red-Figured Vases of Lucania, Campania, and Sicily: Second Supplement.* London: University of London, Institute of Classical Studies.
  1987 *The Red-Figured Vases of Paestum.* London: British School at Rome.
  1989 *Red Figure Vases of South Italy and Sicily.* London: Thames and Hudson.
  1990 "On the Divergence of South Italian from Attic Red-Figure Vase-Painting." In *Greek Colonists and Native Populations,* edited by Jean-Paul Descoeudres, pp. 218–30. Canberra: Humanities Research Centre.
  1992 "A New Early Apulian *Phlyax* Vase." *Bulletin of the Cleveland Museum of Art* 79 (January), pp. 2–15.
Trendall, A. D., and Alexander Cambitoglou
  1978 *The Red-Figured Vases of Apulia.* Vol. 1, *Early and Middle Apulian.* Oxford: Clarendon Press.
  1982 *The Red-Figured Vases of Apulia.* Vol. 2, *Late Apulian.* Oxford: Clarendon Press.
  1983 *First Supplement to the Red-Figured Vases of Apulia.* London: University of London, Institute of Classical Studies.
  1991–92 *Second Supplement to the Red-Figured Vases of Apulia.* London: University of London, Institute of Classical Studies.

Trendall, A. D., and T. B. L. Webster

1971 *Illustrations of Greek Drama*. London: Phaidon.

Uhlenbrock, Jaimee P.

1988 *The Terracotta Protomai from Gela: A Discussion of Local Style in Archaic Sicily*. Rome: "L'Erma" di Bretschneider.

Vogel, Julius

1886 *Scenen euripideischer Tragödien in griechischen Vasengemälden*. Leipzig: Verlag von Veit & comp.

Watzinger, Carl

1899 "Studien zur unteritalischen Vasenmalerei." PhD diss., Rheinische Friedrich-Wilhelms-Universität Bonn.

Winter, Nancy A.

1974 "Terracotta Representations of Human Heads Used as Architectural Decoration in the Archaic Period." PhD diss., Bryn Mawr College.

1978 "Archaic Architectural Terracottas Decorated with Human Heads." *Mitteilungen des Deutschen Archaeologischen Instituts, Roemische Abteilung* 85, pp. 27–58.

2009 *Symbols of Wealth and Power: Architectural Terracotta Decoration in Etruria and Central Italy, 640–510 B.C.* Ann Arbor: University of Michigan Press for the American Academy in Rome.

Wuilleumier, Pierre

1939 *Tarente: Des origines à la conquète romaine*. Paris: E. de Boccard.

Zuntz, Günther

1971 *Persephone: Three Essays on Religion and Thought in Magna Graecia*. Oxford: Clarendon Press.

LILLIAN BARTLETT STONER

A Bronze Hellenistic Dwarf in the Metropolitan Museum

Representations of dwarfs in the Hellenistic world include a blending of realistic and imagined elements, and they are a fascinating subcategory of the "Hellenistic grotesque," representations of the ill, destitute, or handicapped. Small-scale bronze statuettes of dwarfs, of which one in The Metropolitan Museum of Art is an important example (figs. 1a–c), were frequently displayed in Roman domestic settings and seem to have been particularly popular during the Late Republican and Early Imperial periods (ca. 100 B.C.–A.D. 100). In this context, images of dwarfs were emblematic of the mania for all things "Egyptian" that reached a fever pitch in the decades leading up to and following the Battle of Actium in 31 B.C. This article explores the various associations that dwarfs came to embody through a long and complex process of appropriation (Egyptian to Greek to Roman), in an attempt to elucidate how the Metropolitan Museum's statuette was displayed and what it might have meant to the Roman viewer.

The small bronze dwarf is displayed in the Museum's Hellenistic gallery, in a case populated by other genre statuettes. Henry Gurdon Marquand, a discerning collector and well-known patron of the arts, gave the statuette to the Museum in 1897, the same year he became its second president. The donation of his fine collection of Roman bronzes, as well as a wealth of European paintings, transformed the Museum's collection before the turn of the century.[1]

The statuette, measuring 3⅛ inches in height, is solid cast in bronze and, despite surface damage and aggressive cleaning, is in remarkably good condition.[2] The green patina has been worn off in places, leaving blotches of a more golden color. The left side has sustained the most damage: the outer arm, hand, and shin are badly abraded. The face has also suffered, with a break at the left nostril and wear on the chin making those features appear respectively rather hooked and sharp. Areas of pitting are visible on the forehead, right knee and ankle, and the bottom of the tray. Two fingers are missing on the right hand. A shallow hole at the top of the head retains traces of lead solder, encircled by a worn, raised molding—this feature gives the most valuable clues to the statuette's ancient display context.

The dwarf stands on his left foot and steps forward in a toddling, bowlegged stride. The legs are chubby, with bulky, softly modeled calf and thigh muscles. The buttocks are prominent and boxy in shape, and the phallus is completely exposed and abnormally large,

figs. 1a–c Statuette of a Dwarf. Late Hellenistic or Early Imperial, ca. 100 B.C.–A.D. 100. Bronze, with silver in the eyes, H. 3⅛ in. (7.9 cm). The Metropolitan Museum of Art, Gift of Henry G. Marquand, 1897 (97.22.9)

reaching to the soles of the feet. The feet themselves seem unlikely to have ever supported the figure, as they are somewhat curved. The protruding stomach and broad breast are covered by an apron of thick material, tied at the nape of the neck. A small, square pouch hangs from the belt on the left side, and the left wrist is encircled by what appears to be a blockish bracelet. He holds a large, deep dish laden with small, round edibles—perhaps fruits or cakes—and is sampling one with his right hand. Despite its small size, the statuette is full of a cheeky malevolence; the mouth is open to receive the treat he has pilfered, revealing both upper and lower rows of teeth. The brow is prominent and furrowed with dramatic, stylized eyebrows conveying a sinister effect. The eyes are inlaid in silver with deeply incised pupils, once likely filled with gemstones or glass-paste, now missing.[3] The use of a precious metal is a deliberate choice intended to draw focus to the eyes and additionally served to increase the expense and prestige of the statuette. The bald head is encircled by a crude wreath consisting of stylized leaves and clusters of grapes or berries.

In terms of physiognomy, it is clear that the artist was portraying disproportionate dwarfism (achondroplasia), the result of a genetic mutation that is characterized by short stature, stunted arms and legs, and "normal" sized trunk and head.[4] However, the oversize phallus and exaggerated facial features are figments of artistic imagination that impart the effect of caricature. Although more than two hundred bronze dwarf statuettes of this approximate scale have survived from

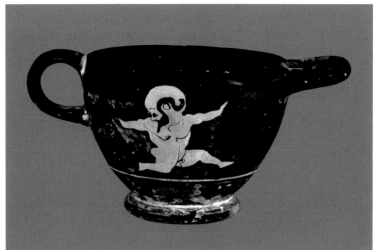

figs. 2a,b Gamboling Dwarf on a Red-figure Skyphos. Attributed to the Manner of the Sotades Painter. Greek, from Capua, ca. 460 B.C. H. 3 in. (7.7 cm). Musée du Louvre, Paris (G 617)

antiquity,[5] the silver eyes and impish animation of the Metropolitan's example make it especially compelling and deserving of a closer look.

Dwarfism was an acknowledged reality in ancient Mediterranean societies, and images of dwarfs were often depicted in the arts of New Kingdom Egypt and Classical Greece.[6] The different responses that the condition generated in these periods found partial reconciliation in Hellenistic and eventually Roman culture. Dwarfs featured prominently in Egyptian art and mythology, particularly in relation to scarab beetles and the dwarfish gods Ptah and Bes, their images circulating widely around the ancient Mediterranean, notably as symbols of apotropaic power.[7] These associations evidently influenced the treatment of dwarfs positively: they were frequently included in the retinue of elite households as special servants and enjoyed important roles in the religious sphere as ritual dancers and guards of temple precincts.[8]

In Archaic and Classical Greece dwarfs did not enjoy an elevated status such as they had in Egypt. Several popular Greek myths feature dwarfs; the most famous is the Battle of Pygmies versus Cranes, a tale from the *Iliad* in which a migrating flock of cranes wages war on a tribe of pygmies residing near the source of the Nile.[9] In general, no clear distinction between pygmies and dwarfs was made in Greek literature and art, an ambiguity that persisted through the Roman period. The words *pygmaios* and *nanos* (and their Latinized equivalents) were used interchangeably to describe both African pygmies[10] (in modern terms, a dark-skinned, sub-Saharan ethnic group characterized by their small size) and indigenous dwarfs, whose physical disproportion was caused by genetic mutation.[11] In one of the earliest artistic depictions of the Pygmies versus

Cranes episode, on the foot of the François Krater (ca. 570–560 B.C.), the pygmies (both cavalrymen and infantry) are small, proportionate humans.[12] In a later representation from ca. 480–470 B.C., now in the State Hermitage Museum, Saint Petersburg, and in the majority of cases, they are shown as disproportionate dwarfs, suggesting that dwarfs in the local population were used as visual inspiration.[13]

Another myth involving abnormally small characters is set during the life of Herakles. In this story the Kerkopes, diminutive, mischievous twin brigands, are caught red-handed while trying to steal from the hero.[14] Once they are hog-tied and slung over Herakles' shoulder, they earn their freedom by amusing him with their coarse jokes.[15] This myth can be read as an early precursor to the comedic, foulmouthed dwarfs described in Roman literature.

In Greek representations unrelated to these specific myths, dwarfs are nearly always shown balding or bearded, perhaps in an effort to distinguish them from children.[16] A charming red-figure skyphos in Paris shows a male dwarf gamboling on each side and displaying all of the iconographic conventions typical of the period: mostly bald, bearded, with prominent forehead and snub nose (figs. 2a, b). These stylized facial features and those of satyrs are markedly similar, and perhaps because of this contrived resemblance, dwarfs began to be associated with Dionysos—a tendency that intensified through the Roman period.[17]

The burgeoning popularity of dwarfs in the art and literature of the Hellenistic period builds upon their earlier roles in dynastic Egypt and Classical Greece. While older associations (as servants, attendants of Dionysos, and mischievous foreigners) remain, for the first time dwarfs become the subject of heavy-handed

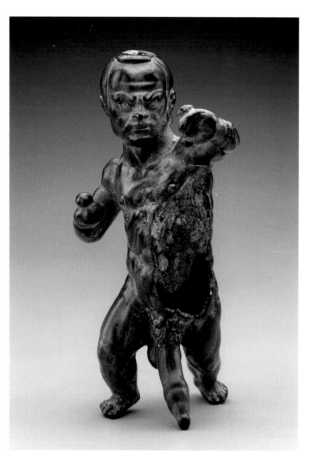 

fig. 3 Dwarf Boxer. Greek, 150 B.C.–A.D. 10. Bronze, 4⅜ in. (11.1 cm). Museum of Fine Arts, Boston (RES.08.32k)

fig. 4 Dwarf Gladiator. Bronze, 2⅜ in. (6 cm). British Museum, London (1922,0712.4)

humor: their smallness, combined with surprising and distinctly adult characteristics, is the butt of the joke.

Dwarfs are often referred to in literature as entertainers and servants in elite households. Athenaeus writes of Ptolemy IV processing publicly in Alexandria, followed by a retinue of dancing dwarfs in an enactment of a Dionysiac procession.[18] In this case, the practice of keeping dwarfs for amusement is a continuation of the much older Pharaonic tradition, but with a distinctly Greek twist. In such a grandiose display, Ptolemy IV presented himself as the new Dionysos, and the cavorting dwarfs filled in as real-life satyrs. Dwarfs were assimilated into Ptolemaic court ideology of luxury and hedonistic excess, which in Roman times was recalled (sometimes with admiration) as an example of excessive moral decadence. Not only did dwarfs preserve their function as novelty servants, but their humorous size and cultivated exoticism were transformed into symbols of godlike luxury. They were soon viewed this way throughout the Roman world.

In the Roman period, dwarfs were strongly associated with Egyptian culture, more so than they had been in Classical Greece. Special interest in Egypt developed in the second century B.C., as Rome became a major international force and found itself increasingly in

contact (and at odds) with the powerful Hellenistic kingdoms of the East. Egyptian cults became fashionable in Rome, and interior spaces were decorated with Egyptian ethnological scenes, one of the most famous and earliest examples coming from Palestrina.[19] As Rome confronted Egypt's captivating history, images of dwarfs entered Roman culture as part of the newly adopted "Egyptianizing" repertoire.

Mark Antony is the first notable Roman known to have adopted the tradition of keeping dwarfs in his home.[20] Given Antony's reported enjoyment of luxuries typically associated with the decadent "East," his ownership of dwarfs likely deliberately echoed the Ptolemaic practice.[21] Retaining dwarfs quickly became popular, even in the highest levels of Roman society, as a status symbol. Augustus's renegade daughter, Julia, kept two, although Suetonius writes of the emperor's personal dislike of the fashion.[22] The fact that Mark Antony and Julia were characterized as owning dwarfs is highly significant, given how well known they were in literature as intemperate consumers of wine, sex, and other excesses associated in the Roman mind with the "East." Dwarfs had come to represent the extravagances of Hellenistic despots that the most conservative fringe of Roman society—with the emperor Augustus at its forefront—disdained as utterly un-Roman. His endorsement of traditional Roman mores could not stop the spread of a culture of "Eastern" luxury, and the popularity of dwarf-attendants in Rome persisted.

Roman authors refer to dwarfs as entertainers, performing in public and private spheres. Statius describes with admiration a display of pugilist dwarfs in the Roman arena: "They give wounds fighting hand to hand and threaten each other with death—what fists!"[23] Their aggressive demeanor and unexpected power are emphasized as a counterpoint to their smallness, eliciting amusement and amazement in a cosmopolitan audience constantly seeking novel forms of diversion. Other descriptions indicate that dwarfs reenacted the Battle of Pygmies versus Cranes, in an appealing mix of drama, comedy, and brute violence.[24] An even more outlandish combination, in the Colosseum during Saturnalia, featured dwarf gladiators fighting against armed, full-size women, perhaps impersonating Amazons.[25] The uncertain outcome of this bizarre match must have increased the highly valued suspense factor.[26]

Many representations of fighting dwarfs in bronze survive, including a particularly fine boxer now in Boston (fig. 3).[27] The figure's compact, muscular body is poised for action as he grasps the ancient equivalent of brass knuckles in his fists—reminiscent of the class of

fighter that so impressed Statius. Dwarfs are also shown wearing gladiatorial costume, as in a British Museum figure equipped with a crested helmet cuirass and small circular shield (fig. 4). Presumably the spectacle here was intended to be more comic than menacing.

Ancient authors also write of dwarf entertainers in the private sphere. Propertius tells of a dwarf dancing in flickering lamplight to the accompaniment of a flute, and characterizes the troupe as specializing in "Egyptian-style" entertainment.[28] Lucian describes a dinner-party guest who is the target of a rude-mouthed dwarf belonging to the host family, referring to the dwarf as a "tiny Alexandrian man." In another passage, a dwarf recites salacious verses in an Egyptian accent to the delight of his audience.[29] Whether or not these dwarfs were Egyptian by birth or ethnicity, it seems clear that their distinct modes of entertainment—dancing and rehearsing ribald poems—linked them in the Roman mind with Alexandria by the first century B.C.[30]

A large corpus of dancing dwarf statuettes provides clues of what these performances might have looked like. Dancers, alone or in troupes, specialized in performance genres and employed an assortment of costumes and musical instruments. The famous late second-century B.C. dancing dwarfs from the Mahdia shipwreck, clearly a pair, twirl around and play castanets (figs. 5, 6).[31]

fig. 5 Dancing Female Dwarf. Late 2nd century B.C. Bronze, 12⅜ in. (31.5 cm). From the Mahdia shipwreck, ca. 80s B.C. The National Bardo Museum, Tunis (F213)

fig. 6 Dancing Male Dwarf. Late 2nd century B.C. Bronze, 12⅝ in. (32 cm). From the Mahdia shipwreck, ca. 80s B.C. The National Bardo Museum, Tunis (F215)

The female figure caricatures the veiled dancer type, which had strong associations with Alexandria.[32] The so-called Baker Dancer[33] is a particularly beautiful example in the Metropolitan Museum, and the parallels between the two figures in their whirling motion and costume are apparent.

The bronze dwarf in the Museum belongs to a smaller category of surviving dwarf figures that neither fight nor dance, and it should be considered one of the finest existing representations of dwarfs as household attendants. His Dionysian wreath locates him in a symposium or festival context, and the heavily laden tray suggests that he is serving refreshments at such an event. The closest parallel, and perhaps the only other dwarf of this type, is a statuette now in Florence with a similar costume and disposition (fig. 7).[34] Instead of a tray, he clutches a wickerwork basket of fruits or breads and appears to be singing or calling out. Both works may be interpreted as servants misbehaving to the delight of both host and guests, of the sort described by Suetonius, Propertius, and Lucian.

The conspicuously large phallus of the Museum's figure, and so many other surviving dwarf statuettes from the Roman period, can be interpreted in a number of ways. In Greco-Roman art, the male body was frequently represented nude, and across a variety of media, the genitalia of beautiful youths and mature warriors alike were typically rather small. Because of this association, modestly sized penises have regularly been considered a hallmark of the ideal male form.[35] In

fig. 7 Dwarf Carrying a Basket. 1st century B.C.–1st century A.D. Bronze, 3¼ in. (8.2 cm). Museo Archeologico Nazionale, Florence (2300)

contrast, the grotesquely large phallus was reserved for unheroic characters, including comic actors (who wore large strap-ons) and the congenitally misshapen bodies that so captured the artistic imagination in the Hellenistic period.[36] In these contexts, the preposterously outsized phallus was likely used to reinforce an already unattractive aspect, while at the same time providing a humorous gloss. Ancient religion provides another index for understanding the phallus, which is sometimes interpreted as a symbol to repel the evil eye in the Roman period.[37] The phallus reinforces readings of dwarf statuettes as ugly, humorous, and even apotropaic, but also provides a visual manifestation of the paradox between small stature and loud voice, prodigious strength, or sharp wit that is underscored in ancient descriptions.

Neither the provenance nor original display context of the Museum's dwarf statuette is known, but works with secure provenance provide clues as to how it might have been used in antiquity. Bronze dwarfs of similar size and craftsmanship were found by the dozens in ruined houses of Herculaneum, Pompeii, and the surrounding areas.[38] Because the socioeconomic situation of these households is now fairly well understood, it seems reasonable to suggest that objects of this type were used to adorn the homes of prosperous, middle-class owners.[39] They were displayed as decorative objects, independently, in groups, or incorporated in furniture and utensils. Six bronze dwarfs cunningly shaped as oil lamps have been recovered from Herculaneum and Pompeii, the phalluses serving as nozzles from which the wicks and flames would emerge (fig. 8).

The soldered feature on the head of the Museum's statuette may indicate that it was originally part of some type of ornament or utensil. Because the feet are curved to the extent that the figure cannot stand on its own, it seems probable that it was hung by means of a suspension ring fixed to the head. The bronze boxer from Boston (see fig. 3), too, has remains of a soldered-on attachment at the top of the head; given its tripod-like lower body, it most likely supported a candelabrum or some other fitting. Not all examples were functional objects: a female dwarf from the Mahdia shipwreck still has a suspension ring on its back and presumably floated among the proceedings (fig. 9). Such ornaments intended for suspension were often fitted with small bells that would have chimed in the wind or at the passage of a visitor.[40]

Dwarfs attracted many associations in the ancient world. They were alternately revered or ridiculed, or valued as servants or dancers, but always forced into

fig. 8 Oil Lamp in the Shape of a Phallic Dwarf. 1st century A.D. From Pompeii. Bronze, 8⅝ in. (22 cm). Museo Archeologico Nazionale (27871)

fig. 9 Female Dwarf with Suspension Ring. Late 2nd century B.C. Bronze, 11⅝ in. (29.5 cm). From the Mahdia shipwreck, ca. 80s B.C. The National Bardo Museum, Tunis (F214).

the entertaining fringes by way of myth and occupation. Hellenistic representations of dwarfs fall into the grotesque category but ultimately surpass it by retaining older associations as attendants of Dionysos and by embodying Ptolemaic luxury and excess. In the home of a wealthy Roman, the Museum's dwarf would have served as a charming decoration; indeed, as a royal household might surround itself with live dwarf entertainers, so might a middle-class Roman *dominus* populate his house with whimsical statuettes of the same. When displayed in a dining room, the statuette would blend unobtrusively into the lavish decoration perhaps until an inebriated guest spotted it. After a closer look, the diner would recognize the figure as a misbehaving dwarf—he might think of satyrs, lavish festivals, or Eastern despots. Most importantly, he would be caught off guard and enjoy the dwarf's intense gaze and surprising phallus. The diminutive statuette would successfully entertain the room, as its living counterpart might have done in a royal household.

LILLIAN BARTLETT STONER
The Institute of Fine Arts,
New York University

ACKNOWLEDGMENTS

A version of this article was delivered at the Symposium on the History of Art organized by the Frick Collection and the Institute of Fine Arts of New York University (2011), and at the XVIIth International Bronze Congress in Izmir, Turkey (2011). I thank Guido Petruciolli, Beryl Barr-Sharrar, Joan Mertens, Clemente Marconi, Katherine E. Welch, and Günter H. Kopcke for their suggestions. Seán Hemingway of the Department of Greek and Roman Art and Deborah Schorsch of the Sherman Fairchild Center for Objects Conservation at the Metropolitan Museum kindly allowed me to examine the dwarf statuette and shared their insights. Mario Iozzo of the Museo Archeologico Nazionale in Florence was equally gracious.

NOTES

1 Tomkins 1989, pp. 73–75.

2 Casting technique and condition were summarily addressed by Gisela Richter (1915, p. 126). Further analysis is based on my observation and the suggestions of Deborah Schorsch.

3 This is assumed to be the case for another small bronze grotesque with silver eyes and similarly deeply incised pupils at the Metropolitan Museum (12.229.6). See Richter 1913, p. 150.

4 For an extensive description of achondroplasia, see Dasen 1993, pp. 7–10.

5 For a nearly comprehensive catalogue and discussion of surviving bronze dwarf statuettes (although it does not include MMA 97.22.9), see Garmaise 1996.

6 The work of Véronique Dasen is the most thorough for the Egyptian and Classical Greek periods; see Dasen 1988, 1990, and 1993. For further erudite observations on the iconography of dwarfs in the Classical period, see Shapiro 1984.

7 Dasen 1993, pp. 55–103; Meyboom and Versluys 2007, pp. 175–77.

8 Dasen 1993, pp. 156–59.

9 Homer, *Iliad* 3.4–9. After the conquests of Alexander, as the known world expanded, the "little people" of myth were placed farther afield and became associated with Caria, India, and Thule. Ibid., p. 176.

10 For the modern definition of "pygmy," see Cavalli-Sforza 1986, pp. 81–93. Michael Garmaise points out, "Homer may have conceived them as 'tiny' or 'fist-sized men' (from the Greek *pygme*)." Garmaise 1996, pp. 21–23.

11 Dasen believes that stories of pygmies may have emerged to account for the presence of pathologically short people in Greek cities; this supposition explains the absence of descriptions of ethnic characteristics, such as skin color. Dasen 1993, p. 179.

12 Museo Archeologico Nazionale, Florence (4209). *ABV* 76.1 (682).

13 The State Hermitage Museum, Saint Petersburg (b 1818). *ARV* 382.188 (1649).

14 Ibid., pp. 189–93.

15 The oldest surviving literary narrative of the myth of Herakles and the twin brigands is recounted by Nonnos (6th century A.D.) and presumably was born out of a longer literary tradition. For a succinct survey of the myth's literary and iconographic development, as well as its significance in the western colonies, see Marconi 2007, pp. 150–59.

16 The perceived similarities between children and dwarfs owing to their size and proportions persisted in both comedic and scientific texts. Most famously, Aristotle (*De partibus animalium* 4.10.686, 1–20) noted that "all children are dwarfs. . . ."

17 For instance, dwarfs are often shown with thyrsoi, garlands, and wine. See, for example, a stamnos fragment attributed to the Peleus Painter at the Friedrich-Alexander-Universität in Erlangen (I707) (*ARV* 1039.6). In representations of the Kerkopes harassing a sleeping Herakles, the Kerkopes were occasionally replaced by satyrs, underscoring the connection between these groups of comical and otherworldly beings. See McPhee 1979, pp. 38–40, pl. 15.1–3.

18 Athenaeus, *Deipnosophistae* 5.201e; 6.246c.

19 Meyboom 1995, app. 13, pp. 150–54; Meyboom and Versluys 2007, p. 176. See also De Vos 1980.

20 Philodemus, *De signis* 4.

21 Horace, *Satirae* 1.3.46–47.

22 Suetonius, *Divus Augustus* 83. That Augustus presented himself as a true Roman in opposition to Antony (who had been corrupted by the luxury and effeminacy of the East) is another way to interpret his dislike of the practice of keeping dwarfs in the home.

23 Statius, *Silvae* 1.6.57–64.

24 Duke 1955, pp. 223–24; Brunet 2004, pp. 145–70.

25 Carcopino 1940, p. 240.

26 I thank Katherine E. Welch for this suggestion.

27 Comstock and Vermeule 1971, p. 129, no. 145.

28 Propertius, 4.8.39–42.

29 Lucian, *Symposium* 18–19.

30 Garmaise 1996, p. 46.

31 Pfisterer-Haas 1994, pp. 483–88.

32 Thompson 1950.

33 MMA 1972.118.95.

34 Arbeid and Iozzo 2015, pp. 186–87, no. 165.

35 Dover 1989, pp. 126–27; McNiven 1995.

36 For excellent discussions of the "Hellenistic grotesque" as a type, see Himmelmann 1983; Giuliani 1987; and Fischer 1998.

37 See, for example, Stewart 1997, pp. 225–27.

38 Garmaise 1996, pp. 148–64.

39 See, for example, Jongman 1988.

40 These tintinnabula are known from many works. Even the bronze oil lamp shown in fig. 8 is fitted with small rings from which small bells were presumably attached. More complete examples abound; see, for instance, Cantarella 1998, pp. 66, 88, 104, 116–17.

ABBREVIATIONS

ABV   Beazley 1956
ARV   Beazley 1963

REFERENCES

Arbeid, Barbara and Mario Iozzo, eds.

2015 *Piccoli grandi bronzi: Capolavori greci, etruschi e romani delle collezioni mediceo-lorenesi nel Museo Archeologico Nazionale di Firenze.* Exh. cat., Museo Archeologico Nazionale, Florence. Florence: Edizioni Polistampa.

Beazley, J. D.

1956 *Attic Black-Figure Vase-Painters.* Oxford: Clarendon Press.

1963 *Attic Red-Figure Vase-Painters.* 2nd ed. 3 vols. Oxford: Clarendon Press.

Brunet, Stephen

2004 "Female and Dwarf Gladiators." *Mouseion* 4, pp. 145–70.

Cantarella, Eva

1998 *Pompei: I volti dell'amore.* Milan: Mondadori.

Carcopino, Jérôme

1940 *Daily Life in Ancient Rome: The People and the City at the Height of the Empire.* New Haven: Yale University Press.

Cavalli-Sforza, Luigi Luca, ed.

1986 *African Pygmies.* Orlando, Fla.: Academic Press.

Comstock, Mary, and Cornelius Vermeule

1971 *Greek, Etruscan, and Roman Bronzes in the Museum of Fine Arts, Boston.* Boston: Museum of Fine Arts.

Dasen, Véronique

1988 "Dwarfism in Egypt and Classical Antiquity: Iconography and Medical History." *Medical History* 32, pp. 253–76.

1990 "Dwarfs in Athens." *Oxford Journal of Archaeology* 9 (May), pp. 191–207.

1993 *Dwarfs in Ancient Egypt and Greece.* Oxford: Clarendon Press.

De Vos, Mariette

1980 *L'egittomania in pitture e mosaici romano-campani della prima età imperiale.* Leiden: Brill.

Dover, K. J.

1989 *Greek Homosexuality.* Cambridge, Mass.: Harvard University Press.

Duke, T. T.

1955 "Women and Pygmies in the Roman Arena." *Classical Journal* 50 (February), pp. 223–24.

Fischer, Jutta

1998 "Der Zwerg, der Phallos und der Buckel: Groteskfiguren aus dem ptolemäischen Ägypten." *Chronique d'Egypte* 73, no. 146, pp. 327–61.

Garmaise, Michael

1996 "Studies in the Representation of Dwarfs in Hellenistic and Roman Art." PhD diss., McMaster University, Hamilton, Ont.

Giuliani, Luca

1987 "Die seligen Krüppel: Zur Bedeutung von Mißgestalten in der hellenistischen Kleinkunst." *Archäologischer Anzeiger,* pp. 701–21.

Himmelmann, Nikolaus

1983 *Alexandria und der Realismus in der griechischen Kunst.* Tübingen: Wasmuth.

Jongman, Willem

1988 *The Economy and Society of Pompeii.* Amsterdam: J. C. Gieben.

Marconi, Clemente

2007 *Temple Decoration and Cultural Identity in the Archaic Greek World: The Metopes of Selinus.* Cambridge and New York: Cambridge University Press.

McNiven, Timothy J.

1995 "The Unheroic Penis: Otherness Exposed." *Source: Notes in the History of Art* 15 (Fall), pp. 10–16.

McPhee, Ian

1979 "An Apulian Oinochoe and the Robbery of Herakles." *Antike Kunst* 22, no. 1, pp. 38–42.

Meyboom, Paul G. P.

1995 *The Nile Mosaic of Palestrina: Early Evidence of Egyptian Religion in Italy.* Leiden: Brill.

Meyboom, Paul G. P., and Miguel John Versluys

2007 "The Meaning of Dwarfs in Nilotic Scenes." In *Nile into Tiber: Egypt in the Roman World; Proceedings of the 3rd International Conference of Isis Studies, Faculty of Archaeology, Leiden University, May 11–14, 2005,* edited by Laurent Bricault, Miguel John Versluys, and Paul G. P. Meyboom, pp. 170–208. Leiden: Brill.

Pfisterer-Haas, Susanne

1994 "Die bronzenen Zwergentanzer." In *Das Wrack: Der antike Schiffsfund von Mahdia,* edited by Gisela Hellenkemper Salies, vol. 1, pp. 483–505. Cologne: Rheinland-Verlag.

Richter, Gisela M. A.

1913 "Grotesques and the Mime." *American Journal of Archaeology* 18 (April–June), pp. 149–56.

1915 *Greek, Etruscan, and Roman Bronzes.* New York: MMA; Gilliss Press.

Shapiro, H. A.

1984 "Notes on Greek Dwarfs." *American Journal of Archaeology* 88 (July), pp. 391–92.

Stewart, Andrew

1997 *Art, Desire, and the Body in Ancient Greece.* Cambridge: Cambridge University Press.

Thompson, Dorothy Burr

1950 "A Bronze Dancer from Alexandria." *American Journal of Archaeology* 54 (October–December), pp. 371–85.

Tomkins, Calvin

1989 *Merchants and Masterpieces: The Story of The Metropolitan Museum of Art.* Rev. ed. New York: Henry Holt.

CHRISTOPHER S. LIGHTFOOT

Ennion, Master of Roman Glass: Further Thoughts

During The Metropolitan Museum of Art's recent exhibition "Ennion: Master of Roman Glass" (2014–15), I had the opportunity to study at close quarters the twenty-two intact or nearly complete vessels from Ennion's workshop that formed the core of the show.[1] Indeed, only four other vessels by Ennion have survived in such a complete condition. They were not in the exhibition but are featured or mentioned in the catalogue (cats. 3, 25 and figs. 5, 6 in that volume). This short article serves as an addendum, providing some corrections and adding further thoughts that were prompted by visitors' questions. In the following discussion, catalogue numbers refer to the numbers assigned to vessels in the exhibition and its publication.[2]

THE INVENTION OF GLASSBLOWING

The glassblowing technique was introduced at some point in the first century B.C., probably in the Near East.

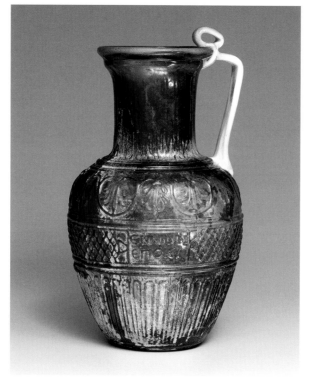

The first archaeological evidence for attempts at using a short ceramic blowpipe to inflate small bubbles of glass comes from Jerusalem and dates to about 50 B.C. However, no true blown glass can be dated any earlier than the last decades of the first century B.C., putting the actual invention in the time of the first emperor Augustus (r. 27 B.C.–A.D. 14).[3] Blown glass only starts to appear in any quantity at archaeological sites dating to the early years of the first century A.D.[4]

The question of how glassblowing came to be invented can probably never be answered, but it is worthwhile considering why it did. In the Classical (ca. 480–323 B.C.) and Hellenistic (ca. 323–31 B.C.) periods, glassworkers made glass vessels that were either luxury cast tableware, often quite large and elaborately decorated, or core-formed containers that were also attractive but time-consuming to make. Today we might think that glassworkers who first experimented with the blowpipe did so in order to make their work easier and their products thus less expensive, but these are unlikely to be the reasons for the invention. A more compelling argument is that they needed a quicker method of making glass in sufficient quantities to compete with pottery as tableware and containers. The first century B.C. witnessed a great increase in pottery production, which exploited the expansion of markets and international trade by Roman merchants. Glassworkers wanted to be part of this boom, but with the existing technologies of core forming and casting, their output was limited. Their solution was to develop a new production method.

Once the blowing technique had been perfected, the glass industry experienced an unprecedented expansion, not just in the size of its output but also in the variety of shapes, sizes, and types of vessels and objects (including window glass) that was produced. At first, it seems, Roman glassworkers continued to make luxury glass, such as cameo glass, which remained costly and time-consuming to produce, but they also created very plain and functional free-blown perfume bottles, perhaps made expressly for funereal purposes.[5] Between these two extremes came mold-blown glass, which served to furnish the market with good-quality tableware that could be mass-produced. The idea of using molds was probably taken from the Roman pottery industry, where this technique allowed potters to make large quantities of decorated tablewares, as well as terracotta oil lamps, of a consistent size and quality, enabling them to flood the market quickly with their goods.

Makers of glassware were so successful at applying and developing the blowing technique that, during the course of the first century A.D., their products not only competed with similar wares in pottery but also, in some cases, supplanted them.[6] In addition, the invention of glassblowing brought some beneficial and, perhaps, unexpected consequences. As glass grew more readily available, it also became fashionable and popular; its qualities and advantages were more widely appreciated, and finally, as demand for glassware rose, so the production of raw glass increased. This led to the fall in price of the raw material, which in turn was passed on to the consumer, making glass more affordable for a larger percentage of the population. As early as the first decades of the first century A.D., Strabo was able to claim that in Rome it was possible to purchase a glass bowl or small drinking cup for the price of a bronze coin.[7] By the second half of the first century A.D., the poet Martial referred to peddlers in Rome who

fig. 3 Cup signed by Aristeas. Translucent light green, H. 2⅜ in. (6 cm), Diam. 3½ in. (9 cm). Strada Collection, Scaldasole, Pavia (68). Cat. 27

collected up broken glass in exchange for dry tinder soaked in sulfur.[8]

Ennion, however, did not want to flood the market with cheap glass containers. Rather, he set up his workshop, probably in Sidon, Lebanon, in the first decades of the first century A.D., in order to compete with the local glass industry that was already producing cast tablewares.[9] His surviving signed vessels show that he strove to produce quality blown glass that was attractive yet affordable. He put his name on the molds, clearly wanting customers to recognize them as his. He was, so far as is known, the first maker of glassware to do so.

SEQUENCING ENNION'S GLASSWARE

The sequence in which Ennion made his glassware has long been debated. For example, it has been argued that he first made the jugs and then turned to making the cups. Nevertheless, this view, derived from the theory that he transferred his workshop from the East to the West, cannot be taken as a valid basis for understanding how his repertoire developed. Instead, it might be argued that as his skill and experience at making and using multipart molds increased, the forms of, and decoration on, his wares became more sophisticated. Thus, it could be reasoned that Ennion's earliest products were the two-handled cups of the so-called Geometric style (cats. 21, 22, one of which was found in a tomb at Caresana, near Vercelli, Italy) or the globular bowls (cats. 23, 24, both of which are said to come from Sidon), since they have simpler and more regular forms of decoration. There is, however, no evidence to prove this was actually the case.

A more valid and worthwhile approach may be to examine the inscriptions and to argue that his first attempts at labeling would be those that are poorly formed in terms of either grammar or layout. The largest of his cups, the single-handled examples from Tremithus, Cyprus, and Adria, Italy (cats. 11, 12), bear inscriptions in a plain square panel (fig. 1 [cat. 11]). They run on into four lines and appear to have been poorly planned. His signed inscription, for example, although it consists of only two words, is arranged so that his name is divided between lines 1 and 2, and the verb is spread out across three lines with the final letter appearing on its own in line 4. In other words, as a label it is very badly designed, suggesting that it might be one of Ennion's first attempts at putting his name on his products. Perhaps, too, the plain frame is earlier than the *tabula ansata* (a rectangular frame with projecting handles at the sides) that appears on the majority of the signed vessels from his workshop. Certainly,

the latter design is striking, calling attention to the labels and, as has been mentioned before, exploiting a well-known feature of Roman inscriptions.[10] In addition, it may be argued that the molds for these large cylindrical cups were easier to make and, especially, to use than those for the vessels with more elaborate profiles or of smaller size (such as the two-handled cups cats. 15–20).

We may speculate that Ennion first made his large cups (that is, cats. 11–13, which are one-handled, and 14, a two-handled example) and that he followed with his smaller two-handled cups, all of which have inscriptions within the *tabula ansata* frame. Other reasons may also be put forward for this sequence. Perhaps Ennion initially wanted to make large and impressive cups but subsequently found their functionality disappointing: such a vessel, filled with liquid, presumably wine, must have been very difficult to hold and prone to overbalancing. Thereafter, Ennion may have turned to making smaller cups with two handles that were better suited for use. By then, too, his labeling was more refined. He adopted the Roman *tabula ansata* and organized the inscription so that all of his name appeared on the first line (see cats. 1–7, 9, 15–26). The final version of his "brand label" may well be ΕΝΝΙΩΝ ΕΠΟΙΕΙ in two lines (fig. 2 [cat. 1]). Of the twenty-six surviving vessels mentioned above, nearly half have this form of inscription. It should be noted that all of these examples, which include cups, beakers, bowls, and jugs, have convex or concave curving sides (rather than straight profiles) where the vertical sections of the mold were used. Aristeas, probably following Ennion, used the same label design for his products (fig. 3 [cat. 27]), inserting the word ΚΥΠΡΙΟC as an additional line in the case of his bowl (cat. 28). However, it is notable that fragments of two Aristeas cups found at Narona and Burnum in Croatia bear similar inscriptions, but in those the last letter of Aristeas's name appears on the second line and the last letter of ΚΥΠΡΙΟC spills over

4

5

6

figs. 4–8:
Examples of anomaly
(ringed) on the back,
opposite the *tabula ansata*
and to right of seam 2

fig. 4 Detail of fig. 2 (cat. 1)

fig. 5 Detail of two-handled
jug (amphora) signed by Ennion
(see also fig. 11). Translucent blue
green with handles in same color,
H. 6⅞ in. (17.5 cm). Shlomo
Moussaieff Collection. Cat. 2

fig. 6 One-handled jug signed by
Ennion. Translucent amber brown
with handle and pedestal foot in
same color, H. (to rim, including
restored foot) 8¼ in. (21.1 cm), H. (to
handle) 9⅜ in. (23.8 cm), diam. (rim)
2⅞ in. (7.2 cm). diam. (max.) 4¼ in.
(10.8 cm). The Corning Museum of
Glass, Corning, New York (59.1.76).
Cat. 4

7   8

from the second onto the last line. The fragments belong to vessels of two different shapes and designs, one with cylindrical sides and the other with a convex profile.[11] So it would appear that Aristeas, too, experimented with the arrangement of his labels.

ENNION'S MOLDS

Previous detailed studies of the glass vessels signed by Ennion have allowed scholars to identify several as coming from the same molds. Thus, for example, the two globular bowls (cats. 23, 24) come from the same set of molds, and several of the different types of cups were also made in the same molds (cats. 16, 22). Although Donald Harden stated in 1935 that figures 2 and 6 (cats. 1, 4) were blown in the same mold, detailed comparison of all the jugs with the same decoration has not been attempted.[12]

Having all of the known surviving examples on display together at The Metropolitan Museum of Art, however, provided the opportunity for close inspection and comparison. Particular attention was paid to the mold seams on the upper part of the body since

they provide fixed points of reference. On all of the examples, they occur in the same places. Seam 1 runs through the downturned palmette with inward-facing leaves to the left of the *tabula ansata*; seam 2 is located at the rear, diametrically opposite the *tabula*, again splitting a downturned palmette with inward-facing leaves; and seam 3 is to the right of the *tabula*, running through another downturned palmette with inward-facing leaves.[13] Just to the right of seam 2 at the rear on the horizontal ridge above the net pattern, there occurs an anomaly in the form of a slightly raised bump that extends upward. It is visible in five vessels (figs. 4–8 [cats. 1, 2, 4–6]), and it may be taken as a good indication that all of these jugs were blown in the same vertical mold sections. Sadly, the jug from Jerusalem (fig. 9 [cat. 7]) lacks this part of the body, but other details appear to confirm that this jug, too, was made in the same set of molds around the upper body. For example, the inscription and the network pattern, especially its arrangement to either side of the *tabula ansata*, match very closely on all of the jugs, although these details appear to be much crisper and better

fig. 7 Detail of one-handled jug signed by Ennion (see also fig. 13). Translucent cobalt blue with handle and pedestal foot in same color, H. 8⅝ in. (22 cm). Glass pavilion collection, Eretz Israel Museum, Tel Aviv (MHG1200.58). Cat. 5

fig. 8 Detail of one-handled jug signed by Ennion (see also fig. 14). Translucent pale blue green with handle and pedestal foot in same color, H. (including restored foot) 9½ in. (24 cm). Shlomo Moussaieff Collection. Cat. 6

fig. 9 Jug signed by Ennion. Translucent pale green with pedestal foot in same color, H. (including restored foot) 5¾ in. (14.6 cm). Israel Antiquities Authority, on permanent exhibition at The Israel Museum, Jerusalem (1982-1105). Cat. 7

fig. 10 Detail of fig. 13, showing left side of the *tabula ansata*. Cat. 5

defined on the fragmentary Jerusalem example (see also figs. 2, 10 [cats. 1, 5]).[14]

If it is accepted that the same three vertical mold sections were used for all the jugs, the question then has to be asked whether the same bowl-shaped mold in which the lower body was formed was employed for all of them as well. Donald Harden, in stating that the Metropolitan Museum's flat-bottomed jug (fig. 2 [cat. 1]) and the pedestal-footed example now in the Corning Museum of Glass (fig. 6 [cat. 4]) were "blown in the same mould," clearly believed that such was the case.[15] In order to explain the different ways in which the base was finished, he argued that the bowl-shaped mold "must have been open at the base." This seems unlikely, and a more convincing explanation is needed that still allows for the use of the same mold. Harden also later stated, followed by Yael Israeli, that the jug now in the Eretz Israel Museum (fig. 13 [cat. 5]) came "from the same mold" as the jugs in figures 2 and 6 (cats. 1, 4), but he added that they were "finished off differently at the base," since the plain, curving bulb below the bottom register of decoration on the footed jugs is pushed in on the Metropolitan Museum's flat-bottomed jug.[16] It is also worth noting that, whereas the handles on the jugs in figures 2 and 11 (cats. 1, 2) are applied in different ways, those on figures 6, 13, and 14 (cats. 4–6) are remarkably similar—so much so that they were probably formed by the same hand.

It is difficult to identify telltale marks on all the jugs that prove they were all blown in the same set of molds. Nevertheless, it does seem possible to identify one common anomaly: a small projecting bump, which is visible just above one of the vertical flutes formed in the bowl-shaped mold. Remarkably, this feature is more easily seen with the naked eye than captured in a photograph, but it does exist. Furthermore, the anomaly is found in exactly the same position on all the jugs—that is, it is to the left of seam 1 vertically below the right side of the next downturned palmette with outward-facing leaves (figs. 11–14 [cats. 2, 4–6]; see also fig. 2 [cat. 1]). The fact that the anomaly is located in the same position on all of the jugs strongly suggests that the mold sections were locked together in a set order. Although the bump is hard to detect on the fragmentary jug from Jerusalem (see fig. 9 [cat. 7]), other details (as noted above) indicate that this vessel may also have been blown in the same molds.

Little has been said in previous publications about the splayed foot, and one good reason for this reticence is that it has survived on only two of the jugs (figs. 9, 13 [cats. 5, 7]), together with the fragmentary foot of another jug (cat. 8). No mold seams can be detected on these examples, implying that they were made in a mold that had three parts—one for the foot itself and two detachable side elements for the moil (the excess glass between the blowpipe and the foot).[17] The molds used for figures 9 and 13 (cats. 7, 5) appear very similar, but there is one clear difference on the finished jugs, for on the fragmentary jug from the Old City in Jerusalem (fig. 9), there is a solid horizontal ring around the top of the foot where it joins the base of the body. It may be, therefore, that different molds were employed to make the feet, just as different molds were used for the bottom section of some cups (see cat. 15). As pointed out by David Hill, the foot moil played an important role during the making of the jugs, especially during the adding of the handle and the shaping of the rim.[18] The foot in effect served as the punty during the finishing of the vessel; it is not necessary to envisage the use of "some sort of clamp-like tool."[19] However, this does not resolve the question of how the vessels with flat bases (figs. 2, 11 [cats. 1, 2] and cat. 3) were held during the finishing process.

If I am right in claiming that all of the jugs in the exhibition, regardless of whether they had a flat bottom or a pedestal base, were blown in the same molds, then there is good reason for believing that Ennion used only one set for jugs such as those in figures 2, 6, 9, 11, 13 and 14 (cats. 1, 2, 4–7). If he had made several versions of these molds, the chances are remote, at best, that none of the jugs blown in the other molds would have survived. Obviously, he did make another set of four molds, as the two-handled jug from Panticapaeum, in the Crimea (cat. 3), demonstrates, but the design there is more elaborate and the vertical sections of the mold extend from the neck to the base. Only the *tabula ansata* and its inscription remain the same. I would place this type of jug later than the others in his sequence of production.

FURTHER OBSERVATIONS

Finally, some addenda and corrigenda to the exhibition catalogue can now be offered. For the one-handled jug in the Metropolitan's collection, an indent was noted on the upper side of the body (see fig. 4 [cat. 1]), although no attempt was made to explain this feature.[20] In fact, the flattened area was probably caused when the jug was laid on its side in the annealing oven, the floor of which was too hot, making the glass become slightly soft.[21] This explanation, however, raises the question of why it was necessary or desirable to lay the vessel on its side when it presumably already had a finished flat bottom.

In the catalogue it was stated that the two-handled cup from the Shlomo Moussaieff Collection (cat. 14) was blown in a three-part mold.[22] Close inspection of the piece during installation revealed three vertical mold seams, indicating that it was, in fact, blown in a four-part mold. The mold seams run across the rosette near the handle to the right of the Ennion inscription, to the left of the palmette to the left of the Ennion inscription, and along the right edge of the other inscribed panel on the back. Likewise, with regard to the cup found at Vercelli in 1981 (cat. 20), I was unwisely critical of the description provided in its first publication, where it was argued that one of the handles had been malformed or damaged during production.[23] My firsthand observation of the cup showed that there are two raised areas on the side of the vessel where the handle should be. These were not left jagged or smoothed over by grinding, as would be expected if the handle had broken off during use; rather, they appear to be fire-worked, a treatment that can only have been done in the workshop.

11

12

figs. 11–14:
Examples of anomaly
(ringed) to the left of
seam 1

fig. 11 Cat. 2 (see fig. 5)
fig. 12 Cat. 4 (see fig. 6)
fig. 13 Cat. 5 (see fig. 7)
fig. 14 Cat. 6 (see fig. 8)

FUTURE RESEARCH

Many questions about Ennion and his glassware remain unanswered and await further study and future archae-ological discoveries. Nevertheless, the exhibition "Ennion: Master of Roman Glass," in bringing together so many examples of his work, undoubtedly has pro-vided a welcome and unparalleled opportunity to study this enigmatic craftsman and to acknowledge his major contribution to the Roman glass industry. Indeed, this new study of Ennion's workshop has wider implications for our understanding of Roman trade, commerce, and industry.[24] Glass clearly played a role in long-distance trade, and Ennion was at the forefront in creating a market for it by using his name as a label and so devel-oping a recognizable brand. As a result, it may be argued that he was more famous in his own day than he is now.

Did he also play a leading role in the invention of glassblowing? Many years ago Harden espoused the view that mold blowing was the first stage of blowing glass.[25] In 1971 the discovery in Jerusalem of material providing evidence of glassblowing activity as early as the mid-first century B.C. swept away Harden's conten-tion, and it is now generally accepted that free blowing preceded mold blowing.[26] Some reservations have been voiced, notably by David Grose, who saw the introduc-tion of the metal blowpipe as the key element in the creation of a blown-glass industry.[27] Ennion must have used the metal blowpipe, but can it be proved that he did so in imitation of glassworkers making small, free-blown glass bottles?[28] Or was he, perhaps, instrumental in its invention, as well as in the revolutionary use of molds in which to blow glass?

Finally, since Ennion used molds to create multiple examples of the same object, can his surviving works be regarded as art? Does the fact that we have five or, possibly, six jugs all blown in the same set of molds

13

14

detract from their artistic merit? They cannot be regarded as exact replicas of a single prototype but are mass-produced copies, all of equal merit.

The vessels' mass production is not the only reason why Ennion (and much of Roman glassware in general) is not discussed in most books on Roman art. Rather, I would contend that his work is often over-looked because there is no iconography to study; his products are devoid of human, allegorical, or mythologi-cal figures. Was it beyond his skill to carve them on his molds? It certainly was not impossible to do, as is shown by the fragment of a cast or mold-pressed bowl in the exhibition (cat. 42). Or was his choice dictated by other factors? Again, contemporary makers of cameo glass showed no such inhibitions, but in fact very little glass-ware before Ennion's time was decorated with figural scenes. Roman cameo glass led the way in this respect,

and it was inspired not by earlier types of glass but by hardstone carving, which its makers attempted to imitate.[29] Perhaps, then, we should not expect Ennion to have thought of everything, despite his genius, his technical skill, and his entrepreneurship.

CHRISTOPHER S. LIGHTFOOT
Curator, Department of Greek and Roman Art,
The Metropolitan Museum of Art

NOTES

1 The exhibition, held at The Metropolitan Museum of Art between December 9, 2014, and April 13, 2015, was made possible by Diane Carol Brandt, The Vlachos Family Fund, and The David Berg Foundation. I am grateful to the glassmaker David Hill (www.romanglassmakers.co.uk) for many fruitful and instructive discussions via email on the subject of Roman mold blowing.

2 For the vessels signed by Ennion and Aristeas, see Lightfoot 2014, pp. 70–115, nos. 1–28.

3 For discussion of the enigmatic find of a blown perfume bottle at En-Gedi in the Judaean Desert, thought to date before about 40 B.C., see Grose 1977, p. 11, and Stern 1977, p. 31.

4 Israeli 1991, especially pp. 47, 53; Stern 1999, pp. 446–47; Di Pasquale 2004, p. 34; Stern 2004, pp. 82–89; Israeli 2005, pp. 55–56; Antonaras 2012, pp. 22–24; see also the caveat in Price 2012, p. 256.

5 It is far from proven that the Portland Vase and other examples of early Roman cameo glass were blown; *pace* Lightfoot 2014, p. 34, with n. 115 (and references).

6 Grose 1977, p. 9.

7 *Geography* 16.2.25: "ὅπου γε καὶ τρυβλίον χαλκοῦ πρίασθαι καὶ ἐκπωμάτιον ἔστιν." For this and other Roman sources, see Di Pasquale 2004, pp. 34–35.

8 *Epigrams* 1.41.3–4: "Transtiberinus ambulator, qui pallentia sulphurata fractis permutat vitreis." See also Juvenal, *Satires* 5.46; Whitehouse 1999, p. 78; Lightfoot 2007, pp. 18–19.

9 Zrinka Buljević in Lightfoot 2014, pp. 19, 26.

10 Ibid., p. 27.

11 Lightfoot 2014, pp. 66–67, figs. 58, 51, nos. 13a–c.

12 Harden 1935, p. 168.

13 See Wight 2014, p. 53, figs. 41–43.

14 David Hill has explained in an email that good, sharp impressions from the mold resulted when the glassblower blew with sufficient force. In other cases, where the design is less distinct (as on cats. 18, 19), the glass has not been forced into the details of the mold.

15 He thought then that the jugs were made in a tripartite mold; Harden 1935, p. 168 and n. 12. This error was later corrected; see Harden et al. 1987, p. 166, no. 87.

16 Harden 1944–45, pp. 89–90; Israeli 1964, pp. 34–35. It is interesting to note that this blue jug was sold by Dikran Kelekian in New York directly to Dr. Walter Moses, the founder of the Museum Haaretz (personal communication from Nanette Kelekian); Kelekian died in 1951, Moses in 1955. See www.metmuseum.org/exhibitions/listings/2012/buried-finds/dikran-kelekian, and www.eretzmuseum.org.il/e/113/. It should be noted that Kelekian started his business in Istanbul (Constantinople), where the Metropolitan's jug (fig. 2 [cat. 1]) was acquired in the late nineteenth century.

17 For the complete definition of a moil, see Whitehouse 1993, p. 58, s.v. "Overblow"; Ignatiadou and Antonaras 2008, p. 184, s.v. "Moil/Moile" (with helpful illustration).

18 Email from David Hill, January 18, 2015.

19 *Pace* Wight 2014, p. 54.

20 During the installation of the Ennion exhibition at the Corning Museum of Glass in April 2015, it was noticed that one side of the Moussaieff footed jug (fig. 14 [cat. 6]) is also slightly flattened.

21 I am grateful to William Gudenrath for pointing this out to me.

22 The description follows that in Israeli 2011, p. 32.

23 Gabucci and Spagnolo Garzoli 2013, p. 44.

24 Roman shipwrecks containing raw and/or worked glass provide some insight into the nature and size of the trade; see, most recently, Fontaine and Cibecchini 2014.

25 Harden 1969, pp. 46–47.

26 Israeli 1991.

27 Grose 1984, pp. 32–34.

28 It has been argued, however, that the iron blowpipe replaced clay ones only in about A.D. 70; Stern and Schlick-Nolte 1994, pp. 81–82. This date is too late for Ennion's production; see Lightfoot 2014, p. 26.

29 See Roberts, Whitehouse, and Gudenrath 2010, pp. 18–19.

REFERENCES

Antonaras, Anastassios
2012 *Fire and Sand: Ancient Glass in the Princeton University Art Museum*. Princeton: Princeton University Art Museum.

Di Pasquale, Giovanni
2004 "Scientific and Technological Use of Glass in Graeco-Roman Antiquity." In *When Glass Matters: Studies in the History of Science and Art from Graeco-Roman Antiquity to Early Modern Era*, edited by Marco Beretta, pp. 31–76. Florence: Leo S. Olschki.

Fontaine, Souen, and Franca Cibecchini
2014 "An Exceptional Example of Maritime Glass Trade: The Deep Wreck *Cap Corse 2* (France, Corsica)." *Journal of Glass Studies* 56, pp. 354–57.

Gabucci, Ada, and Giuseppina Spagnolo Garzoli
2013 "Vetri bollati dal Piemonte romano (Transpadana occidentale e Liguria interna)." In *Per un corpus dei bolli su vetro in Italia: XIV Giornate Nazionali di Studio sul Vetro, Trento, 16–17 ottobre 2010*, edited by Maria Grazia Diani and Luciana Mandruzzato, pp. 43–58. Venice: Comitato Nazionale Italiano dell'Association Internationale pour l'Histoire du Verre.

Grose, David F.
1977 "Early Blown Glass: The Western Evidence." *Journal of Glass Studies* 19, pp. 9–29.
1984 "Glass Forming Methods in Classical Antiquity: Some Considerations." *Journal of Glass Studies* 26, pp. 25–34.

Harden, Donald B.
1935 "Romano-Syrian Glasses with Mould-Blown Inscriptions." *Journal of Roman Studies* 25, pp. 163–86.
1944–45 "Two Tomb-Groups of the First Century A.D. from Yahmour, Syria, and a Supplement to the List of Romano-Syrian Glasses with Mould-Blown Inscriptions." *Syria* 24, nos. 1–2, pp. 81–95, and nos. 3–4, pp. 291–92 (postscript).
1969 "Ancient Glass II: Roman." *Archaeological Journal* 126 (pub. 1970), pp. 44–77.

Harden, Donald B., Hansgerd Hellenkemper, Kenneth Painter, and David Whitehouse
1987 *Glass of the Caesars*. Exh. cat., Corning Museum of Glass, Corning, N.Y.; British Museum, London; Römisch-Germanisches Museum, Cologne. Milan: Olivetti.

Ignatiadou, Despina, and Anastassios Antonaras
2008 *Yalourgia, archaia kai mesaiōnikē: Orologia, technologia kai typologia / Glassworking, Ancient and Medieval: Terminology, Technology, and Typology; a Greek-English, English-Greek Dictionary*. Translated by Deborah Brown Kazazis. Thessaloniki: Kentro Hellēnikēs Glōssas, Tmema Lexikographias.

Israeli, Yael
1964 "Sidonian Mold-Blown Glass Vessels in the Museum Haaretz." *Journal of Glass Studies* 6, pp. 34–41.
1991 "The Invention of Blowing." In *Roman Glass: Two Centuries of Art and Invention*, edited by Martine Newby and Kenneth S. Painter, pp. 46–55. Occasional Paper (Society of Antiquaries of London), n.s., 13. London: Society of Antiquaries of London.
2005 "What Did Jerusalem's First-Century BCE Glass Workshop Produce?" In *Annales du 16ᵉ Congrès de l'Association Internationale pour l'Histoire du Verre*, pp. 54–57. Nottingham: AIHV.
2011 *Mi-sadnato shel Enyon/Made by Ennion*. Exh. cat. Jerusalem: Israel Museum.

Lightfoot, Christopher S.
2007 *Ancient Glass in National Museums Scotland*. Edinburgh: National Museums Scotland.
2014 *Ennion: Master of Roman Glass*. Contributions by Zrinka Buljević, Yael Israeli, Karol B. Wight, and Mark T. Wypyski. Exh. cat. New York: MMA.

Price, Jennifer
2012 "Urban and Maritime Glass Assemblages in the Western and Eastern Mediterranean." *Antiquity* 86 (March), pp. 254–57.

Roberts, Paul, David Whitehouse, and William Gudenrath
2010 "British Museum Cameo Glass in Context." In Paul Roberts, William Gudenrath, Veronica Tatton-Brown, and David Whitehouse, *Roman Cameo Glass in the British Museum*, pp. 9–23. London: British Museum Press.

Stern, E. Marianne
1977 *Ancient Glass at the Fondation Custodia (Collection Frits Lugt), Paris*. Archaeologica Traiectina 12. Groningen: Wolters-Noordhoff.
1999 "Roman Glassblowing in a Cultural Context." *American Journal of Archaeology* 103 (July), pp. 441–84.
2004 "The Glass *Banausoi* of Sidon and Rome." In *When Glass Matters: Studies in the History of Science and Art from Graeco-Roman Antiquity to Early Modern Era*, edited by Marco Beretta, pp. 77–120. Florence: Leo S. Olschki.

Stern, E. Marianne, and Birgit Schlick-Nolte
1994 *Early Glass of the Ancient World, 1600 B.C.–A.D. 50: Ernesto Wolf Collection*. Ostfildern: Verlag Gerd Hatje.

Whitehouse, David
1993 *Glass: A Pocket Dictionary of Terms Commonly Used to Describe Glass and Glassmaking*. Corning, N.Y.: Corning Museum of Glass.
1999 "Glass in the Epigrams of Martial." *Journal of Glass Studies* 41, pp. 73–81.

Wight, Karol B.
2014 "The Mold-Blowing Process." In Lightfoot 2014, pp. 49–55.

MIKI MORITA

The Kizil Paintings in the Metropolitan Museum

Among the many intriguing, less well-known holdings of The Metropolitan Museum of Art is a group of small mural painting fragments from the ruins of Buddhist cave complexes in the areas of Kucha, Khotan, and Turfan, in northwestern China. These sites, scattered in a deserted area in the Xinjiang Uyghur Autonomous Region, played essential roles in the transmission of Buddhism from India to East Asia. Among them, Kizil is noted for its size and its abundant, flamboyant murals, which provide rare visual information about the culture of the Kucha Kingdom, a renowned Buddhist center from the third through the seventh century. The Metropolitan Museum's collection of Kizil mural fragments consists of twelve pieces depicting various Buddhist figures in styles associated with particular caves or groups of caves. These and many other Kizil mural fragments now in collections in the United States were once part of a German collection

fig. 1 View of Kizil

that was amassed during expeditions to the site in the early twentieth century. Determining the original locations of the fragments is essential for ascertaining the function of the site and understanding the religious practices of the Kucha Kingdom. This essay attempts to identify the caves in which the Metropolitan Museum's Kizil mural fragments originated.

The Kizil caves served as Buddhist temples and as domiciles for monks (fig. 1). The complex comprises more than two hundred caves carved into the sandstone cliffs along the Muzart River, about forty-three miles west of present-day Kucha.[1] The earliest known direct reference to a kingdom called Kucha appears in *Han shu* (History of the Han), a history of the Western Han Dynasty (202 B.C.–A.D. 8) in China written in the first century A.D.[2] It is not certain when Buddhism was transmitted to Kucha, but we know from primary Chinese sources that Buddhist monks were active in the Kucha Kingdom in the middle of the fourth century, and that by the seventh century, Buddhism was the predominant religion there.[3]

Centuries later, the cave temples were abandoned, and their artistic contents fell into oblivion. Beginning in the late nineteenth century, a series of expeditions set out from Europe, Russia, and Japan to study Central Eurasia, a region then virtually unknown. In the Xinjiang Uyghur Autonomous Region, these undertakings resulted in the discovery of many deserted cultural sites known only through local legends.[4] Among these sites, the Kizil caves were investigated most thoroughly by German expedition teams.

Four German expeditions led by Albert Grünwedel (1856–1935) and Albert von Le Coq (1860–1930) explored Central Asia between 1902 and 1914.[5] The teams documented the sites and sent home many examples of the paintings and statues they found there, thus endowing

Germany with the largest collection of Kizil art outside China. A majority of the mural fragments carried off by the German expeditions initially went to the Museum für Völkerkunde (Museum of Ethnology), Berlin. Then, in the 1920s, a portion of these works was sold off to finance the museum's publishing projects.[6] Some of the Kizil fragments eventually made their way into private collections and museums in the United States, including the Smithsonian Institution and The Metropolitan Museum of Art.[7]

Most of the Metropolitan Museum's pieces were purchased in the 1940s and 1950s from dealers and private collectors. Although acquired from diverse sources, the Museum's fragments show evidence of having been removed from Kizil as a group. Inscriptions on the back of each piece identify which of the four expeditions removed the work, the general area on the Kizil site where it was found, and the location of the specific cave from which it was taken. Some of the fragments carry additional information, such as the number of the container in which they were placed. One bears a French customs stamp; another, the name of Le Coq (see fig. 17b).[8] The inscriptions reveal that most of the Museum's fragments were removed from the caves during the fourth expedition, which was led by Le Coq from June 1913 to February 1914.

In 1928, Alan Priest, curator of Far Asian Art at the Metropolitan Museum, submitted a proposal to purchase ten seventh-century Buddhist paintings from Turfan, a site about 420 miles northeast of Kizil. The proposal, which was not acted upon, stated that the works were brought to the market by Le Coq through the Chinese art dealer Edgar Worch (1880–1972).[9] While this information relates to fragments from Turfan, it resonates with the partial sale of the German collection in the 1920s and helps to explain the works' early dispersal abroad.[10]

DATING THE KIZIL MURAL PAINTINGS

Lack of historical documentation makes dating the wall paintings one of the most difficult challenges in studying the Kizil caves. Following are representative opinions concerning when the works were created. There is still no consensus on the matter.

Grünwedel's early division of the paintings into stylistic groups was adopted with modifications by Ernst Waldschmidt, who factored into his classifications paleographic studies of Brāhmī script and identifications of Kuchean royals' names from inscriptions and manuscripts discovered in the Kizil caves.[11] Waldschmidt

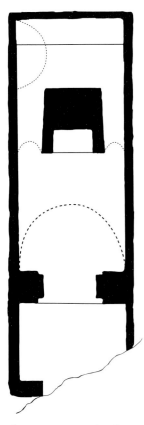

fig. 2 Interior Plan of Kizil Cave 224

proposed a three-stage stylistic evolution incorporating elements of Indian, Iranian, and Chinese art. The earliest style, which Waldschmidt called Indo-Iranian style I, flourished from about A.D. 500 to 550. Displaying characteristics of Gandharan art, it features warm colors, such as orange and yellow, and flexible handling of line and detail, resulting in natural-seeming depictions of the human figure. The second style, Indo-Iranian style II, from the seventh century, is regarded as the locally mature phase of the preceding style. The palette is predominantly cool. Blue, derived from lapis lazuli, and green appear frequently. Sharp chromatic contrasts are favored, as is a stiffer, more linear treatment of the human form. The third style is heavily influenced by Chinese painting, which is thought to have been transmitted to the area when the Tang dynasty (A.D. 618-907) extended its influence between the eighth and ninth centuries, during the late period of Kuchean Buddhist art.[12]

While much earlier dates, based on comparative materials from the Northern Liang (A.D. 397-439) and Northern Wei (A.D. 386-534) periods, were subsequently proposed, Waldschmidt's dating was generally accepted until new scientific, archaeological, and art-historical methodologies were adopted about 1980.[13] A Beijing University project led by Su Bai from 1979 to 1981 classified the Kizil caves according to their interior plans and the styles and themes of their mural paintings, and it employed radiocarbon dating to estimate the caves' age.[14] The caves examined in the Beijing study were classified into three approximate time periods: 310±80-350±60, 395±65-465±65 to the early sixth century, and 545±75-685±65 and later.[15] Since the completion of the Beijing study, radiocarbon dating has become a primary tool in the study of the Kizil caves and has been used by research teams from China, Japan, and Germany to examine more than one hundred Kizil samples.[16] Nevertheless, there is still no consensus on the dating of the Kizil caves: the results of a radiocarbon test conducted in 2011 places the origins of one of the cave murals in the first century B.C., earlier than many scholars think plausible.[17]

In recent years, Giuseppe Vignato has studied a subset of the Kizil caves: those with core units that were added to in later periods. Vignato designated two main types of cave groups: one with a central pillar cave, the other without. He then divided the caves into four time periods, proposing A.D. 550 to 750 as the fourth and latest period and assigning to it about half of the caves.[18] This late period witnessed the intense development of the cave groups containing central pillar caves.[19]

Hiyama Satomi notes that the stylistic features of Cave 224 are similar to those of Cave 205, a central pillar cave containing an inscription referring to a Kuchean noble who lived at the end of the sixth century.[20] In light of the findings outlined above, it is tempting to speculate that several of the Museum's pieces, which, as it will be shown, possibly originated in Cave 224 or in other caves with central pillars, were painted in the sixth or seventh century. However, this dating is provisional, subject to future archaeological and art-historical developments in the study of the Kucha Kingdom.[21]

THE STRUCTURE OF THE KIZIL CAVES

While the caves have lost most of their sculpture, about a third of them are decorated with murals.[22] Among those that are not, some have lost their paintings to natural decay or vandalism, but many were never decorated in the first place. Some of the caves' principal uses can be inferred from their designs.[23] Monks' residences, which were not decorated, usually consisted of a main room with a fireplace and a window.[24] Some had an additional, small room carved out behind the back wall of the hallway.

Caves with a single square chamber also may have been used for communal religious activities such as lectures on Buddhist scriptures.[25] Some square caves were furnished with altars and decorated with statues and murals, the latter done mainly in the first pictorial style.[26]

Central pillar caves (fig. 2), which have a large, square pillar in the middle of the main chamber, were used for liturgical purposes. Designed as spaces for prayer, their interiors share common iconography and pictorial programs. The front side of the pillar usually contained a large niche for a statue that would have functioned in dialogue with a mural to represent the Buddha preaching in Indra's cave, a common theme in Gandharan art also. The side walls were often covered with preaching scenes, and a large part of the ceiling displayed episodes from *jātaka* (tales of the Buddha's previous lives) and more scenes of the Buddha preaching, each individually framed within a border. The back wall, decorated with a scene of *nirvāṇa*, featured a painted or sculpted image of the recumbent Buddha.[27] The side corridors and entrance wall of the cave were also painted.[28] A variant of the central pillar cave, known as the "monumental image cave," was distinguished by the presence of a large statue of the Buddha standing in front of the central pillar. In some monumental image caves, the statue was probably carved directly into the wall of the cliff, with a wide area around the statue's legs hollowed out to create the space at the back of the chamber.[29]

All of the caves considered here as possible original locations for the Metropolitan Museum's Kizil paintings are of the central pillar type.[30] The caves' similar interior plans and their murals' shared figurative elements and thematic content allow for typological categorization and cross-referencing in identifying the paintings' themes.

IDENTIFICATION OF THE ORIGINAL LOCATIONS

In the following discussion, eight relatively well-preserved Kizil fragments (three of which are treated as a group) in the Metropolitan Museum's collection are introduced and their original locations proposed. In cases where there is sufficient evidence, the fragments' possible themes are investigated. It should be noted that some of the pieces have probably undergone partial restoration, resulting in minor alterations in their appearance. These modifications are not so significant as to affect the research presented here.[31]

Monk Holding a Lotus

The most complete fragment in the Metropolitan Museum's Kizil collection represents a standing monk holding a lotus flower (fig. 3). Seen against a light blue backdrop, the figure has its head turned slightly to the left; the round face is rendered in three-quarter view, and light orange shading applied over the pale beige tone of the skin gives an impression of volume. The arms are bent and the left hand is clasped. The open right hand with palm facing outward delicately holds the stem of a lotus flower between thumb and index finger. The flowing brown robe both conceals and reveals the monk's elongated frame: the graceful folds of drapery falling across the torso and the gentle outward curve of the right hip indicate a contrapposto stance.

According to an inscription on the reverse, *Monk Holding a Lotus* was taken from the *Tür-wand* (door wall) of the *Figuren Höhle* (Figures Cave), also known in the early German nomenclature as the *Höhle der Statuen* (Cave of the Statues) and in current scholarship as Cave 77.[32] Yet Grünwedel makes no mention of this figure in his description of Cave 77.[33] Moreover, comparison of the fragment with the surviving murals in Cave 77 makes it clear that the monk on a blue background does not correspond to the images remaining in situ, where brown and other warm colors predominate.

However, a perfect match for the Metropolitan Museum's monk is seen in the image of standing

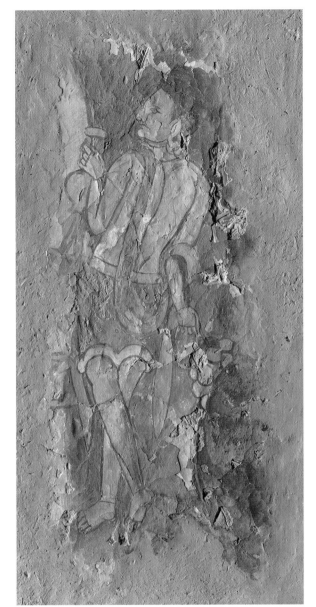

monks on a mural fragment titled *Monks and Stupas* (fig. 4), now in Berlin. The Berlin piece was formerly thought to have originated in Cave 7 (also known as the *Höhle mit dem Frescofussboden* [Cave with the Frescoed Floor]).[34] Among the shared elements of the two works are their light blue backdrops and floral motifs, the figures' height, the angle of the faces, the clasped left hands and contrapposto poses, long-sleeved brown undergarments, robes patterned with U-shaped folds, and the bright green delineation of the compositions' bottom edges.[35]

There can be no doubt that *Monk Holding a Lotus* was once part of the procession of monks on the Berlin fragment. It is now known that the assignment of *Monks and Stupas* to Cave 7 was a mistake: photographs from the German expedition show this frag-

ment in situ in Cave 13.[36] Therefore it is likely that *Monk Holding a Lotus*, too, is from Cave 13.[37]

Monk Holding a Lotus and *Monks and Stupas* probably depict donor figures in procession. Murals showing similar processions of monks survive in several Kizil caves, where they are painted on the walls flanking the central pillars.[38]

Attendant

Attendant (fig. 5) is a small fragment depicting a standing male figure from behind. The head is turned to show the face in left profile, the hair is knotted on top of the head, and a large circular earring is worn in the left ear. The contours of the upper body are defined by gently curving black lines, whereas the legs are stiff, as

fig. 8 *Warrior*. China (Xinjiang Uyghur Autonomous Region), Kizil, ca. 6th–7th century. Pigments on mud plaster, 9¼ × 5⅜ in. (23.5 × 13.7 cm). Inscribed on reverse: *IV Reise Qieszil. Gr. Anl. / Blaue Höhle / g. No. 2*. The Metropolitan Museum of Art, Fletcher Fund, 1951 (51.94.1)

indicated by their nearly straight lines. The figure wears a long green scarf and a sarong-like garment that wraps around the waist and is gathered between the legs. The left hand holds a long-necked flask, and the right holds a string attached to a cluster of spherical objects. The attendant gazes toward a figure whose presence is suggested by the edges of a white mandorla and a throne. At the lower right, a dark blue shape partly overlaps the cluster of spherical objects below the attendant's right hand. Green and blue, colors associated with the second style of Kizil mural paintings, predominate.

Penciled notations on the back of the work indicate that it is from the *Blaue Höhle* (Blue Cave), also called *Höhle mit dem Musikerchor* (Cave with the Choir), today referred to as Cave 38. A photograph from the German expeditions showing the arched ceiling of Cave 38 (fig. 6) enables us to trace the original location of *Attendant* to what is now a small rectangular section of the ceiling's mud wall (fig. 7). The image reveals that the dark shape partly covering the spherical objects in the fragment perfectly corresponds to the upper left side of the lozenge-shaped border seen immediately below the attendant in the mural. What is more, Grünwedel's detailed description of Cave 38 mentions the presence, near a Buddha looking to his

left, of a standing male figure seen from the back. This figure is said to be wearing a loincloth and holding a bottle in his left hand.[39] These archival records leave no doubt that *Attendant* was originally located on the ceiling of Cave 38.

The figure in this fragment most likely represents a character in the Buddha's sermon scenes, which were frequently depicted on the ceilings of the Kizil caves.[40] Each scene, framed by a lozenge-shaped border, had a seated Buddha figure at the center and smaller figures alongside, and each scene was associated with a particular tale. The rich variety of the narratives makes it difficult to determine which stories are represented in these small segments. So far, the Metropolitan's *Attendant* has not been identified with specific tale. Painted images of a partially clothed figure with a topknot and bottle are present in other Kizil caves also; the figure is often associated with non-Buddhist mendicants, especially with Brahmanical ascetics.[41]

The round objects trailing from the attendant's right hand are possibly flowers.[42] Attendant figures in Kizil cave paintings are often represented offering flowers to Buddha. For example, on the outer wall of a corridor in Cave 163, the attendant of a large standing Buddha holds a similar "bouquet."[43] That attendant, too, is scantily clad, his torso covered only by a tightly tied sash and a narrow scarf that hangs loosely from his shoulders. In his proper right hand, raised to revere the Buddha, he holds multiple circular objects attached to straight, stem-like lines like the ones seen in *Attendant*. Although his other hand is empty, the main elements of his pose—face in profile and back to the viewer—resemble those of the Metropolitan Museum's *Attendant*. These figures possibly represent the same character, but additional comparative materials are needed to identify the narrative with which he is associated.[44]

Warrior

The mustached *Warrior* (fig. 8) holds a small black banner trimmed with white triangles and attached to a pole. Horizontally striped armor covers the figure's torso, arms, and legs, and the curved, trapezoidal helmet is topped with a semicircular black ornament. The warrior sits cross-legged on a chair and turns diagonally to the left, toward a figure suggested by the edge of a large mandorla. A cone-shaped form similar to the ones in the border surrounding *Attendant*'s scene (see fig. 6) is present on the lower right.

The inscription *Blaue Höhle* (Blue Cave), penciled on the reverse, is the same as that found on the back

fig. 9 Two Bodhisattvas. China (Xinjiang Uyghur Autonomous Region), Kizil, ca. 6th–7th century. Pigments on mud plaster, 16⅜ × 9¾ in. (41.6 × 24.8 cm). Inscribed on reverse: *IV. Reise. Qieszil / gr. Anlg. / 3 Höhle in d* [?]. The Metropolitan Museum of Art, Fletcher Fund, 1951 (51.94.5)

fig. 10 Archival photograph of preaching scene in Cave 175, with tops of parasols outlined in red. China (Xinjiang Uyghur Autonomous Region). Museen zu Berlin, Museum für Asiatische Kunst (MIK B 544)

fig. 11 Preaching scene from Cave 178, with tops of parasols outlined in red. China (Xinjiang Uyghur Autonomous Region), Kizil. Pigments on mud plaster, 28⅜ × 36¼ in. (72 × 92 cm). Staatliche Museen zu Berlin, Museum für Asiatische Kunst (detail of MIK III 8725 a,b)

of *Attendant*, indicating that *Warrior*, too, is from Cave 38.[45] The painting's predominantly green and blue colors match the color scheme of that cave, and it is clear from the figure's position between the large mandorla and the conical form on the lower right that the fragment was taken from a lozenge-shaped segment on the ceiling. The rectangular patch of mud immediately to the left of the spot once occupied by *Attendant* is most likely the original location of this fragment, since *Warrior*'s bright green background and the beige conical form slot perfectly into this position. The white and blue concentric arcs on the warrior's proper right complete the mandorla of the Buddha figure still found in this lozenge-shape segment on the south side of the ceiling in Cave 38. Grünwedel's record supports the argument that this was indeed the *Warrior*'s original location. It describes the figure in this particular rhomboid as "Buddha, meditating and seated, left, an armored knight."[46]

Like *Attendant*, *Warrior* is associated with one of the tales of the preaching Buddha. While unidentified, the narrative was probably referenced repeatedly in the ceiling paintings of Kizil, as a similar armored figure with a flag is found in Cave 192 and elsewhere on the site.[47]

Two Bodhisattvas

A fragment with beautiful contrasts of bright blue, white, and orange (fig. 9) shows two bodhisattvas facing diagonally to the right, their arms raised above their shoulders and their hands closed in a grip. A horizontal bar decorated with zigzag patterns is seen above the hands of each figure, and on the right, a shorter length of the same type of bar is depicted above a segment of a large halo. The upper and lower edges of the bars are lined with dotted bands, and below the bars are areas of solid white. Beneath her blue and white halo, the upper bodhisattva wears a headdress decorated with a triangular ornament at the center and blue and white ribbons attached at the sides; the headdress of the lower figure is adorned with three disks outlined in blue.

The penciled inscription on the back of the fragment is partly illegible. The decipherable portion reads: *IV. Reise. Qieszil gr. Anlg. 3 Höhle in d*[. . .] (4th trip, Kizil, largest segment, 3rd cave in the [. . .]). This information suggests that the piece possibly came from a cave with the word *third* in its title or from one that was designated as the third cave in a certain section of Kizil. While the word "third" occurs in the German titles of two Kizil caves (*Drittletzte Höhle* for Cave 184, and *Dritte Höhle von vorn* for Cave 188), the paintings on the walls of those caves do not share the *Two Bodhisattvas*'s most salient features: strong contrasts of bright blue and white, the three distinctive disks on the headdress of the lower figure, and the figures' round, stylized faces. However, an archival photograph of the preaching scene from Cave 175 (fig. 10) as well as the remnants of that mural in situ show a marked resemblance to the Metropolitan Museum's fragment, as do the painted figures in Cave 178 (fig. 11).[48] Moreover, as the following section will make clear, the same patterns that appear on the "bars" in *Two Bodhisattvas* also decorate the "bars" represented in the murals of Caves 175 and 178. These two caves are considered part of a group of caves that share geographic proximity as well as stylistic and architectural similarities.[49] Judging from the close formal and stylistic relationship of the murals in Caves 175 and 178 to the Metropolitan Museum's fragment, either of these two caves, or one of several others nearby, could be the original location of *Two Bodhisattvas*.[50]

The pose of the figures in *Two Bodhisattvas* recurs in several other Kizil cave paintings, where it is held by parasol bearers. Such is the case in the murals found in Caves 175 and 178, where bars decorated with zigzag patterns are seen between two seated Buddha figures. Directly in front of and at the left end of each bar, a figure holds both hands at shoulder height, like the

figures in the Metropolitan Museum's fragment. In the murals in Caves 175 and 178, it is possible to discern that each bar is surmounted by a low, dome-shaped top (see figs. 10, 11). These tops reveal that the "bars" are in fact parasol rims, and that the white areas below them are the parasols' undersides. In light of this, there can be little doubt that the Metropolitan Museum's bodhisattvas, whose gestures and overhead "bars" are nearly identical to those of the comparison figures, also hold parasols, albeit with poles merely hinted at by the positions of the figures' hands.

It is probable that the Metropolitan's parasol bearers illustrate a different narrative from the one referenced by their counterparts in Caves 175 and 178. The murals in those two locations show beneath each parasol a pair of seated figures with elaborate headdresses and halos. In addition, the mural in Cave 175 features a three-headed male figure standing behind the Buddha on the left, who also has a prostrate monk at his feet. These remarkable figures have been identified with a protagonist in the story of the conversion of King Bimbisāra of Magadha during the lifetime of the Buddha.[51] Based on the similarity of the crowned, seated figures in Caves 175 and 178, it is likely that the parasol bearers in these scenes are the attendants of high-ranking individuals such as the king.

Unlike the parasol bearers portrayed in Caves 175 and 178, both figures in *Two Bodhisattvas* have halos and wear headdresses. The absence of additional figures beneath their parasols indicates that the parasols do not

fig. 12 Mural depicting the
Buddha surrounded by parasol
bearers. China (Xinjiang
Uyghur Autonomous Region),
Kizil, Cave 189.

function to shelter high-ranking individuals. Part of a third parasol is visible on the right, directly above the segment of a very large halo designating the presence of a figure of great importance—undoubtedly a Buddha. The lack of aristocratic figures and the implied presence of a central figure, now missing, surrounded by attendants suggest that this fragment was once part of a mural depicting the offering of parasols to the Buddha.

A related composition is found in the remnants of a mural surviving in situ in Cave 189 (fig. 12). The scene features a large standing Buddha surrounded by haloed attendants holding parasols. Although the theme has not yet been identified conclusively, certain scholars believe that it alludes to the twin miracles performed by the Buddha when he overwhelmed the non-Buddhist heretics in Śrāvastī.[52] In Cave 189, the miracles are represented in depictions of the Buddha levitating as flames burst from his shoulders and water gushes under his feet. More recently, the mural has been interpreted as representing the Buddha crossing the Ganges River to save victims of epidemics in the state of Vaiśālī.[53] The story tells of the sky filling with thousands of parasols offered to the Buddha by King Bimbisāra, the people of Vaiśālī, *nāgas* (snake deities), and other spirits and deities. Although the central figure

in *Two Bodhisattvas* is missing, the compositional similarity of this fragment to the wall painting in Cave 189 suggests that the two works might share as their theme one of these narratives from the life of Śākyamuni Buddha.

Seated Bodhisattva

Seated Bodhisattva (fig. 13) is a fragment depicting a Buddhist figure seated with crossed legs. The figure's face, portrayed in three-quarter view to left, is tilted slightly upward. The hair is tied in a topknot. Encircling the head is a band decorated with grid patterns and knots on each side. At its center, a large triangular ornament is embellished near the top by a spherical element, perhaps a flower. The ornaments on the headdress match the figure's earrings and choker. The features of the face, with its arched eyebrows and piercing gaze, are accented with reddish brown lines that follow the dark contours but do not convey a sense of three-dimensionality. The figure's dark brown robe is draped over one shoulder, leaving the other exposed. The border of what is possibly an undergarment appears as a bright green diagonal across the figure's upper torso; reddish brown necklaces and bracelets adorn the chest and wrists. The halo, composed of concentric circles of dark blue and brown, identifies the figure as a bodhisattva.

The style of *Seated Bodhisattva* and the inscription on its reverse closely match those of at least six other fragments in collections in the United States, Germany, and Japan.[54] Common to all of the images are their color schemes, the figures' piercing gaze and arched eyebrows,

fig. 13 Seated Bodhisattva.
China (Xinjiang Uyghur
Autonomous Region), Kizil,
ca. 6th–7th century. Pigments
on mud plaster, 19⅜ × 11½ in.
(49.2 × 29.2 cm). Inscribed on
reverse: M.Ö.Q. gr. Anlag. /
II Schlucht. II Höhle / in d. Ecke
gefunden. The Metropolitan
Museum of Art, From the
Collection of A. W. Bahr,
Purchase, Fletcher Fund, 1947
(47.18.27)

fig. 14 Fragment of a mural
painting. China (Xinjiang Uyghur
Autonomous Region), Kizil,
ca. 6th–7th century. Pigments
on mud plaster, 9½ × 9 in.
(24.1 × 22.9 cm). The University
of Pennsylvania Museum of
Archaeology and Anthropology,
Purchase from A. W. Bahr, 1924
(C413A)

fig. 15 *Bodhisattva* in Cave 176. China (Xinjiang Uyghur Autonomous Region)

the rendering of the hair with thick, bold lines, and the design of the figures' accessories (fig. 14). The inscriptions on all of these fragments read in part: *gr. Anlag[e], II Schlucht, II Höhle in d. Ecke gefunden* (largest section, second gorge, second cave, found in the corner).[55] A label attached to the fragment in the Museum für Asiatische Kunst (Museum of Asian Art) in Berlin identifies the cave mentioned in the inscription as Cave 179.[56] For this reason, the fragments in this group are generally considered to have originated in Cave 179.[57]

Fortunately, Cave 179 still retains some of its original mural paintings.[58] A comparison of these in situ murals

with the group of related fragments reveals a general correspondence of stylistic features but disparities in the details. For example, the necklaces worn by several large figures in Cave 179 are decorated with small white dots, which clearly differ from the squarish elements adorning the chokers and headdresses depicted on the fragments. More closely akin to the fragments in both its general characteristics and its details is the figure of a standing bodhisattva (fig. 15) in Cave 176, located near Cave 179. Not only does the figure's facial expression recall the Metropolitan's *Seated Bodhisattva*, but so do his earrings, rimmed with curved, petal-like forms. The sinuous trailing end of the hair tie and the spherical ornament attached to it are like those seen in *Seated Bodhisattva*, and the design of the standing bodhisattva's choker matches the design of the chokers worn by all of the figures in this group. Such similarities necessitate a reconsideration of the fragments' assignment to Cave 179, and they suggest Cave 176 as another possibility for the fragments' place of origin.[59]

The iconography of *Seated Bodhisattva* is so general that it is impossible at this time to link the image to a specific narrative. Judging from the small size and the generic quality of all of the figures in this group of fragments, they probably represent attendants of larger, more significant figures.

Cave 224 fragments

Three Celestial Attendants (fig. 16), *Three Bodhisattvas* (figs. 17a,b), and *Buddha with Two Disciples* (fig. 18) are a stylistically related set of mural fragments in the Metropolitan Museum's collection. Each image contains three figures and is beautifully colored bright blue and green. Although their inscriptions differ, these

fig. 16 *Three Celestial Attendants.* China (Xinjiang Uyghur Autonomous Region), Kizil, ca. 6th–7th century. Pigments on mud plaster, 8¾ × 15¾ in. (22.2 × 40 cm). Inscribed on back: *M [?] Q. [or A.?] / gr. Höhle Vorhalle / loin gr. [. . .] / [. . .] 71.* The Metropolitan Museum of Art, Fletcher Fund, 1951 (51.94.4)

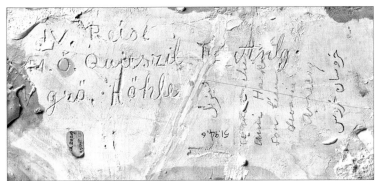

fig. 17a Three Bodhisattvas. China (Xinjiang Uyghur Autonomous Region), Kizil, 6th–7th century. Pigments on mud plaster, 9½ × 15⅜ in. (24.1 × 39.1 cm). Inscribed on reverse (see fig. 17b). The Metropolitan Museum of Art, Fletcher Fund, 1951 (51.94.6)

fig. 17b Inscription on reverse of fragment shown in fig. 17a: *IV. Reise / M. Ô. Quitszil [III?] Anlg. / grö. Höhle*. At right, sideways, in pencil: *A mon cher ami Hack* [?] *son bien* [?] *devoué* [?] *A. LeCoq* and undeciphered words in Arabic script transliterated as *Khurusaan Khurus füzibal* [*füzi'l*]

fig. 18 Buddha with Two Disciples. China (Xinjiang Uyghur Autonomous Region), Kizil, 6th–7th century. Pigments on mud plaster, 9⅛ × 10½ in. (23.2 × 26.7 cm). Inscribed on back: *II Hohle, II Anl. Kyzil*. The Metropolitan Museum of Art, Purchase, Fletcher Fund, 1951 (51.94.7)

three fragments possibly originated in the same cave and therefore will be discussed together.

The heads depicted in *Three Celestial Attendants* have similar features: the faces are oval, with long, narrow noses, half-open eyes squared off at the inner corners, and small mouths with full lower lips. While all are presented in three-quarter view, the heads differ in color, hairstyle, and ornamentation. The figure on the right has gray skin with darker gradations and white highlighting; its blue headband is decorated with white dots and a large brown disk, also dotted with white. The other two figures gently tilt their heads and look away from one another. The head at the center is dark beige with light brown shading and white highlights. It wears white-dotted headbands of brown and blue and, attached to its headdress, a white flower and spherical ornaments of green and dark brown. The figure on the left looks diagonally to the left. Its skin is light beige with orange shading and white highlighting. Above its wavy hairline are white-dotted headbands of brown and blue surmounted by blue spherical ornaments decorated with small, four-pointed stars in reddish brown and possibly beige, and by a white flower with a green center.

The heads' halos are composed of concentric rings of white, green, blue, and dark brown. The spaces between the halos were originally filled with floral motifs, two of which are still visible below the composition's upper border. The flowers' gray, curled petals surround a reddish brown center ringed with white, and from each bloom three filaments rise, supporting anthers. A solid white border edged with blue runs along the top of the fragment.

The figures on the left and at the center of *Three Bodhisattvas* closely resemble their counterparts in *Three Celestial Attendants*. The figure on the right, seen in profile, looks to its proper left. Its face is painted in the same manner as the other two in the composition, and its headdress consists of dotted bands adorned with a white flower of the type worn by the figure on the left in *Three Celestial Attendants*. The background of this fragment was originally decorated with floral motifs, as can be inferred from a single anther visible between the halos of the figures at left and center; as in *Three Celestial Attendants*, the white border at the top is edged with blue.

Buddha with Two Disciples features three male figures without halos. The skin of the central figure is painted white with orange shading; the face, turned toward the left, is shown in three-quarter view. The index finger of the right hand, raised to the chest, points to the figure itself. The folded fingers of the heavily damaged left hand can just be seen beside the right hand. The figure wears a bright green robe and appears to converse with the bearded, blue-robed figure on its proper right. Their conversation is closely attended by the figure shown in profile on the right. The skin of this figure is painted gray-beige, with tattoo-like markings visible under the eye and on the cheek. A pair of hands placed together in front of the figure belongs to a different figure, now missing. The bearded figure has rounded eyes, thick eyebrows, and prominently exposed collarbones, features that set him apart from his companions. The background is bright blue, and a green belt with white dots hangs down from above.

These three fragments are thought to have originated in Cave 224 by reason of an inscription on the reverse of *Three Bodhisattvas* (fig. 17b) and also owing to the fragments' stylistic similarity to mural paintings still found in that cave. The inscription reads in part [*III?*] *Anlg. grö. Höhle* ([third] district largest cave). While the *III* preceding *Anlg.* is abraded, Aki Ueno notes that the inscription refers to the "3rd district," a crucial piece of information that would link the fragment to Cave 224.[60] Other Kizil mural fragments in collections outside Germany bear the same inscription, and, thanks to Grünwedel's detailed records, the original locations of some of these pieces have been more or less pinpointed in Cave 224.[61] However, *Three Bodhisattvas*'s probable spot of origin has not yet been found.[62]

The inscriptions on *Three Celestial Attendants* and *Buddha with Two Disciples* differ from one another as well as from those on *Three Bodhisattvas* and the fragments that are known to come from Cave 224.[63] However, because of their stylistic proximity to those fragments, *Three Celestial Attendants* and *Buddha with Two Disciples*, too, may have originated in Cave 224.[64] As to their locations within the cave, it is possible that *Three Celestial Attendants* occupied a position on the east wall of the main chamber, where in situ murals contain floral motifs like those seen in the background of this piece.[65] Comparison of the many fragments thought to be from Cave 224 with paintings that survive in the cave itself will lead to more conclusive knowledge of the works' origins.

The figures portrayed on the Metropolitan Museum's set of three related fragments lack distinguishing characteristics such as multiple heads or prostrate poses that would help to link them to specific Buddhist narratives.[66] *Three Celestial Attendants* and *Three Bodhisattvas* probably represent generic attendant figures of the kind found between the principal figures in many of the Kizil caves' sermon scenes. If *Buddha with Two Disciples* is indeed

fig. 19 Head of Buddhist Image. China (Xinjiang Uyghur Autonomous Region), Kizil, ca. 6th–7th century(?). Pigments on mud plaster, 6 × 6¾ in. (15.2 × 17.1 cm). Inscribed on reverse: *IV. Reise Qieszil / gr. Anlg. 3te Höhle / rechte Sete i. d. K1 Schlucht / g. No. 33 / (Kiste 74)*. The Metropolitan Museum of Art, Rogers Fund, 1944 (44.77.1)

fig. 20 Head of a Buddha. China (Xinjiang Uyghur Autonomous Region), Kizil, ca. 6th–7th century(?). Pigments on mud plaster, 4¾ × 4¾ in. (12.1 × 12.1 cm). Inscribed on reverse: *Kiste 74 / IV. Reise / Qieszil. gr. Anlg. / 2 letzte Hohle in d. K1. / Schlucht / g. No. 16.* The Metropolitan Museum of Art, Rogers Fund, 1944 (44.77.2)

from Cave 224, it was probably located near the center of the cave's preaching scenes, and its three figures most likely represent attendants rather than the characters suggested in the title. Not only do none of the figures display the main identifying features of the Buddha, such as *uṣṇīṣa* (protuberance on the top of the head) and *ūrṇā* (curl between the eyebrows)—but in Cave 224, the Buddha is depicted as a seated figure with a large green, white, and blue mandorla.[67]

Although the Kizil paintings in the Metropolitan Museum's collection are fragmentary and do not contain major figures, careful examination has enabled us to identify their possible caves of origin. The identification of even minor fragments such as these advances the project of reconstructing the murals of the Kizil caves. This preliminary study of the Museum's fragments also aspires to contribute to the larger objective of improving understanding of the Buddhist culture of Kucha and its surrounding regions.

ADDENDUM: FOUR SMALL FRAGMENTS WITH FACES

In addition to the works discussed above, the Metropolitan Museum's collection of Kizil paintings includes four smaller mural fragments, all depicting single heads. Owing to the limited number of stylistic and iconographic features present in these fragments, it is not yet possible to trace their original locations on the Kizil site. However, many fragments with similar subjects and styles exist in collections in the United States and abroad. These widely scattered fragments remain to be studied as a group. This research, when carried out, may lead to the identification of these works' caves of origin. Following are descriptions of the Museum's four fragments.

Head of Buddhist Image (fig. 19) shows a haloed figure in profile wearing a headdress with circular ornaments in blue and white. The inscription on the back reads in part: *gr. Anlg. 3te Höhle / rechte Sete i. d. K1 Schlucht* (largest segment, 3rd cave, right side in the small gorge).[68]

Head of a Buddha (fig. 20) features a round face in three-quarter view with details delineated in dark red, in the manner of figure 19. The remnants of a head ornament indicate that this is probably not a Buddha figure. According to the inscription, the fragment was found in *gr. Anlg. 2 letzte Höhle in d. K1. Schlucht* (largest segment, 2nd-to-last cave in the small gorge)."[69]

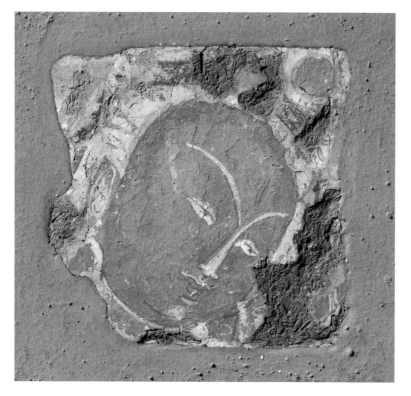

Head of Bodhisattva (fig. 21) presents an oval face in three-quarter view. The skin is dark gray, and on the headdress is a circular ornament that was once painted blue. An inscription on the back gives the fragment's origins as *Gr. Anlg. 2te letzte Höhle in d. kl. Schlucht, 1[l?]. Seite* (Largest segment, 2nd-to-last cave in the small gorge, left side).[70]

Buddha (fig. 22) includes part of the arms and chest of a round-faced figure. The inscription on the reverse reads in part: *gr. Anlg. 4te Höhle link. Seite in d. Kl Schlucht* (largest segment, 4th cave on the left in the small gorge).[71]

ACKNOWLEDGMENTS

This article is based on research undertaken by the author in 2012 as the Sylvan C. Coleman and Pamela Coleman Memorial Fellow at the Metropolitan Museum. My sincere thanks go to Denise Leidy, Brooke Russell Astor Curator of Chinese Art, for her supervision, assistance, and encouragement. I am grateful also to Satomi Hiyama, Zhao Li, Wicky Tze, Monika Zin, Lilla Russell-Smith, Deng Jie, and Chen Lei.

MIKI MORITA
Research Affiliate, Department of Art and Art History, Georgetown University, Washington, D.C.

fig. 21 *Head of Bodhisattva*. China (Xinjiang Uyghur Autonomous Region), Kizil, ca. 6th–7th century(?). Pigments on mud plaster, 5⅛ × 5¼ in. (13 × 13.3 cm). Inscribed on reverse: *Privat [. . .] / IV. Reise, Qieszil gr. Anlg./ 2te letzte Höhle in d. Kl. Schlucht, l [1?]. Seite / g. No. 23.* The Metropolitan Museum of Art, From the Collection of A. W. Bahr, Purchase, Fletcher Fund, 1947 (47.18.61)

fig. 22 *Buddha*. China (Xinjiang Uyghur Autonomous Region), Kizil, ca. 6th–7th century(?). Pigments on mud plaster, 12¾ × 9⅜ in. (32.4 × 23.8 cm). Inscribed on reverse: *IV. Reise. Qieszil / gr. Anlg. 4te Höhle link. Seite / in d. Kl. Schlucht / g. no. 38 / Kiste 74.* The Metropolitan Museum of Art, Fletcher Fund, 1951 (51.94.2)

NOTES

1 In most of the caves, the walls' soft surfaces were cemented with mud plaster mixed with straw. After being pressed and buffed, they were then covered with calcareous material that served as the base for painting. Pigments were mixed with glues for stabilization. For an overview of the scientific studies of Kizil mural paintings, see Taniguchi 2010.

2 The Kucha Kingdom is mentioned many times in *Han shu*. A compilation of these and other primary-source references to the Kucha Kingdom is found in Xinjiang Weiwu'er zizhiqu wenwu guanli weiyuanhui and Baicheng xian Kezi'er qianfodong wenwu baoguansuo 1983–85.

3 Kumārajīva (A.D. 344–413), a renowned Buddhist monk and translator of Buddhist texts, was a member of a Kuchean noble family and was active as a translator in China in the early fifth century. According to his biography in Sengyou's *Chu sanzang jiji*, Kucha was home to more than ten thousand Buddhist monks during his time. For this account, see *Taishō shinshū Daizōkyō* 55, no. 2145: 100a–102a. The dominance of Buddhism in Kucha was attested in Xuanzang, *Da Tang xiyu ji* (*Taishō shinshū Daizōkyō* 51, no. 2087, 870a–870c). According to Hyecho (A.D. 704–787), a Buddhist monk in Korea's Silla Kingdom, Buddhist monks of Han Chinese ethnicity in Kucha practiced Mahāyāna Buddhism (*Wang ocheonchukguk jeon; Taishō shinshū Daizōkyō* 51, no. 2089, 979a). Furthermore, Xuanzang and Hyecho both report that Kuchean monks practiced "lesser vehicle Buddhism" (*Taishō shinshū Daizōkyō* 51, no. 2087, 870a; and 51, no. 2089, 979a). Analysis of manuscripts written in Sanskrit and Tocharian B, the language used in the Kucha region suggests that Kuchean monks were followers of the school of the Sarvāstivādins (Ogihara 2013, pp. 95–99, 111). For further information on Buddhism and Buddhist manuscripts in Kucha and Central Asia, see Sander 1991; Hartmann 1999; Ogihara 2013, and other works by these authors.

4 For the German expeditions, see Härtel and Yaldiz 1982, pp. 24–46. Japanese expeditions were organized by Ōtani Kōzui (1878–1948), the twenty-second abbot of the Nishi Honganji branch of Jōdo Shinshū Buddhism; see Dainobu 2002 and Galambos and Kitsudō 2012. For an overview of European and American expeditions to the region, see Hopkirk 1984.

5 Grünwedel was a scholar of Central Asian archaeology, Indology, Tibetology, and Buddhist studies. See Dreyer 2012 for more on Grünwedel. Le Coq started his career in his forties as a volunteer researcher at the Museum für Völkerkunde in Berlin and served as the director of the museum's department of Indian art from 1923 to 1925 (Dreyer, Sander, and Weis 2002, p. 7). The two men's writings remain essential references in the art history of northwestern China. See Dreyer 2012. Theodor Bartus, the technician of the Museum für Völkerkunde, was the only one to participate in all four expeditions (Härtel and Yaldiz 1982, p. 34). See also Van Tongerloo, Knüppel, and Gabsch 2012.

6 Ueno 1978, p. 113; Zhao 2009, p. 93.

7 The Smithsonian Institution possesses the largest collection of the Kizil paintings in the United States. Other U.S. institutions with noteworthy holdings of Kizil paintings include the Fogg Museum, Cambridge, Mass.; the Nelson-Atkins Museum of Art, Kansas City, Mo.; the Museum of Fine Arts, Boston; the Detroit Institute of Arts; and the Museum of Archaeology and Anthropology of the University of Pennsylvania, Philadelphia.

8 A French customs stamp is attached to the reverse of MMA 51.94.1. Le Coq's name appears on the back of MMA 51.94.6 (see fig. 17b) in a penciled notation that reads, in part, *A mon cher ami Hack* [?] *son bien* [?] *devoué* [?] *A. Lecoq*. Aki Ueno (1980a, pp. 59–61, and n. 13) reconstructs this inscription as "A mon cher ami Hackin son bien dévoué A. Le Coq" and believes that this fragment was a gift from Le Coq to Joseph Hackin (1886–1941), a renowned French archaeologist. Next to Le Coq's notation are two inscriptions in Arabic script, which can be read as "Khurusaan Khurus" and "fiizi'l" or "fiizibal."

9 Recommendation for purchase, April 11, 1928, Purchases – Recommended but not purchased – Paintings (Far East) – A–Z, Office of the Secretary Records, MMA Archives. The present writer has discovered similar information concerning the provenance of Kizil fragments in the archives of the University of Pennsylvania Museum of Archaeology and Anthropology. There, a notation on the accession card for C412, a mural fragment from Turfan, states that the museum's Central Asian mural fragments were purchased from A. W. Bahr in 1924 and, further, that Bahr obtained the fragments from Worch, who "got them from Le Coq."

10 Although these fragments were recorded as originating in Turfan, they may have included Kizil mural fragments. It was recently affirmed that a fragment numbered C411 in the museum of the University of Pennsylvania originated in Kizil Cave 38. The same fragment is identified as "Fresco from Turfan" on a card of earlier date, which also bears a notation questioning whether the piece might be from Kizil rather than from Turfan.

11 Le Coq and Waldschmidt 1922–33, vol. 3 (1924), pp. 22–23; Waldschmidt 1933, pp. 24–31. Inscriptions on the murals associated with each stylistic group were identified with archaic or later "Turkistani Brahmi" scripts, based on the paleographic study of Heinrich Lüders. Waldschmidt further mentions that the manuscripts discovered in Caves 66 and 67 contain the names of six Kuchean kings, two of them identified with kings from the seventh century mentioned in Chinese primary sources. Also according to Waldschmidt, a name inscribed on a wall of Cave 205 is that of a wife of another Kuchean king of the sixth and the early seventh centuries. For an explanation of cave numbering, see note 20 below.

12 The consecutive chronological ordering of the first two styles has been questioned. The challenges involved in dating the Kizil caves are discussed in Howard 1991; Ma 1998; Zhao 2002; and Hiyama 2013, pp. 143–46.

13 Earlier dates were proposed by Alexander Soper and Benjamin Rowland in 1958 and 1974, respectively. Soper's analysis of the assimilation of cave structure, artistic style, and certain motifs found in Dunhuang murals from the Northern Liang period (A.D. 397–439) presupposes the existence of prototypes in the Kucha region at an earlier date. Rowland, probably based on Soper's analysis, places the Kizil paintings of both the first and second styles in the late fourth to early sixth century; see Soper 1958, pp. 145–64; Howard 1991, p. 68. The views held by several others on the Kizil chronology present little challenge to Waldschmidt's dating; Howard 1991, pp. 68–69.

14 Su 1989, pp. 19–20.

15 Ibid., p. 20. Nakano Teruo (1992) disputes the Beijing study's chronology, proposing the mid-sixth century as the height of the second style and the seventh to the eighth century for the third style. His view is based on a study comparing the second style of the Kizil murals with the Dunhuang murals of the Northern Wei (A.D. 386–534) and Northern Zhou (A.D. 557–81) periods.

16 Zhao 2002, p. 151; Nakagawara et al. 2012; Yaldiz 2010.

17 Nakagawara et al. 2012, pp. 130–33.

18 Vignato 2008, p. 36. Vignato further divides the two cave group types into subtypes based on their combination of architectural elements, such as the different kinds and numbers of chambers they contain, their elevation on the cliff sides, and the presence of suspended balconies. The site of the Kizil caves is divided into seven districts, each of which has a concentration of caves and cave groups with similar structures. Vignato (2006b, pp. 410–11) suggests that the structural differences seen in the two cave types might relate to the types of Buddhism practiced in each. For the criteria applied in the caves' categorization, see pp. 365–69.

19 According to Vignato, the most reliable dates of specific caves are A.D. 625–47 for Cave 69 and the end of the sixth century for Cave 205. These dates are based on cave inscriptions believed to refer to Kuchean royals (Vignato 2006b, pp. 405–6). The cave groups are not necessarily tied to a single period. As modifications and additions were made to the core units in each group, the development of some of the cave groups would have extended through several periods.

20 Hiyama 2013, p. 152. For the inscription in Cave 205, see note 11 above and Waldschmidt 1933, pp. 28–29. The cave numbers used in this essay follow the numbering system currently in standard use. Initially, German scholars named caves after distinguishing artistic features, such as "Cave with the Choir," now commonly known as Cave 38.

21 A number of recent studies contest the view that the Kizil mural styles arose in neat chronological fashion. Klimburg and Ma propose that the second style predated and lasted longer than the first; see Klimburg 1974, p. 325; Ma 1998, p. 91; and Hiyama 2013, p. 144. Vignato's holistic analysis (2006b, pp. 409–10) of the Kizil site, the cave structures, and the content and style of the paintings indicates that these two styles coexisted from the second phase of his periodization.

22 Vignato 2006b, pp. 359–60n1.

23 For the various designs of Kizil caves, see Su 1989.

24 Ibid., p. 12.

25 Vignato 2005, pp. 122–23; Su 1989, p. 15.

26 Su 1989, p. 15; Vignato 2006b, p. 409.

27 Li 2002, pp. 133–48; Vignato 2006b, p. 409.

28 The themes used in the decoration of side corridors vary and may include stupas, donor figures, and scenes from the life of the Buddha. The lunettes on the entrance walls often contain depictions of the preaching scene of Maitreya in Tushita heaven. Li 2002, p. 141.

29 Su 1989, p. 17.

30 Cave 188, mentioned for its descriptive German name below in the present essay, is the only cave cited here that does not have a central pillar. The ceiling and walls of Cave 188 are painted.

31 See Kijima and Satō 2012, pls. 1–3, for an example of the original and restored states of a Kizil fragment documented using infrared photography and ultraviolet-induced visible fluorescence photography. On color changes caused by the deterioration of the murals over time, see Nakagawara 2010, p. 29.

32 The complete inscription reads: M. Ô. Q., Gr. Anlage / Figuren Höhle / Stück 8 / Kiste 29 / Tür-wand.

33 Grünwedel 1912, pp. 91–95.

34 Le Coq and Waldschmidt 1922–33, vol. 6 (1928), pp. 72–73, pl. 9.

35 In an email of October 2013, Monika Zin and Satomi Hiyama informed the writer that they and other scholars, including Giuseppe Vignato, believe that monastic figures wearing undergarments with sleeves represent females. A mural in Ajanta cave XVII features two groups of monastic figures: the males' right shoulders are bare, while the figures with female charac-teristics wear long-sleeved undergarments that cover the shoulders. A similar observation on the gender of monastic figures in Cave 114 is made in Nakagawara 1999, p. 96.

36 Zhao 2004, pp. 57, 59; Zhao 2009, pp. 94, 96.

37 An image reproduced in Zhao 2009, p. 94, shows a fragment formerly in the collection of the Museum für Asiatische Kunst, Berlin (IB 9177) but lost during World War II. This fragment, like Monks and Stupas (MIK III 8859), depicts a procession of monks with lotus flowers and most likely originated in the same cave as MIK III 8859. Although similar, the two compositions exhibit obvious differences: in MIK III 8859, the procession moves to the left and the usual number of lotus flowers between the monks is four, whereas in IB 9177, the procession moves to the right and the number of lotus flowers separating the monks is greater than four. The monk at the far right on MIK III 8859 turns to the right, unlike the other monks represented, and on that figure's proper left side there are more than four lotus flowers. According to Nakagawara Ikuko, lines of donor figures depicted on the walls of side corridors in central pillar caves are generally portrayed as moving in one direction; see Nakagawara 1999, pp. 92, 102–3. The fragment with an anomalous figure on the far right was probably mistakenly reconstructed as part of MIK III 8859. As the direction of the figure and the number of flowers beside it suggest, the fragment was almost certainly originally part of IB 9177. Judging from the current condition and size of the inner walls of Cave 13, it is possible that the MMA's Monk Holding a Lotus is part of MIK III 8859.

38 Other paintings depicting monks in procession are found in Caves 114, 175, and 184. According to Nakagawara, monks' processions were represented briefly during the early developmental phase of donor figures in the second style of Kizil mural painting. Monks' processions in this early phase in Kizil caves might have served as an intermediary phase to the later depictions on these walls of lay donor figures processing in flamboyant attire in the sacred and liturgical space; see Nakagawara 1999, pp. 97, 106. Nakagawara (p. 97) further argues that the monks in procession in Caves 114 and 13 (listed as Cave 7 by Nakagawara based on Le Coq's publication) represent types rather than specific individuals, while she considers that the monks depicted in Caves 175 and 184 are eminent monks in Buddhist history and narratives. See Nakagawara 1999 for more on the study of Kizil donor figures.

39 Grünwedel 1912, pp. 72–73 (description of ceiling segment 21).

40 Some Kizil cave scholars call these scenes avadāna (noble deeds) tales. Jātaka, the other sources of popular themes in Kizil ceiling paintings, contain accounts of the Buddha's previous lives. On the well-preserved ceilings of Cave 38, scenes from jātaka tales alternate with images derived from the sermon scenes.

41 Grünwedel (1912, p. 72) suggests that the figure represents a "brâhmaṇa." Many Gandharan Buddhist reliefs contain figures of ascetics with knotted hair and holding a bottle. For example, in sculptural representations, Maitreya bodhisattva holds a bottle in one hand when portrayed in a manner associated with Brahmanical ascetics (Miyaji 1992, pp. 282–90). In Kizil Cave 80, a large mural depicting the Buddha vanquishing six non-Buddhist masters features two figures in the front row and one in the second row holding black bottles in their left hands and raising their right hands in reverence to the Buddha, at center. See Zhao 1995.

42 Fewer spherical objects are apparent in fig. 6, which shows Attendant in situ, than in fig. 5, indicating that fewer were initially depicted than are now visible on the fragment. The somewhat abstract ensemble of these objects is shaped like a bouquet.

43 Xinjiang Qiuci shiku yanjiu suo 2008, pl. 59; Lesbre 2001, p. 335.

44 Some of the figures shown offering flowers to the Buddha in Kizil murals are identified as the bodhisattva Megha (one of Śākyamuni Buddha's previous incarnations) from the narrative of Dīpaṃkara Buddha, one of the Buddhas from the past. The number of flowers associated with Dīpaṃkara Buddha is either five or seven, as can be seen on a mural in Cave 34 of the Kumtura caves, which include Kuchean Buddhist caves and are located near the Kizil site (Xinjiang Qiuci shiku yanjiu suo 2008, pl. 209).

45 The complete inscription reads: *IV Reise Qieszil. Gr. Anl. / Blaue Höhle / g. No. 2*. Numbers preceded by *g* or *G* are found on other fragments also. They were possibly written later, when the works were inventoried; Ueno 1980a, p. 49.

46 Grünwedel 1912, p. 72 (description of ceiling segment 20).

47 Figures wearing the same type of armor as the MMA's *Warrior* featured prominently in *The Division of the Buddha's Relics by Eight Kings*, from Kizil Cave 224. (Formerly in the Berlin collection [IB 8438], that mural is now lost.)

48 The location of this painting is often given erroneously as Cave 181. See Zhao 2004, pp. 57, 59, and Zhao 2009, pp. 93, 96.

49 Vignato 2006b, pp. 380–81, table 1.

50 Based on Vignato's classification of Kizil caves and his division of the Kizil site into seven districts, *Two Bodhisattvas* could have originated in Caves 175 or 178, or in a cave belonging to their group, or in a cave belonging to a different group but located in the same district. See Vignato 2006b, pp. 380–82; Ueno 1980a, pp. 50–51.

51 See Waldschmidt 1930 (1967) and Mori 2001. The narrative tells of events that occurred after the conversion of the Kāśyapa brothers, renowned brahmans who revered fire. When the Buddha and Uruvilvā-Kāśyapa, one of the three brothers and a disciple of the Buddha, were greeted by King Bimbisāra and his ministers in Magadha, Uruvilvā-Kāśyapa performed miracles, one of which involved creating shadow clones of himself: These clones are represented by the three-headed figure. It is also said that Uruvilvā-Kāśyapa prostrated himself before the Buddha to show his devotion. Another interpretation identifies the three heads with the three Kāśyapa brothers. They were converted by the Buddha, who performed miraculous deeds for them, including the subjugation of the fire dragon. The figure's multiple heads are thought to represent the three brothers. See Ding, Ma, and Xiong 1989, p. 193.

52 Ding, Ma, and Xiong 1989, p. 194.

53 Zin 2013, p. 13. This painting is one of a pair that covers the interior door wall in Cave 189. The second painting in the pair also features a standing Buddha figure; its theme is identified by Zin (pp. 5–9) as the Buddha descending from Trāyastriṃśa, the Heaven of Indra, where he taught dharma to Māyā, his deceased mother. Another composition showing the Buddha figure standing on crisscrossing snakes, as in fig. 12, features two figures holding parasols; it is part of a mural in Kumtura Cave 23, to the left of the entrance. Compositions and iconographic features comparable to those in the paintings in Kizil Cave 189 and Kumtura Cave 23 have been identified in two mural fragments from Kizil Cave 184 that are now in the collection of the Museum of Asian Art, Berlin (MIK III 525 and III 526); ibid., pp. 9–11. Zin believes there must have been a reason why depictions of the Buddha descending from Trāyastriṃśa and standing on crisscrossing snakes were commonly paired in Kizil caves; pp. 11, 13. Although the door walls of Caves 175 and 178, both of which are considered candidates for the original location of fig. 9 (MMA 51.94.5), are mostly lost, further analysis of the pictorial programs of these caves might help to identify the theme of the MMA fragment. The reproductions in Zin of formerly unpublished murals from Cave 184 show clear stylistic differences between those paintings and MMA 51.94.5, and therefore decrease the probability that Cave 184 was the original location of that piece (ibid., fig. 1). I am grateful to Monika Zin for sharing this important information and for allowing me to see her article before it was published.

54 The related fragments are in the Fogg Museum (1926.2), the Museum of Asian Art, Berlin (MIK III 8485; also IB 8483 and IB 8484, both now lost), the University of Pennsylvania Museum of Archaeology and Anthropology (C413A), and a private collection, Japan.

55 The inscriptions from all of the related fragments except for those in the MMA, the University of Pennsylvania museum, and the two lost pieces from Berlin's Museum für Asiatische Kunst are cited in Ueno 1978, pp. 114–16. The slightly damaged inscription on the piece in the collection of the University of Pennsylvania museum was recently recorded by the present writer.

56 Ibid., p. 115.

57 German scholars named Cave 179 *Japaner Höhle* (Japanese Cave) because it had been examined by Japanese expeditions organized by Ōtani Kōzui prior to the arrival of the German teams. Unlike the inscriptions on other fragments, which begin with the identification of the expedition (e.g., *IV Reise*), all notations on the fragments in this group begin with the identification of the site and end with *in d. Ecke gefunden* (found in the corner). Ueno (ibid., pp. 114–16) explains this anomaly by suggesting that Le Coq may have found these fragments already separated from the wall and lying in a corner of the cave, where they probably had been left by Ōtani's team.

58 Zhongguo bihua quanji bianjiweiyuanhui 1995, vol. 2, pls. 152–57.

59 According to Vignato, Caves 176 and 179 share physical proximity and architectural elements, and they belong to the same cave group. Cave 179 is one of the early caves in the group; Cave 176 evinces later development; see Vignato 2006b, pp. 380–81, 391, table 1.

60 Ueno (1980a, n. 13) states that the inscription indicates that this fragment was taken from "the largest cave of the third district." According to Ueno's study (1980a), the inscriptions on stylistically similar fragments in U.S. collections show a *III* before *Anlage*. The present writer has confirmed this on fragments in the Smithsonian's Freer and Sackler Galleries and considers the abraded character in the inscription of MMA 51.94.6 to be *III*.

61 For example, the origins of two mural fragments now housed in the Freer Gallery of Art, Washington, D.C. (Long-term loan from the Smithsonian American Art Museum; gift of John Gellatly; LTS 1985.1.325.4, and .5), have been traced respectively to the upper and lower parts of the west wall of the main room of Cave 224, thanks to Ueno's identification of figures depicted on the fragment with descriptions and drawings published in Grünwedel 1912, pp. 174–77, figs. 405, 407. See Ueno 1980a, pp. 54–56.

62 Based on her comparison of *Three Bodhisattvas* with Grünwedel's description of the murals in Cave 224, Ueno (1980a, pp. 59–60) believes that the fragment was originally located on the east wall, in the section directly above the seated Buddha on the far left of the upper half of the wall.

63 The legible portion of the inscription on *Three Celestial Attendants* reads: *M* [?] *Q* [or *A*?] *gr. Höhle Vorhalle* [loin?] [gr?] [. . .] ([Kizil Thousand Caves (?)] large [or larger/largest] cave, entrance hall). The MMA's database gives the inscription on *Buddha with Two Disciples* as *II Höhle, II Anl. Kyzil*. (2nd cave, 2nd district), which may correspond to Cave 218. However, Grünwedel (1912, p. 145) reported that this cave was badly damaged and its paintings destroyed. An archaeological report

published in 2000 mentions no paintings remaining in Cave 218 (Xinjiang Qiuci shiku yanjiu suo and Xinjiang Weiwu'er Zizhiqu wenhuating shiku yanjiusuo 2000, p. 243). A stylistically related fragment in the the Smithsonian's Freer and Sackler Galleries (Long-term loan from the Smithsonian American Art Museum; gift of John Gellatly; LTS 1985.1.325.1) bears the inscription *II Anlage gr* [. . .]*chhohle* [. . .] [Stupa?] *Wand*, suggesting that *Buddha with Two Disciples* and the Smithsonian fragment might have originated in a cave in the second district. Further cross-over research is anticipated.

64 *Buddha with Two Disciples* may be associated with a different district on the Kizil site. See the note 63 above.

65 Xinjiang Weiwu'er zizhiqu wenwu guanli weiyuanhui, Baicheng xian Kezi'er qianfodong wenwu baoguansuo, and Beijing daxue kaoguxi 1989–97, vol. 3, pl. 137.

66 See note 51 above.

67 Xinjiang Weiwu'er zizhiqu wenwu guanli weiyuanhui and Baicheng xian Kezi'er qianfodong wenwu baoguansuo 1983–85, vol. 3, pls. 136–40.

68 Also inscribed: *g. no. 33* and *Kiste* 74. Ueno (1980a, pp. 50–51) links this fragment to Cave 188.

69 Additional notations: *G. no. 16* and *Kiste* 74. Ueno (ibid.) links this fragment to Cave 176.

70 Additional notation: *g. no. 23*. Ueno (ibid.) links this fragment to Cave 176.

71 Additional notations: *g. no. 38* and *Kiste* 74. Ueno (ibid.) links this fragment to Cave 177.

REFERENCES

Primary Sources

Chu sanzang jiji 出三藏記集 [Compilation of notices on the translation of the Tripiṭaka]. Edited by Sengyou 僧佑 (445–518). *Taishō shinshū Daizōkyō* 55, no. 2145.

Da Tang xiyu ji 大唐西域記 [Great Tang records on the Western Regions]. Xuanzang 玄奘 (602–664); edited by Bianji (d. 652). *Taishō shinshū Daizōkyō* 51, no. 2087.

Han shu 漢書 [History of the Han]. Ban Gu 班固 (32–92) et al. 12 vols. Beijing: Zhonghua shuju, 1962.

Wang ocheonchukguk jeon 往五天竺國傳 [Record of travels in five Indian regions]. In *Youfangji chao* 遊方記抄 [Selected records of itinerant monks]. Hyecho 慧超 (8th century A.D.). *Taishō shinshū Daizōkyō* 51, no. 2089, 975a–979b.

Secondary Sources

Dainobu Yūji 臺信祐爾
    2002 Ōtani kōzui to s*aiiki bijutsu* 大谷光瑞と西域美術 [Ōtani kōzui and the art of the Western Regions]. Vol. 434 of *Nihon no bijutsu* 日本の美術 [Arts of Japan]. Tokyo: Shibundō.

Ding Mingyi 丁明夷, Ma Shichang 馬世長, and Xiong Xi 雄西
    1989 "Kezi'er shiku de fozhuan bihua" 克孜爾石窟的佛傳壁畫 [Mural paintings of the life of the Buddha in the Kizil Caves]. In Xinjiang Weiwu'er zizhiqu wenwu guanli weiyuanhui, Baicheng xian Kezi'er qianfodong wenwu baoguansuo, and Beijing daxue kaoguxi 1989–97, vol. 1, pp. 185–222.

Dreyer, Caren
    2012 "Albert Grünwedel—Ein Leben für die Wissenschaft." In Gabsch 2012, pp. 14–29.

Dreyer, Caren, Lore Sander, and Friederike Weis
    2002 *Dokumentation der Verluste.* Vol. 3, *Museum für Indische Kunst.* Berlin: Staatliche Museen zu Berlin.

Gabsch, Toralf, ed.
    2012 *Auf Grünwedels Spuren: Restaurierung und Forschung an zentralasiatischen Wandmalereien.* Exh. cat., Museum für Asiatische Kunst, Staatliche Museen zu Berlin. Leipzig: Koehler & Amelang.

Galambos, Imre, and Kōichi Kitsudō
    2012 "Japanese Exploration of Central Asia: The Ōtani Expeditions and Their British Connections." *Bulletin of the School of Oriental and African Studies* (University of London) 75 (February), pp. 113–34.

Grünwedel, Albert
    1912 *Altbuddhistische Kultstätten in Chinesisch-Turkistan.* Berlin: Georg Reimer.

Härtel, Herbert, and Marianne Yaldiz
    1982 *Along the Ancient Silk Routes: Central Asian Art from the West Berlin State Museums.* Exh. cat. New York: MMA.

Hartmann, Jens-Uwe
    1999 "Buddhist Sanskrit Texts from Northern Turkestan and Their Relation to the Chinese Tripiṭaka." In *Collection of Essays 1993: Buddhism across Boundaries: Chinese Buddhism and the Western Regions,* edited by Erik Zürcher and Lore Sander, pp. 107–36. Sanchung, Taiwan: Fo Guang Shan Foundation for Buddhist & Culture Education.

Hiyama Satomi 檜山智美
    2013 "Kucha no daiichi yōshiki hekiga ni mirareru Efutaru ki no mochīfu ni tsuite" クチャの第一様式壁畫に見られるエフタル期のモチーフについて [Study on the first-style murals of Kucha: Analysis of some motifs related to the Hephthalite's period]. In *Buddhism and Art in Gandhāra and Kucha: Buddhist Culture along the Silk Road; Gandhāra, Kucha, and Turfan, Section I,* edited by Miyaji Akira, pp. 125–63. Kyoto: Ryukoku University.

Hopkirk, Peter
    1984 *Foreign Devils on the Silk Road: The Search for the Lost Cities and Treasures of Chinese Central Asia.* Amherst: University of Massachusetts Press.

Howard, Angela F.
    1991 "In Support of a New Chronology for the Kizil Mural Paintings." *Archives of Asian Art* 44, pp. 68–83.

Kijima, Takayasu, and Ichiro Satō
    2012 "Superhochauflösende Digital-Fotografie von Wandmalereien aus Kizil." In Gabsch 2012, pp. 181–82.

Klimburg, Maximilian
    1974 "Die Entwicklung des zweiten indo-iranischen Stils von Kutscha." In *Sprache, Geschichte und Kultur der altaischen Völker: Protokollband der XII. Tagung der Permanent International Altaistic Conference 1969 in Berlin,* edited by György Hazai and Peter Zieme, pp. 317–25. Schriften zur Geschichte und Kultur des Alten Orients 5. Berlin: Akademie-Verlag.

Kumagai Nobuo 熊谷宣夫
    1962 "Seiiki no bijutsu" 西域の美術 [Art of the Western Regions]. In *Seiiki bunka kenkyū,* edited by Seiiki Bunka Kenkyūkai 西域文化研究會 [Society for the Study of Culture of the Western Regions], vol. 5, pp. 31–170. Kyoto: Hōzōkan.

Le Coq, Albert von, and Ernst Waldschmidt
    1922–33 *Die Buddhistische Spätantike in Mittelasien.* Ergebnisse der Kgl. Preussischen Turfan-Expeditionen. 7 vols. Berlin: D. Reimer.

Lesbre, Emmanuelle
    2001 "An Attempt to Identify and Classify Scenes with a Central Buddha Depicted on Ceilings of the Kyzil Caves (Former Kingdom of Kutcha, Central Asia)." *Artibus Asiae* 61, no. 2, pp. 305–52.

Li Chongfeng 李崇峰
    2002 *Zhong Yin fojiao shikusi bijiao yanjiu: Yi tamiao ku wei zhongxin* 中印佛教石窟寺比較研究: 以塔廟窟為中心 [Indian and Chinese Buddhist chētiyagharas: A comparative study]. Xinzhu: Caituan faren juefeng fojiao yishu wenhua jijin hui [Juefeng Foundation of Buddhist Art and Culture].

Ma Shichang 馬世長
    1998 "Guanyu Kezi'er shiku de niandai" 關於克孜爾石窟的年代 [On the chronology of the Kizil Caves]. In *Faxiang chuanzhen: Gudai fojiao yishu* 法相傳真: 古代佛教藝術 / *In the Footsteps of the Buddha: An Iconic Journey from India to China,* edited by Rajeshwari Ghose, Puay-peng Ho 何培斌, and Chuntang Yang 楊春棠, pp. 88–92. Exh. cat. Hong Kong: University Museum and Art Gallery, University of Hong Kong.

Miyaji Akira 宮治昭
    1992 *Nehan to Miroku no zuzōgaku: Indo kara Chūō Ajia e* 涅槃と彌勒の圖像學: インドから中央アジアへ [Iconology of *nirvāna* and Maitreya: From India to Central Asia]. Tokyo: Yoshikawa Kōbunkan.

Mori Michiyo 森美智代

2001 "Kucha no seppō zu ni kansuru ichi kōsatsu" クチャの説法圖に關する一考察 [A study of the paintings of preaching scenes in Kucha]. *Waseda daigaku daigakuin bungaku kenkyūka kiyō dai san bunsatsu* 早稻田大學大學院文學研究科紀要第三分冊 [Bulletin of the graduate division of literature of Waseda University] 3, no. 47, pp. 149–64.

Nakagawara Ikuko 中川原育子

1999 "Kucha chiiki no kuyōsha zō ni kansuru kōsatsu—Kijiru ni okeru kuyōsha zō no tenkai o chūshin ni" クチャ地域の供養者像に關する考察—キジルにおける供養者像の展開を中心に [A study on the donors depicted in cave temple of the Kucha region—Case study of Kizil]. *Nagoya daigaku bungakubu kenkyū ronshū Tetsugaku* 名古屋大學文學部研究論輯 哲學 [Journal of the Faculty of Letters, Nagoya University. Philosophy], no. 45, pp. 89–120.

2010 "Kijiru kenkyūno genzai—Kijiru sekkutsu no genba to nihon ni okeru kijiru kenkyū o chūshin ni" キジル研究の現在—キジル石窟の現場と日本におけるキジル研究を中心に [Kizil research today—Mainly on Kizil studies by Kucha Caves Research Institute and in Japan]. In *Chō Aikō shiruku rōdo kijiru sekkutsu hekiga mosha tenrankai* 張愛紅 シルクロード 龜茲石窟壁畫模寫展覽會 [Exhibition of Zhang Aihong's copy of mural paintings of the Kizil Caves], edited by Satō Ichirō, pp. 25–29. Tokyo: Tokyo geijutsu daigaku bijutsu kenkyū ka aburaga kenkyū shitsu.

Nakagawara Ikuko 中川原育子, Taniguchi Yōko 谷口陽子, Satō Ichirō 佐藤一郎, and Nakamura Toshio 中村俊夫

2012 "Berurin ajia bijutsukan shozō no kijiru shōrai hekiga no hōshasei tanso nendai" ベルリンアジア美術館所藏のキジル將來壁畫の放射性炭素年代 [Radiocarbon dating of the Kizil mural paintings collected in Museum für Asiatische Kunst, Berlin]. *Nagoya daigaku kasokuki shitsuryō bunsekikei gyōseki hōkokusho* 名古屋大學加速器質量分析計業績報告書 [Summaries of researches using AMS at Nagoya University], no. 23, pp. 127–37.

Nakano Teruo 中野照男

1992 "Kijiru sekkutsu no setsuwaga no keishiki to nendai" キジル石窟の説話畫の形式と年代 [A proposal for a revised chronology of the Kizil caves]. In *Kijiru o chūshin to suru seiiki bukkyō bijutsu no shomondai* キジルを中心とする西域佛教美術の諸問題 [Studies on the Buddhist art of Central Asia], edited by Fujisawa Norio 藤澤令夫, pp. 11–14. Kyoto: Bukkyō Bijutsu Kenkyū Ueno Kinen Zaidan Josei Kenkyūkai.

Ogihara Hirotoshi 荻原裕敏

2013 "Tokara go shahon・meibun kara mita Kucha no bukkyō" トカラ語寫本・銘文から見たクチャの仏教 [The Buddhism of Kucha from a Tocharian paleological perspective]. In *Buddhism and Art in Gandhāra and Kucha: Buddhist Culture along the Silk Road: Gandhāra, Kucha, and Turfan, Section I*, edited by Akira Miyaji, pp. 75–114. Kyoto: Ryukoku University.

Riederer, Josef R.

1977 "Technik und Farbstoffe der frühmittelalterlichen Wandmalereien Ostturkistans." In *Beiträge zur Indienforschung: Ernst Waldschmidt zum 80. Geburtstag gewidmet*, pp. 353–423. Berlin: Museum für Indische Kunst.

Rowland, Benjamin

1974 *The Art of Central Asia*. New York: Crown.

Sander, Lore

1991 "The Earliest Manuscripts from Central Asia and the Sarvastivada Mission." In *Corolla Iranica: Papers in Honour of Prof. Dr. David Neil MacKenzie on the Occasion of His 65th Birthday on April 8th, 1991*, edited by Ronald E. Emmerick and Dieter Weber, pp. 133–50. Frankfurt am Main: Peter Lang.

Soper, Alexander C.

1958 "Northern Liang and Northern Wei in Kansu." *Artibus Asiae* 21, no. 2, pp. 131–64.

Su Bai 宿白

1989 "Kezi'er bufen dongku jieduan huafen yu niandai deng wenti de chubu tansuo" 克孜爾部分洞窟階段割分與年代等問題的初步探索 [Questions concerning the periodization and chronology of part of the caves in Kizil]. In Xinjiang Weiwu'er zizhiqu wenwu guanli weiyuanhui, Baicheng xian Kezi'er qianfodong wenwu baoguansuo, and Beijing daxue kaoguxi 1989–97, vol. 1, pp. 10–23.

Taishō shinshū Daizōkyō

1924–32 *Taishō shinshū Daizōkyō* 大正新修大藏經 [Taishō Tripiṭaka]. Edited by Takakusu Junjirō 高楠順次郎 and Watanabe Kaigyoku 渡邊海旭. 85 vols. Tokyo: Taishō Issaikyō Kankōkai.

Taniguchi Yōko 谷口陽子

2010 "Kijiru senbutsudō no bukkyō hekiga ni kansuru saishiki zairyō to gihō chōsa—Doitsu, Roshia nado ni yoru senkō kenkyū to, hon kenkyū ni okeru hi sesshoku bunseki hō ni yoru yobi chōsa hō" キジル千佛洞の佛教壁畫に關する彩色材料と技法調査—ドイツ、ロシア等による先行研究と、本研究における非接觸分析法による予備調査法 [Research on the pigments and painting techniques of Buddhist mural paintings of the Kizil Thousand Buddha Caves: Previous studies of Germany and Russia and a preliminary research through non-contact analysis]. In *Chō Aikō shikuru rōdo kijiru sekkutsu hekiga mosha tenrankai* 張愛紅 シルクロード 龜茲石窟壁畫模寫展覽會 [Exhibition of Zhang Aihong's copy of mural paintings of the Kizil caves], edited by Satō Ichirō, pp. 30–35. Tokyo: Tokyo geijutsu daigaku bijutsu kenkyū ka aburaga kenkyū shitsu.

van Tongerloo, Aloïs, Michael Knüppel, and Toralf Gabsch

2012 "Theodor Bartus: Forschungsreisender, Museumstechniker und Restaurator." In Gabsch 2012, pp. 30–49.

Ueno Aki 上野アキ

1978 "Ru・Kokku shūshū saiiki hekiga chōsa, 1: Kijiru nihonjin dō no hekiga" ル・コック收輯西域壁畫調査 1-キジル日本人洞の壁畫 [Research on the mural paintings from the Western Regions collected by Le Coq, 1: Mural paintings from Japaner Höhle in Kizil]. *Bijutsu kenkyū* 美術研究 [Journal of art studies], no. 308 (October), pp. 113–20.

1980a "Ru・Kokku shūshū saiiki hekiga chōsa, 2: Kijiru dai san ku maya dō hekiga seppō zu - jō" ル・コック收輯西域壁畫調査 2: キジル第三區マや洞壁畫説法圖—上 [Research on the mural paintings from the Western Regions collected by Le Coq, 2: Mural paintings of preaching scenes in Māyāhöhle, 3. Anlage, first part]. *Bijutsu kenkyū* 美術研究 [Journal of art studies], no. 312 (February), pp. 48–61.

1980b "Ru・Kokku shūshū saiiki hekiga chōsa, 2: Kijiru dai san ku maya do hekiga seppō zu - jō - zoku" ル・コック收輯西域壁畫調査2: キジル第三區マや洞壁畫説法圖—上 (續) [Research on the mural paintings from the Western Regions collected by Le Coq, 2: Mural paintings of preaching scenes in Māyāhöhle, 3. Anlage, first part (sequel)]. *Bijutsu kenkyū* 美術研究 [Journal of art studies], no. 313 (March), pp. 91–97.

Vignato, Giuseppe

2005 "Kizil: Characteristics and Development of the Groups of Caves in Western Guxi." *Annali dell'Università degli Studi di Napoli "l'Orientale,"* no. 65, pp. 121–40.

2006a "The Wooden Architecture of the Kizil Caves." *Journal of Inner Asian Art and Archaeology* 1, pp. 11–27.

2006b "Archaeological Survey of Kizil: Its Groups of Caves, Districts, Chronology, and Buddhist Schools." *East and West* 56, no. 4, pp. 359–416.

2008 "Towards a More Reliable Chronology for the Site of Kizil." In *Kizil on the Silk Road: Crossroads of Commerce & Meeting of Minds*, edited by Rajeshwari Ghose, pp. 32–39. Mumbai: Marg Publications; National Centre for the Performing Arts.

Waldschmidt, Ernst

1930 "Wundertätige Mönche in der osttürkischen Hīnayāna-Kunst." *Ostasiatische Zeitschrift*, n.s., 6, pp. 3–9. Reprinted in Waldschmidt, *Von Ceylon bis Turfan* (Göttingen: Vandenhoeck & Ruprecht, 1967), pp. 27–33.

1933 "Beschreibender Text." In Le Coq and Waldschmidt 1922–33, vol. 7, pp. 15–31.

Wei Zhengzhong 魏正中 [Giuseppe Vignato]

2013 *Quduan yu zuhe: Qiuci shiku siyuan yizhi de kaogu xue tansuo* 區段與組合: 龜茲石窟寺院遺址的考古學探索 [Districts and groups: An archaeological investigation of the rock monasteries of Kucha]. Shanghai: Shanghai guji chubanshe.

Xinjiang Qiuci shiku yanjiu suo 新疆龜茲石窟研究所 [Kucha Caves Research Institute]

2008 *Zhongguo Xinjiang bi hua: Qiuci* 中國新疆壁畫: 龜茲 [Mural paintings in Xinjiang of China: Qiuci]. Wulumuqi: Xinjiang meishu sheying chubanshe.

Xinjiang Qiuci shiku yanjiu suo 新疆龜茲石窟研究所 [Kucha Caves Research Institute] and Xinjiang Weiwu'er Zizhiqu wenhuating shiku yanjiusuo 新疆維吾爾自治區文化廳研究所 [Research Institute of Xinjiang Uyghur Autonomous Region Department of Culture], eds.

2000 *Kezi'er shiku neirong zonglu* 克孜爾石窟內容總錄 [Comprehensive record of the contents of Kizil grottoes]. Wulumuqi: Xinjiang meishu sheying chubanshe.

Xinjiang Weiwu'er zizhiqu wenwu guanli weiyuanhui 新疆維吾爾自治區文物管理委員會 [Xinjiang Uyghur Autonomous Region Heritage Management Committee] and Baicheng xian Kezi'er qianfodong wenwu baoguansuo 拜城縣克孜爾千佛洞文物保管所 [Institute of Kizil Caves in Baicheng County]

1983–85 *Chūgoku sekkutsu: Kijiru sekkutsu* 中國石窟: キジル石窟 [The Grotto Art of China: Kizil Grottoes]. 3 vols. Tokyo: Heibonsha.

Xinjiang Weiwu'er zizhiqu wenwu guanli weiyuanhui 新疆維吾爾自治區文物管理委員會 [Xinjiang Uyghur Autonomous Region Heritage Management Committee], Baicheng xian Kezi'er qianfodong wenwu baoguansuo 拜城縣克孜爾千佛洞文物保管所 [Institute of Kizil Caves in Baicheng County], and Beijing daxue kaoguxi 北京大學考古系 [Department of Archaeology, Beijing University]

1989–97 *Zhongguo shiku: Kezi'er shiku* 中國石窟: 克孜爾石窟 [The Grotto Art of China: Kizil Grottoes]. 3 vols. Beijing: Wenwu chubanshe.

Yaldiz, Marianne

2010 "Evaluation of the Chronology of the Murals in Kizil, Kucha Oasis." In *From Turfan to Ajanta: Festschrift for Dieter Schlingloff on the Occasion of His Eightieth Birthday*, edited by Eli Franco and Monika Zin, vol. 2, pp. 1029–43. Bhairahawa, Rupandehi: Lumbini International Research Institute.

Zhao Li 趙莉

1995 "Kezi'er shiku jiangfu liushi waidao bihua kaoxi" 克孜爾石窟降伏六氏外道壁畫考析 [A study of the murals of vanquishing heretics in the Kizil Grottoes]. *Dunhuang yanjiu* 敦煌研究 [Dunhuang research], no. 1, pp. 146–55.

2002 "Kezi'er shiku fenqi niandai yanjiu zongshu" 克孜爾石窟分期年代研究綜述 [Overview of studies on the chronology of the Kizil caves]. *Dunhuang xue jikan* 敦煌學輯刊 [Journal of Dunhuang Studies], no. 41, pp. 147–56.

2004 "Deguo Bolin Yindu yishu bowuguan guancang bufen Kezi'er shiku bihua suochu dongku yuanwei yu neirong" 德國柏林印度藝術博物館館藏部分克孜爾石窟壁畫所出洞窟原位與內容 [Original caves and contents of the Kizil mural paintings in the collection of the Museum of Indian Art in Berlin, Germany]. *Dunhuang yanjiu* 敦煌研究 [Dunhuang research], no. 6 (no. 88), pp. 56–61.

2009 "Kezi'er shiku bufen liushi bihua yuanwei kaozheng yu fuyuan" 克孜爾石窟部分流失壁畫原位考證與復原 [Historical retrospect on the loss of mural paintings of Kizil caves and the verification of their original location]. *Zhongguo wenhua yichan* 中國文化遺產 [China cultural heritage], no. 3, pp. 88–99.

Zhongguo bihua quanji bianjiweiyuanhui 中國壁畫全集編輯委員會 [Editorial Committee of *Zhongguo bihua quanji*]

1995 *Zhongguo Xinjiang bihua quanji* 中國新疆壁畫全集 [Corpus of mural paintings in Xinjiang, China]. 6 vols. Tianjin: Tianjin renmin meishu chubanshe.

Zin, Monika

2013 "The Identification of Kizil Paintings VI." *Indo-Asiatische Zeitschrift*, no. 17, pp. 5–15.

IAIN BUCHANAN

Giovanni Battista Lodi da Cremona and the *Story of Mercury and Herse* Tapestry Series

Among the exceptional Renaissance tapestries in The Metropolitan Museum of Art, *Mercury Entering the Bridal Chamber of Herse* (fig. 1) and *Mercury Changes Aglauros to Stone*[1] stand out as two of the most historically significant. They compose part of an eight-piece set of the *Story of Mercury and Herse* woven about 1570 in the workshop of the Brussels tapestry maker Willem de Pannemaker. Scholars now attribute the design of the series to the Italian artist Giovanni Battista Lodi da Cremona, who is documented in the Low Countries from the 1540s to about 1566. This article synthesizes documentary sources that reconstruct Lodi's activities in Flanders, and it uses newly discovered archival evidence to glean further insight into his relationship with the Affaitadi firm of bankers and merchants. Moreover, the traditional sequence of the *Story of Mercury and Herse*, as given by Edith Standen in 1985 and recently upheld by

fig. 1 Here titled *Mercury Entering the Bridal Chamber of Herse* from the *Story of Mercury and Herse*. Design attributed to Giovanni Battista Lodi da Cremona (Italian, active 1540–ca. 1566), ca. 1540. Tapestry woven under the direction of Willem de Pannemaker (Netherlandish, active 1535–78, d. 1581), Brussels, ca. 1570. Wool, silk, silver, and silver-gilt-wrapped threads, 14 ft. 5 in. × 17 ft. 8 in. (439 × 538 cm). The Metropolitan Museum of Art, Bequest of George Blumenthal, 1941 (41.190.135)

Concha Herrero Carretero in 2010, is here challenged and a new reading of the iconography proposed. Finally, a revised chronology of the woven editions of the series is presented.

GIOVANNI BATTISTA LODI DA CREMONA IN BRUSSELS AND LIER

Of the Italian artists resident in the Low Countries during the sixteenth century who were engaged in the local tapestry industry, Giovanni Battista Lodi da Cremona remains one of the most mysterious. Lodi has been linked to several important tapestry series either as the possible designer or as responsible for carrying out the tapestry cartoons.[2] They comprise: (1) *Fructus Belli*, an eight-piece set made by the Brussels weaver

Jehan Baudouyn for Ferrante Gonzaga about 1545–47, of which six tapestries survive (Musée National de la Renaissance, Château d'Ecouen; Edward James Foundation, West Dean College, Chichester, England; Royal Museums of Art and History, Brussels); (2) *Life of Moses* (Châteaudun Castle, Monuments Historiques, France), a twelve-piece set woven by Willem Dermoyen (and possibly Peter van Oppenem) for Ferrante Gonzaga between 1545 and 1550; (3) *Puttini* (Giannino Marzotto collection, Trissino), a six-piece set woven by Willem de Pannemaker for Ferrante Gonzaga between 1552 and 1557;[3] and (4) *Story of Mercury and Herse*, an eight-piece series of which one complete and two partial sets are extant.[4] The earliest of the existing editions of the *Story of Mercury and Herse*, once in the collection of Prince

Thomas of Savoy Carignan-Soisson, survives in three pieces in the Palazzo del Quirinale, Rome, and was woven about 1545–50 by Willem Dermoyen (fig. 2).[5] The edition that included the Metropolitan Museum's *Mercury Entering the Bridal Chamber of Herse* and *Mercury Changes Aglaurus to Stone* was woven, as noted above, by the workshop of Willem de Pannemaker about 1570 and formerly belonged to the dukes of Medinaceli (see fig. 1).[6] A third set, now consisting of six tapestries and two fragments in the Diputació Provincial, Barcelona, was made for Don Fernando of Toledo by Willem de Pannemaker about 1571.[7]

A document confirms that Lodi had been active as an artist in Brussels from at least 1540, when he judged four chimneypieces painted by Frans Borremans, showing the imperial coat of arms and crown with putti and antique figures, after cartoons by Pieter Fabri van Aelst, in the New Gallery of the Brussels Coudenberg Palace.[8] Further, in a letter from Jehan Baudouyn, the weaver of the *Fructus belli*, to Ferrante Gonzaga, written from Brussels on June 15, 1547, Baudouyn requested additional funding for the tapestries and mentioned that Lodi and Giovanni Balbani, an Antwerp-based merchant from Lucca, would evaluate the completed set.[9] He also stated that Balbani had advanced him 250 *carolusgulden* and refused further credit. Subsequently, on August 31, 1547, Baudouyn wrote again to Gonzaga,

noting that he would be pleased for "Gian Battista" and unspecified merchants to inspect the finished tapestry.[10] In 1552, Lodi again acted as an adviser to Ferrante Gonzaga concerning a set of unnamed tapestries that Gonzaga wished to commission in Brussels. In a letter to Gonzaga, written from Lier on February 5, 1552, Lodi recommended a Brussels weaver who was then making the tapestry set of the *Conquest of Tunis* for Charles V.[11] Although Lodi did not mention his name, this weaver must have been Willem de Pannemaker, whose mark appears on the *Conquest of Tunis*. The unnamed tapestry series Gonzaga desired to commission was probably the *Puttini*, which would indeed be woven by Pannemaker between 1552 and 1557, after a design usually attributed to Lodi.[12]

The greatest sources of information on Lodi are two documents related to the painter Conrad Schot.[13] In a disposition made in Brussels for the *procureur général* of Brabant in December 1553, the twenty-six-year-old Schot stated that he had been the apprentice to an Italian artist named "Johan Baptista," living in the Hoochstrate, for a period of about four or five years. Schot must have been with Lodi from about 1544 to 1549, afterward working under Anthonis Mor for a year and a half, and with Jan Maes for three years after that. As both Mor and his pupil Maes specialized in painting portraits, it is possible that Schot also trained with

fig. 2 *The Metamorphosis of Aglauros and Mercury's Departure* from the *Story of Mercury and Herse*. Design attributed to Giovanni Battista Lodi da Cremona, ca. 1540. Tapestry woven in the workshop of Willem Dermoyen (active 1520–ca. 1548 in Brussels), ca. 1545–50. Wool and silk thread, 13 × 21 ft. (400 × 640 cm). Palazzo del Quirinale, Rome (O. D. P., no. 22)

fig. 3 Paolo Veronese (Italian, 1528–1588). *Hermes, Herse and Aglauros*, 1576–84. Oil on canvas, 91½ × 68¼ in. (232.4 × 173.4 cm). Fitzwilliam Museum, Cambridge, England (143)

Lodi in painting. This same "Jan Baptista" was described in a second, longer document as "an Italian and a rich man" who subsequently abandoned painting "for he had enough to live on and was old in years" and traveled to Lier to live with Signor Jan Carlo. This "Jan Carlo" was Gian Carlo Affaitadi, a merchant and banker who was the head of the Affaitadi firm in Antwerp.[14]

Gian Carlo Affaitadi was born in Cremona in 1500, active as a merchant in Antwerp from 1514, and died in Lier on December 24, 1555.[15] A wealthy man with a number of valuable properties, he lived in a large house in Antwerp's Groenplatz until 1535.[16] His summer residence, the château of Selzaten at Wommelghem near Antwerp, was purchased that year for 8,300 florins from the children of Thomas and Barbe Werneer.[17] From 1549, Gian Carlo Affaitadi lived in Lier, apparently under the same roof as Lodi. He owned three houses in the town: a princely residence called De Lier in the Kerkhofstraat; the Chanoine Brabant; and another house opposite the residence of the Antwerp financier and merchant Conrad Schetz, son of Erasmus Schetz, the noted banker and merchant.[18]

In 1550 and 1551, Affaitadi donated two large stained-glass windows, executed by Goyvaert van der Vliet, to the Church of Saint Gummarus in Lier.[19] They were placed on the east side of the south transept of the church and depicted the Transfiguration of Christ on Mount Tabor and the Last Judgment, the former with an inscription stating that it was a gift from Gian Carlo Affaitadi and providing the date 1550. Next to Affaitadi's windows, in the nave, was another large window showing the Adoration of the Kings, donated by Erasmus Schetz. In 1910 all three windows were removed for conservation and then mysteriously disappeared during World War I along with the only photographs that had been taken of them. Erasmus Schetz's other son, Balthazar, married Gian Carlo's widow, Lucretia, after Gian Carlo's death in 1555. At this time, his brother Gian Battista Affaitadi took over as head of the firm until his own death in 1576, when it ceased activity.

The Affaitadi served as bankers and merchants in much the same way as did other foreign firms in Antwerp such as the Fuggers and the Weslers of Augsburg. The Affaitadi were involved in the Portuguese spice trade and dealt in pastel and alum (both important for the textile industry), tapestries, silks for weavers, canvas, cotton, cloth, wool, cereals, precious stones, and jewels.[20] In 1551 they purchased the Suikerhuis, a local sugar refinery, in partnership with the Lucchese merchant Giovanni Balbani.[21] This was the same Balbani who had advanced funds to

fig. 4 Pierre Milan (French, active 1545–57) after Giovanni Jacopo Caraglio (Italian, ca. 1500/1505–1565), 1520–39. *Mercury Visiting Herse* from Caraglio's *Loves of the Gods*. Engraving, 6⅞ × 5¼ in. (17.5 × 13.3 cm). British Museum, London (1866,0623.10)

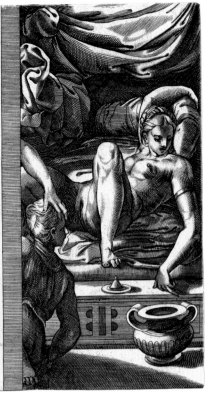

Baudouyn, the weaver of Ferrante Gonzaga's *Fructus Belli*, and who had been charged to evaluate the finished set, together with Lodi. As bankers, the Affaitadi granted loans to the city of Antwerp (for fortifications), the government of the Low Countries, Charles V, his son Philip II, and his sister Mary of Hungary, regent of the Low Countries.[22]

The Affaitadi were involved in the sale of silks to tapestry weavers and in selling the finished tapestries they produced. They supplied a number of important weavers with silk thread, among them, Roderigo Dermoyen, Cornelis de Ronde, Gios van Grimbergen, François Schavart, Gios Rampart, Willem de Pannemaker of Brussels, and Adrien Blumard and Dietrich Mas of Oudenaarde.[23] In 1550, Count Gian Battista Affaitadi of Cremona, who may have been a relation, bought three tapestry verdures from the firm.[24] The most significant recorded sale of tapestries by the firm was to the duke of Alba in 1556 for a now-lost set of *reposteros* (armorial tapestries) woven by Willem de Pannemaker and costing 4,400 florins.[25] Payment was made through Philip II's treasurer, Domingo d'Orbea, and the tapestries were dispatched to the duke of Alba in Naples, where he had just been appointed viceroy. The firm also had dealings with the Brussels weaver Jan Dermoyen and in 1557 paid Dermoyen 387 livres for five unnamed tapestries.[26]

While living with Gian Carlo Affaitadi, Lodi also held an account with the firm. From 1548 to 1566 regular payments are recorded in two surviving *grandes livres* of 1578 and 1580 and in the firm's inventory of 1566.[27] Between 1548 and 1566 Lodi was paid ("per il benificio de sua dinari") the sums of 244 livres, 1 stuiver, and 6 deniers; 335 livres; and 389 livres, 1 stuiver, and 6 deniers, probably as the accrued interest on money that he had invested with the Affaitadi.[28] When Gian Carlo died in 1555, Lodi was a beneficiary named in his will.[29] Evidently, Lodi was still alive in 1566, but there is no subsequent record of him in the Affaitadi papers. The documentary evidence shows, then, that while in Brussels and Lier, Lodi lived with and maintained a close working relationship with the powerful Affaitadi family, affording him an essential connection to supplies and patronage that fostered his successful career.

THE *STORY OF MERCURY AND HERSE*: A NEW RECONSTRUCTION OF THE SERIES

The *Story of Mercury and Herse* series is based on Ovid's account of the metamorphosis of Aglauros from *Metamorphoses* (2.708–835). However, four extra subjects have been added to those described by Ovid, probably to give more emphasis to the story of Mercury and Herse than to Aglauros. Ovid recounts how Mercury, while flying over Athens, noticed and fell in love with the daughter of King Cecrops, Herse, who was among a group of maidens making their way to the Temple of Minerva. When Mercury approached the royal palace, Herse's sister Aglauros stopped him on the steps and demanded payment for her assistance in Mercury's pursuit. Aglauros's action so enraged Minerva that she sought out Envy in order to infect Aglauros with jealousy of Herse. When Mercury returned to the palace and again found his way barred by Aglauros, he changed her to stone and then flew away. Ovid does not describe any sexual encounter between Mercury and Herse, but according to Apollodorus (*Bibliotheca* 3.14.3), Mercury and Herse had a son named Cephalus, who was later carried off by Eos.

Although the scene is not mentioned by Ovid, there is a visual tradition of showing Mercury in the bedchamber of Herse after Aglauros has been turned to stone. The episode is depicted in Paolo Veronese's painting *Hermes, Herse, and Aglauros* (fig. 3). It also appears in various engravings: Jacopo Caraglio's *Mercury Visiting Herse* (fig. 4), the fourth engraving of the series *Loves of the Gods*; Antonio Tempesta's *Mercury Turning Aglauros to Stone* (fig. 5); and Hendrick Goltzius's *Mercury Entering Herse's Room after Changing Aglauros to Stone* (fig. 6), from his Ovid series. Thus it appears likely that, contrary to the traditional reading,

which positions the bridal chamber scene as a jealous vision of Aglauros and penultimate to her transformation into stone, *Mercury Entering the Bridal Chamber of Herse* is the final tapestry in the series. The composition and some of the details of this tapestry are based on Lucian's description of the wedding of Alexander and Roxana, which was taken from a print by Caraglio of the subject. Ovid's basic story of four scenes is expanded into eight in the tapestries of the series, which can be reconstructed as follows:

1. *The Flying Mercury Sees Herse among the Athenian Maidens Going to the Temple of Minerva* (Colección Duques de Alba)
2. *Mercury Walking with Herse toward Athens* (Museo Nacional del Prado, Madrid)
3. *Aglauros Bars Mercury from Entering the Palace; Minerva Flies Off to Visit Envy* (Fundación Casa Ducal de Medinaceli)
4. *King Cecrops Greets Mercury* (Museo Nacional del Prado, Madrid)
5. *Mercury Banqueting with Cecrops and His Three Daughters; Envy Infecting Aglauros* (Colección Duques de Cardona)
6. *Dancing and Music in Cecrops's Palace* (Fundación Casa Ducal de Medinaceli)
7. *Mercury Changes Aglauros to Stone* (The Metropolitan Museum of Art)
8. *Mercury Entering the Bridal Chamber of Herse* (The Metropolitan Museum of Art)

THE *STORY OF MERCURY AND HERSE*: THE THREE VERSIONS AND THEIR BORDERS

As has long been remarked, the three surviving sets of the *Story of Mercury and Herse* were, rather surprisingly, woven by two different Brussels weavers. The earliest extant edition bears the weaver's mark of Willem Dermoyen. This set may have been acquired originally by Emanuel Philibert, duke of Savoy (1528–1580), when he was governor of the Low Countries between 1557 and 1559. Its three remaining pieces are now in the Palazzo del Quirinale, Rome (see fig. 2), formerly in the collection of Madame S. Horst, Lausanne, and in the collection of the Château d'Espeyran, Saint-Gilles-du-Gard, France.[30] Its border design of flowers, fruit, and small animals is common to Dermoyen's tapestries of the 1530s and 1540s, such as the *Hunts of Maximilian* (Musée du Louvre, Paris) and the *Story of Joshua* (Kunsthistorisches Museum, Vienna). These comparisons suggest that this edition of the *Story of Mercury and Herse* was made by Willem Dermoyen about 1545 to 1550.

The weaver's mark of Willem de Pannemaker appears on the other two known sets of the *Story of Mercury and Herse*, which were probably woven in the 1570s, the last important decade of Willem de Pannemaker's production. One was made by Pannemaker about 1570, according to the date woven on the first tapestry of the set.[31] First documented in 1603 in the collection of Francisco Gómez de Sandoval y Rojas, 5th marquis of Denia and 1st duke of Lerma (1553–1625), the set subsequently entered the Medinaceli collection in 1673 as a gift from Feliche Enríquez de Cabrera, widow of the 2nd duke of Lerma, Francisco Gómez de Sandoval y Rojas Manrique de Padilla (1598–1635).[32] After the death of the duchess of Denia and Tarifa, widow of the 15th duke of Medinaceli, in 1903, the set was broken up when certain of the tapestries were sold by her heirs in 1908, by which means two of the pieces eventually entered the Metropolitan Museum as a bequest of George Blumenthal (see fig. 1).[33] This set displays a border design different from that of Dermoyen's edition, with the lateral borders representing the Seven Virtues, the Four Elements, the Three Fates, the Four Seasons, the Seven Liberal Arts, and the Muses, reusing designs first developed for the tapestries of Raphael's *Acts of the Apostles* in the Vatican Collection, woven by Pieter van Aelst in Brussels for Pope Leo X and delivered to Rome between 1519 and 1521.[34] The lower borders, including scenes of Prometheus, Justice or Good Government, Opportunity, Fortune, the Virtues, and Hercules, were employed first for the three reeditions of the *Acts of the Apostles* woven by the Brussels weavers Jan van Tieghem and Frans Ghieteels. They are: one made in the 1540s for Cardinal Ercole Gonzaga (Palazzo Ducale, Mantua); another first recorded in the 1598 inventory of Philip II (Patrimonio Nacional, Madrid, series 12); and one originally made for Henry VIII and first listed in a 1542 inventory of Whitehall Palace. The latter work was later in Berlin and is now lost.[35]

The other partially surviving *Story of Mercury and Herse* set made by Willem de Pannemaker was originally owned by Don Fernando of Toledo, prior of Castile and captain general of Catalonia, and was acquired from him in 1578 by the Diputació Provincial, Barcelona, where it remains.[36] One of the tapestries in the set originally had the date of 1571 woven (or embroidered) onto the border. Unlike the other two tapestries, this set was woven by Pannemaker without metal thread. With a different border again, this set reuses the designs of landscapes populated by animals and mythical figures that first appeared on the *History of Noah*, also woven by Pannemaker, for Philip II between 1562 and 1565.[37] Don Fernando of Toledo also owned a ten-piece set of the same *History of Noah* with the same type of border design, acquired in 1583 and probably intended to match his earlier set of the *Story of Mercury and Herse*. Three of Don Fernando's *Noah* tapestries remain in the collection of the Palace of the Diputació General of Catalonia, Barcelona: *God Orders Noah to Construct the Ark, God Establishes His Covenant with Noah,* and the *Drunkenness of Noah.*[38]

Famously, in 1560–61, Willem de Pannemaker rewove six of the eight tapestries of the *Apocalypse* (Patrimonio Nacional, Madrid, series 11), originally woven by Willem Dermoyen for Philip II, after the original set of the *Apocalypse* was lost in a storm at Laredo in 1559.[39] The two pieces that survived the shipwreck bear Willem Dermoyen's mark, and the six replacement tapestries have the mark of Willem de Pannemaker. Thus either Pannemaker was involved with Dermoyen in the weaving of the original set or he was able to obtain Dermoyen's original cartoons. In the case of the three editions of the *Story of Mercury and Herse,* the production dates point to the likelihood that Pannemaker obtained the original cartoons from the descendants of Willem Dermoyen. Not only did Pannemaker revive these cartoons through his later versions, but he also apparently obtained existing cartoons for the borders from Jan van Tieghem's workshop. As such, the *Story of Mercury and Herse* provides a compelling case of the reuse, revival, and continued appreciation of existing compositions in tapestry production, causing Giovanni Battista Lodi da Cremona's designs to be woven over more than two decades.

IAIN BUCHANAN
Associate Professor, University of Auckland

NOTES

1 See fig. 1 in "Collecting Sixteenth-Century Tapestries in Twentieth-Century America: The Blumenthals and Jacques Seligmann," by Elizabeth Cleland, in the present volume.

2 On Giovanni Battista Lodi da Cremona, see Delmarcel in Brown and Delmarcel 1996, pp. 170–71, 185, 191; Campbell 2002, pp. 393–94; Cleland 2008; and Forti Grazzini 2010.

3 For the *Fructus Belli*, the *Life of Moses*, and the *Puttini*, see Delmarcel in Brown and Delmarcel 1996, pp. 158–73, 194–205, 184–91.

4 For the most recent discussions of the *Story of Mercury and Herse*, see Standen 1985, pp. 87–99, no. 10; and Forti Grazzini 1994, vol. 1, pp. 170–82, no. 76.

5 See Ferrero Viale 1959; Standen 1985, pp. 88–89; and Forti Grazzini 1994, vol. 1, p. 174.

6 See Standen 1985, pp. 88–89; and Forti Grazzini 1994, vol. 1, p. 174. The eight-piece set was reunited for the exhibition "Los amores de Mercurio y Herse: Una tapicería rica de Willem de Pannemaker," Museo Nacional del Prado, Madrid, 2010; see Herrero Carretero and Forti Grazzini 2010.

7 See Puig y Cadafalch and Miret y Sans 1909–10, pp. 456–70; Donnet 1912; Rubio y Cambronero 1972, pp. 51–89; Standen 1985, p. 89; and Forti Grazzini 1994, vol. 1, p. 174.

8 The document is printed in Schneebalg-Perelman 1982, p. 279; see also Roobaert 2004, pp. 96–97, 115–16.

9 The letter of June 15, 1547, is now lost, but its contents are discussed in Hymans 1910, pp. 23–24.

10 The letter of August 31, 1547, is printed in ibid., pp. 160–61, and in Brown and Delmarcel 1996, pp. 96–97.

11 *Conquest of Tunis*, Patrimonio Nacional, Madrid, series 13. The letter of February 5, 1552, from Lodi to Ferrante Gonzaga is printed in Brown and Delmarcel 1996, p. 104 (doc. 32).

12 See Delmarcel in Brown and Delmarcel 1996, p. 191.

13 The two documents concerning Conrad Schot are printed and discussed in Hymans 1910, pp. 36–43. They were discovered by Alexandre Pinchart (see Papiers Pinchart, Département des Manuscrits, Bibliothèque Royale de Belgique, Brussels).

14 On Gian Carlo Affaitadi, see Denucé 1934.

15 Ibid., p. 72.

16 Ibid., p. 54.

17 Ibid., p. 70.

18 Ibid., pp. 70–74.

19 On the stained-glass windows, see d'Hulst 1956, pp. 75–77, 86–88, and Helbig 1968.

20 Denucé 1934, pp. 54–65.

21 Ibid., p. 64.

22 Ibid., pp. 58–61.

23 Stadsarchief Antwerp, Insolvente Boedelskamers (hereafter SAA, IB) 1579, Affaitadi Grootboek C (1555–1556), fols. 335, 422, 450, 458, 461–62, 477–78, 480, 523.

24 Denucé 1934, p. 11.

25 SAA, IB 1579, fols. 428, 494; Denucé 1934, pp. 52–53; Archivo de la Casa Alba, Palacio de Leria, Madrid, C169-14 (161).

26 SAA, IB 1580, fol. 160. See Roobaert 2004, p. 208.

27 SAA, IB 1578, Affaitadi Grootboek A; SAA, IB 1580, Affaitadi Grootboek D. The 1568 Inventory is printed in Denucé 1934.

28 SAA, IB 1578 (1548–1551), fol. 142; SAA, IB 1580 (1557–1560), fol. 42; Denucé 1934, p. 205.

29 Denucé 1934, pp. 15, 224, 231: "Mr Bapte le peintre 7 livres, 1 stuiver, 10 gros."

30 See Ferrero Viale 1959; Standen 1985, pp. 88–89; and Forti Grazzini 1994, vol. 1, pp. 170, 174.

31 According to information kindly supplied by Concha Herrero Carretero.

32 See Herrero Carretero 2010.

33 See "Collecting Sixteenth-Century Tapestries in Twentieth-Century America: The Blumenthals and Jacques Seligmann," by Elizabeth Cleland, in the present volume.

34 For Raphael's *Acts of the Apostles,* see Shearman 1972, pp. 84–90, and Campbell 2002, pp. 187–218.

35 For the Gonzaga set, see Delmarcel in Brown and Delmarcel 1996, pp. 148–57. For the Madrid set, see Junquera de Vega and Herrero Carretero 1986, pp. 63–72, and Delmarcel 1999, pp. 165, 170. For Henry VIII's set, see Campbell 2007, pp. 261–67.

36 See Puig y Cadafalch and Miret y Sans 1909–10, pp. 456, 469, and Donnet 1912, p. 201.

37 On the *History of Noah*, see Buchanan 2006.

38 See Rubio y Cambronero 1972, pp. 51–52, illus. on pp. 74, 75, 76.

39 On the *Apocalypse*, see Steppe 1968, pp. 734–48, and Buchanan 1999, pp. 134–37.

REFERENCES

Brown, Clifford M., and Guy Delmarcel, with Anna Maria Lorenzoni
   1996 *Tapestries for the Courts of Federico II, Ercole, and Ferrante Gonzaga, 1522–63.* Monographs on the Fine Arts, 52. Seattle: College Art Association.

Buchanan, Iain
   1999 "The Tapestries Acquired by King Philip II in the Netherlands in 1549–50 and 1555–59: New Documentation." *Gazette des Beaux-Arts,* ser. 6, 134 (October), pp. 131–52.
   2006 "The Contract for King Philip II's Tapestries of the 'History of Noah.'" *Burlington Magazine* 148 (June), pp. 406–15.

Campbell, Thomas P.
   2002 *Tapestry in the Renaissance: Art and Magnificence.* Contributions by Maryan W. Ainsworth et al. Exh. cat. New York: MMA.
   2007 *Henry VIII and the Art of Majesty: Tapestries at the Tudor Court.* New Haven: Yale University Press for the Paul Mellon Centre for Studies in British Art.

Cleland, Elizabeth
   2008 "Christ Appearing to Mary Magdalene ('Noli me tangere')." In Koenraad Brosens et al., *European Tapestries in the Art Institute of Chicago,* pp. 103–7. Exh. cat. Chicago: Art Institute of Chicago.
   1999 "Le Roi Philippe II d'Espagne et la tapisserie: L'Inventaire de Madrid de 1598." *Gazette des Beaux-Arts,* ser. 6, 134 (October), pp. 153–78.

Delmarcel, Guy
   1999 "Le Roi Philippe II d'Espagne et la tapisserie: L'inventaire de Madrid de 1598." *Gazette des Beaux-Arts,* ser. 6, 134 (October), pp. 153–78.

Denucé, Jean
   1934 *Inventaire des Affaitadi, banquiers italiens à Anvers de l'année 1568.* Collection de documents pour l'histoire de commerce 1. Antwerp: Editions de Sikkel.

Donnet, Fernand
   1912 "Note sur quelques tapisseries bruxelloises à Barcelone." *Académie Royale d'Archéologie de Belgique, Bulletin,* pp. 191–204.

Ferrero Viale, Mercedes
   1959 "Essai de reconstitution idéale des collections de tapisserie ayant appartenu à la maison de Savoie au XVIIᵉ et XVIIIᵉ siècle." In *Het herfsttij van de Vlaamse tapijtkunst: Internationaal colloquium, 8–10 October 1959,* pp. 269–300. Brussels: Paleis der Academiën.

Forti Grazzini, Nello
   1994 *Gli arazzi.* 2 vols. Il patrimonio artistico del Quirinale. Rome: Editoriale Lavoro; Milan: Electa.
   2010 "El cartonista de *Las bodas de Mercurio.*" In Herrero Carretero and Forti Grazzini 2010, pp. 47–59.

Helbig, Jean
   1968 *Les Vitraux de la première moitie du XVIᵉ siècle conservés en Belgique: Province d'Anvers et Flandres.* Corpus vitrearum Medii Aevi 2. Brussels: Impr. F. van Buggenhoudt.

Herrero Carretero, Concha
   2010 "Una tapicería rica recuperada: *Las bodas de Mercurio* del duque de Lerma y la Casa de Medinaceli." In Herrero Carretero and Forti Grazzini 2010, pp. 7–23.

Herrero Carretero, Concha, and Nello Forti Grazzini
   2010 *Los amores de Mercurio y Herse: Una tapicería rica de Willem de Pannemaker.* Exh. cat. Madrid: Museo Nacional del Prado.

d'Hulst, Henri
   1956 *Kunstglasramen in de Collegiale kerk van Sint-Gummarus te Lier.* Antwerp: De Vlijt.

Hymans, Henri
   1910 *Antonio Moro: Son Oeuvre et son temps.* Brussels: G. Van Oest.

Junquera de Vega, Paulina, and Concha Herrero Carretero
   1986 *Catálogo de tapices del Patrimonio Nacional.* Vol. 1, *Siglo XVI.* Madrid: Editorial Patrimonio Nacional.

Puig y Cadafalch, Josep, and Joaquim Miret y Sans
   1909–10 "El Palau de la Diputació General de Catalunya." *Institut d'Estudis Catalans: Anuari* 3, pp. 385–480.

Roobaert, Edmond
   2004 *Kunst en kunstambachten in de 16de eeuw te Brussel.* Archives et bibliothèques de Belgique, numéro spécial/Archief- en Bibliotheekwezen in België, extranummer 74. Brussels: Archief- en Bibliotheekwezen in België.

Rubio y Cambronero, Ignacio
   1972 *El Palacio de la Diputación Provincial de Barcelona.* 2nd ed. Barcelona: Diputación Provincial.

Schneebalg-Perelman, Sophie
   1982 *Les Chasses de Maximilien: Les Enigmes d'un chef-d'oeuvre de la tapisserie.* Brussels: Chabassol.

Shearman, John
   1972 *Raphael's Cartoons in the Collection of Her Majesty the Queen, and the Tapestries for the Sistine Chapel.* London: Phaidon.

Standen, Edith Appleton
   1985 *European Post-Medieval Tapestries and Related Hangings in The Metropolitan Museum of Art.* 2 vols. New York: MMA.

Steppe, Jan-Karel
   1968 "Vlaams tapijtwerk van de 16de eeuw in Spaans koninklijk bezit." In *Miscellanea Jozef Duverger: Bijdragen tot de Kunstgeschiedenis der Nederlanden,* vol. 2, pp. 719–65. 2 vols. Ghent: Uitg. Vereniging voor de Geschiedenis der Textielkunsten.

ELIZABETH CLELAND

Collecting Sixteenth-Century Tapestries in Twentieth-Century America: The Blumenthals and Jacques Seligmann

In the summer of 2010, a complete, eight-piece tapestry set, the *Story of Mercury and Herse*, probably designed by the Italian Giovanni Battista Lodi da Cremona, was reunited to magnificent effect in the temporary exhibition "*Los amores de Mercurio y Herse*: Una tapicería rica de Willem de Pannemaker" at the Museo Nacional del Prado, Madrid.[1] Although six of the tapestries were already in Spain, documented there since 1603, the final two pieces, *Aglauros's Vision of the Bridal Chamber of Herse*[2] and *Mercury Changes Aglauros to Stone* (fig. 1), were lent by The Metropolitan Museum of Art, having been sold by their Spanish owners at the dawn of the twentieth century. The circumstances of these tapestries' more recent provenance draw attention to two of the Metropolitan Museum's most inspired donors. The unusual relationship between these collectors and the dealer from whom they acquired the tapestries, and the survival of their correspondence, sheds some light on the often impenetrable world of art dealing in the first quarter of the twentieth century.

In beauty of design, quality of execution, condition, and the sumptuousness of their raw materials, *Aglauros's Vision of the Bridal Chamber of Herse* and *Mercury Changes Aglauros to Stone* are keystones of the Metropolitan Museum's tapestry collection.[3] It is, therefore, perhaps all the more surprising that these tapestries were not part of the primary edition of the *Story of Mercury and Herse*, only one piece of which survives in the Palazzo del Quirinale, Rome.[4] Instead they were woven some thirty years later, about 1570, under the direction of the great Brussels-based master weaver Willem de Pannemaker as part of a breathtakingly sumptuous reedition, the richness of which is remarkable even among characteristically splendid Renaissance tapestries. In this edition, the decorative elements of the designs have been noticeably embellished, the bright palette toned down to accentuate the glow of silver and gilded-silver metal-wrapped threads, and the weaving technique ramped up to include large areas of virtuoso effects, such as embroidery-like basket weave.

Though the cartoons were approaching three decades old when they were reused to weave this set, the outlay of cost to afford such materials and workmanship implies that de Pannemaker was almost certainly working on commission. The patron has not been documented, but by 1603 the set was already included in an inventory of the collection of Francisco Gómez de Sandoval y Rojas, 5th marquis of Denia and 1st duke of Lerma (1553–1625), and his wife, Catalina de la Cerda, daughter of the 4th duke of Medinaceli.[5] After the tapestries had remained for centuries together, in 1903, at the death of the duchess of Denia and Tarifa (1827–1903), widow of the 15th duke of Medinaceli, they were split among six of her heirs. A note in the Medinaceli family archives, written in June 1909, recorded the allocations: the first piece, *Mercury Seeing Herse*, passed to the duchess of Híjar (1854–1923); the second, *Mercury Walking with Herse*, to the 2nd duke of Tarifa (1864–1931); the third, *Aglauros Stopping Mercury*, the fifth, *Aglauros Is Overcome by Envy*, and the sixth, *Dancing in Cecrops' Palace*, all to the 17th duke of Medinaceli (1880–1956); the fourth, *Cecrops Welcoming Mercury*, to the duchess of Uceda (1849–1923); the seventh, *Aglauros's Vision of the*

fig. 1 *Mercury Changes Aglauros to Stone* from the *Story of Mercury and Herse*. Design attributed to Giovanni Battista Lodi da Cremona (Italian, active 1540–ca. 1566), ca. 1540. Tapestry woven under the direction of Willem de Pannemaker (Netherlandish, active 1535–78, d. 1581), Brussels, ca. 1570. Wool, silk, and precious-metal-wrapped threads, 14 ft. 9 in. × 23 ft. 6 in. (449.6 × 716.3 cm). The Metropolitan Museum of Art, Bequest of George Blumenthal, 1941 (41.190.134)

Bridal Chamber of Herse, to the 14th duke of Lerma (1860–1936); and the eighth, *Mercury Changes Aglauros to Stone*, to the countess of Valdelagrana (1865–1949).[6]

By November 1909, the duke of Lerma and the countess of Valdelagrana had both sold their tapestries, which passed in rapid succession from a Parisian antiquarian, Raoul Heilbronner, to the dealer Jacques Seligmann, based in Paris and New York, to collectors George and Florence Blumenthal.[7] On November 17, 1909, the two tapestries arrived at the Metropolitan Museum, to which, apparently immediately after the tapestries' acquisition, the Blumenthals presented them on loan.[8] The loan was celebrated in the Museum's *Bulletin* in March 1910.[9]

George Blumenthal was a self-made millionaire.[10] Born in Frankfurt am Main, Germany, in 1858, he worked as a banker and found his niche in the buying and selling of securities. By the time he was twenty-eight, Blumenthal had already been chosen by the legendary moneyman John Pierpont Morgan to work with him and Jacob H. Schiff on forming a syndicate to successfully halt the gold crisis that was on the brink of wiping out the American economy. J. P. Morgan impressed the younger bankers not solely as a business mentor but also with his voracious pursuit of fine art. Both Schiff and Blumenthal emulated Morgan's tapestry

collecting, but while Schiff was content to commission inexpensive modern copies woven in New York, Blumenthal spent part of his fortune buying the real thing.[11] Employed by the firm of Lazard Frères, by his late thirties Blumenthal had become director of the New York branch, and his phenomenal success was already the stuff of caricature (fig. 2).

Although Blumenthal's work occupied him on both shores of the Atlantic, and his wife, Florence (fig. 3), had been born and raised in California, the Blumenthals lived much of their married life in France: it was in Paris that their hospital for sick children was built; that they gave to the Sorbonne, sponsored new inner-city parks, and funded prizes for struggling artists; and that Florence established their philanthropic Fondation Blumenthal. Indeed, in 1929, Florence was presented with France's Legion of Honor, her husband receiving his slightly later.[12]

Nonetheless, stateside, the couple needed a suitably impressive New York base. In 1920, the Blumenthals unveiled their brand-new New York town house, built on the corner of East Seventieth Street and Park Avenue. It is likely that the *Mercury and Herse* tapestries were acquired, eleven years earlier, with that specific location already in mind. The New York mansion, long in the planning, had been designed around the Blumenthals' art collection, with each room taking as its focus a particular star possession. Seligmann's son, Germain Seligman (he dropped the second *n* from his name), would later report that "every capital work of art was to be chosen before the actual building began . . . so that it would fit ideally into the place planned for it both in physical proportion and in relation to the aesthetic scheme."[13] Not long after the Blumenthals acquired the tapestries from Seligmann, they also bought from him another Renaissance masterpiece, the early sixteenth-century marble patio from the castle of Los Vélez, in Vélez Blanco, Almería, Spain, which would ultimately provide the inimitable setting for the tapestries' display. Sourced, like the tapestries, from Spain, the patio came via Seligmann's agent Heilbronner.[14] Though the Blumenthals' house was demolished in 1945—an event deemed newsworthy enough for a headline in the *New York Times*—most of the art collection survives, and written accounts and archival photography provide a sense of the home's extraordinary atmosphere.[15]

The heart of the house was the patio (figs. 4, 5). Within it, the two *Mercury and Herse* tapestries faced each other across the space, the walls nearby adorned with Florentine terracotta armorial tondi, a painted and gilded stucco relief of the Virgin and Child also from Florence, Justus of Ghent's great cloth painting *The Adoration of the Magi* (which Blumenthal acquired from the younger Seligman), and, on opposite sides of the room's upstairs gallery, two massive fifteenth-century Spanish polyptychs: the *Virgin and Child with the Pietà and Saints* by an anonymous Castilian painter, and the Aragonese *Virgin and Child Enthroned with Scenes from the Life of the Virgin* attributed to the Master of the Morata Retable.[16] Lining the upstairs gallery were early sixteenth-century *Hunting Parks* tapestries.[17] In the windows were set sixteenth-century Flemish stained glass, and the room was lit by candles held in massive, mostly Spanish, sixteenth-century iron freestanding candelabra. The Florentine fountain in the center of the room bore the arms of Jacopo de' Pazzi; it had been rescued from the Pazzi Gardens, which were destroyed in 1865.

Next door to the patio was the Ballroom, decorated with eighteenth-century "flower-strewn" tapestries.[18] The Gothic Hall (also called the Library) on the floor above, featured the tapestry titled *Hawking Party*, acquired from the Charles Mège collection in Paris, conceivably again via Seligmann and/or Heilbronner, both of whom handled works from that collection, and *Shepherd and Shepherdesses*, formerly in the Schutz collection in Paris; covering the cushions scattered on the sofas, visible in period photography, was a set of six Brussels-attributed *Story of Abraham* miniature tapestries, dated to 1600 and sumptuously woven in wool, silk, and precious-metal-wrapped threads, bought by Mrs. Blumenthal from Seligmann.[19] The Formal Dining Room next door centered on the sizable tapestry fragment then called the "Charlemagne Tapestry," bought by the Blumenthals in 1912 from the dealers French & Co. and previously owned by the marquis Henri de Vibraye, from his château at Bazoches du Morvan in the Nièvre region of France, and the very fine altar tapestry of the Lamentation was positioned under a minstrels' gallery.[20] Finally, on the top floor of the house was George Blumenthal's study, in which could be found the splendid tapestry of the Crucifixion, purchased before 1909, also from French & Co.; its former owner, the baron Frédéric d'Erlanger, had acquired it—along with many other tapestries—at the sale of the collection of the duke of Berwick and Alba in 1877.[21]

After a day spent in the house as Florence Blumenthal's guest, the architect William Welles Bosworth wrote to his hostess that she had made "the greatest contribution to the art of domestic architecture in this country."[22] The Parisian dealer René Gimpel noted in his diary that "her house is the only one in New York whose atmosphere is genuinely antique."[23] Another visitor to the house, the connoisseur-dealer Georges Demotte, wrote to Florence that "for the first time in my life, I have visited an ideal home."[24]

In his memoirs, Germain Seligman evocatively recalled visiting the New York town house:

> Once inside, the impression of austerity was replaced by a world of the imagination, far from the material bustle of New York. It was a dream-like oasis of beauty, complete with melodious sound of running water from the patio fountain, often the only sound of greeting. At dusk, the light from a table lamp opposite the entrance gave to the high, wide court a quality at once eerie and intimate, as it reduced the proportions and picked up the warmth of the blooming flowers, green plants, and colorful oriental rugs. It is difficult to explain how so sumptuous and impressive a house could be so intimate; this was but one achievement of an extraordinary woman; he continued: Florence Blumenthal moved about like a fairy-tale princess. . . . In the evening, she often wore Renaissance velvet gowns, in dark jewel-like colors which . . . gave her an air of having been born to this superb environment where every work of art seemed tirelessly at home."[25]

fig. 4 View of the patio in the Blumenthals' New York home, with the *Aglauros's Vision of the Bridal Chamber of Herse* tapestry. Photographic print preserved in the "Home of George and Florence Blumenthal, fifty east Seventieth Street, New York, 192-?" album. Thomas J. Watson Library, The Metropolitan Museum of Art

fig. 5 View of the patio in the Blumenthals' New York home, with *Mercury Changes Aglauros to Stone* tapestry. Photographic print preserved in the "Home of George and Florence Blumenthal, fifty east Seventieth Street, New York, 192-?" album. Thomas J. Watson Library, The Metropolitan Museum of Art

In later years, after Florence's death, George Blumenthal stopped using any electric light in the Court, but instead lit it only by candles—and employed three "candlemen" who were kept solely occupied with the lighting and extinguishing of the hundreds of candles illuminating the cavernous room.[26]

Like so many of their contemporaries, the Blumenthals built up their holdings of European art by acquiring works sold off from the great European collections via a small group of dealers.[27] For a handful of their tapestries, they turned, for example, to French & Co., René Gimpel, and auctions. But the bulk of their tapestries, like much of their other medieval and Renaissance furniture, paintings, sculptures, and stained glass, they acquired from the Seligman(n)s. In addition to the tapestries recorded in their New York mansion, the Blumenthals' collection included two important *Grotesques* tapestries, then believed to have been part of a set of bed hangings for Philip II of Spain, acquired from Seligmann in 1912, and other fine examples of Brussels and Parisian production.[28]

In what was an exceedingly cynical and intensely competitive atmosphere, with the vast sums of money being spent occasioning dealers to nurture and groom clients, the case of the Seligman(n)s and the Blumenthals seems to have been rather exceptional.[29] George Blumenthal and Jacques Seligmann (fig. 6) shared a personal acquaintance that stretched all the way back to boyhood, when both apparently attended the same school in Frankfurt. Aware of the reflected cachet of this connection, the Seligman(n)s, ever canny businessmen, went to some length to present the association as more of a friendship and less of a business relationship, an idea perpetuated by Germain throughout his memoirs.[30] Nonetheless, the letters between the Blumenthals and the Seligman(n)s, preserved in the Jacques Seligmann & Co. Records, do reveal an informality between the correspondents—endorsing the notion that this was indeed more than a business acquaintance. Seligmann, writing to George Blumenthal in French, familiarly addressed him as "tu"; in his correspondence with Mrs. Blumenthal, she signed herself "Florie."[31]

Their letters ranged beyond art collecting. Blumenthal, for example, gave the younger Seligman advice about stocks and shares.[32] Motivated by their shared Jewish heritage, Jacques Seligmann noted to "George" a request from a "Mr. Warburg" to send him something for Jewish charities (which he did).[33] As proof of their friendship, the Blumenthals sent the Seligman(n)s food hampers on a regular basis.[34] A glimpse into the Blumenthals' domestic life is also

offered by Florence's correspondence with Germain, written in a conspiratorial tone, regarding the acquisition of her husband's Christmas present in December 1928.[35] George Blumenthal's relationship with Seligmann was familiar enough for the dealer to ask Blumenthal to recommend him to John D. Rockefeller Jr.[36]

Blumenthal's support of Seligmann's endeavors led him to lend some of his most splendid tapestries to the ambitious loan exhibitions that Seligmann hosted in his Parisian showroom. In 1913, Blumenthal withdrew both of the *Mercury and Herse* tapestries from their loan at the Metropolitan Museum and had them shipped to France so that Seligmann could show them at his exhibition "Medieval and Renaissance Art," ostensibly organized by the marquise de Ganay to raise funds for the French Red Cross. In 1927, the Blumenthals lent the Crucifixion that Seligmann had previously admired hanging in what he called "George's den" in the New York mansion to the loan exhibition of religious art organized to benefit the Basilica of the Sacré Coeur and sponsored by Louis Cardinal Dubois, archbishop of Paris, and Patrick Cardinal Hayes, archbishop of New York.[37]

At face value, these exhibitions were noncommercial ventures: none of the tapestries or other works were for sale, and the events were, in name at least, curated by luminaries of the social scene, with proceeds going to charity. In actuality, they provided Seligmann, as host, with a respectable veneer of philanthropy and served as a marvelous advertisement, reuniting many works that had passed through his hands, showcasing an impressive roster of influential clients and, as Germain later put it, "bringing the art-minded public, as well as the choice collectors, to [their premises in the former Hôtel de] Sagan."[38]

The Blumenthals' special relationship with Seligmann also provides the key to explaining the otherwise puzzling paucity of transactions between Blumenthal and the ubiquitous dealer Sir Joseph Duveen. Blumenthal never apparently acquired any tapestries from Duveen's stock and had little or no dealings with the Duveen firm in general. The correspondence between the Blumenthals and the Seligman(n)s is remarkably candid in their mutual abhorrence of Duveen, strengthening the idea that, long before they became subject to investigation by modern observers, the questionable tactics of the Duveen firm and, in particular, Duveen's business relationship with the art historian Bernard Berenson were already being remarked upon by their contemporaries.[39] Seligmann wrote to Blumenthal: "It is terrible to think that a country like America is undermined by such intelligent and nasty people as that lot [Duveen and associates], but it cannot be helped. That 'bande noire' wants to be in possession of all of America, and the means which are employed are really terrible. . . . Well, it is no use to talk about all those terrible, undermining businesses."[40]

When another collector questioned Jacques Seligmann's refusal to provide attributional guarantee, Seligmann took a veiled swipe at what he regarded as Duveen's questionable transactions with art "experts."[41] In 1921 Seligmann went so far as to suggest that he and Blumenthal were united against all that Duveen represented, and that Duveen's associate, Berenson, had occasioned an intrigue around a painting attributed to Titian owned by Blumenthal simply to "what we call in French, 'nous brouiller' [cause trouble between us]!"[42] Almost three years later, Germain wrote to Florence Blumenthal that "you would be surprised indeed to hear of the machinations already set afoot against me by the combination at the head of which the same people [Duveen and associates] remain."[43]

The particularly bitter antagonism between the Seligman(n)s and the Duveens probably originated with Henry Duveen's perceived double cross back in 1901 when he maneuvered Jacques Seligmann, his erstwhile partner in the scheme, out of the sale at vastly inflated cost of the *Mazarin Tapestry* to J. P. Morgan.[44] Nor can it have helped that Duveen continued to

engage in business with Jacques's estranged brother, Arnold.[45] But in general terms, the atmosphere of suspicion and distrust among the principal dealers of tapestries operating about this time was part of a wider phenomenon: the small band of dealers frequently pitted one against another and kept a wary eye on one another's activities. When George Blumenthal, for example, later bought another tapestry, *Gentleman*, from the *Figures in a Rose Garden* group, at the sale of Raoul Heilbronner's holdings in Paris in June 1921, Joseph Duveen's agent cabled Duveen to remark upon the fact that Jacques Seligmann had accompanied Blumenthal to the sale.[46]

We get the impression of a pack of hounds on the scent of ancient European collections whose owners were amenable to selling. In the midst of negotiations with the Chapter of the Cathedral of Burgos, for instance, for two of its splendid *Story of the Redemption of Man* tapestries, Duveen's agents cabled him this warning: "We must act quickly as Germain Seligman is now in Spain, probably after this business also we must keep very alive as Wildenstein, Larcade, both Seligmanns are searching everywhere for Gothic tapestries and are paying higher prices than we are."[47] Indeed, in 1931, the Spanish agent Raimundo Ruiz would eventually sell the two tapestries from Burgos not to Duveen but to French & Co.[48]

Similarly, in 1913, during an uneasy business collaboration between French & Co. and Heilbronner, pertaining to the duke of Sesto's *Scipio* tapestries (subsequently sold to William Randolph Hearst), a mutual acquaintance urged Heilbronner to be candid with French & Co. about who had already seen the tapestries because "you know exactly what kind of people Duveen and Seligmann are, and if they can damage the goods by talking against them, they will certainly do so."[49] In 1915, at J. P. Morgan's death, Joseph Duveen made an offer to purchase his enormous and important tapestry collection from Morgan's son; Duveen later confided to his gallery manager that "he did not reply. Two days later I heard that Mitchell Samuels of French & Co., backed by [the collector] Joseph Widener, had bought the tapestries. I had lost the market for tapestries which had been created by my father forty years ago and which we had held ever since. I have to do something to get it back."[50]

Given this backdrop, it is perhaps not so surprising to find no explicit reference to sales transactions regarding the *Mercury and Herse* tapestries either in Raoul Heilbronner's papers, preserved in the Library of Congress, or in the Jacques Seligmann & Co. Records, now in the Smithsonian's Archives of American Art. Not only are both of these sets of records incomplete, but more particularly, even if the transactions linked to the *Mercury and Herse* tapestries are preserved among them, the vocabulary used to describe the tapestries would have been kept deliberately vague, lest any competitors caught wind of the tapestries' short-lived availability to the art market.

The speed with which the tapestries passed from their two Spanish owners through the hands of Heilbronner and Seligmann to the Blumenthals, and the seamlessness of the immediate loan to the Metropolitan Museum lend credence to the suggestion that Seligmann had orchestrated a plan well in advance of the actual purchase. Seligmann had apparently been aware of the sumptuous *Mercury and Herse* set since it was first published in 1906; citations for this reference and for a 1907 article appear in the brief object record of the tapestries in the Jacques Seligmann & Co. Records.[51] Once the tapestries had been split between the Medinaceli heirs, Seligmann almost certainly approached them with an offer, already bearing in mind the tapestries' suitability for the Renaissance Hispano-Flemish theme of the planned centerpiece of the Blumenthals' American home.

Heilbronner, who elsewhere dealt in more pedestrian works, is unlikely to have been acting independently and instead seems to have been Seligmann's discreet intermediary, probably again needed to avoid arousing the curiosity of rival dealers. It was Seligmann who handled all the details of the loan to the Museum, acting in the Blumenthals' name. The tapestries were shipped from Europe to Jacques Seligmann & Co.'s New York branch, whence they were transferred to the Museum, where they remained until June 1914, with a brief absence from March to July 1913, when they traveled to Paris for inclusion in Seligmann's exhibition.[52]

Seligmann was apparently right to have been so cautious: French & Co. had photographs of all eight *Mercury and Herse* tapestries among its papers, and the well-informed author of the later note in the Metropolitan Museum's files addressed to John Goldsmith Phillips, then a curator in the Department of Western European Arts, recording Heilbronner, Seligmann, and Blumenthal's transactions for the two *Mercury and Herse* tapestries, was French & Co.'s cofounder and director, Mitchell Samuels.[53] Seligmann's efforts and achievement in obtaining two of the prized *Mercury and Herse* tapestries on behalf of his erstwhile school friend was probably motivated as much by awareness of the cachet the Blumenthals' New York residence would eventually

confer as by their perceived friendship, but it is nonetheless striking that he sold the tapestries to Blumenthal for a very reasonable sum: reportedly $120,000 for both tapestries.[54] To put that in some context, $120,000 in 1909 was roughly equivalent to the price of ten acres of Bronx farmland in that year, and eight times the mayor of New York's annual salary.[55] Had Seligmann made the tapestries available to the market, it is probable that he could have sold them for considerably more than $60,000 each, considering the $80,000 Mrs. Blumenthal paid the dealer René Gimpel for the much smaller and less important *Saint Veronica* tapestry in 1919, or Arthur Lehman's acquisition of the more modest, if appealing, *Holy Family with Saint Anne* for $100,000 from French & Co. in 1916.[56] Inflated tapestry costs achieved by some dealers dwarf the Blumenthals' payment for the prized *Mercury and Herse* works: examples include Henry Duveen's sale of the *Mazarin Tapestry* to J. P. Morgan, mentioned above, for a reputed $500,000 in 1901 and the $350,000 Joseph Duveen persuaded Mrs. George Cooper to pay for a set of Beauvais tapestry-woven chair upholstery and wall panels in 1902.[57]

From 1926 to 1930, the Blumenthals published privately a series of six volumes cataloguing the various facets of their art collection.[58] The pattern behind much of their collecting was the furnishing of their homes: Rococo works in their Parisian home were complemented by medieval and Renaissance pieces for a newly built annex, called the Salle Gothique, partly composed of various salvaged architectural elements, also decorated with tapestries. Period photography of the Salle Gothique (fig. 7) provides glimpses of the *Gentleman* from the *Figures in a Rose Garden* acquired at Heilbronner's sale. European medieval and Renaissance objects dominated the New York mansion and Mrs. Blumenthal's other domestic project, their château in Grasse, near Cannes, France.

Although Jacques Seligmann celebrated George Blumenthal as "superior to the generality of (American) connoisseurs," adding, "there is no body (and this is not to flatter you) in all America of whom you can say, except the Rothschilds, that he possesses such a marvelous chosen collection as yours," sources indicate that it was Florence who was the driving force behind the couple's enthusiasm for art.[59] It was she, and not George, whom Gimpel noted as the purchaser of the *Saint Veronica* tapestry.[60] Works were needed to furnish the Blumenthal homes, but above and beyond decoration, Florence was clearly interested in condition and suitability: in their correspondence, Jacques Seligmann, for example, was careful to be honest with her about

fig. 7 View of the Salle Gothique in the Blumenthals' Parisian home. Photographic print preserved in the George and Florence Blumenthal Scrapbook, Department of European Sculpture and Decorative Arts, The Metropolitan Museum of Art

restorations, candidly admitting that one set of "Gothic" tapestries in which she was interested had "modern borders"; she frequently alluded to objects' proportions and to their appropriateness for the settings she had in mind for them.[61]

Florence Blumenthal also displayed enthusiasm and pride in the sway her husband's status with the Metropolitan Museum gave her: according to an anecdote recounted by Alfred H. Barr Jr., later director of the Museum of Modern Art, New York, when in 1910 Alfred Stieglitz declared that the Metropolitan Museum would never accept the three drawings by Matisse she intended to gift to the Museum, she apparently retorted, "The Museum will take what I offer it," and it did.[62] According to Germain Seligman, Florence sought to emulate the example of her older acquaintance, Bostonian Isabella Stewart Gardner, who had opened the museum housing her art collection in 1903, declaring, "years ago, I decided that the greatest need in our Country was Art. . . . We were a very young country and had very few opportunities of seeing beautiful things, works of art . . . so I determined to make it my life's work, if I could."[63] In turn, Florence herself would provide inspiration for philanthropic art collecting by a wealthy young heiress in Chicago, Kate Buckingham. Folders of letters from 1921 to 1924 in the Seligman(n)s' correspondence reveal the extent of Florence's role as an intermediary introducing Miss Buckingham to the dealers and reassuring her on acquisitions from them.[64] Among the works Buckingham would go on to acquire from the Seligman(n)s was the important tapestry *A Falconer with Two Ladies and a Foot-Soldier*, purchased as one of a group of objects intended to form a great Gothic Hall at the center of the new Art Institute of Chicago.[65]

Above all, it was Florence Blumenthal who, following the tragic death of their only child from illness at eleven years of age, articulated poignantly her motivation behind the couple's ultimately philanthropic collecting, declaring in 1919:

> I'm rich, pampered, elegant, and people think I'm happy. . . . How can I be! I've lost my son. . . . The child whom I created is dead; so I had to create something else, and I made this house, a personality of stone. We'll bequeath it, with the collection, to the city of New York, but its spirit will be gone, for these rugs caress the stones below; the familiars of all this furniture they adorn, will have to be put away, protected behind thick glass.[66]

The couple's philanthropic intentions were perhaps already evident in 1909, when George Blumenthal became the first Jewish trustee of the Metropolitan Museum; from 1928, he donated and handled a fund of $1 million for the Museum; in 1933, three years after Florence's death, he took on the role of the Museum's president.[67] Upon his death, in 1941, he bequeathed to the Museum his entire art collection (more than 630 objects), along with the New York mansion, with the understanding that the Museum could demolish the house to profit from the land sale.[68] After a twenty-year absence, during which time they hung in the Blumenthals' New York mansion, the *Mercury and Herse* tapestries returned to the Metropolitan Museum. When George Blumenthal's second wife, Ann, died two years later, in 1943, she left to the Museum the twenty-one works that had been allowed to stay with her.

The Blumenthals' magnificent collection, of such caliber that more than two hundred of the works are still on display in the Museum's galleries, spanned European paintings, applied arts, and furniture from the eleventh to the eighteenth century. But arguably, it was their tapestries, in particular the *Mercury and Herse* hangings, that most effectively embody Florence Blumenthal's sumptuous aesthetic and the fruits of the canny guidance of Jacques Seligmann.

ELIZABETH CLELAND
Associate Curator, Department of
European Sculpture and Decorative Arts,
The Metropolitan Museum of Art

NOTES

1 See Herrero Carretero and Forti Grazzini 2010. This article is based on a paper delivered at the accompanying symposium, held at the Prado, titled "Los Tapices Flamencos en el Siglo XVI: La Serie de Mercurio y Herse," July 13–15, 2010. Giovanni Battista Lodi da Cremona is the focus of Iain Buchanan's accompanying article in this volume.

2 MMA 41.190.135; see fig. 1 in "Giovanni Battista Lodi da Cremona and the *Story of Mercury and Herse Tapestry Series*, by Iain Buchanan, in the present volume. For analysis of the tapestry's raw materials, see Caro et al. 2014, pp. 163, 164, tables 1 and 2.

3 MMA 41.190.135; 41.190.134; see Standen 1985, pp. 87–99, no. 10.

4 Rome, Palazzo del Quirinale, inv. O.D.P., no. 22; see Forti Grazzini 1994, vol. 1, pp. 170–82, no. 76.

5 "Cuaderno de diferentes tasaciones, unas simples y otras originales, de tapicerías, alfombras, colgaduras, camas, sitiales y otras cosas correspondientes al Exmo. Sr. Duque de Lerma, Año de 1603," El Archivo Ducal de Medinaceli, Hospital de San Juan Bautista, Toledo, Spain, Denia-Lerma microfilm, reel 69, frames 368–456; see Herrero Carretero 2010, p. 7.

6 Today, four of the tapestries remain in the private collections of the extended family; those inherited by the duchess of Uceda and the duke of Tarifa are now in the Prado, the former bequeathed in 1934 and the other purchased in 1965; see Herrero Carretero in Herrero Carretero and Forti Grazzini 2010, pp. 10, 26–29. For an alternate ordering of the seventh and eighth tapestries, see "Giovanni Battista Lodi da Cremona and the *Story of Mercury and Herse Tapestry Series*," by Iain Buchanan, in the present volume.

7 The sale of the tapestries from Heilbronner to Seligmann to the Blumenthals is described in a letter from Mitchell Samuels to John Goldsmith Phillips Jr., October 13, 1943, departmental files, MMA Department of European Sculpture and Decorative Arts. Although it is apparent that Samuels is referring to 41.190.134 and .135, he mistakenly identifies their subject as "Psyche," perhaps thinking of the lost, rich, Brussels-woven, sixteenth-century *Story of Psyche* associated with designs by Michiel Coxcie (see Cleland n.d.a [forthcoming]). The tapestries were similarly wrongly described as "Mercury and Psyche" in the Metropolitan Museum Registrar's paperwork in 1909, although at an unknown date, "Psyche" was crossed out in ink and corrected to "Herse."

8 The receipt for the loan, no. 516, with associated memos and correspondence, is preserved in the Metropolitan Museum Registrar's records for the year 1909. I am indebted to Katharine Baetjer for suggesting this resource, and very grateful to Nina S. Maruca, senior associate registrar, for locating the material for me.

9 Breck 1910a and 1910b.

10 Accounts of Blumenthal's life and achievements are provided by George M. Goodwin (1998, pp. 138–39), by Calvin Tomkins (1989, pp. 218–26, 281–82), and by the Blumenthals' obituaries: "Mrs. Blumenthal, Art Patron, Dead," *New York Times*, September 22, 1930, p. 15, and "Geo. Blumenthal, Museum Head, Dies," *New York Times*, June 27, 1941, p. 17. Recollections of the life and personalities of Mr. and Mrs. Blumenthal are also provided by Florence's niece, Katharine Graham, in her autobiography (1997, p. 8).

11 For J. P. Morgan as a collector, see Seligman 1961, pp. 69–77, and Strouse 2000; for Morgan's biography, see Sinclair 1981. For Schiff's patronage of Baumgarten's looms in the Bronx, see Lorne 1904. For the context of their tapestry collections, see Cleland n.d.b (forthcoming).

12 The full extent of this philanthropy is chronicled in numerous newspaper clippings, from both the American and French press, stored in the George and Florence Blumenthal Scrapbook, preserved in the Library of the Department of European Sculpture and Decorative Arts (hereafter G. & F. B. Scrapbook).

13 Seligman 1961, p. 84.

14 MMA 41.190.482; see Raggio 1964. Additional unpublished documentation pertaining to the transactions between Heilbronner and Seligmann regarding Vélez Blanco can be found in container 5 of the Raoul Heilbronner Papers, preserved in the manuscript division of the Library of Congress, Washington, D.C. (hereafter R. H. Papers).

15 "Blumenthal Home under Demolition," *New York Times*, August 16, 1945, p. 30. Well-illustrated contemporary accounts of the house were published by Augusta Owen Patterson (1930) and by Francis Henry Taylor (1941); there is a very detailed description of the house by Germain Seligman (1961, pp. 142–45). The house is also discussed by Michael C. Kathrens (2005, pp. 294–304). An unpublished album, in the holdings of the Thomas J. Watson Library, MMA (call number 106.1B622F), documents the interior architecture and art collection of the residence in a series of photographic prints.

16 These and all other objects referred to in the following description of the house can now be located in the collection of the Metropolitan Museum: 41.190.43, .44; 41.190.40a; 41.190.21; 41.190.27a–e; 41.190.28a–d; 41.190.457; 41.190.370, 371; 41.100.252–.255; 41.190.471.

17 MMA 41.190.106, .107, .227, .228; see Cavallo 1993, pp. 574–85, no. 49.

18 As described in Seligman 1961, p. 143, and illustrated by Patterson 1930, p. 70.

19 MMA 41.100.195, 41.100.196; see Cavallo 1993, pp. 495–97, no. 37, and pp. 479–82, no. 34 (respectively); and 41.100.57a–.57f; see Standen 1985, pp. 199–203, no. 30. The *Story of Abraham* was the focus of the "Examining Opulence: A Set of Renaissance Tapestry Cushions" installation in the Metropolitan Museum's Antonio Ratti Textile Center (August 4, 2014–January 18, 2015), co-curated by Cristina Carr and Sarah Mallory. I am obliged to Sarah Mallory for identifying these cushion covers in use on the sofas in period photography of the room.

20 MMA 41.100.214, 41.100.215; see Cavallo 1993, pp. 377–412, no. 27, and pp. 278–84, no. 17 (respectively). Another piece from the same tapestry or set as the "Charlemagne Tapestry," also from the marquis's collection, was in a private collection in Geneva in 1921, eventually obtained by the Walters Art Gallery, Baltimore; thence, by exchange, also becoming part of the Museum's collection in 1953, when the two pieces were sewn together with a third fragment, apparently acquired by the Museum from the Duveens, to form a huge composite hanging.

21 MMA 41.190.136; see Standen 1985, pp. 59–64, no. 5.

22 Letter from William Welles Bosworth to Florence Blumenthal, January 6, 1917, in the G. & F. B. Scrapbook.

23 Gimpel 1966, p. 100 (recounted following a visit paid to the house on May 27, 1919).

24 "pour la première fois dans ma vie, j'ai visité une maison idéale." Letter from Demotte to Florence Blumenthal [undated], in the G. & F. B. Scrapbook.

25 Seligman 1961, pp. 142–43.

26 Tomkins 1989, p. 281.

27 For detailed accounts of the tapestry dealers working in Europe and the United States from the late nineteenth to the mid-twentieth century, see Bremer-David 2003–4 and Cleland n.d.b (forthcoming).

28 MMA 41.100.384, .385; see Standen 1985, pp. 105–9, no. 12. Also MMA 41.190.254; 41.190.212a, .212b; 43.163.17, .18; see Standen 1985, pp. 228–30, no. 36, p. 475, no. 69, and pp. 402–4, no. 58 (respectively).

29 For example, already in the early 1880s, Joel Duveen showed a railroad magnate, probably Collis P. Huntington, a set of four Gobelins tapestries designed by Boucher, pretending that they were on order to J. P. Morgan and, by doing so, goading Huntington into making an offer for them: Duveen had purchased them in England for £12,000; he "reluctantly" sold them to Huntington for $150,000 (at that time, approximately £35,000); see Secrest 2004, pp. 25–27. By 1899, Joel's son, Joseph Duveen, would seduce a targeted client with his displays—for example, arranging a set of Boucher-designed, Beauvais-woven *Noble Pastorale* tapestries acquired from château Gâtelier in his salesroom as if in a sumptuous house, to persuade the wealthy soap manufacturer R. W. Hudson how good they would look in his newly acquired country house, as recounted by Edward Fowles (1976, p. 9). Further examples are detailed in Cleland n.d.b (forthcoming). I am very grateful to Charlotte Vignon for corresponding with me in 2006 about the Duveens' tapestry-related transactions.

30 Seligman 1961, pp. 83, 142.

31 Much of this correspondence has been preserved in the Jacques Seligmann & Co., Inc., Records, preserved in the Archives of American Art, Smithsonian Institution, Washington, D.C. (hereafter J. S. & Co. Records).

32 Letter from George Blumenthal to Germain Seligman, November 20, 1929 (J. S. & Co. Records: series 1.3 [General Correspondence], box 15, folder 36).

33 Letter from Jacques Seligmann to George Blumenthal, February 28, 1921 (J. S. & Co. Records: series 1.2 [Paris Office Correspondence], box 6, folder 2).

34 One of many instances being the "case of apples" thank-you letter from Jacques Seligmann to George Blumenthal, January 12, 1921 (J. S. & Co. Records: series 1.2 [Paris Office Correspondence], box 6, folder 2).

35 Letters from Germain Seligman to Florence Blumenthal, December 3, 1928, and from Florence Blumenthal to Germain Seligman, December [n.d.] 1928 (J. S. & Co. Records: series 1.3 [General Correspondence], box 15, folder 36).

36 Letter from Jacques Seligmann to George Blumenthal, October 15, 1921 (J. S. & Co. Records: series 1.2 [Paris Office Correspondence], box 6, folder 2).

37 Reams of surviving correspondence reveal the cost and upheaval of the transatlantic travel to the show of the Crucifixion tapestry and other pieces from the Blumenthals' collection (J. S. & Co. Records: series 1.3 [General Correspondence] box 15, folder 35).

38 See Ricci 1913 and Seligmann 1928; discussed by Seligman 1961, p. 46.

39 See, for example, Simpson 1987.

40 Letter from Jacques Seligmann to George Blumenthal, January 12, 1921 (J. S. & Co. Records: series 1.2 [Paris Office Correspondence], box 6, folder 2).

41 Letter from Jacques Seligmann to Walter Blumenthal, March 6, 1922 (J. S. & Co. Records: series 1.1 [New York Office Correspondence], box 1, folder 4).

42 Letter from Jacques Seligmann to Florence Blumenthal, January 8, 1921 (J. S. & Co. Records: series 1.2 [Paris Office Correspondence], box 6, folder 2).

43 Letter from Germain Seligman to Florence Blumenthal, December 14, 1923 (J. S. & Co. Records: series 1.3 [General Correspondence], box 15, folder 34).

44 According to Fowles 1976, pp. 21–22, and Sinclair 1981, p. 149, J. P. Morgan bought the tapestry for $500,000, apparently prompted to pay more in order to have the honor of subsequently loaning it to Edward VII for his coronation at Westminster Abbey, where it was displayed behind the throne. However, in the more sanitized, "official" account published in Duveen 1935, pp. 130–33, the tapestry was much cheaper, Seligmann was at fault, and the tapestry was never actually used at the coronation. After French & Co. acquired J. P. Morgan's tapestries from his estate, they sold the tapestry to Peter A. B. Widener, whose heir Joseph E. Widener gifted it to the National Gallery of Art (1942.9.446).

45 Numerous transactions and negotiations are included in the Duveen papers—for example, regarding the sale of a set of tapestry-upholstered chairs from Baron Rothschild's collection, in an uneasy alliance between Duveen, Arnold Seligmann, and Wildenstein: cables of May 6 and November 24, 1916, and May 1 and May 5, 1917, between Duveens' New York and Paris offices, (Duveen Brothers Records, Thomas J. Watson Library, MMA, hereafter D. B. Records, box 292, folder 4).

46 Cable, of June 24, 1921, from Paris to New York (D. B. Records, box 250, folder 3). The tapestry is now in the Metropolitan Museum, 41.100.231; see Cavallo 1993, pp. 174–89, no. 8d.

47 Cable, of April 28, 1924, from Paris to New York (D. B. Records, box 293, folder 1).

48 French & Co., stock N.16867 and N.16868. The tapestries are now in the Metropolitan Museum, 38.28, .29; see Cavallo 1993, pp. 421–45, no. 29.

49 Letter from Trade Development Company, N.Y., [signature indiscernible] to Raoul Heilbronner, March 31, 1913 (R. H. Papers, container 8).

50 As recounted by Fowles 1976, p. 114.

51 Mélida 1906 and 1907. Both citations were listed on the single-sheet object record in Seligmann's files (J. S. & Co. Records: series 2.1 [Collectors], box 177, folder 27).

52 Handwritten notes added to the receipt for the initial loan, no. 516, and associated memos and correspondence (Metropolitan Museum Registrar's records for 1909).

53 French & Co.'s negative numbers for the images are N.15299, N.15300, N.15301, N.15302, N.15303, N.15304, N.15305, N.15306; a transcription of the letter from Mitchell Samuels to John Goldsmith Phillips Jr., October 13, 1943, is in departmental files of the Department of European Sculpture and Decorative Arts.

54 Noted by Samuels in the aforementioned letter to John Goldsmith Phillips (see note 53 above).

55 The land sale was reported "In the Real Estate Field," *New York Times*, June 17, 1909, p. 12; the mayor's salary in "The Mayor's Salary," *Commercial West*, November 27, 1909, pp. 8–9. According to the Consumer Price Index, $120,000.00 in 1909 corresponds to just over $3 million today.

56 MMA 41.190.80; see Standen 1985, pp. 74–78, no. 7. For the sale of the *Saint Veronica* tapestry, which Gimpel noted in his diary for the entry on April 8, 1919, see Gimpel 1966, pp. 34, 98. The amount of $80,000 in 1919 equates to approximately $1 million in current terms, according to the Consumer Price Index. MMA 65.181.15; see Cavallo 1993, pp. 342–46, no. 23. The sale to Lehman was reported in the *New York Times*, March 2, 1916, p. 9.

57 For the *Mazarin Tapestry*, now in the National Gallery of Art, Washington, D.C. (1942.9.446), see Fowles 1976, pp. 21–22, and Sinclair 1981, p. 149. For Mrs. Cooper's purchase, see Fowles 1976, p. 28.

58 See Rubinstein-Bloch 1926–30.

59 The first phrase cited in Seligman 1961, p. 38; the subsequent compliment paid in a letter from Jacques Seligmann to George Blumenthal, January 12, 1921 (J. S. & Co. Records: series 1.2 [Paris Office Correspondence], box 6, folder 2).

60 Gimpel 1966, pp. 34, 98.

61 Letter from Jacques Seligmann to Florence Blumenthal, December 1, 1921 (J. S. & Co. Records: series 1.1 [New York Office Correspondence], box 1 folder 4); for example, letters from Florence Blumenthal to Germain Seligman, December 2, 1921, and December 30, 1921 (J. S. & Co. Records: series 1.1 [New York Office Correspondence], box 1, folder 4).

62 Barr 1974, p. 115.

63 Seligman 1961, p. 83; Mrs. Gardner's statement was made in a letter to Edmund Hill, June 21, 1917, Isabella Stewart Gardner Museum files, cited by Chong 2007, p. 213.

64 For example, in Mrs. Blumenthal's correspondence with the firm (J. S. & Co. Records: series 1.1 [New York Office Correspondence], box 1 folder 4); there are also numerous references to Mrs. Blumenthal in Miss Buckingham's letters to and from the Seligman(n)s (J. S. & Co. Records: series 1.1 [New York Office Correspondence], box 1 folder 5 and series 1.2 [Paris Office Correspondence], box 6, folder 2). In his memoirs, Seligman (1961, p. 89) alluded to the Blumenthal influence over Buckingham. However, toward the end of their acquaintance, Mrs. Blumenthal's sway seems to have waned: one particular exchange, from May to June 1924, details a particular transaction in which Miss Buckingham, very embarrassed, requests Germain Seligman to take back and reimburse her (almost $3,000) for a group of furniture that Mrs. Blumenthal had urged her to buy; she also expressly asks Seligman not to mention this to Mrs. Blumenthal (box 6, folder 2).

65 The Art Institute of Chicago, 1922.5370; see Brosens et al. 2008, pp. 56–61, no. 5.

66 As recounted by Gimpel (1966, pp. 100–101). This tragedy as impetus for Mrs. Blumenthal's collecting activities was also alluded to by Seligman (1961, p. 144). An unsigned, typewritten eulogy for Florence Blumenthal, pasted into the G. & F. B. Scrapbook, reiterates her devotion to the child and the shadow his death cast.

67 Discussed in context by Calvin Tomkins (1989, pp. 218–26, 281–82).

68 A second unpublished scrapbook, in the holdings of the Thomas J. Watson Library (call number N5220.B681941Q) documents the objects in the Blumenthal collection received by the Metropolitan Museum as gifts, and also includes typewritten excerpts from the last will and testament of George Blumenthal. In 1943, a special installation was opened, accompanied by a publication: *Masterpieces in the Collection of George Blumenthal* (Ivins 1943).

REFERENCES

Barr, Alfred H., Jr.
1974 *Matisse: His Art and His Public*. New York: Museum of Modern Art. First published 1951.

B[reck]., J[oseph].
1910a "Two Tapestries Woven by Wilhelm de Pannemaker." In "The Wing of Decorative Arts," supplement to *MMAB* 5, no. 3 (March), p. 31.
1910b "Two Tapestries Woven by Wilhelm de Pannemaker, a Further Note." *MMAB* 5, no. 7 (July), pp. 166–68.

Bremer-David, Charissa
2003–4 "French & Company and American Collections of Tapestries, 1907–1959." *Studies in the Decorative Arts* 11, no. 1 (Fall–Winter), pp. 38–68.

Brosens, Koenraad, et al.
2008 *European Tapestries in the Art Institute of Chicago*. Contributions by Pascal-François Bertrand, Charissa Bremer-David, Elizabeth Cleland, Guy Delmarcel, Nello Forti Grazzini, Yvan Maes De Wit, and Christa C. Mayer Thurman. Chicago: Art Institute of Chicago; New Haven and London: Yale University Press.

Caro, Federico, Giulia Chiostrini, Elizabeth Cleland, and Nobuko Shibayama
2014 "Redeeming Pieter Coecke van Aelst's *Gluttony* Tapestry: Learning from Scientific Analysis." *MMJ* 49, pp. 151–64.

Cavallo, Adolfo Salvatore
1993 *Medieval Tapestries in The Metropolitan Museum of Art*. New York: MMA.

Chong, Alan
2007 "Mrs. Gardner's Museum of Myth." In "Museums—Crossing Boundaries," *Res: Anthropology and Aesthetics*, no. 52 (Autumn), pp. 213–20.

Cleland, Elizabeth
n.d.a "From Brussels to Paris. Repurposing Sixteenth-Century Flemish Designs in Seventeenth-Century French Tapestries." In *La Tapisserie en France*, edited by Pascal-François Bertrand and Audrey Nassieu Maupas. Rennes: Presses Universitaires de Rennes. Forthcoming.
n.d.b "An Unbiased Eye? Early Tapestry Scholarship, Stateside." In *Historiographie des arts décoratifs*, edited by Pascal-François Bertrand. Le Kremlin-Bicêtre: Editions Esthétiques du Divers. Forthcoming.

Duveen, James Henry
1935 *Collections and Recollections: A Century and a Half of Art Deals*. London: Jarrolds.

Forti Grazzini, Nello
1994 *Gli arazzi*. 2 vols. Il patrimonio artistico del Quirinale. Rome: Editoriale Lavoro; Milan: Electa.

Fowles, Edward
1976 *Memories of Duveen Brothers*. London: Times Books.

Gimpel, René
1966 *Diary of an Art Dealer*. New York: Farrar, Straus & Giroux.

Goodwin, George M.
1998 "A New Jewish Elite: Curators, Directors, and Benefactors of American Art Museums." *Modern Judaism* 18, no. 2 (May), pp. 119–52.

Graham, Katharine
1997 *Personal History*. New York: Random House.

Herrero Carretero, Concha

    2010 "Una tapicería rica recuperada: *Las bodas de Mercurio* del duque de Lerma y la Casa de Medinaceli." In Herrero Carretero and Forti Grazzini 2010, pp. 7–23.

Herrero Carretero, Concha, and Nello Forti Grazzini

    2010 *Los amores de Mercurio y Herse: Una tapicería rica de Willem de Pannemaker.* Exh. cat. Madrid: Museo del Prado.

Ivins, W. M., Jr.

    1943 *Masterpieces in the Collection of George Blumenthal: A Special Exhibition.* Exh. cat. New York: MMA.

Kathrens, Michael C.

    2005 *Great Houses of New York, 1880–1930.* New York: Acanthus Press.

Lorne, H. M.

    1904 "Gobelins Tapestry Weaving in America." *Broadway Magazine* 13, no. 5 (August), pp. 23–31.

Mélida, José Ramón

    1906 "Les Tapisseries flamandes en Espagne: Les Fables de Mercure." *Les Arts anciens de Flandre* 1, fasc. 4, pp. 169–71.

    1907 "Una tapiceria inédita." *Forma* 2, pp. 245–48, 262–74.

Patterson, Augusta Owen

    1930 "The Residence of Mr. George Blumenthal." *Town and Country* 84 (March 1), pp. 63–70.

Raggio, Olga

    1964 "The Vélez Blanco Patio: An Italian Renaissance Monument from Spain." *MMAB* 23, no. 4 (December).

Ricci, Seymour de

    1913 *Exposition d'objets d'art du Moyen Age et de la Renaissance: Tirés des collections particulières de la France et de l'étranger; organisée par la Marquise de Ganay à l'ancien Hôtel de Sagan (Mai–Juin 1913).* Paris: Emile Lévy.

Rubinstein-Bloch, Stella

    1926–30 *Catalogue of the Collection of George and Florence Blumenthal, New York.* Vol. 1, *Paintings: Early Schools;* vol. 2, *Sculpture and Bronzes: Mediaeval and Renaissance;* vol. 3, *Works of Art: Mediaeval and Renaissance (Ivories, Enamels, Majolica, Stained Glass, etc.);* vol. 4, *Tapestries and Furniture: Mediaeval and Renaissance;* vol. 5, *Paintings, Drawings, Sculptures: XVIIIth Century;* vol. 6, *Furniture and Works of Art: XVIIIth Century.* Paris: privately printed, A. Lévy.

Secrest, Meryle

    2004 *Duveen: A Life in Art.* Chicago: University of Chicago Press.

Seligman, Germain

    1961 *Merchants of Art, 1880–1960: Eighty Years of Professional Collecting.* New York: Appleton-Century-Crofts.

Seligmann, Jacques

    1928 *Loan Exhibition of Religious Art: For the Benefit of the Basilique of the Sacré Coeur in Paris, at the Galleries of Jacques Seligmann and Company, Inc., March–April 1927.* New York and Paris: La Gazette du Bon Ton.

Simpson, Colin

    1987 *The Partnership: The Secret Association of Bernard Berenson and Joseph Duveen.* London: Bodley Head.

Sinclair, Andrew

    1981 *Corsair: The Life of J. Pierpont Morgan.* Boston and Toronto: Little, Brown.

Standen, Edith A.

    1985 *European Post-Medieval Tapestries and Related Hangings in The Metropolitan Museum of Art.* 2 vols. New York: MMA.

Strouse, Jean

    2000 "The Collector J. Pierpont Morgan." In *Collectors, Collections, and Scholarly Culture: Proceedings of the Session Presented at the American Council of Learned Societies Annual Meeting on May 6, 2000,* pp. 25–34. ACLS Occasional Paper, no. 48. New York: American Council of Learned Societies.

Taylor, Francis Henry

    1941 "The Blumenthal Collection." *MMAB* 36, no. 10 (October), pp. 193, 195–98.

Tomkins, Calvin

    1989 *Merchants and Masterpieces: The Story of The Metropolitan Museum of Art.* Rev. ed. New York: Henry Holt. First published 1970.

Di drento.

½   ½

½

¼

⅓

⅓ì fatto questa fanolatonda
perdie si stermiano duna
al chia altrimentinons
faina

FEMKE SPEELBERG
FURIO RINALDI

Vincenzo de' Rossi as Architect: A Newly Discovered Drawing and Project for the Pantheon in Rome

Although Vincenzo de' Rossi (1525–1587) is principally known as a sculptor today, early written sources suggest that this eminent pupil of Baccio Bandinelli (1493–1560) also had a career as an architect. In the 1568 edition of his *Vite*, Giorgio Vasari (1511–1574) introduced the artist among the "accademici del disegno" as "Vincenzo de' Rossi of Fiesole sculptor, and also architect and member of the Florentine Academy."[1] Raffaello Borghini (1537–1588), in his short account of Vincenzo's life in *Il Riposo* (1584), similarly referenced his work as an architect: "He [Vincenzo] also loved architecture, and with his designs many works have been made."[2]

Given the fact that Vincenzo seems to have been generally known as an architect by his contemporaries, it seems surprising that no architectural project or building has, to date, been assigned to his name. The second part of Borghini's sentence quoted above, which

fig. 1 Vincenzo de' Rossi (Italian, 1525–1587). *Design for a Fountain with the Labors of Hercules*, ca. 1559–62. Black chalk, 17 × 11 in. (43.3 × 27.8 cm). Cooper Hewitt, Smithsonian Design Museum, New York (1942-36-1)

fig. 2 Vincenzo de' Rossi. *Design for a Fountain with Hercules and Cerberus*, ca. 1559–62. Black chalk, with pen and brown ink (?), 17¾ × 14¼ in. (45.2 × 36.1 cm). Location unknown (formerly Colnaghi)

fig. 3 Here attributed to Vincenzo de' Rossi. *Design for an Altar Surmounted by a Crucifix*, ca. 1546–47. Pen and brown ink, brush and gray-brown washes, over traces of black chalk, ruling and compass work; annotated by the artist in pen and brown ink, 23 × 16¾ in. (57.3 × 42.6 cm). The Metropolitan Museum of Art, Purchase, Brooke Russell Astor Bequest, 2013 (2013.205)

implies that the execution of Vincenzo's architectural designs was often left to others, provides some explanation as to why so little is known about this side of his career. It still leaves us with questions, however, concerning what those designs were for and what they may have looked like.

In an effort to explain Vasari's and Borghini's references to Vincenzo as an architect, Barbara Castro, in her 1998 biography of the artist, referred to the *Design for a Fountain with the Labors of Hercules*, now in the collection of the Cooper Hewitt Smithsonian Design Museum (fig. 1), as an example of his designs for architecture.[3] A second drawing of similar subject matter appeared on the art market in 1983 (fig. 2).[4] Together the two designs can be considered to represent the start of a small oeuvre, but while fountains occupy a middle ground between sculpture and architecture, they can hardly provide the sole basis for understanding Vincenzo's career as an architect.

A drawing newly attributed to the artist, acquired by The Metropolitan Museum of Art in 2013,[5] more persuasively substantiates the references found in the sixteenth-century sources and sheds new light on Vincenzo's activities as a draftsman and architect.

The *Design for an Altar Surmounted by a Crucifix* (fig. 3) is inscribed and signed *Vincentio Rossi* by the artist at bottom right (fig. 4) and can be considered the first genuine architectural drawing known by his hand. Moreover, it is almost certainly connected to an early and prestigious commission in Rome for an altar in the Pantheon, by then the dedicated church of Santa Maria ad Martyres, that was awarded to the artist by the influential Confraternita dei Virtuosi.

THE DRAWING AND ITS AUTHORSHIP

The altar design is executed on a sheet of monumental size and contains four different views of the structure, placed on the sheet in a correlated manner, with three projections of the elevation depicted on a horizontal axis above the floor plan of the altar. In the center, the frontal elevation is worked out in pen and brown ink with a light, gray-brown wash. The overall construction consists of a protruding tabernacle supported by Tuscan columns on top of a podium with three steps. The tall frieze above the columns is decorated with a combination of triglyphs with guttae, and metopes filled with symbols of the liturgy: from left to right, a bishop's miter; the host above a chalice and paten; Veronica's veil with the *vera icon*; a trophy of the crucifix and other instruments of the Passion; and a trophy consisting of a ewer and censer. The cornice is crowned by an arched pediment, which is left undecorated, and on top are placed three figural

sculptures supported by rectangular pedestals. The main sculpture in the center is an elongated crucifix with the rocks of Golgotha and the skull and bones of Adam at the base. It is flanked on either side by a figure of a crouching cherub holding up a lance—on the right side combined with the Holy Sponge. An altar table placed underneath the tabernacle consists of a thin slab supported by balusters. The plinth above the altar supports a reliquary in the form of a small central-plan building, of which only half is worked out in the round, flanked at left and right by three candelabra. In the wall above, a shallow compartment or niche with a semicircular top has been outlined by a frame with beveled edges.

The elevation of the altar is combined with three more views: the floor plan (depicted directly under the elevation), the side view from the exterior (on the right, marked *di fuoro* [from outside]), and a section of the side view (on the left, marked *Didrento* [sic] [from inside]). These additional views elucidate various details of the design. They make clear, for example, that the *mensa* (the altar's tabletop) protrudes from the tabernacle, and that shallow Tuscan pilasters are added to the structure behind the main columns of the tabernacle. The elevation and side views are combined with inscriptions providing relevant measurements in Florentine *braccia*. From these measurements it can be calculated that the main architectural body of the altar measures approximately 4.8 × 2.8 × 1 meters, and that the structure at its full reach, including sculpture and pedestal, covers almost double the

drawing's surface, with approximate measurements of 7.9 × 4.2 × 2 meters.[6]

Aside from these notes, the sheet contains two other inscriptions written in the same hand but at different times. The four-line inscription at the bottom right is executed in an ink of similar hue to the ink of the drawing and includes the artist's signature: *Avete a chonsiderare dalli ischalini insu / echorre la misura della tavola dipinta che / va i[n] mezo de dua membretti che sono fralli / 2 pilasstri rinchontro alle cholonne / Vincentio Rossi*[7] (From the small steps and up, you have to take into consideration the measurement of the painted panel that goes in between the two members that are between the 2 pilasters behind the columns, Vincenzo Rossi).[8]

The second inscription, which is placed in the central compartment over the altar, is written in a different, nearly black-brown ink. It appears to have been added later and rather quickly, because the cursive is less neat in comparison to the first inscription, and the text partially runs over the lines of the drawing: *Se fatta questa tavola tonda / perche si servivano duna / vechia altrimenti nonsi / faceva*[9] (This panel has been made with an arched top, because they were using an old one, otherwise this would not have been done [designed] in this manner).[10]

Despite the presence of the artist's signature below the inscription at the lower right, the drawing was not connected to Vincenzo de' Rossi prior to its acquisition by the Metropolitan Museum, and it had been on the art market as an anonymous, sixteenth-century Florentine design. This omission in attribution is perhaps explained by the drawing's subject matter, which has no direct connection with the artist's known sculpted oeuvre.

A comparison of the handwriting (fig. 4) with that in a note written and signed by Vincenzo de' Rossi—addressed to the learned courtier Vincenzo Borghini (1515–1580) and pasted on the verso of one of the artist's few firmly attributed drawings, in the Musée du Louvre, Paris[11]—leaves no doubt, however (figs. 5, 6). Both inscriptions display the distinct *cancellaresca* cursive, the same use of flourishes on the letter *e*, and an almost identical signature by the artist as "Vincentio Rossi."

The draftsmanship of the two sheets is otherwise difficult to compare, owing to their different functions. The figural drawing in the Louvre, *Hercules' Descent into Hades* (fig. 6), was conceived as a compositional study for a bronze relief to be placed under one of the statues of Hercules commissioned from Vincenzo about 1562 by Cosimo I de' Medici (1519–1574), grand duke of Tuscany. The Louvre drawing was primarily meant to convey the composition and expressive properties of the relief, while the overall style of the architectural structure of the altar in the Museum's sheet is descriptively objective and focused on a clear portrayal of the details of the construction. The character of the sculpted figures on top of the altar, particularly the quick and effective pen strokes seen in the two crouching cherubs holding the instruments of the Passion (figs. 7, 8), nevertheless unmistakably exposes the influence of Vincenzo's master, Baccio Bandinelli.[12]

THE COMMISSION

While the inscription and style of the altar drawing confirm the attribution to Vincenzo de' Rossi, at first sight they do not reveal much that can help to identify the specific commission for which this design was made. The Central Italian watermark in the paper (fig. 9) is known to have been in use between 1529 and 1580—a time span that encompasses most of Vincenzo's working life—and therefore does not provide any helpful clues, either.[13]

Viewed within the context of Vincenzo's career, however, the relatively sober character of the altar design indicates an early work. In this respect the design is reminiscent of the overall structure of the tombs of

figs. 7, 8 Details of cherubs in fig. 3

the Medici popes Leo X (r. 1513–21) and Clement VII (r. 1523–34) in the church of Santa Maria sopra Minerva in Rome—a commission obtained by Vincenzo's master, Bandinelli, in 1536. To complete the complex project, Bandinelli supervised a team of Tuscan artists that included the architect Antonio da Sangallo the Younger (1484–1546), who created the overall structure, and the sculptors Raffaello da Montelupo (1504/5–1566/67) and Nanni di Baccio Bigio (1512/13–1568), who were responsible for the final execution of the statues of Popes Leo X and Clement VII.[14] Although he is not mentioned by name, the young Vincenzo de' Rossi, who began an apprenticeship in Bandinelli's workshop at the age of nine, is generally presumed to have assisted in the execution of the two tombs, which were completed by June 15, 1542, when the ashes of the popes were transferred from Saint Peter's to Santa Maria sopra Minerva.[15]

Following his assistance on the two Medici tombs, Vincenzo appears to have worked for Bandinelli in Florence between 1541 and 1545, but his first recorded commissions as an independent artist were also in Rome, where he executed the marble reliefs for the tomb of Pietro Mates (1474–1545) in the church of San Salvatore in Lauro (ca. 1545)[16] and the freestanding sculpture group *Saint Joseph with the Christ Child* for the main altar of the Chapel of Saint Joseph in the Pantheon (fig. 10). Commissioned in August 1545 to "mastro Vincentio scultore,"[17] the latter sculpture can still be

found on the altar of the first chapel on the left when one enters the building.

The Chapel of Saint Joseph is one of the four subsidiary spaces within the Roman building, and it was donated in 1541 by Pope Paul III (r. 1534–49) to the newly founded Confraternita dei Virtuosi al Pantheon, later known as the Confraternita di San Giuseppe in Terrasanta (Brotherhood of Saint Joseph in the Holy Land). The confraternity was founded in March 1541 by the Cistercian monk and canon of the Pantheon, Desiderio de Adiutorio (ca. 1481–1546), who remained at its head until his death. The members of the confraternity came from religious and secular backgrounds, and among them were many prominent artists active in Rome at the time, including Antonio da Sangallo the Younger, Antonio Salamanca (1479–1562), Perino del Vaga (1501–1547), Livio Agresti (ca. 1508–1579), Jacopino del Conte (ca. 1515–1598), Francesco Salviati (1510–1563), Marcello Venusti (ca. 1512–1579), and Girolamo Siciolante da Sermoneta (1521–ca. 1580).[18]

The confraternity became a pontifical academy that survives to this day, and the minutes of the meetings, regularly held by its members, are kept in the Archivio Storico dei Virtuosi al Pantheon in Rome.[19] The minutes of the early meetings provide detailed information about the commission and execution of, and payment for, the statue of Saint Joseph, and they also contain crucial records about a subsequent commission extended to Vincenzo by the confraternity that has so far gone unnoticed. This second commission entailed the erection of an altar in the same chapel that was to house the statue Vincenzo had made. It is this commission that provides us with a plausible context for the newly discovered drawing.

The minutes of the confraternity record that the chapel remained unfurnished during the first two years after the official concession and, through use, gradually became cluttered and disorderly. For this reason, by October 14, 1543, Desiderio decided to commission works to furnish the chapel and decorate it with a statue. The chapel was also meant to house one of the most precious objects in the confraternity's possession: a marble reliquary containing earth from the Holy Land that had been collected by Desiderio himself during two visits to Jerusalem and Mount Sinai in the 1520s. The relics had miraculously survived the Sack of Rome in 1527, when so many others were lost, and found a proper home in the chapel of the confraternity, which was therefore in need of a more dignified appearance.[20]

Initially, the confraternity meant to dedicate its chapel to the Crucifixion and outfit it with sculptures of the crucified Christ, the Virgin Mary, and Saint Joseph. During the meeting of October 1543, however, the members discussed the fact that another altar in the Pantheon was already dedicated to the same subject (the first chapel to the left of the main altar), and they subsequently decided to choose Saint Joseph as their principal patron saint. In response to this change, Antonio da Sangallo the Younger—an important member of the confraternity since its founding and, together with Raffaello da Montelupo, one of the surveyors of the chapel's refurbishment—suggested that he knew a suitable "antique" sculpture ("statua antiqua") that could serve their purpose, and Desiderio immediately set out to obtain it.[21]

Unsuccessful in this endeavor, Desiderio instructed the two surveyors in May 1545 to give the commission to "un mastro excellente" of their acquaintance—who, as the minutes of August 1545 show, was none other than Vincenzo de' Rossi. Just two months after the members of the confraternity had discussed and decided on the iconography of the statue of Saint Joseph, Vincenzo was able to show them an initial clay model. This *bozzetto*, although not yet completed, was highly praised by members of the confraternity ("qual modello piacque molto"), and they gave Vincenzo further instructions to ensure that the final marble version would "please all, in every respect."[22]

Between September 22, 1546, and May 7 of the following year, the marble sculpture of Saint Joseph was completed, and during their meetings, the members of the confraternity began to discuss the subsequent commission for a proper altar, referred to as a large window, to accommodate it. Since Antonio da Sangallo, their principal architect, had died in August 1546, the confraternity decided to entrust this matter either to Raffaello da Montelupo or to Vincenzo.[23]

Close reading of the minutes reveals that the satisfactory execution of the statue of Saint Joseph induced the members to invite its author to furnish the rest of the chapel as well: "The sculptor who made the statue of our Saint Joseph, having brought it to good result by now, also planned to begin to decorate the place where it was to be placed."[24] To execute the design, Vincenzo requested a draft with the specific requirements from the members of the confraternity,[25] who assigned this task to Raffaello da Montelupo and Antonio Labacco (also known as Antonio dell' Abacco; 1495–1570), Sangallo's close collaborator and successor as artistic consultant to the confraternity. That Vincenzo was indeed chosen to design an altar for the chapel is confirmed further by the minutes of the meeting of

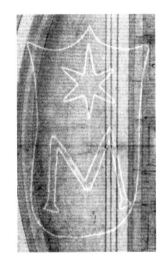

fig. 9 Detail of fig. 3, showing watermark (letter *M* under star in shield)

fig. 10 Vincenzo de' Rossi. *Saint Joseph with the Christ Child,* 1546–47. Marble. Detail of the Altar of the Confraternita dei Virtuosi al Pantheon (fig. 13), Santa Maria ad Martyres (Pantheon), Rome

August 1547, when the artist was asked to report on his progress with the statue and his plans for the site where it was to be placed.[26]

Records of the meetings held in November and December of the same year show that most of the work on the altar had been completed to the satisfaction of the confraternity, and arrangements were made to pay Vincenzo and the craftsmen he employed.[27] This passage in the minutes contains crucial information on the various elements of the altar Vincenzo had designed: "On the day of the 11th of December . . . were settled the accounts with master Vincenzo the sculptor, both for the rest that was owed to him for the statue he made and for the works he commissioned for the window in which the above-mentioned statue was placed, as well as the pilasters, architraves, frieze, cornice, the stone slabs and carving [?] all of it done perfectly."[28]

Several parallels can be drawn between the documentary evidence of the confraternity's commission and details of *Design for an Altar Surmounted by a Crucifix* in the Metropolitan's collection (see fig. 3). First, the most characteristic architectural elements of this otherwise rather sober altar design—such as the "architrave" and "stipiti"—are mentioned expressly in the minutes on several occasions with regard to the "finestrone," or large window. Second, the sculptural decorations on top of the pediment recall the confraternity's original intention to dedicate its chapel to the Crucifixion. Although this subject was rejected in favor of Saint Joseph, its presence in the design bespeaks the order's principal devotion and is warranted by the importance of Christ's sacrifice as the central focus during the Eucharist, an element that is further emphasized in the decoration of the metopes.

A third important link is the prominence that the design gives to the reliquary on the altar (see frontis and fig. 3). This receptacle can be connected to the relics from the Holy Land that had been in the confraternity's possession since its founding. Whether the reliquary in the drawing reflects an already existing object, or whether this, too, is a design by Vincenzo, is unknown. What is significant is that it takes the form of an octagonal temple, in clear reference to the centralized building structure of the Church of the Holy Sepulchre in Jerusalem. A receptacle of this shape would have been the ideal repository for the confraternity's cherished relics.

The two inscriptions on the drawing with Vincenzo's comments on his plans contain further indications that the design is related to the commission in the Pantheon. His directions at the lower right seem to be meant for the craftsmen who assisted him in the execution of the altar, reminding them of measurements and particulars of the construction. The mention of a "tavola dipinta," or painted panel, in this inscription is somewhat mystifying in the context of the Pantheon commission, since it cannot be adequately reconciled with the records of the altar's construction as chronicled in the minutes of the confraternity. Panels and paintings are mentioned there several times, but not in direct connection with the chapel or the altar.[29] However, in the drawing, the compartment above the *mensa* is portrayed as a relatively shallow space, better suited to a painting than to Vincenzo's sculpture of Saint Joseph and the Christ Child.

This fact, inevitably, raises some doubt about the veracity of the identification of the altar design in the Metropolitan's newly discovered drawing with the confraternity's commission to Vincenzo, unless it may be presumed that the sculpture was not placed directly on the altar but positioned elsewhere in the chapel, contrary to the summary wording in the records ("the window in which the above-mentioned statue was placed"). This hypothesis is partially sustained by the recent analysis of the confraternity's records by Regine Schallert. In her written reconstruction of the chapel, which is based purely on the documentary evidence at hand, she concludes that the confraternity discarded the idea of having the statue decorate the altar in favor of placing it in a simple niche. The latter solution was thought to conform more to the "antique" appearance of the Pantheon, in which each subsidiary space had

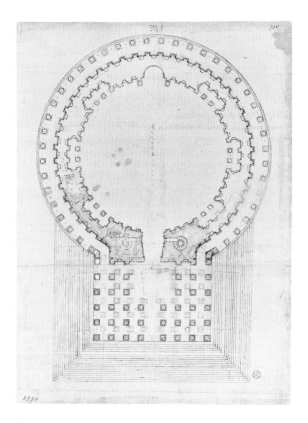

fig. 11 Antonio da Sangallo the Younger (Italian, 1484–1546). *Design for the Floorplan of the Pantheon*, ca. 1535. Pen and brown ink, traces of black chalk, ruling and compass work, 23⅛ × 17⅛ in. (58.9 × 43.4 cm). Gabinetto Disegni e Stampe degli Uffizi, Florence (3990A)

three rectangular niches in the back wall. This would have been in line with sixteenth-century efforts to restore the original character of the building—a project in which many members of the confraternity actively participated.[30] The idea that the statue of Saint Joseph might have been given a separate place within the chapel seems substantiated further by the fact that Vincenzo selected a pillar from the church of Santi Giovanni e Paolo from which to fashion a base.[31] Schallert does not discuss the matter of the altar further, but it is unlikely that the confraternity would have done without an altar for its chapel, both for practical reasons related to the liturgy and because of the frequent mention of "l'altare di San Giuseppe" in the confraternity's records that predate the construction of the current Baroque altar, toward the end of the seventeenth century.[32]

While the content of the first inscription may generate some doubt about the identification of the altar as the commission by the confraternity, the second inscription, placed over the central niche of the altar, speaks highly in its favor. Most likely written at a later time, the inscription (quoted above) shows Vincenzo in defense of his design. He explains that the niche has been made round because he had to conform to specific conditions, in this case presumably a painted panel with an arched top.

The implication is that someone wondered about this specific element while looking at the design drawing, prompting Vincenzo to respond—a scenario that might be explained by the context of the altar within the Pantheon. Indeed, the overall design closely follows the model of the *aediculae*, or tabernacles, in the main hall of the building. The most significant departures from the building's structure are the order of the columns (Tuscan in the drawing, instead of Corinthian) and the fact that Vincenzo decided, or was forced, to make his niche round, whereas the *aediculae* all have rectangular niches.

PANTHEON SANGALLENSIS

The decision to follow the general shape of the *aediculae* may have been influenced, or even prescribed, by Antonio da Sangallo the Younger. Annotations and sketches preserved in several of his drawings, now in the Gabinetto Disegni e Stampe degli Uffizi, Florence, reveal Sangallo's profound interest in the Pantheon.[33] Rather than being in awe of its design, however, the architect focused on the defects he noted in the building's architectural structure and set out to correct them, if not in real life, then at least on paper.[34] Sangallo's rendition of a new floor plan for the building (fig. 11) of about 1535 can be considered the culmination of this so-called *Pantheon Sangallensis*, in which all irregularities have been removed and the building answers to one uniform scheme.[35]

Antonio da Sangallo's role as principal surveyor of the building activities of the Confraternita dei Virtuosi provided him with direct access to the architecture of the building. Although he did not execute the altar for the confraternity personally, it may be presumed that his stature as the architect of highest renown and seniority, and his role as surveyor, granted him the right to advise and exercise his influence on the plans, either through Raffaello da Montelupo, who survived him, or possibly directly through Vincenzo, whom he seems to have known from their collaboration on the papal tombs in Santa Maria sopra Minerva. Most of Sangallo's emendation plans for the Pantheon, in fact, date from that period, when the two were working so near the antique building. That Sangallo knew Vincenzo well is further attested to by the fact that Vincenzo's brother, Nardo de' Rossi (ca. 1520–1570/72), was an active member of the Sangallo workshop until Sangallo's death in 1546 and was also connected to the Sangallo family by marriage. A letter from Nardo to Sangallo written on the verso of a drawing in the Uffizi dated January 9, 1546, includes greetings from his brother and reveals that Vincenzo was staying with Nardo in Rome at the time of the Pantheon commission.[36]

fig. 12 Antonio da Sangallo the Younger. *Design for a Freestanding Tomb Seen in Elevation and Plan*, 1530–35. Pen and brown ink, brush and brown wash, over extensive, compass-incised and stylus-ruled construction with pinpricked measurements, on off-white paper now partly darkened, 15¾ × 7⅜ in. (40.1 × 18.8 cm). The Metropolitan Museum of Art, Edward Pearce Casey Fund, 1998 (1998.265)

The Metropolitan Museum's sheet itself also sheds light on the relationship between Vincenzo and Antonio da Sangallo. It is clear, for example, that Vincenzo had become acquainted with the particular drawing practice of the architect's workshop. Over the course of his career and influenced by the methods of his father, Antonio da Sangallo the Elder (1455/62–1534), his uncle Giuliano da Sangallo (1443/45–1516), and Donato Bramante (1444–1514), Antonio da Sangallo the Younger had perfected a systematic way of portraying architecture by integrating plans, projections, and sections into one fully comprehensive design that enlightened the viewer about every aspect of the construction. This revolutionary system became particularly important in Sangallo's work after the Sack of Rome in the late 1520s and 1530s, when he was working on his survey of the architecture of antiquity and his commentary on Vitruvius.[37]

Though often criticized for a certain loss of spontaneity, the comprehensive end result was informed by a series of preparatory drawings, as demonstrated, for example, by the surviving designs by Sangallo for a freestanding tomb, often identified as a monument for Pope Clement VII meant for Santa Maria sopra Minerva.[38] A comparison of Sangallo's *Design for a Freestanding Tomb Seen in Elevation and Plan* in the Metropolitan Museum (fig. 12) and Vincenzo's altar shows how Vincenzo adopted the expository manner of portraying the architectural form, as well as Sangallo's use of wash, to enhance the spatial effects of the construction. Vincenzo does not seem to have used the latter technique for his figural drawings, or he may have abandoned the use of wash later, after returning to Florence, for a system of hatching, closer to Bandinelli's approach (see fig. 6).

The decorative components of the altar—the choice of Tuscan columns and a frieze of triglyphs and decorated metopes—are also reminiscent of Sangallo's

preferred vocabulary, which was prevalent as early as 1519 in a design for part of the facade of Saint Peter's.[39] Vincenzo's design is also especially close to another sheet by Sangallo, dated 1542–43, with ideas for the Porta Santo Spirito in Rome.[40]

The shared history of Antonio da Sangallo the Younger and Vincenzo de' Rossi, and the latter's knowledge of (or possibly even training in) Sangallo's comprehensive system of architectural representation, reveals a closer connection between the two artists than was previously known. It is thus not surprising that the young Vincenzo's candidacy for the confraternity's two commissions was so strongly endorsed by the architect and his colleagues. In the execution of the altar and the decision to follow the shape of the *aediculae* in the nave of the Pantheon, Vincenzo was able to realize at least a small part of Sangallo's vision of bringing more unity to the interior structure of the antique building.

THE FATE OF VINCENZO'S ALTAR

Despite the many reproductions of the Pantheon in drawings, prints, and books, no interior views portraying the chapel of the confraternity with the completed altar appear to have survived.[41] The confraternity's records indicate that the altar remained in place until 1691, when both the statue of Saint Joseph and the altar were deemed to be in need of renovation.[42] Although Vincenzo's sculpture underwent restorative treatments and was returned to the chapel in the Pantheon, the altar itself was demolished to give way to a more modern structure. The confraternity's records report that a design for the renovations was prepared by Mattia De Rossi (1637–1695), a pupil of Gian Lorenzo Bernini (1598–1680) and member of the confraternity, although the marble tabernacle with a convex frame and broken pediment still visible in the chapel today (fig. 13) is also attributed to Filippo Leti (active Rome, 1677–1711).[43] It was only at this time, it seems, that the decision was made to place the statue of Saint Joseph and the Christ Child centrally, in a niche above the altar. To accommodate this change, it was necessary to "expand the altar towards the front [of the chapel] and to this effect, demolish the old one."[44] Also mentioned as part of the renovation work was the relocation of the confraternity's relics from their original repository into a deeper-set compartment within the new altar.[45] Whether the original tabernacle was discarded or put to new use elsewhere is not known, but it is no longer part of the chapel's inventory today.

fig. 13 Vincenzo de' Rossi. *Saint Joseph with the Christ Child*, 1546–47; Mattia De Rossi (1637–1695) or Filippo Leti (active Rome, 1677–1711), marble altar, 1691. Chapel of Saint Joseph, Santa Maria ad Martyres (Pantheon), Rome

fig. 14 Antonio da Sangallo the Younger and Vincenzo de' Rossi. Detail of *Tomb of Angelo Cesi and Franceschina Carduli Cesi*, ca. 1554–60. Cesi Chapel, Santa Maria della Pace, Rome

VINCENZO'S DRAFTSMANSHIP RECONSIDERED

The general paucity of drawings securely attributable to Vincenzo de' Rossi has led modern scholars to conclude that the artist was not a prolific draftsman and preferred his sculpting tools to pen and ink.[46] While the drawings assigned to Vincenzo are few compared to the large corpus of drawings by his principal master, Baccio Bandinelli, the rediscovery of the Metropolitan's drawing, with its architectural subject matter, raises the question of whether there might still be others waiting to be uncovered, or to be correctly attributed to his hand.

A new, more accurate portrait of Vincenzo de' Rossi as a draftsman emerges from this design together with the few other securely attributable drawings by him, including his signed sheet at the Louvre (see fig. 6) and the two designs for fountains (see figs. 1, 2). Dating from different moments in his career and executed in different media and styles, his drawings seem far more diverse and his artistic personality more multifaceted than has been previously proposed in the scholarly literature, which generally maintains that, on paper, Vincenzo was a less skilled and less energetic imitator of Bandinelli.[47] The four individual sheets discussed here clearly show Vincenzo's ability to change and adapt to the taste of his time and patrons, and to the specific requirements of particular commissions. This flexibility is also manifest in his oeuvre as a sculptor. The archaic look of the confraternity's Saint Joseph has often been criticized by modern art historians, but it was greatly appreciated and praised by its contemporary audience.

Vincenzo may have deliberately adopted an archaizing style for the statue in order to conform to an Early Christian ideal; such an approach would have been in line with the confraternity's initial plan to place a "statua antiqua" on the altar of their chapel.[48]

The newly discovered drawing also provides us with tangible evidence that Vincenzo de' Rossi was indeed active as an architect, or designer of architecture, from an early moment in his career. His implementation of the vocabulary and rendering techniques of Antonio da Sangallo the Younger suggests that he may well have been trained in Sangallo's studio during his time in Rome. The connections between the drawing and Vincenzo's further activities for the Confraternita dei Virtuosi at the Pantheon, heretofore overlooked in favor of the details concerning the commission for the still-extant statue of Saint Joseph, are compelling and noteworthy. If correctly identified, the sheet in the Metropolitan Museum thus reinstates a part of Vincenzo's early career and provides a key to understanding his subsequent Roman commissions that display striking architectural components, such as the funerary monument of Uberto Strozzi in Santa Maria sopra Minerva (1553) and the completion of Antonio da Sangallo's renovation and decoration of the Cesi Chapel in Santa Maria della Pace (fig. 14).[49]

ACKNOWLEDGMENTS

We thank Carmen C. Bambach, who kindly commented on an early draft of this article, stimulating the final form of this contribution. In addition, we thank other colleagues in the Department of Drawings and Prints, Stijn Alsteens and George R. Goldner. For their kind help during the preparation of this article, we are indebted to Federica Kappler, Università degli Studi di Roma Tor Vergata; Giorgio Marini, Gabinetto Disegni e Stampe degli Uffizi; Bénédicte Gady, Département des Arts Graphiques, Musée du Louvre; Gayle Davidson and Caitlin Condell, Department of Drawings, Prints, and Graphic Design, Cooper Hewitt, Smithsonian Design Museum; and Marco Simone Bolzoni, Rome.

FEMKE SPEELBERG
Associate Curator, Department of Drawings and Prints, The Metropolitan Museum of Art

FURIO RINALDI
Research Assistant, Department of Drawings and Prints, The Metropolitan Museum of Art

NOTES

1 "Vicenzio de' Rossi da Fiesole scultore, anch'egli architetto ed accademico Fiorentino": Vasari (1568) 1966–87, vol. 6, p. 274.

2 "Si è dilettato etiandio dell'architettura, e co' suoi disegni si sono fatte più fabriche": Borghini 1584, p. 598.

3 Cooper Hewitt, Smithsonian Design Museum, New York (1942-36-1). Black chalk, 17 × 11 in. (43.3 × 27.8 cm), Central Italian watermark ("lozenge containing six-pointed star in circle," Diam. 4.5 cm) close to Woodward 292 (Rome, ca. 1555–59) and Briquet 6097 (Lucca ca. 1556–72), annotated at right in pen and brown ink: *Baccio 46*; collector's mark of Sir Joshua Reynolds (1723–1792; Lugt 2364). See Utz 1971, pp. 360–61, fig. 23; Castro 1998, pp. 120, 127n35; and Michael W. Cole in Cole 2014, pp. 222–24, no. 39, with incorrect transcription of the annotation. The same annotation *Baccio* in pen and brown ink, followed by a number written in a different ink, occurs on other drawings by or attributed to Baccio Bandinelli, such as British Museum inv. 1946,0713.261 (*Baccio 37*) and Christ Church, Oxford inv. 0090 (*Baccio / Bandinelli*)—and on a drawing recently acquired by the Metropolitan Museum attributed to Bernardo Buontalenti (2014.466, annotated in the same handwriting *Benvenuto Cellino 4.*).

4 Location unknown, formerly Colnaghi, London. Black chalk, 17¾ × 14¼ in. (45.2 × 36.1 cm). See Colnaghi 1983, no. 2, ill.

5 The provenance of the work is as follows: possibly George Ramsey, 8th earl of Dalhousie (d. 1787); possibly his son George Ramsey, 9th earl of Dalhousie (1770–1838); his son James Ramsey, 10th earl and 1st marquess of Dalhousie (1812–1860); his eldest daughter, Lady Susan Broun Ramsey (d. 1898); her great-niece Edith Christian Baird, from 1921 Lady Broun Lindsay (still living in 1965); her grandson (by descent); *Old Master Drawings*, Sotheby's, New York, January 25, 2012, lot 40 (as Anonymous, Florentine, 16th-century).

6 These measurements are based on the common assumption that 1 Florentine *braccio* corresponds to 23 in. (58.3 cm). While the drawing principally contains measurements for the height and depth of the altar, the width can be approximated with relative accuracy, supposing that the design is to scale.

7 Inscription has been normalized in transcription: u = v.

8 Paraphrased translation by authors; artist's signature has been modernized.

9 Inscription has been normalized in transcription: u = v.

10 Paraphrased; interpretative translation by authors.

11 *Hercules' Descent into Hades*, ca. 1562, Musée du Louvre, Département des Arts Graphiques, Paris (1573, fig. 6). Pen and brown ink, over traces of black chalk, 13⅞ × 17⅝ in. (35.2 × 44.8 cm), signed by the artist on the lower right of the recto in pen and gray-brown ink: *Vincentio Rossi*. The inscription on the verso, meant for Vincenzo Borghini, reads: *Reverendo Priore delli innocenti (a) questo e il disegnio / che sua. al.[tez]za S.[erenissi]ma mi a ordinato pelle isstorie / sotto li Hercholi che sieno di bronzo .V.[ostra] S.[ignoria] ne dicha il suo / parere vi bacio la mano quanto alla favola / Vincentio Rossi / (a) Vincenzo Borghini. [in a different hand]."* (Honorable prior of the Innocenti [a], this is the drawing that His Highness ordered from me for the stories under the Hercules statues that should be made in bronze. Awaiting your opinion on these fables, I kiss your hand, Vincenzo Rossi / [a] Vincenzo Borghini [later inscription to identify Borghini].) The verso has not been reproduced previously; see Heikamp 1964, pp. 38, 39, pl. 49; Utz 1971, p. 352, fig. 9; Monbeig-Goguel 1972, pp. 105–8, no. 125, ill.; Scorza 1984,

pp. 316–17, fig. 2; Schallert 1998, p. 142, fig. 156; and Louis A. Waldman in Franklin 2009, p. 184, fig. 42.1. A preparatory study showing the central figure of Hercules is in an Italian private collection and is published in Scorza 1984, pp. 315–17, pl. 41.

12 Compare the draftsmanship of the two cherubs with Bandinelli's compositional drawing in the Uffizi (539F), for which see Petrioli Tofani 1991, p. 229, ill., and Waldman in Franklin 2009, pp. 262–63, no. 92.

13 The watermark (letter *M* under star in shield) is close to Briquet 8390 (documented Florence 1529) and Woodward 324 (documented Ancona 1569).

14 For the collaborative commission of the Medici tombs, see Frommel 2003, pp. 335–57; Götzmann 2005; Carmen C. Bambach in Franklin 2009, pp. 182–83, no. 41; and Partridge 2014.

15 The presence of the young Vincenzo de' Rossi during this commission is endorsed by Schallert 1998, pp. 259–60, and Castro 1998, p. 111. The first official surviving archival evidence that links Bandinelli and Vincenzo dates from June 27, 1541, and relates to his position as stonecutter in the Opera del Duomo in Florence; see Waldman 2004, p. 218, doc. 355.

16 See Marini 2001.

17 Archivio Storico della Pontificia Insigne Accademia di Belli Arti e Lettere dei Virtuosi al Pantheon, Rome (hereafter AVP), "Libro I delle Congregazioni (1543–1597)," 1545, fol. 6v; see Schallert 1998, pp. 28–36, 232–33, no. 1.

18 On Desiderio de Adiutorio and the early history of the Confraternita dei Virtuosi al Pantheon, see Visconti 1869; Orbaan 1915; Cherubini 1987; and especially Tiberia 2000, 2002, and 2005.

19 Part of the documents from the "Libro I" of the confraternity, encompassing the years 1543 to 1597, were published in Schallert 1998, pp. 233–35, and Tiberia 2000, pp. 51–242.

20 Visconti 1869, pp. 41–43; Cherubini 1987, p. 193. Referred to as the "Terre Sante," the relics are mentioned in the first statutes of the confraternity drawn up in 1545, when it was determined that the confraternity's chapel in the church devoted to the Holy Mother would be the perfect place to keep them safe. Specific mention is made of the placement of the relics under an altar in this chapel. "[Desiderio] consider che in tal Tempio consecrato alla Gloriosiss.a Vergine, et a tutti li santi martiri sarebbero bene collocate dette Terre S[an].te, et visto esservi un luogho bello per una Cappella, qual non si usava, né era ad altri destinato, lo domnandò et gratiosamente . . . ottenne per fundavi una Cappella, et sotto l'altare di quelle collocare dette Terre S.te." AVP, "Primo Statuto della Compagnia di San Giuseppe di Terrasanta," 20 Dicembre 1545; Tiberia 2000, pp. 231–32. The reliquary containing the earth is still recorded among the confraternity's possessions in the confraternity's minutes of January 14, 1691; Tiberia 2005, p. 437.

21 AVP, "Libro I," 1543, fol. 3v, 1544, fol. 4r; see Visconti 1869, pp. 41–43, and Schallert 1998, p. 233.

22 "acciò faciessi la statua di marmore che in tutto piaciessi": AVP, "Libro I," 1545, fol. 6v; see Schallert 1998, pp. 233–34.

23 AVP, "Libro I," 1546, fol. 11r: "si risolse che si dessin le dui tavole di marmo o al nostro mastro Rafael da Montelupo o allo scultore detto et che si acconciassi el finestrone dove ha da star la statua di san Josef, pingendolo et ponendovi li stipiti et architravi come ha da stare"; see Schallert 1998, p. 235, and Tiberia 2000, p. 76.

24 "lo scultore qual fa la statua del nostro san Josef, avendola hormai a buon porto, disegnava cominciare di adornare el loco dove

si aveva da ponere": AVP, "Libro I," 1547, fols. 13v–14r; see Schallert 1998, p. 235.

25 AVP, "Libro I," 1547, fol. 13v–14r: "voleva dalli signori confratri el disegno."

26 Ibid., fol. 15r: "14 d'Agosto . . . fu sollecitato mastro Vincentio scultore che dessi perfectione et alla statua del nostro Santo et al luogo dove ha da stare"; see Schallert 1998, p. 235.

27 After Desiderio's death, the confraternity had trouble raising the money for their commissions and frequent mention is made of payments due to Vincenzo for his work in the chapel until the end of 1549; see Tiberia 2000, pp. 86–98.

28 "Adi 11 di Dicembre . . . si erano saldati li conti con mastro Vincentio scultore, si del restante diquel si li doveva per conto della statua fatta da esso et sí del lavoro fatto fare da esso nel finestrone dove si è posta decta statua sopra allo altare, di sti-piti, architrave, fregio, cornicie et lastrone et conducitura di tutto a perfetione": AVP, "Libro I," 1547, fol. 16v; see Schallert 1998, p. 236, and Tiberia 2000, pp. 86–87.

29 Early mention is made of a "tavola," with a description of the various "Terre Sante," which was to be placed on one of the walls of the chapel (January 1, 1543). On June 21, 1545, Perino del Vaga and Nanni di Baccio Bigio were invited to decorate the left and right sides of the chapel, respectively. Whether any of these decorations were realized remains unclear. After Desiderio's death and during the time Vincenzo was employed by the confra-ternity, the members sold a painted "ritratto del Nostro Signore" (on August 8, 1546) and a "ritratto del Papa," most likely Paul III (on September 22 of the same year), both from the possessions left behind by Desiderio, to come up with the funds to pay Vincenzo. During the same meeting, the members also agreed to give two marble panels ("dui tavole di marmo") to Vincenzo for the execution of the altar—which are most likely the same pan-els mentioned again in the payment records of December 11, 1547, where it is specified that they were meant to be joined together to form one panel ("dui pezi di tavole di mischio per fare una tavola"). In addition, some paintings ("bellisime pitture") were considered, on November 23, 1547, to be part of the decor of the chapel after the completion of the altar. A commission to Federico Zuccaro (1540/42–1609) was considered from 1597 onward after Pope Clement VIII complained about the barren state of the confraternity's chapel, but the program was never executed. The frescoes currently flanking the altar in the chapel were commissioned to the painter Fabrizio Chiari (1621–1695) but, owing to his absence, then assigned to Francesco Cozza (1605–1682) and added only in 1659. AVP, "Libro I," 1547, fol. 16v; see Schallert 1998, pp. 234–36; Tiberia 2000, pp. 34, 65, 74–75; and Tiberia 2005, pp. 38, 288.

30 Schallert 1998, pp. 95, 96, and nn. 90, 95; Buddensieg 1968; Buddensieg 1971; Buddensieg 1976. For reconstructions of the antique Pantheon, see Grasshoff et al. 2009.

31 Schallert 1998, p. 235; Tiberia 2000, p. 84.

32 For the construction of this new altar, see below in this article.

33 See the drawings in the Gabinetto Disegni e Stampe degli Uffizi, Florence (306A, 841A, 874A, 1241A), discussed and illustrated by Arnold Nesselrath in Frommel and Adams 2000, pp. 134–35, 158–59, 172–73, 221, 268–69, 347, 369, 380, 424, ill.

34 Sangallo had set out to measure all antique buildings in Rome with the help of his workshop to prove that they answered to the architectural rules as communicated by Vitruvius. Where devia-tions were noted, these were explained as mistakes made by the ancient architects. In the specific case of the Pantheon, a myth was put forward in the sixteenth century, described by, among others, Vasari in his *Vite* of 1568 (1966–87, vol. 4, pp. 273–74), that the building had been realized by a total of three architects; the beautiful and "correct" parts were built by the first architect, but when his work was continued after his death, his successors misunderstood the plans and made the apparent mistakes. See Frommel and Adams 2000, pp. 3, 4; Buddensieg 1971, p. 265; and Buddensieg 1976, p. 343. Sangallo first studied the Pantheon as a source of inspiration while working with Donato Bramante on the Dome of Saint Peter's. In his later sketches and annota-tions concerning the Pantheon, Sangallo instead set out to cor-rect the irregularities and thus went a step further than many of his predecessors and contemporaries who created a large group of drawings of the Pantheon during the late fifteenth and early sixteenth centuries (some from observation, others by copying). Most of these drawings, which predominantly record the vesti-bule and parts of the interior, can be considered as observa-tional studies rather than as acts of criticism in Sangallo's sense. For the early Italian drawings, see Shearman 1977; Wurm 1984, p. 473; and Scaglia 1995, pp. 9–28; for a group of French draw-ings in the collection of the Metropolitan Museum and related material, see Yerkes 2013.

35 *Design for the Floorplan of the Pantheon*, ca. 1535, Gabinetto Disegni e Stampe degli Uffizi, Florence (3990A; fig. 11). Pen and brown ink, traces of black chalk, ruling and compass work, 23⅛ × 17⅛ in. (58.9 × 43.4 cm). Annotated at the top in pen and brown ink: *299.* and *100*; at lower left, in blue graphite: *3990*; at lower right, collector's stamp of the Uffizi (Lugt 929); see Arnold Nesselrath in Frommel and Adams 2000, pp. 268–69, 476, ill.

36 Nardo di Raffaele de' Rossi was a stonecutter who worked with Antonio da Sangallo the Younger and was married to an uniden-tified Sangallo daughter. In 1541 he drew up an inventory of objects left behind by Baccio Bandinelli in his house in Rome, indicating that Bandinelli either stayed with Nardo or was at least a close contact of his whom he trusted with his belongings after leaving Rome for Florence. Later, Nardo would also work with Nanni di Baccio Bigio and Pirro Ligorio, and between 1560 and 1564 he assisted Michelangelo in the completion of sculp-tures for the Porta Pia. The drawing with the above-mentioned letter from Nardo to Sangallo is Gabinetto Disegni e Stampe degli Uffizi (302A); see Bertolotti 1884, p. 41; Ferri 1885, p. 164; Utz 1971, pp. 363–65, under docs. 6 and 10; Schallert 1998, p. 173n108; and Waldman 2004, pp. 214–17, doc. 351.

37 Frommel and Adams 1994, pp. 10–51. We would like to thank Carmen C. Bambach for pointing out this important connection.

38 For the Metropolitan Museum's drawing by Sangallo, *Design for a Freestanding Tomb Seen in Elevation and Plan*, 1530–35 (1998.265; fig. 12), see Bambach 2007, pp. 81–82, fig. 95; Bambach 2008, p. 128, fig. 3; and Bambach in Franklin 2009, pp. 182–83, no. 41. Other autograph and workshop drawings related to the same project are in the Gabinetto Disegni e Stampe degli Uffizi, Florence (183A, 185A, 1129A).

39 Gabinetto Disegni e Stampe degli Uffizi, Florence (122A). Pen and brown ink, brown wash, straightedge, compass, stylus, pin, 18⅞ × 21⅞ in. (48 × 55.6 cm); see Frommel and Adams 2000, pp. 108, 321 (ill.) (dated to 1519).

40 Gabinetto Disegni e Stampe degli Uffizi, Florence (1096A). Pen and brown ink, 8 × 10⅝ in. (20.3 × 27.1 cm); see Frommel and Adams 1994, pp. 195–96, 388 (ill.) (dated to 1542–43).

41 Most of the artists reproducing the building during the Renaissance and Baroque periods focused on recording the

parts of the building that were considered antique and not the "modern additions." This changed in the eighteenth century, with portrayals of the contemporary interior such as the panel by Giovanni Paolo Panini in the Statens Museum for Kunst, Copenhagen (4594); see Shearman 1977; Wurm 1984, p. 473; Scaglia 1995; and Yerkes 2013, p. 87.

42 AVP, "Libro III delle Congregazioni," 14 Gennaio 1691, cited from Tiberia 2005, pp. 42–43, 296–97, 437–38. An earlier restoration was necessary in 1610, and a further plan to enlarge the altar was formulated in 1660 but apparently not executed owing to a lack of funds; see Tiberia 2002, pp. 35, 36, and Tiberia 2005, p. 39.

43 Schallert 1998, p. 232.

44 "dilatare piu avanti l'altare et a questo effetto demolire il vecchio": AVP, "Libro III delle Congregazioni," 14 Gennaio 1691, cited from Tiberia 2005, pp. 437–38.

45 AVP, "Libro III delle Congregazioni," 14 Gennaio 1691, cited from Tiberia 2005, pp. 42–43, 296–97, 437–38, 474–75.

46 See Heikamp 1964, p. 40.

47 Based on this small group of securely attributed drawings, the further body of works attributed to Vincenzo de' Rossi needs careful revision and consideration. In the past, his hand has been sought mainly in the vast body of works from the circle of Bandinelli; see Heikamp 1964; Vitzthum 1965; Utz 1971; Scorza 1984; Schallert 1998; and Louis A. Waldman in Franklin 2009. Not all of these attributions are convincing, however.

48 This idea is also brought to the fore by Schallert 1998, pp. 97–104.

49 On the Strozzi and Cesi commissions, see Schallert 1998, pp. 126–27, 155–201, 242–47.

REFERENCES

Bambach, Carmen C.

2007 "Tuscan Drawings of the Quattrocento and Cinquecento in The Metropolitan Museum of Art, 1998–2005." In *Invisibile agli occhi: Atti della giornata di studio in ricordo di Lisa Venturini, Firenze, Fondazione Roberto Longhi, 15 dicembre 2005*, edited by Nicoletta Baldini, pp. 77–95. Florence: Fondazione di Studi di Storia dell'Arte Roberto Longhi.

2008 "Drawings in Dresden: Further Newly Identified Works by Italian Masters." *Apollo* 167, no. 552 (March), pp. 126–31.

Bertolotti, Antonio

1884 *Artisti subalpini in Roma nei secoli XV, XVI e XVII: Ricerche e studi negli archivi romani*. Mantua: Mondovi.

Borghini, Raffaello

1584 *Il Riposo di Raffaello Borghini in cui della pittura, e della scultura si favella. . . .* Florence: Appresso Giorgio Marescotti. Edited by Mario Rosci. 2 vols. Milan: Edizioni Labor. Vol. 1 is a facsimile of the edition published in Florence, 1584.

Buddensieg, Tilmann

1968 "Raffael's Grab." In *Munuscula discipulorum: Kunsthistorische Studien, Hans Kauffmann zum 70. Geburtstag 1966*, edited by Tilmann Buddensieg and Matthias Winner, pp. 45–70. Berlin: B. Hessling.

1971 "Criticism and Praise of the Pantheon in the Middle Ages and the Renaissance." In *Classical Influences on European Culture, A.D. 500–1500: Proceedings of an International Conference Held at King's College, Cambridge, April 1969*, edited by R. R. Bolgar, pp. 259–67. Cambridge: Cambridge University Press.

1976 "Criticism of Ancient Architecture in the Sixteenth and Seventeenth Century." In *Classical Influences on European Culture, A.D. 1500–1700: Proceedings of an International Conference Held at King's College, Cambridge, April 1974*, edited by R. R. Bolgar, pp. 335–48. Cambridge: Cambridge University Press.

Castro, Barbara

1998 "Vincenzo de' Rossi." In *Scultori del Cinquecento*, edited by Stefano Valeri, pp. 110–28. Rome: Lithos Editrice.

Cherubini, Paolo

1987 "De Adiutorio, Desiderio." In *Dizionario biografico degli Italiani* 33, pp. 193–94. Rome: Instituto della Enciclopedia Italiana.

Cole, Michael W., ed.

2014 *Donatello, Michelangelo, Cellini: Sculptors' Drawings from Renaissance Italy*. Essays by Michael W. Cole, Davide Gasparotto, Alina Payne, Oliver Tostmann, and Linda Wolk-Simon. Exh. cat. Boston: Isabella Stewart Gardner Museum.

Colnaghi

1983 *An Exhibition of Old Master Drawings*. Exh. cat. London: P. & D. Colnaghi & Co.

Ferri, Pasquale Nerino

1885 *Indice geografico-analitico dei disegni di architettura civile e militare esistenti nella R. Galleria degli Uffizi in Firenze*. Rome: Presso i Principali Librai.

Franklin, David, ed.

2009 *From Raphael to Carracci: The Art of Papal Rome*. With essays by Sebastian Schütze, Carlo Gasparri and Ingrid D. Rowland. Exh. cat. Ottawa: National Gallery of Canada.

Frommel, Christoph Luitpold

2003 "Disegni sconosciuti di Sangallo per le tombe di Leone X e Clemente VII." In Christoph Luitpold Frommel, *Architettura alla corte papale nel Rinascimento*, pp. 335–57. Milan: Electa.

Frommel, Christoph Luitpold, and Nicholas Adams, eds.

1994 *The Architectural Drawings of Antonio da Sangallo the Younger and His Circle.* Vol. 1, *Fortifications, Machines, and Festival Architecture.* New York: Architectural History Foundation.

2000 *The Architectural Drawings of Antonio da Sangallo the Younger and His Circle.* Vol. 2, *Churches, Villas, the Pantheon, Tombs, and Ancient Inscriptions.* New York: Architectural History Foundation.

Götzmann, Jutta

2005 "Der Triumph der Medici: Zur Ikonographie der Grabmäler Leos X. und Clemens' VII. in Santa Maria sopra Minerva." In *Praemium Virtutis.* Vol. 2, *Grabmäler und Begräbniszeremoniell in der italienische Hoch- und Spätrenaissance*, edited by Joachim Poeschke, Britta Kusch-Arnhold, and Thomas Weigel, pp. 171–200. Münster: Rhema.

Grasshoff, Gerd, Michael Heinzelmann, Nikolaos Theocharis, and Markus Wäfler, eds.

2009 *The Pantheon in Rome.* Vol. 1, *Contributions to the Conference, Bern, November 9–12, 2006.* Vol. 2, *The Bern Digital Pantheon Project, Plates.* Zürich: LIT Verlag.

Heikamp, Detlef

1964 "Vincenzo de' Rossi disegnatore." *Paragone,* no. 169, pp. 38–42.

Marini, Maurizio

2001 "Modelli classici e rapporti con l'antico nell'inedito monumento funebre del patrizio spagnolo Pietro Mates nella Chiesa romana di San Salvatore in Lauro." In *El coleccionismo de escultura clásica en España: Actas del simposio*, edited by Matteo Mancini, pp. 101–14. Madrid: Museo Nacional del Prado.

Monbeig-Goguel, Catherine

1972 *Inventaire général des dessins italiens.* Vol. 1, *Maîtres toscans nés après 1500, morts avant 1600: Vasari et son temps.* Paris: Editions des Musées Nationaux.

Orbaan, Johannes Albertus Franciscus

1915 "Virtuosi al Pantheon: Archivalische Beiträge zur römischen kunstgeschichte." *Repertorium für Kunstwissenschaft* 37, pp. 17–52.

Partridge, Loren W.

2014 "Le tombe dei papi Leone X e Clemente VII." In *Baccio Bandinelli: Scultore e maestro (1493–1560)*, edited by Detlef Heikamp and Beatrice Paolozzi Strozzi, pp. 168–87. Exh. cat., Museo Nazionale del Bargello, Florence. Florence: Giunti Editore.

Petrioli Tofani, Annamaria

1991 *Gabinetto Disegni e Stampe degli Uffizi. Inventario: Disegni di figura.* Vol. 1. Florence: Leo S. Olschki.

Scaglia, Gustina

1995 "Eleven Facsimile Drawings of the Pantheon's Vestibule and the Interior in Relation to the Codex Escurialensis and Giuliano da Sangallo's Libro Drawings." *Architectura* 25, pp. 9–28.

Schallert, Regine

1998 *Studien zu Vincenzo de' Rossi: Die frühen und mittleren Werke (1536–1561).* Hildesheim, Zürich, and New York: G. Olms.

Scorza, Rick

1984 "A Life Study by Vincenzo de' Rossi." *Master Drawings* 22, no. 3 (Autumn), pp. 315–17, 375.

Shearman, John

1977 "Raphael, Rome and the Codex Escurialensis." *Master Drawings* 15, no. 2 (Summer), pp. 107–46, 189–96 (pls. 1–8).

Tiberia, Vitaliano

2000 *La Compagnia di S. Giuseppe di Terrasanta nel XVI secolo.* Galatina, Lecce: M. Congedo.

2002 *La Compagnia di S. Giuseppe di Terrasanta nei pontificati di Clemente VIII e Leone XI e Paolo V (1595–1621).* Galatina, Lecce: M. Congedo.

2005 *La Compagnia di S. Giuseppe di Terrasanta da Gregorio XV a Innocenzo XII.* Galatina, Lecce: M. Congedo.

Utz, Hildegard

1971 "The *Labors of Hercules* and Other Works by Vincenzo de' Rossi." *Art Bulletin* 53, no. 3 (September), pp. 344–66.

Vasari, Giorgio

1966–87 *Le Vite de' più eccellenti pittori, scultori e architettori nelle redazioni del 1550 e 1568.* 6 vols. Edited by Rosanna Bettarini and Paola Barocchi. Florence: Sansoni; Studio per Edizioni Scelte.

Visconti, Carlo Ludovico

1869 *Sulla istituzione della insigne artistica Congregazione Pontificia dei Virtuosi al Pantheon: Notizie storiche.* Rome: Tipografia di E. Sinimberghi.

Vitzthum, Walter

1965 "A Drawing by Vincenzo de' Rossi." *Master Drawings* 3, no. 2 (Summer), pp. 165, 219 (pls. 35a, 35b).

Waldman, Louis A.

2004 *Baccio Bandinelli and Art at the Medici Court: A Corpus of Early Modern Sources.* Philadelphia: American Philosophical Society.

Wurm, Heinrich

1984 *Baldassare Peruzzi: Architekturzeichnungen.* Tübingen: Verlag Ernst Wasmuth.

Yerkes, Carolyn

2013 "Drawings of the Pantheon in the Metropolitan Museum's Goldschmidt Scrapbook." *MMJ* 48, pp. 87–120.

ASHER ETHAN MILLER
SOPHIE SCULLY

The Pont Neuf: A Paris View by Johan Barthold Jongkind Reconsidered

In 1980 The Metropolitan Museum of Art acquired *The Pont Neuf*, a view of Paris by Johan Barthold Jongkind (1819–1891). The painting was not accompanied by historical documentation other than the names of the donors, New York collectors Mr. and Mrs. Walter Mendelsohn.[1] Owing to a thick and discolored varnish, its condition was difficult to assess and its composition was difficult to read. As the result of recent research and conservation treatment, a collaborative undertaking by the authors, the picture can be appreciated anew (fig. 1) and situated in the context of other views of Paris that Jongkind painted about 1850. This study presents findings about the artist's working process and approach to composition in *The Pont Neuf* as well as in other of his early reckonings with the Paris cityscape.

Jongkind initially trained in his native Holland with the landscape painter Andreas Schelfhout (1787–1870).

fig. 1 Johan Barthold Jongkind (Dutch, 1819–1891). *The Pont Neuf*, 1849–50, after treatment. Oil on canvas, 21½ × 32⅛ in. (54.6 × 81.6 cm). Signed and inscribed at lower right: *Souvenir du Pont Neuf / Jongkind*. The Metropolitan Museum of Art, New York, Gift of Mr. and Mrs. Walter Mendelsohn, 1980 (1980.203.3)

He was noticed in 1845 by the visiting French marine painter Eugène Isabey (1803–1886), a leading figure of the Romantic generation, and in 1846 he received a royal stipend that enabled him to move to Paris.[2] There he spent the following decade under Isabey's wing, working with him often and joining him on excursions to the Channel coast in the summers of 1847, 1850, and possibly 1851.

Jongkind's first extended Parisian sojourn, which ended in 1855, coincided with a time of transition in the arts: Ingres and Delacroix were still at the height of their powers; the Barbizon painters were beginning to receive their due; photography was in ascendance; and another recent arrival in the capital, Jongkind's exact contemporary Gustave Courbet, was gaining notoriety. During this decade Jongkind exhibited at the Salons of 1848, 1850, 1852, 1853, and 1855, and he reached collectors through at least two dealers, Adolphe Beugniet and Pierre-Firmin Martin. He returned to Holland in 1855, remaining there until 1860, when he reestablished himself in Paris. Two

years later, in 1862, the twenty-one-year-old Claude Monet (1840–1926) would encounter Jongkind for the first time, and the two artists painted together in 1864. Monet reflected on their initial meeting: "From this moment on, he was my true master, and it is to him that I owe the final education of my eye."[3] Jongkind's legacy is often seen through the prism of this remark, but his own work, and his Paris views in particular, have rarely been singled out for close study.

In Paris, Jongkind pioneered a burgeoning genre of urban-picturesque views, so called because they truly take the city as their subject, integrating all its distinctive details, however mundane, as part of the aesthetic whole. He searched for the technical and compositional means suitable to this end, characteristically employing a sketch-like technique in paintings that bear comparison to contemporary landscapes by Charles-François Daubigny (1817–1878) and seascapes by Eugène Boudin (1824–1898), artists who, like himself, are considered catalysts in the development of "The New Painting" of the 1860s. In the 1840s and

1850s, Paris was in a state of constant transformation that encompassed growth at its edges as well as urban renewal in its historic center, but it had not yet assumed the form envisioned by Baron Haussmann. Jongkind was open to experimenting with a variety of approaches to picture making appropriate to a city taken hold by change but not yet redefined by the wide, tree-lined boulevards, public parks, and architecture of spectacle announced in 1855 with the first in a series of universal expositions that would take place every decade or so until 1900. The banks of the Seine in particular were just then luring artists of all stripes, even inspiring a touch of poetry in such prosaic writers as Félix Lazare and Louis Lazare, for whom the river evoked "the appearance of one of those floating cities that abound on the great rivers of China."[4]

Jongkind's affinity for urban subject matter did not take root immediately upon his arrival in Paris in 1846. It was only after concluding an eleven-month visit to Holland in May 1849 that he evidently began to regard Paris with new eyes.[5] In a sketchbook already partially filled with scenes of the Dutch countryside, he also recorded scenes along the Seine.[6] On one sheet (fig. 2) Jongkind drew spontaneous sketches, or croquis, depicting the Cathedral of Notre Dame at the top and bottom, and two groups of laundresses at the center. Together, these modest sketches form the kernel of Jongkind's earliest known Paris view in oil, *The Cathedral of Notre Dame de Paris, Seen from the Pont de l'Archevêché*, which

fig. 2 Johan Barthold Jongkind. Sketchbook page: *Three Parisian Scenes*, 1849. Pencil on paper, sheet 12⅛ × 8⅝ in. (30.8 × 22 cm). Musée du Louvre, Paris, Jongkind Album 31, fol. 22 recto (RF 11636,38)

fig. 3 Johan Barthold Jongkind. *The Cathedral of Notre Dame de Paris, Seen from the Pont de l'Archevêché*, 1849. Oil on canvas, 13¾ × 23⅞ in. (35 × 60.6 cm). Signed, dated, and inscribed at lower left: *Paris 1849 Jongkind*. Santa Barbara Museum of Art, Museum purchase with funds provided by 19th-century Acquisition Fund (1999.1)

fig. 4 Johan Barthold Jongkind. *The Cathedral of Notre Dame de Paris, Seen from the Left Bank of the Seine*, 1849. Red chalk on paper, sheet 8⅝ × 12¼ in. (21.9 × 31.1 cm). Musée du Louvre, Paris (RF 10970)

fig. 5 Johan Barthold Jongkind. *The Cathedral of Notre Dame de Paris, Seen from the Left Bank of the Seine*, 1849. Pencil on paper, sheet 8⅝ × 15¾ in. (22 × 40 cm). Musée du Louvre, Paris (RF 3426 recto)

is signed and dated 1849 (fig. 3).[7] The development of this composition can be traced through other surviving drawings. Its essential features were set in place in a spirited sheet executed in red chalk (fig. 4), whose registration lines at the top and bottom correspond to the framing of the sketchbook croquis as well as to a very fine pencil drawing (fig. 5), and to the finished painting.[8] The meticulous structure and rendering of details in the pencil drawing suggests that the artist employed an optical device, perhaps a camera obscura. Although such tools had been available to artists for centuries, the prospect of Jongkind's having used one for the execution of this highly polished drawing is intriguing because it is arguably as close as he came to similar compositions by colleagues such as the pioneering photographer Henri Le Secq (1818–1882), another habitué of Isabey's studio. Le Secq was probably acquainted with Jongkind by the late 1840s, and Jongkind was undoubtedly familiar with his work.[9] The influence of photography on the development of landscape painting at this moment is widely accepted, and there is every reason to suppose that Jongkind experimented with a parallel technique in conjunction with his painting practice.[10] Similar views would soon be adopted by other artists, including the etcher Charles Meryon (1821–1868).[11]

While there was nothing new or exceptional about the process of working up a painting through preparatory sketches, *The Cathedral of Notre Dame* is notable for the means by which Jongkind confidently filled the canvas with a veritable tapestry of constructive brushstrokes that give the impression of form and volume entirely by means of color and light. Vertical strokes of paint that describe stripes of stonework on the wall of the quai of the Île de la Cité are extended up through the recently restored buttresses of the cathedral and down through their reflections in the Seine. Together, they balance the composition's otherwise emphatic horizontality. Not only is the sense of detail conveyed by the pencil study (fig. 5) maintained and even enhanced in the painting, but the sweeping sense of movement imparted by the converging diagonals in the red chalk drawing (fig. 4) is carried over as well, grafting a characteristic feature of the Dutch canalscape to a vision of Paris complete with two tricolors, one on the right tower of Notre Dame and the other in the cityscape to the left of the cathedral.

The genesis of *The Pont Neuf* (see fig. 1) is traceable to the same moment, but Jongkind worked on this picture in a very different fashion and for a longer period of time. The bridge—specifically, its southern span—is depicted from the base of the Quai de Conti on the

Left Bank of the Seine, looking across to the Île de la Cité, with the towers of Notre Dame in the distance. The viewer is situated down on the riverbank, which is dominated by masses of debris, a few sketchy figures, and, on the far right, an overturned boat. A walkway connects the bank to the tangle of *bateaux-lavoirs*, or laundry barges, and other boats that crowd the river. At the right of the composition, a stairway and ramp lead up to the quai. In the lower right corner a slightly blurred inscription reads *Souvenir du Pont Neuf / Jongkind*.

Prior to the treatment of the painting in the Metropolitan's Sherman Fairchild Center for Paintings Conservation from August 2013 through February 2014, an aged varnish masked flaws in its condition. These included a network of wide drying cracks rooted in Jongkind's painting process; flattening of raised impasto, which occurred during an early lining of the canvas; and abrasion of the uppermost layers of the paint surface during an insensitive past cleaning. Once it was determined that the varnish could be safely removed, it became apparent that cleaning was likely to produce favorable results. While the condition of the picture was being assessed, its history was investigated. Layers of inaccurate references in the literature, including erroneous measurements and the confusion of the present work with other representations of the same subject, had obscured its early history.[12] Beginning with the posthumous sale of the collector Emile Vial in 1918, photographs of the painting were reproduced in auction catalogues; these provided the key to retracing the work's succession of owners, as the drying cracks visible in all of them match those in the Metropolitan's picture (figs. 6a,b).[13]

The removal of the varnish had a transformative effect on the picture's appearance, permitting a new appreciation of Jongkind's quiet yet dramatic use of light. The dynamic play of gray and white in the clouds as they move across the Paris sky allows for unexpected incidents of brightness. One ray of sunlight falls on the near bank and illuminates the laundresses poised at the edge of the river. Another catches the railings to the right, breaking up the bluish-green shadow of the ramp and the stairs. In this painting Jongkind studied the effects of light on different surfaces and used these sunlit passages to guide the eye around the scene. The highlights on the Seine draw the eye back and into the center of the composition. Reflections in the puddle on the near bank and in the river correspond to bright, clear blue patches in the sky above them.

The subtlety of Jongkind's palette and brushwork could only be surmised prior to cleaning. This primarily brown and gray urban scene, dominated by stone, wood, and dirt, is enlivened by a nuanced use of color. Jongkind contrasted the steely sky with the warm golden light that turns the quai along the far bank a pale pinkish brown and the houses above the quai a mauve-gray to create the distinctively Parisian effect of contre-jour. The bridge, intermittently in light and shadow, is simultaneously warm and cool in tone; here, in addition to the lead white, iron earth, and bone or ivory black that one would expect the artist to have used to depict the grayish-brown stone, cobalt blue, vermilion, and copper-containing green pigments—most likely verdigris or malachite—are mixed in as well.[14]

fig. 6a Detail of an early photograph of *The Pont Neuf* (fig. 1) overlaid with red lines tracing cracks in the painting's surface

fig. 6b Detail of *The Pont Neuf* (fig. 1) before treatment, with cracks in the painting's surface traced in red

Increased legibility following the removal of the old varnish also called attention to a passage that now appears less than successful. The point of intersection where the quai of the Île de la Cité meets the Pont Neuf is ill-defined, with uncharacteristically inarticulate brushwork denoting the top of the quai (fig. 7). The awkward rendering of this juncture prompted an examination of Jongkind's construction of perspective, which revealed that the composition is not based on a unified perspectival scheme. The angles of both quais in relation to the bridge are incongruent. The left side of the bridge and the far quai intersect at an overly obtuse angle; from the viewer's position on the riverbank, the opposite quai should be further foreshortened, as indicated by the broken red lines seen at the left in figure 8. Alternatively, if the perspective on the left side of the bridge is assumed to be correct, the angle of the wall on the right side should be further foreshortened, perhaps closer in appearance to the broken red line seen at the right. Moreover, the railings of the staircase and ramp, indicated by the solid red lines, have been painted at angles that are slightly off-kilter in either scenario. Thus, one may see that the major perspective lines on both sides of the bridge do not correlate, with the result that the foreground is overly wide in relationship to the background.

fig. 7 Detail of *The Pont Neuf* (fig. 1) showing the juncture of the Pont Neuf and the Île de la Cité

fig. 8 *The Pont Neuf* (fig. 1) with alternative perspective lines indicated by broken red lines, and with the angles of the ramp and staircase highlighted in solid red

Given the formal clarity of *The Cathedral of Notre Dame de Paris, Seen from the Pont de l'Archevêché*, the possibility that artistic license underlay the faulty perspective in *The Pont Neuf* was considered and the actual topography of the depicted site studied.[15] Jongkind's rendering of the view diverged from its actual appearance in several ways. First, the Pont Neuf has five arches, and always has, although Jongkind depicted the bridge with only four. Jongkind well knew how many arches support the bridge, as evinced by a drawing (fig. 9) that can be dated to 1849 since it appears in the same Louvre sketchbook as the sheet of studies (see fig. 2) that served as his starting point for *The Cathedral of Notre Dame*.[16] Another significant departure from the actual view is the addition of the bell towers of Notre Dame. This motif derives from another drawing in the Louvre sketchbook (fig. 10), for which the artist positioned himself farther to the east, with the Pont Neuf behind him; the bridge depicted before Notre Dame in the sketch is the Pont Saint-Michel.[17] Jongkind probably referred to both sketches while developing the composition for the Metropolitan's *Pont Neuf*.[18]

He also left certain things out of this hybrid scene, notably, at the far left, the place Dauphine, located at the intersection of the Pont Neuf and the Île de la Cité (at which point the bridge continues across the Seine's northern arm). As part of his decision to include the towers of Notre Dame, Jongkind omitted this early seventeenth-century square, an iconic landmark that he included in other renderings of the site.[19]

Topographical analysis makes clear that *The Pont Neuf* is a composite view. With the source material

fig. 9 Johan Barthold Jongkind. *Two Views of the Pont-Neuf, Paris*, 1849. Pencil on two sketchbook pages, each sheet 8⅝ × 12⅛ in. (22 × 30.8 cm). Fol. 10 inscribed at top right: *M. Forget*. Musée du Louvre, Paris, Jongkind Album 31, fols. 9 verso and 10 recto (RF 11636,16–17)

fig. 10 Johan Barthold Jongkind. *The Pont Saint-Michel and the Cathedral of Notre Dame, Paris*, 1849. Pencil on sketchbook page, sheet 8⅝ × 12⅛ in. (22 × 30.8 cm). Musée du Louvre, Paris, Jongkind Album 31, fol. 12 recto (RF 11636,20)

fig. 11 X-radiograph of *The Pont
Neuf* (fig. 1). The lines in red
trace features of the painting's
original composition visible only
in the X-radiograph; the green
lines trace the main features of
the final composition.

fig. 12 *The Pont Neuf* (fig. 1)
overlaid with tracing in red of
the original five arches evident
in fig. 11

for the composition—the two sketchbook drawings—
in mind, a further question arises: did Jongkind set out
to paint a hybrid view or, given the relative lack of
resolution in the painted passages on the far bank (see
fig. 7), did he change course at some point during the
painting process?

An X-radiograph of the painting indicates that
Jongkind reworked the composition. Owing to the high
concentration in Jongkind's paint mixtures of lead
white (a radiopaque pigment that appears white in
X-radiographs), the image is difficult to read, but the
changes become visible in a diagram (fig. 11) in
which the main features of the painting are traced in
green onto the X-radiograph. In the same diagram, the
tracing in red shows that some elements visible in the
X-radiograph are not related to the final composition.
These include, most notably, the bridge's five arches,
which extend farther to the left and have a steeper arc—
an accurate portrayal of the structure of the Pont Neuf
about 1850. Legible too in the X-radiograph is a slight
adjustment to the angle of the staircase railing, which
was originally almost vertical. It is also revealing to
see the position of the five arches from the painting's
earlier state traced onto a photograph of the finished
painting (fig. 12).

The X-radiograph provides evidence that Jongkind
began painting the Pont Neuf with all five of its arches.
At some point during the process, he painted out the
leftmost arch, giving over more of the composition to
the wall of the quai on the far bank. In doing so, he
improvised directly on the canvas. This reworking
sheds light on how Jongkind arrived at the inaccuracies
of perspective described above. In order to insert the
quai on the far bank, he was forced to flatten the intersection of the bridge and the quai. He then compen-
sated for that change on the right side by shifting the
position of the ramp and/or the staircase. Unfortunately,
the concentration of lead white in the sky obscures any
clues to possible alterations in the buildings, and so one
cannot venture to say with any degree of certainty that
Jongkind envisioned including the towers of Notre
Dame from the outset.

Considering the clarity of the topographically
straightforward picture now in Santa Barbara (see fig. 3),

it is fair to ask why Jongkind complicated the present view through the introduction of hybrid elements. One has only to compare it with a slightly later picture by Isabey (fig. 13), with whom Jongkind was closely aligned at the time, to understand the pictorial strategy with which he was experimenting. Jongkind's painting, like Isabey's, employs strong opposing diagonals, one for the foreground and another for the background, to contribute an element of Romantic drama that complements its tenebrous sky.

Whatever aspects of irresolution were introduced in the course of revising his picture, Jongkind arrived at a composition that he found satisfying enough to produce a second, smaller version, which is dated 1850 (fig. 14).[20] It presents the view as seen in the final state of the Metropolitan picture, showing that it was executed subsequently. The composition of this dated painting establishes that Jongkind had arrived at the larger painting's composition by 1850. It is not possible to know, however, when the artist last worked on the Metropolitan picture. The inscription *Souvenir du Pont Neuf* implies that he returned to it at some point, if only to add the inscription, perhaps for a dealer or collector. Its first documented owner, Emile Vial, was acquainted with Jongkind at least as early as the 1870s, although when or from whom he acquired the painting is unknown.[21] What is now clear is that while painting *The Pont Neuf*, the artist made substantial revisions of an exploratory nature, and the painting defies simple categorization: it is not a preparatory sketch, nor is it unfinished. It reached a state that pleased the artist, who felt that he had resolved the picture sufficiently to add an inscription and replicate the composition.

Jongkind's openness to seemingly disparate approaches to composition and the handling of his materials is manifest in the third and last subject by the artist to be considered here, a composition that he developed over a period of at least two years, *View from the Quai d'Orsay*, which is signed and dated 1854 (fig. 15).

The earliest known treatment of this motif is a sketchbook drawing in the Louvre (fig. 16), which is entirely in the vein of the studies he used for his paintings of Notre Dame and the Pont Neuf.[22]

But a watercolor study of the crane (fig. 17) represents a departure from the freedom of handling that he characteristically employed in the medium.[23] This superlative pencil and wash drawing, reminiscent of the pencil study of Notre Dame in its precision (see fig. 5), depicts a motif that is a far cry from the cathedral's Gothic grandeur, yet the artist's determination to record its engineering accurately reflects a keen appreciation for the modernity of his subject and, by extension, his enterprise.

A loosely painted yet assured oil study on paper in the Fondation Custodia, Paris (fig. 18), appears to have been sketched out of doors to establish the values and tones of the composition before the artist worked up his first "finished" version of the subject, now in the Musée des Beaux-Arts Salies, Bagnères-de-Bigorre (fig. 19).[24] This first version of the composition painted on canvas is dated 1852. There is also an unlocated watercolor version (fig. 20), although it has not been possible to establish whether it served a preparatory role either in its current state or in an earlier state.[25] As it is signed and dated 1852, it may well be a variant of the finished painting.

The Metropolitan's *View from the Quai d'Orsay* (fig. 1) is Jongkind's final essay of this subject. Here he opens up the view to more air, space, and light. Examination with infrared reflectography indicates that, in working toward this aim, he made slight

adjustments to the composition. The infrared photograph (fig. 21) shows that Jongkind initially positioned the wheel on the crane higher and painted more ropes entwining the beams, including a dangling line with a hook at left. He subsequently reduced the size of the wheel and painted out the ropes, effectively eliminating clutter that detracted from the strong form of the central motif. The crane was clearly a critical motif for Jongkind, as indicated by the small changes to its structure and position in each of the preparatory studies, in which he fine-tuned an already meticulously developed composition. This protracted consideration of the smallest details stands in sharp contrast to his improvisational approach in composing *The Pont Neuf*. Close examination of *The Pont Neuf* reveals an artist still experimenting with his technique and method, whereas in *View from the Quai d'Orsay*, executed some four years later, Jongkind carefully presents himself as a modern painter of Paris.

View from the Quai d'Orsay was one of three paintings, all of them Paris views, that Jongkind showed at

fig. 19 Johan Barthold Jongkind. *Crane on the Quai d'Orsay, Paris*, 1852. Oil on canvas, 10⅝ × 16⅛ in. (27 × 41 cm). Signed and dated at lower right: *Jongkind 52*. Musée des Beaux-Arts Salies, Bagnères-de-Bigorre (169)

fig. 20 Johan Barthold Jongkind. *View of the Seine at Paris*, 1852. Watercolor on paper, 8 × 11¼ in. (20.3 × 28.5 cm). Signed at lower right: *Jongkind*; inscribed and dated at lower left: *Paris 52*. Location unknown

the Universal Exposition of 1855—not in the Dutch section, but as a French painter.[26] As in the view of Notre Dame painted in 1849 (see fig. 3), one detects the tricolor. It can be seen not only atop the central pavilion of the Tuileries palace, at left, but also, perhaps, in the costume of the worker seated at the edge of the quai, in the center of the picture. Jongkind's first Paris sojourn ended soon after he completed the picture, and although he departed with a sense of having failed to gain traction in his career as a painter, he had sown the seed for the relative success he would achieve after he returned five years later, in 1860.

In memory of our friend and colleague Walter Liedtke

ACKNOWLEDGMENTS

This article was developed from a lecture, "The Paris Views of Johan Barthold Jongkind: Between Romanticism and Impressionism," presented by the authors at the symposium "Interactions: Drawings and Oil Sketches," at the Morgan Library and Museum, New York, on April 30, 2014. Sophie Scully previously presented portions of these findings in her talk "The Study and Treatment of *The Pont Neuf* by Johan Barthold Jongkind," at the Metropolitan Museum's Fellows Colloquium "Painters and Paintings," held at the Museum on March 14, 2014. The authors thank Charlotte Hale and Michael Gallagher in the Department of Paintings Conservation for their invaluable advice and Alice Panhard for her generous assistance.

ASHER ETHAN MILLER
Assistant Curator, Department of European Paintings, The Metropolitan Museum of Art

SOPHIE SCULLY
Research Scholar, Department of Paintings Conservation, The Metropolitan Museum of Art

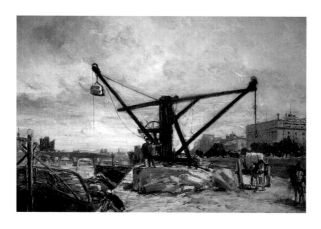

fig. 21 Detail of infrared photograph of fig. 15, showing original state of crane

NOTES

1 The painting a partial gift in 1980; the gift was completed in 1996.

2 The most reliable source for Jongkind's chronology is Auffret 2004.

3 Quoted in Thiébault-Sisson 1900, p. 3, as translated in Tinterow 1994, p. 66; for the juxtaposition of views of Sainte-Adresse by Jongkind and Monet, see ibid., pp. 62–63, fig. 82 (no. 80) and fig. 83 (no. 118).

4 "L'aspect d'une de ces villes flottantes qui pullulent sur les grands fleuves de la Chine." Félix Lazare and Louis Lazare, in *Le Moniteur*, August 4, 1854, quoted by Darin 1999, pp. 98, 100n59.

5 Before the end of the year, Achille Jubinal would write: "We have seen in the studio of Mr. Jongkind, a young Dutch painter who has an annual stipend from his king, several marine subjects that our best painters would not have blushed to sign. The banks of the Seine, old seaports, [and] canals have been represented by him with admirable talent." ("Nous avons vu chez M. Jongkind, jeune peintre hollandais, qui touche de son Roi une pension annuelle, plusieurs marines que nos premiers peintres n'auraient pas rougi de signé. Les bords de la Seine, de vieux ports de mer, des canaux ont été représentés par lui avec un admirable talent.") Jubinal in *Handelsblad*, November 4, 1849, quoted in French in Auffret 2004, p. 61.

6 The sketchbook (Musée du Louvre, Jongkind Album 31, RF 11636), which bears the maker's label of Dupin Papetier, located at 38 Notre-Dame-de-Lorette, Paris, is dated 1849 on a second label that was applied subsequently. Drawings of windmills, evidently made in Holland, are interspersed with marine subjects and Paris views, in no apparent order.

7 See Hefting 1975, no. 59; Stein et al. 2003, no. 66; and Simon Kelly in Kelly and Watson 2013, no. 1. The sketchbook sheet (see fig. 2) described here as a source for this picture was related by Carla Gottlieb (1967) to another, later painting (not in Hefting 1975; Stein et al. 2003, no. 124, as private collection). That work, which measures 44 × 65 cm and is dated 1854, is a variant of an earlier composition, *Notre Dame de Paris Seen from the Quai de la Tournelle*, 1852, oil on canvas, 11 × 16 in. (28 × 40.5 cm); signed and dated at lower left: *Jongkind 52*; Musée des Beaux-Arts de la Ville de Paris, Petit-Palais, inv. PP-PDUTO1193; see Stein et al. 2003, no. 91.

8 The sheet with the red chalk sketch was once loosely inserted into the Louvre's Jongkind Album 28. A faint offset remains on the otherwise blank folio 12 verso (Musée du Louvre, RF 11636,20 verso).

9 The closest composition by Le Secq is *Cathédrale Notre Dame, vaisseau sud*, 1850s, which exists in a photographic negative on waxed paper in the Musée des Arts Décoratifs, Paris. On Le Secq and Isabey, see Hefting 1969, p. 7. A sense of Jongkind's broader milieu during his first Paris sojourn may be gained from the list of contributors to the auction organized in 1860 to help reestablish him financially in Paris. It was organized by the collector Armand Doria with the help of the painter Adophe-Félix Cals and the dealer Pierre-Firmin Martin. The catalogue of the sale, *Tableaux offerts par divers artistes à un de leurs confrères* (Hôtel Drouot, Paris, April 7, 1860), lists sixty-six lots contributed by as many artists, including Anastasi, Berchère, Bonvin, Braquemond, Cals, Corot, Diaz, Harpignies, Isabey, Jacque, Lavieille, Nadar, Pils, Théodore Rousseau, and Ziem. Le Secq contributed lot 35, a painting entitled *Le Retour du Marché*.

For Jongkind's return to Paris and the auction, see Auffret 2004, pp. 106–10.

10 On the connection between early photography and landscape painting, see, for example, Stuffmann 1993.

11 On Meryon's etching *The Apse of Notre Dame, Paris*, 1854 (five impressions in the MMA) and speculation that it was influenced by Jongkind's painting, see Burke 1974, p. 76. For a comparable photographic view by Jules Couppier (d. 1860), see Stuffmann 1975, p. 145, no. P 15, ill. on p. 161.

12 The early histories of the majority of these works are murky and, to complicate matters further, there are descriptions of images by Jongkind that cannot be linked to works known today. The earliest example identified is a "Vue du Pont-Neuf," which the artist abandoned in Paris when he returned to Holland in 1855; the painting was included in the studio sale organized by the dealers Boussaton (*commissaire-priseur*) and Martin (*expert*) to pay off his debts (*Tableaux, études & dessins par M. Johan-Barthold Jongkind, Éleve de M. Eugène Isabey*, Hôtel des Commissaires-Priseurs, Paris, March 11, 1856, lot 10). It was sold for 27 francs, a low price although not exceptionally so, to Thirault; see Moreau-Nélaton 1918, p. 42, and Auffret 2004, p. 97.

13 The early history of the painting is unknown. Its first owner was Louis-Charles-Emile Vial (d. 1917), a successful pharmacist; his wife was a cousin of Joséphine Fesser (1819–1891), Jongkind's friend and companion from 1860 onward. Vial was in contact with Jongkind by 1876 at the latest; see Auffret 2004, p. 223. The provenance of the work is as follows: Vial's estate sale, Hôtel Drouot, Paris, March 6–7, 1918, lot 32, as "Le Vieux Pont-Neuf à Paris," for Fr 12,900); Myran Eknayan (until 1926; his sale, Hôtel Drouot, Paris, June 12, 1926, lot 37, as "Le Vieux Pont-Neuf à Paris vers 1850"); vicomte de Beuret (until 1931; his sale, Galerie Georges Petit, Paris, May 11–12, 1931, lot 21, for Fr 19,000); Gula Investments Ltd., London (until 1965; sale, Christie's, London, July 9, 1965, lot 111, for £3,150 to Mendelsohn); Mr. and Mrs. Walter Mendelsohn, New York (1965–80). In the literature, Hefting 1975, p. 84, no. 88 (under 1851) gives dimensions erroneously as 27 × 41 cm; the date and dimensions are repeated in Hefting 1992, p. 45; Stein et al. 2003, p. 84, no. 69. Adolphe Stein was the first to present the painting with accurate, if partial, documentation. The first known exhibition to include the painting was "Cathédrales, 1789–1914, un mythe moderne," held at the Musée des Beaux-Arts, Rouen, and the Wallraf-Richartz-Museum, Cologne, in 2014–15; see Amic and Le Men 2014.

14 Pigments were identified from a cross section using Raman spectroscopy and SEM-EDS by Silvia Centeno and Mark Wypyski, both of the Department of Scientific Research, MMA. The strategy of using color in place of blacks and browns would later be used to exaggerated effect by the Impressionists, who largely eliminated black from their palettes. See Bomford et al. 1990, pp. 71–72, 90.

15 The Pont Neuf crosses the Seine in two parts: the northern section is a seven-arch span linking the Right Bank to the western end of the Île de la Cité at the place Dauphine, and the southern section is a five-arch span linking the island to the Left Bank. It was originally constructed between 1578 and 1607 according to designs by Jean-Baptiste Androuet du Cerceau, Pierre des Iles, and Guillaume Marchant; for a comprehensive history of the bridge, see Boucher 1925. During Jongkind's first Parisian

sojourn the bridge and the adjacent quais on the Left Bank of the Seine underwent considerable renovation: the bridge's arches were lowered and roofs that had been added to the projecting bays in the eighteenth century were removed. Several sources must be consulted for an overall impression of the transformation, whose chronology remains vague. See especially Lazare and Lazare 1855, pp. 179, 294, 651; Duplomb 1911, pp. 198–99; Boucher 1925, vol. 1, pp. 120–21; and Lambert 1999, pp. 98, 209–10. For an etched view of the bridge showing its appearance close to the date of Jongkind's painting, see Charles Meryon's *Pont-Neuf, Paris*, 1853–54 (three impressions in MMA). Early photographic views include an anonymous daguerreotype of ca. 1845–50, *The Pont-Neuf and the Louvre* (Danmarks Fotomuseum, Herning, inv. 148-00-696; see Marrinan 2009, p. 377, fig. 162), and a photograph of the bridge by Le Secq from 1852 (reproduced in Stuffmann 1975, pp. 145, 159, no. P 13).

16 The inscription *M. Forget* at the top of fol. 10 (see fig. 9) refers to someone hitherto unidentified but who was in all likelihood the artist and critic Charles-Gabriel Forget (b. 1807), a pupil of Eugène Isabey and Théodore Rousseau (see Bellier de la Chavignerie and Auvray 1882–87, vol. 1, pp. 565–66). Forget's estate sale, which included no works by Jongkind, was held at Hôtel Drouot, Paris, March 17–19, 1873; the author of the prefatory biographical notes in the accompanying catalogue was Alfred Sensier.

17 Bird's-eye views by two contemporary photographers help to make sense of the space between the Pont Neuf and Notre Dame: Louis-Adolphe Humbert de Molard (1800–1874), *View of Paris, with Notre Dame and the Pont Saint-Michel*, 1850 (Musée d'Orsay, Paris); and the slightly later photograph depicting nearly the same view: Auguste-Hippolyte Collard (1812–188?), *Pont Saint-Michel [à Paris]: Vues photographiques des phases principales des travaux de reconstruction de ce pont exécutés en 1857*, Paris, 1857 (example in the Bibliothèque Nationale de France, Paris, FOL-VE-1035).

18 The two pages were reproduced together, one above the other, by Etienne Moreau-Nélaton, an early owner of the sketchbook in which they are found, in his 1918 monograph, which also includes a photograph of the picture now in the Metropolitan. Moreau-Nélaton may well have first seen the painting in the Vial sale and recognized a connection between it and the drawings at that time, but if he did, he left it unremarked. See Moreau-Nélaton 1918, p. 14, figs. 15 (the painting, dated about 1850) and 16, 17 (the drawings).

19 For example, *Le Pont-Neuf à Paris avec la Statue de Henri IV*, oil on unknown support, 14¾ × 18 in. (37.5 × 45.7 cm); signed and dated (lower left): *Jongkind 1851*. Private collection; Hefting 1975, p. 228, no. 556; Stein et al. 2003, p. 245, no. 619 (as ca. 1870). There is a related composition in watercolor and gouache on paper, measuring 10⅝ × 17⅜ in. (27 × 44 cm); whereabouts unknown. It is similarly inscribed *Paris 1851* and bears the artist's atelier stamp (Hefting 1975, no. 96; see Galerie Schmit 1988, no. 38). Hefting (1975, p. 228, no. 556) noted that the painting's frame bore an inscription in Jongkind's hand: *Le Pont neuve a Paris 3 juin 1851 rive gauche avec la Statue de Henri IV, au fond de la cité de Paris – quai des orfèvres* (The Pont Neuf, Paris, June 3, 1851, left bank with the statue of Henri IV, at the end of [the Île de] la Cité in Paris – Quai des Orfèvres). Nevertheless, she concluded that the year 1851, which appears on the painting and its frame, refers to the date

of the watercolor, and that the painting itself was executed in 1871. Stein et al. affirm Hefting's view.

20 Not in Hefting 1975; Stein et al. 2003, no. 70; sold Sotheby's, New York, November 4, 2011, lot 85. The authors did not see this painting firsthand nor was an X-radiograph available for comparison.

21 In Vial's collection the Metropolitan picture was complemented by another treatment of the subject, *The Seine at the Pont-Neuf*, oil on canvas, 13 × 16⅞ in. (33 × 43 cm); signed and dated (lower left): *Jongkind 1851* (it was lot 39 in the Vial sale; see note 13 above). Not in Hefting 1975; Stein et al. 2003, no. 80. Sold at Sotheby's, London, on June 28, 1989 (lot 109), the painting is now in a private collection. As with Hefting 1975, no. 556 / Stein et al. 2003, no. 619 (see note 19 above), the artist himself inscribed this work with the year 1851. Moreau-Nélaton (1918, p. 111), however, thought that the painting was datable on stylistic grounds to the early 1870s, despite the presence of incidental details that would have been anachronistic by then. (Stein et al. accepted the date of 1851.) Moreau-Nélaton even suggested that it might be the picture mentioned by Emile Zola in a description of the artist's rue Chevreuse studio in *La Cloche*, January 24, 1872: "A study of the Pont-Neuf; in the background, the [Île de] la Cité; horses bathing in a pool at the foot of the staircase on the quai; one imagines Paris buzzing above this tranquil river scene." ("Une étude du Pont-Neuf; au fond, la Cité; des chevaux se baignant dans l'abreuvoir, au pied de l'escalier du quai; on devine Paris bourdonnant au-dessus de cette rivière tranquille.") Alternatively, François Auffret proposed (in Poitout 1999, p. 130n395) that Hefting 1975, no. 556 / Stein et al. 2003, no. 619 (see note 19 above) was the work seen by Zola.

22 On this and other studies relating to the Metropolitan's *View from the Quai d'Orsay*, see Gottlieb 1967.

23 See ibid., pl. 46; and see Sérullaz 1991, p. 198, no. 252.

24 For the oil study at the Fondation Custodia, see Hefting 1975, no. 117 (as ca. 1853); Stein et al. 2003, no. 74 (as 1850). For the painting in Bagnères-de-Bigorre, see Gottlieb 1967, fig. 2; Hefting 1975, no. 106 (with incorrect dimensions); Stein et al. 2003, no. 92.

25 A photograph of the watercolor was published in an advertisement for M. Newman Ltd., London, in *The Connoisseur* 119 (June 1947), p. 11. See Gottlieb 1967, fig. 3.

26 The other two exhibited works were: *View of Notre Dame from the Pont de la Tournelle*, 1849, and *Moonrise near Paris* (both unidentified; see Auffret 2004, pp. 86–87n49). In this regard it is appropriate to recall Jongkind's oft-quoted reference to himself as "the painter of Paris" ("le peintre de Paris") in a letter he wrote to Martin from Holland on March 21, 1860, at the time he was planning his return to Paris, which would remain his center of operation for the rest of his career. See Hefting 1969, p. 115, letter no. 153.

REFERENCES

Amic, Sylvain, and Ségolène Le Men, eds.

2014 *Cathédrales, 1789–1914: Un Mythe moderne.* Exh. cat., Musée des Beaux-Arts, Rouen; Wallraf-Richartz-Museum & Fondation Corboud, Cologne. Paris: Somogy.

Auffret, François

2004 *Johan Barthold Jongkind, 1819–1891: Héritier contemporain & précurseur; biographie illustrée.* Paris: Maisonneuve et Larose.

Bellier de la Chavignerie, Émile, and Louis Auvray

1882–87 *Dictionnaire général des artistes de l'école française depuis l'origine des arts du dessin jusqu'à nos jours.* 3 vols. Paris: Librairie Renouard.

Bomford, David, et al.

1990 *Impressionism.* Exh. cat. London: The National Gallery.

Boucher, François

1925 *Le Pont-Neuf.* 2 vols. Paris: Le Goupy.

Burke, James D.

1974 *Charles Meryon, Prints & Drawings.* Exh. cat., Toledo Museum of Art, Toledo, Ohio; Yale University Art Gallery, New Haven; Saint Louis Museum of Art. New Haven: Yale University Art Gallery.

Darin, Michaël

1999 "Les Bouleversements urbains [1848–1877]." In Lambert 1999, pp. 92–100.

Duplomb, Charles

1911 *Histoire générale des ponts de Paris.* Vol. 1, *Première Partie: Les Ponts sur la Seine.* Paris: J. Mersch.

Galerie Schmit

1988 *Maîtres français, XIXᵉ–XXᵉ siècles.* Exh. cat. Paris: Galerie Schmit.

Gottlieb, Carla

1967 "Observations on Johan-Barthold Jongkind as a Draughtsman." *Master Drawings* 5 (Autumn), pp. 296–303, pls. 44–49.

Hefting, Victorine

1969 as editor. *Jongkind d'après sa correspondance.* Utrecht: H. Dekker & Gumbert.

1975 *Jongkind: Sa Vie, son oeuvre, son époque.* Paris: Arts et Métiers Graphiques.

1992 *J. B. Jongkind: Voorloper van het impressionisme.* Amsterdam: Bakker.

Kelly, Simon, and April M. Watson

2013 *Impressionist France: Visions of Nation from Le Gray to Monet.* Exh. cat. Saint Louis: Saint Louis Art Museum and The Nelson-Atkins Museum of Art.

Lambert, Guy, ed.

1999 *Les Ponts de Paris.* Paris: Action Artistique de la Ville de Paris.

Lazare, Félix, and Louis Lazare

1855 *Dictionnaire administratif et historique des rues et monuments de Paris.* 2nd ed. Paris: Au Bureau de la Revue Municipale.

Marrinan, Michael

2009 *Romantic Paris: Histories of a Cultural Landscape, 1800–1850.* Stanford: Stanford University Press.

Moreau-Nélaton, Etienne

1918 *Jongkind raconté par lui-même.* Paris: Henri Laurens.

Poitout, Louis Adolphe

1999 *Johan Barthold Jongkind (1819–1891) vu par un ami de la famille Fesser; Manuscrit de Louis Adolphe Poitout (1857–1913), fin de rédaction dans les années 1905–1910.* Preface and notes by François Auffret. Paris: Société des Amis de Jongkind.

Sérullaz, Arlette

1991 *De Corot aux impressionnistes, donations Moreau-Nélaton.* Exh. cat., Galeries Nationales du Grand Palais, Paris. Paris: Editions de la Réunion des Musées Nationaux.

Stein, Adolphe, Sylvie Brame, François Lorenceau, and Janine Sinizergues

2003 *Jongkind: Catalogue critique de l'oeuvre.* Vol. 1, *Peintures.* Paris: Brame & Lorenceau.

Stuffmann, Margret

1975 *Charles Meryon: Paris um 1850; Zeichnungen, Radierungen, Photographien.* Exh. cat., Städelsches Kunstinstitut und Städtische Galerie, Frankfurt am Main; Hamburger Kunsthalle; Haags Gemeentemuseum. Frankfurt am Main: Städelsches Kunstinstitut und Städtische Galerie.

1993 "Zwischen der Schule von Barbizon und den Anfängen des Impressionismus: Zur Landschaftsphotographie von Gustave Le Gray / Between the Barbizon School and the Beginnings of Impressionism: The Landscape Photography of Gustave Le Gray." In *Pioniere der Landschaftsphotographie; Gustave Le Gray, Carleton E. Watkins: Beispiele aus der Sammlung des J. Paul Getty Museums, Malibu / Pioneers of Landscape Photography; Gustave Le Gray, Carleton E. Watkins: Photographs from the Collection of the J. Paul Getty Museum,* by Margret Stuffmann et al., pp. 90–106. Exh. cat., Graphische Sammlung, Städtische Galerie im Städelschen Kunstinstitut, Frankfurt am Main. Mainz: H. Schmidt.

Thiébault-Sisson, François

1900 "Claude Monet, les années d'épreuves." *Le Temps,* November 26, p. 3.

Tinterow, Gary

1994 "The Realist Landscape." In Gary Tinterow and Henri Loyrette, *Origins of Impressionism,* pp. 55–93. Exh. cat. New York: MMA.

OLIVIER HURSTEL
MARTIN LEVY

Charles Lepec and the Patronage of Alfred Morrison

Since the second half of the twentieth century, the appreciation of nineteenth-century European decorative arts has evolved by fits and starts. For British design, the revival was arguably initiated by the exhibition "Victorian and Edwardian Decorative Arts," held at the Victoria and Albert Museum, London, in 1952.[1] Interest in French and other continental European manufacture began later and did not immediately take hold. In France, this interest increased with the decision in 1978 to create the Musée d'Orsay, Paris, specifically devoted to the art of the nineteenth century.[2] Writing that same year in the introductory essay to the catalogue for the seminal exhibition originating in Philadelphia "The Second Empire, 1852–1870: Art in France under Napoleon III," Jean-Marie Moulin acknowledged that this particular period "has been ignored—one might almost say erased—by French art historians. . . . Those who have had the experience of working on the

Second Empire in the area of the arts have felt the scorn (sometimes tinged with indulgence) that has surrounded the period, even—and perhaps especially—among the specialist and the knowledgeable layman."[3]

The ambivalence toward French decorative arts from the middle decades of the nineteenth century can perhaps be understood against the backdrop of a sense of loss for the dignified and aristocratic grandeur encapsulated by the culture of the ancien régime. France was dominated by the bourgeoisie by the time of the Second Empire, and the frequently backward-looking decoration of this period tended toward the showy: the taste of the nouveaux riches. But this viewpoint has come to be seen as representing an incomplete and unfair assessment of a fertile period, in which technical and artistic invention introduced a great degree of originality, with such work now appreciated for its distinctly nineteenth-century aesthetic merit.

Charles Lepec (1830–1890), who was at his most active during the Second Empire period,[4] exemplifies this sophisticated strand of French creativity. He was an artist who excelled in the medium of enamels, and, as will be shown, was particularly original and technically innovative. Many of his contemporaries working in the medium depended on compositions prevalent during the Renaissance. The 1978 Second Empire exhibition drew attention to many of the period's leading manufacturers, some of whom are now represented in the collection of The Metropolitan Museum of Art, which acquired them subsequently. These include the bronze founder and enamel manufacturer Ferdinand Barbedienne (1810–1892); the cabinetmaker

Charles-Guillaume Diehl (1811–?1885); the ceramist Théodore Deck (1823–1891); and the silversmith and maker of enamels and electroplated wares Christofle et Cie (1830–present).[5]

The leading Parisian manufacturers were major participants in the series of world's fairs that dominated the second half of the nineteenth century, beginning with the Great Exhibition in London in 1851. These massive international expositions, attended by millions of visitors, served as shop windows, enabling French firms to attract the patronage of British royalty, the aristocracy, and the newly powerful plutocrats.[6] Notable English purchasers from French manufacturers included Queen Victoria and Prince Albert;[7] William Ward, 1st Earl of Dudley (1817–1885);[8] and, most significant of all, Lepec's patron, the Victorian Maecenas, Alfred Morrison (1821–1897).

With France particularly hard hit by the worldwide depression that dominated the 1870s, England became an increasingly important market not only for French manufacturers, several of whom—for example, Deck and Barbedienne—had London-based outlets, but also for some craftsmen who joined English firms, such as Marc-Louis Solon (1835–1913), who in 1870 left Sèvres for Minton.[9] Like so many nineteenth-century French designers and manufacturers admired during their lifetimes, the *peintre-émailleur*[10] Charles Lepec almost disappeared from view in the twentieth century.

In 1971 Lepec's sumptuous enamel and gold *nef* (table ornament in the form of a ship) (fig.1), exhibited at the Exposition Universelle in Paris in 1867, was sold by Lord Margadale (1906–1996),[11] grandson of Alfred Morrison and in 1976 it entered the collection of the Badisches Landesmuseum, Karlsruhe.[12] It was not until 1980, when Daniel Alcouffe published his magisterial "Les Emailleurs français à l'Exposition Universelle de 1867," that Lepec was finally reappraised.[13] Alcouffe presented Lepec as the most original and outstanding enamel artist of the nineteenth century, the master of an art form at which the French had excelled since the Renaissance—but who had been somewhat forgotten since then.[14]

Alcouffe also gave details of the enamel work of Lepec's contemporaries who exhibited at the Paris Exposition Universelle, 1867, although not in the same category[15]—a notable coterie that included Alexis Falize (1811–1893), Charles Duron (1814–1872), Charles Dotin (b. 1820), Claudius Popelin (1825–1892), and Alfred Meyer (1832–1904).[16] While enamels by Popelin and Meyer, for example, generally depend directly on Renaissance prototypes for their style of painting,

Lepec's Renaissance-inspired creations show a greater degree of inspired originality and a finer mastery of technique. If the forms of some of Lepec's vessels reveal their historic sources, the decoration, as seen in his work for Morrison, is utterly creative in its composition and coloration. Duron is best known for his interpretations and copies of mounted hardstone vessels from the French royal collection, housed in the Musée du Louvre, Paris.[17]

Alcouffe's review of Lepec's career was based on contemporary criticism and on records of works published and exhibited during the artist's lifetime, but Alcouffe identified and illustrated only three surviving objects, including the nef and *Clémence Isaure* (fig. 2). In 1982, the Musée d'Orsay acquired *Clémence Isaure*, formerly in the collection of Henry Bolckow (1806–1878), a German-born iron magnate, member of Parliament, and first mayor of Middlesbrough, who lived at Marton Hall.[18] More recently, both Katherine Purcell, in connection with Alexis Falize, and Charlotte Gere and Judy Rudoe, with regard to jewelry, have touched briefly, but significantly, on Lepec.[19]

Since the early 1980s many more examples of Lepec's work in enamel have been identified, as well as paintings, drawings, designs, and carvings. In 2004 the Metropolitan Museum acquired the *Bouteille vénitienne* (Venetian flask) (fig. 21), and in 2010 the *Carved Panel, with a Portrait of Mabel Morrison* (fig. 28); both were formerly in the collection of Alfred Morrison. In addition to a greatly increased body of work, it is now possible to add substantially to the biographical details given by Alcouffe. As a preface here, we outline hitherto unrecognized and significant aspects of Lepec's life.[20]

Central to Lepec's career, as is made clear by Alcouffe and others, was Alfred Morrison, who was the son of the fabulously rich collector James Morrison (1789–1857), a man obsessed with money, status, class, and power, but also public-spirited and passionate about his family.[21] James Morrison built his fortune on the simple motto "small profits and quick returns." Although his elder son, Charles (1817–1909), emulated James in terms of business acumen, it was Alfred who matched and exceeded his father as a collector and patron. James had been a typical collector in the tradition of the nineteenth-century nouveaux riches, an autodidact who took the advice of his architect J. B. Papworth (1775–1847) and others in forming an outstanding collection of old master and contemporary English paintings. His decor included the typical rich man's accumulation of Boulle furniture and Sèvres vases.

Alfred preserved much of his father's collection but stands out as a discerning patron of contemporary craftsmen (and, to a lesser extent, painters). The younger Morrison should be seen as a successor to great amateurs such as William Beckford (1760–1844) and Thomas Hope (1769–1831).[22] Alfred Morrison patronized in depth those whose work he admired, many of whom are now considered among the outstanding manufacturers of the period. These include the innovative jeweler Alessandro Castellani (1823–1883); the reviver of enameled glass in the Islamic taste Philippe-Joseph Brocard (1831–1896); Lucien Falize (1839–1897), whose remarkable gold, silver, amethyst, diamond, and enamel clock made for Morrison is now in the Metropolitan Museum;[23] and the maker of damascened ironwork Plácido Zuloaga (d. ca. 1910). Lepec's work would have glowed in such company. Among other areas in which Morrison collected voraciously were engravings, textiles,

fig. 3 Studio of Nadar [Gaspard-Félix Tournachon] (French, 1820–1910). *The Painter Lepec N° 848*, n.d. Albumen print from glass negative, 3⅜ × 2¼ in. (8.5 × 5.8 cm). Bibliothèque Nationale de France, Paris (FT-4-NA-235 [2])

and, famously, autographs.[24] Chinese porcelain and enamels and Japanese works of art, including many cloisonné enamels, were also a passion of Morrison's.[25]

The taste for enamels began to revive toward the end of the reign of Louis Philippe (1773–1850).[26] During the 1850s, collectors were principally interested in medieval and Renaissance enamels, but following the opening of Japan to the West in the mid-1850s and the sacking of the Summer Palace in Peking (now Beijing) in 1860, connoisseurs had a greater opportunity to study and acquire Asian enamels. Morrison's collecting is distinguished, however, by his pursuit of contemporary European enamels, alongside older Asian creations.

But Morrison's interests extended beyond the works of art he commissioned and collected. The influential and innovative architect, designer, and design theorist Owen Jones (1809–1874) was engaged by Morrison to create the furniture and interiors at Carlton House Terrace, London, and at Fonthill, in Wiltshire; the work was carried out by the talented London cabinetmaker Jackson & Graham (active ca. 1840–85).[27]

CHARLES LEPEC

Charles Florent Joseph Lepec (fig. 3) was born in Paris on April 5, 1830, and died in Reux, France, on May 19, 1890.[28] He was the son of Charles Antoine Lepec, who

was born at Reux on April 19, 1791, and died in Paris on March 12, 1875. A descendant of the noble family of Costentin de Tourville,[29] Lepec père was a lawyer, the author of several books on law,[30] and a recipient of the Legion of Honor (as would be his son). His wife, Florence Jeanne Raimonde Demetria Rodriguez, was of Spanish origin.[31] Despite the conventions of the time, the couple did not marry until May 1, 1832, two years after the birth of their only child. The family lived at 11, rue Gaillon, a former *hôtel particulier* by then divided into apartments. The building was fashionably located at the bottom of the chaussée d'Antin, between the Place Vendôme and the Palais-Royal. The spacious apartment also housed the office of Lepec père until his death in 1875.

The Lepec family owned property, including land and orchards, in Reux, near Pont-l'Evêque, Normandy, which suggests that they enjoyed a degree of financial stability and social standing. Thus it could be argued that Charles Lepec grew up in a privileged environment. He attended the Lycée Condorcet, the great liberal school on the Right Bank, much favored by the Parisian bourgeoisie. His father was a long-standing member of the prestigious Cercle des Arts, a meeting place for painters, sculptors, musicians, writers, and art lovers.[32]

Proximity to this group surely influenced Charles Lepec's choice of career. However, despite its relatively prosperous position, his family clearly wanted the young Lepec to have the advantage of a formal education. Although he did not go on to pursue a career in law or one of the other professions for which he might have been eligible, the benefits of his academic learning would become evident in his erudite artistic output. As Auguste Luchet noted of Lepec's early life: "Happy is he who is able to enter the Arts through the noble door of Letters and Sciences."[33]

Contemporary accounts, published about the time of the 1867 Exposition Universelle, suggest that Lepec's principal artistic development occurred under the supervision of the artist Hippolyte Flandrin (1809–1864).[34] After an early career as a painter, exhibiting at the Salons of 1857 and 1859,[35] by 1860 Lepec had turned to the enamel work that would be his major preoccupation until the early 1870s.[36] By 1861, he was living at 61, rue du Faubourg-Montmartre, Paris; in 1865 he was at 52, rue de Bourgogne; and by 1869 he had moved to 12, rue de Pré-aux-Clercs. When Lepec married his pupil Jeanne Marie Thierry in 1882, he lived at 13, rue Bonaparte. It is clear that Lepec also spent time from the 1860s onward at Reux, and seems eventually to have made it his main place of residence.[37]

fig. 4 J. Smith (English). *Alfred Morrison*, Photograph. Fonthill Estate Archive

LEPEC, ROBERT PHILLIPS, AND ALFRED MORRISON

Lepec exhibited at the 1862 London International Exhibition,[38] where he may have had his first encounter with Robert Phillips, the jeweler based at 23 Cockspur Street, London, who would shortly become the agent for his work in England.[39] At this world's fair, during a period when modern enamels appealed mainly to a small number of elite connoisseurs, Lepec made his first sales to Alfred Morrison, who would become his most significant patron (fig. 4).[40] Phillips and Morrison were, in effect, to shape Lepec's career. The considerable Morrison archive, part of the Fonthill Estate Archive, contains documents and letters with direct bearing on the relationships between Lepec and Phillips, Lepec and Morrison, and Lepec and his fellow Parisian craftsmen.[41] This remarkably well-preserved source provides unique insights into the relationship between a patron and his agent, and those whose work was commissioned.

A simple six-page list on lined paper, certainly prepared by Phillips's clerk,[42] records purchases made by Morrison at the "International Exhibition 1862." The list demonstrates the range and depth of Morrison's approach to the work of contemporary manufacturers, even at this early stage of his collecting career. From Lepec, Morrison bought "9 Plaques of Enamel. Reduced from 12000 to 9,000.

£360" and "Models of Coffrets & Enamel⁵ 2000 frs. £80." Morrison acquired a number of paintings at the International Exhibition, generally noted by country of origin rather than by artist. He also bought from leading French manufacturers, including the cabinetmakers Fourdinois and Guillaume Grohé and the metalworkers Christofle and Barbedienne (who on this occasion first exhibited his cloisonné enamels).[43] He bought an ebony and ivory étagère from Jackson & Graham (some years before the firm became responsible for supplying Morrison with large quantities of Owen Jones–designed furniture); work by the Italians Giovanni Battista Gatti,[44] Angiolo Barbetti, and Pietro Giusti (all three famous for their Renaissance-revival furniture); and ceramics from Minton and Sèvres. In all, Morrison spent £7,762 14s 8d, reduced after various discounts—for example, of 5 percent from Fourdinois—to £7,557 15s 8d. In an account from Phillips to Morrison covering 1862–63, which includes items from Elkington, Royal Worcester Porcelain Company, Jackson & Graham, and Gatti, there are two payments to Barbedienne, including one dated October 9, 1863, for "2 Lepec Enamels 500 fr. [£]20." The authors have not been able to establish the circumstances surrounding this transaction or its significance.[45]

Almost certainly purchased in 1862 is the small rectangular plaque, probably depicting Venus (fig. 5), inscribed on the reverse, according to a 1975 Sotheby's catalogue, "IPY [*sic*] 1861 no. 73."[46] Alcouffe speculates, probably correctly, that this work might be the one exhibited in 1867 and described at length in 1893 by Lucien Falize as "a study of a female nude, Venus or Psyche, softly and lightly clad."[47] When this piece was sold at Sotheby's, the catalogue entry quoted the critic and curator Alfred Darcel (1818–1893) as saying that Lepec's nudes had a *gentillesse banale* (ordinariness) and that such works had an unfortunate resemblance to colored lithographs.[48] This criticism should, in fact, be seen as an interesting observation when looked at in light of Lepec's (and others') use of another relatively modern invention, photography.[49]

From his position as Morrison's agent at the 1862 London International Exhibition, it is clear that Phillips was already acting as an intermediary between manufacturers and Morrison.[50] Other retailers and manufacturers that appear in Morrison's address-notebook in the early 1860s include Thomas Goode (retailers of ceramics), Hatfield ("Brass Cleaner"), and Fannière Frères (silversmiths). Over the next five years, Phillips's role as an intermediary helped Morrison become Lepec's most important patron. Lepec would later highlight many of the creations from this period when he participated in the 1867 Paris Exposition Universelle.[51]

In 1864, Phillips himself first exhibited Lepec's work in London. The *Morning Post* (January 7) reported:

> An enamelled tazza of remarkable beauty, designed and executed by Signor Charles Lepec. It is as perfect a work in its particular style of art as can well be imagined . . . In the cavity of the cup is a picture—classic in conception, . . . representing Venus gliding swiftly over the surface of the sea in a car drawn by mermaids, while overhead hovers in mid-air Cupid with a torch in one hand, and in the other the silken reins wherewith he gently guides the water-nymphs. . . . In the rim of the cup, which is concave, are medallion miniatures, exquisitely painted, of some of the most celebrated women who, whether in the records of historic or of imaginative literature, have exercised the most potent influence. . . .

fig. 5 Charles Lepec. *Venus*, 1861. Enamel with silver-gilt mount in ebonized and glazed frame, excluding frame 4¾ × 1¾ in. (12 × 4.5 cm). Reportedly inscribed on the reverse *IPY* [probably *V* rather than *Y*] *1861 no. 73*. Private collection

> The outside of the tazza is elaborately ornamented with flowers and foliage, painted in a manner to resemble the lack[*sic*]-work of the Japanese.[52]

This passage is quoted at length because this tazza (unlike *La Fantaisie*, dated 1864 and also exhibited by Phillips; see figs. 6, 7) has disappeared from sight since it was sold at auction in 1994 and thus cannot be illustrated.[53] Identified here as *La Volupté*, this piece, formerly in Morrison's collection, was also exhibited at the 1867 Exposition Universelle (see Appendix and fig. 8, top).

The earliest surviving letter from Lepec to Phillips in the Fonthill Estate Archive is dated July 26, 1863. Its tone establishes the cordial bond and professional relationship that had developed between the two since their encounter, probably at the London International Exhibition, the previous year. In it, Lepec discusses a piece he had been working on since about April: after three months of constant work, he had now finished the foot.[54] He continues by asking if Phillips will be coming to Paris with his client (clearly Morrison) and asks for a few days' notice so that he can return from the country (presumably Reux). Lepec had made alterations to the design and would require at least four more uninterrupted months to finish the work.[55] The artist also asks to be remembered to Phillips's family.

On December 21, 1863, Lepec announced to Phillips that he had finished the *coupe* (a shallow, dish-shaped bowl on a stem) and that a work of such importance would bring credit to them both.[56] In what will be shown to be one of many instances of artistic collaboration with contemporary craftsmen, Lepec notes that Charles Duron has made the mount for the coupe.[57] Lepec will leave for London on December 27 and asks if he might stay at the British Hotel, located at 26–27 Cockspur Street, virtually next door to Phillips (both premises now demolished).[58] Despite the absence of a distinctive foot rim or "mount," logic and timing would suggest that *La Fantaisie* is the coupe to which Lepec refers, and that Duron simply put together the top and stem.

Both *La Volupté* and *La Fantaisie* (see figs. 6–8), lent by Phillips, were shown at the Paris Salon in 1864.[59] In a letter to Phillips dated May 11, 1864, Lepec notes the excellent reception of the two coupes, that he has received more requests for work, and he attributes the success to *La Fantaisie*.[60] To the same letter Lepec attached an English-language news clipping received that day: "We beg, however, to direct attention towards two of the finest enamel paintings we have ever met

fig. 6 Charles Lepec. *La Fantaisie*, 1864. Enamel on metal, with a gold coin on the base, as a washer, 6⅝ × 8½ in. (16.8 × 21.5 cm). Signed and dated *CHARLES LEPEC 1864*, and inscribed *LA FANTAISIE*. Saint Louis Art Museum, Lopata Endowment Fund (129:1994)

fig. 7 Charles Lepec. Detail of the top of *La Fantaisie* shown in fig. 6

fig. 8 A page from the catalogue of the 1867 Paris Exposition Universelle with an illustration (top) of a stemmed bowl, or coupe, identified here as *La Volupté*. *Art-Journal* 1867b, p. 304

THE ART-JOURNAL CATALOGUE OF

M. LEPEC, to whom the Exhibition gave highest rank among the artists of France, supplies us with materials for another page. | All his productions in Enamel are of the best order | of Art; they may be placed, without disadvantage, beside the greatest works of their class, of any age or country. The difficulties

over which he has triumphed, the rare intelli- | gence by which his pencil has been guided, ac- | count for the "success" that has attended all

his later efforts. France may be proud of this | able and admirable artist, who has been justly re- | warded with a "decoration" and a *médaille d'or*.

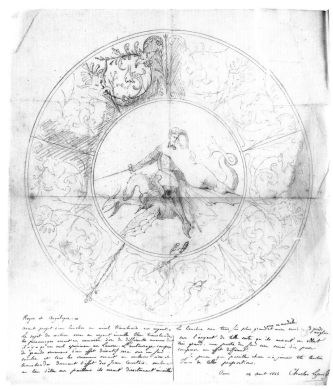

fig. 9 Charles Lepec. Coffret, ca. 1870. Painted and plique-à-jour enamel on gold and gilt-bronze, 5⅞ × 5⅜ × 3⅜ in. (15 × 13.5 × 8.5 cm). Musée des Beaux-Arts de Limoges, Palais de l'Evêché (94.522)

fig. 10 Charles Lepec. *Roger et Angélique*, 1864. Pencil on paper, 16 × 14¼ in. (40.6 × 36.2 cm). Signed and dated *Paris 14 août 1864 Charles Lepec*. Fonthill Estate Archive

with. They are by Lepec (No. 2,305) 'La Volupté' and 'La Fantaisie.' They belong to Mr. Phillips, says the catalogue."[61] *La Fantaisie* was described in the *Gazette des Beaux-Arts* as depicting a wild female "Redskin" riding a chimera. The writer continued, however, by noting that he preferred the portraits shown the year before.[62] Thus, by 1864, Lepec's work in enamel was already receiving critical attention on both sides of the English Channel.

In the chronology of enamels discussed by Lepec in correspondence with Phillips, the next items are three untraced bottles or flasks (*trois flacons*) referred to in a letter dated March 16, 1864.[63] Another work completed in 1864 was a *coffret* (box), which Lepec planned to take to London in early July 1864; this resembled goldsmith's work.[64] Although undocumented and unsigned, the small coffret at the Musée des Beaux-Arts de Limoges, Palais de l'Evêché, might be of similar appearance.[65] Lepec's three-quarter profile portrait on the front of the coffret (fig. 9) resembles *Clémence Isaure* (see fig. 2)—but on a diminutive scale.[66]

Not all the works listed by Pierre Sanchez as exhibited by Lepec at the Paris Salons of 1863–65 have been traced.[67] One such is *Roger et Angélique* (1865 Salon, no. 2615), which was lent by M. H. Durand, who has not been positively identified.[68] Although Morrison was fast becoming Lepec's greatest patron, it did not follow that Morrison acquired everything he was offered The drawing from the Fonthill Estate Archive, *Roger et Angélique* (fig. 10),

is clearly for a major work and surely illustrates the (untraced) object lent by Durand to the 1865 Salon. It is signed and dated *Paris 14 août 1864 Charles Lepec* and is informative about the effect Lepec wished to achieve with translucent colored enamels in an enameled silver *bouclier* (shield) three feet in diameter.[69]

The degree to which Lepec and Phillips's friendship deepened is emphasized in a letter dated August 23, 1864. Lepec expresses concern that Mrs. Phillips has undergone a serious operation. He also comments that his own health has improved. With regard to the bouclier, he says that he is happy that the design is to Phillips's taste and that he will not sell it before giving him the right of first refusal.[70] The bouclier is not referred to again, so we must assume that Morrison, through Phillips, rejected the piece.

The subject of Lepec's shield, characteristically erudite, is based on a section of the romantic epic *Orlando Furioso* by Ludovico Ariosto (1474–1533) and depicts Ruggerio (Roger) rescuing Angelica (Angélique) from a rock where she is about to be attacked by a sea monster.[71] It may not be a coincidence that in 1819 Jean-Auguste-Dominique Ingres painted the same subject to great effect.[72] Paul Mantz, describing the work as *Angélique et Médor*, admires its exquisite technical composition but dislikes its purple hue and overall decorative effect.[73] Meanwhile, Félix Jahyer admires the colors and grace of the dazzling work.[74]

fig. 11 Charles Lepec. Plate, 1865. Enamel on silver, silver-gilt edge, Diam. 8⅝ in. (22 cm). Signed *N. 230. CHARLES LEPEC.I.P.V. 1865.* Musée des Beaux-Arts de Limoges, Palais de l'Evêché

fig. 12 Charles Lepec. Plate, 1865. Enamel on silver, silver-gilt edge, Diam. 8 in. (20.3 cm). Signed *N. 231. CHARLES LEPEC. IPV.1865.* Rijksmuseum, Amsterdam (BK-1995-1)

fig. 13 Charles Lepec. Lepec monogrammed letterhead, ca. 1867. Pen and ink on paper. Fonthill Estate Archive

Two smaller-scale works from 1865, formerly in Morrison's collection and shown at the 1867 Paris Exposition Universelle, each described as an *assiette sujet* (plate depicting a particular subject),[75] give some idea of how Lepec's composition *Roger et Angélique* might have looked. The plates are sequential works; the earlier, number 230 (fig. 11), is now in the collection of the Musée des Beaux-Arts de Limoges.[76] It depicts the blindfolded figure of Fortune beside her wheel, with falling emblems of power to her right. The representation of the crown and scepter recalls a similar treatment on the earlier *Audaces Fortuna Juvat* (1860).[77] The subject of the decoration on the second plate, numbered 231, has not been identified (fig. 12).[78] Both plates have decorative floral borders surmounted by variants of a type of drag-onlike creature, which is something of a leitmotif in Lepec's work and a familiar element of the nineteenth-century interest in medieval mythology.[79] Lepec also incorporated a similar motif into the monogram he created as his own letterhead (fig. 13).

From correspondence relating to these two plates, it would appear that they followed two simpler, untraced examples, one with an overall geometric design and the other with a plain center (see fig. 8, bottom center, left and right), which Morrison also lent to the 1867 Paris Exposition Universelle. In a letter dated October 13, 1865, Lepec tells Robert Phillips to let Morrison know that these new plates, despite their rich decoration, could not possibly fetch the same price as the first two.[80] The following day, Phillips sent Lepec's invoice to Morrison.[81]

The Victoria and Albert Museum holds an important and hitherto unpublished group of designs by Lepec.[82] The sixteen drawings, some of which are dated, range from 1865 to 1886; they were acquired in 1891 from Phillips Brothers of Cockspur Street for £9 12s. Alfred Phillips, in a letter to the museum, refers to the "selection of 16 drawings which you made," tantalizingly suggesting that there were more.[83] In the majority of instances where the design can be associated with an identifiable work,[84] these relate to commissions for Morrison.[85] Although Morrison would seem to have remained Lepec's most significant patron throughout the period 1862–66, we have already seen that *Angélique et Roger* went elsewhere. Another major work not acquired by Morrison was the large-scale *Clémence Isaure* exhibited at the 1866 Paris Salon (see fig. 2).[86] The buyer, as noted above, was Henry Bolckow, who at some point also bought a Lepec-designed gold ring with an enamel of Psyche surrounded by brilliant-cut diamonds; this is now in the collection of the Victoria and Albert Museum.[87]

The year 1866 was to be a very busy one for Lepec, and it seems that he felt the strain. Not only was he creating work on an ambitious scale, but also, as the months went by, he would be increasingly preoccupied by the following year's Exposition Universelle. In a letter dated February 1, 1866, Lepec tells Phillips about difficulties he is having with this 71-by-45-inch creation, on which he has worked for more than a year with the help of his two ablest students.[88] Lepec is delighted by the complex panels making up the arabesque borders but distraught that the 21-inch central panel has been damaged that day in the kiln. He says that he will be devastated if it cannot be recovered in time for the 1866 Salon.[89]

There can be no doubt that the work with which Lepec was struggling is *Clémence Isaure*; the dimensions 71 by 45 inches correspond sufficiently closely with the 180.3 by 113 centimeters given by the Musée d'Orsay.[90] The letter continues in an increasingly despondent vein. Lepec had now failed a second time in firing the central panel, recalling a problem he had had once before with a silver shield (perhaps the Durand bouclier). He says that if he finally succeeds, he will never again attempt a work on such a scale.[91] Lepec clearly did succeed, as *Clémence Isaure* was shown at the 1866 Salon. Toward the end of the letter, Lepec writes that he hopes to be in London at the end of February with the model of the gold cup, although this may be delayed because of the difficulties of the project. Here, surely, is the first mention of the nef (see fig. 1) that was to cause such a stir the following year.

Despite the evident success of *Clémence Isaure* in April 1866, Lepec's health, according to a letter Phillips wrote to Morrison from Paris, was "seriously affected by his recent disappointments."[92] In fact, health seems to have remained a dominant factor in Lepec's life, and one might speculate that he simply could not take the stress involved in creating his time-consuming and accident-prone enamels. In a letter dated January 8, 1879, identified here as to the enameler Claudius Popelin, Lepec notes his exhaustion and ill health on his return from Normandy.[93]

As Alcouffe records (citing Falize), Lepec had the help of Charles Dotin in completing *Clémence Isaure*.[94] In the final part of his survey "Claudius Popelin et la renaissance des émaux peints," Falize notes that *Clémence Isaure* remains one of the largest enamels produced at the time, and that great credit is owed to Dotin, who, like Gagneré for Popelin, was an outstanding craftsman.[95] *Clémence Isaure* was the work highlighted by the *Art-Journal* in an article titled "The Enamels of Charles Lepec," which was intended to introduce "the name of this remarkable artist to our readers" at the time of the 1867 Paris Exposition Universelle:

> One only of M. Lepec's greatest works, the greatest indeed, . . . has Mr. Morrison permitted to pass from Mr. Phillips to any other hands than his own. This admirable enamel, a group of colossal plaques, incorporated so as to form a single composition upwards of six feet in height, is not only by far the most important work of its class that has been executed in modern times, but it also takes precedence of all the greatest enamels that are known to be in existence.[96]

We do not know why Morrison turned down *Clémence Isaure*, but much of what he bought from Lepec and others was more "jewel like" in appearance than this uncharacteristically large-scale work.

Also from 1866 is the Morrison tazza and cover (figs. 14, 15) now in the collection of the Fitzwilliam Museum, Cambridge.[97] All the surviving works for Morrison highlighted so far—*La Volupté*, *La Fantaisie*, the two plates divided between Amsterdam and Limoges, and the tazza and cover—were first resold as "The Property of a Lady" on January 25, 1899, at Christie's. The sale, by Morrison's widow, Mabel, whom he had married in April 1866, included "Vases, caskets, Plaques, Dishes, &c, of Silver and Gilt Metal, Beautifully damascened and enamelled by C. Lepec and P. Zuloaga."[98] Lot 389—"A Silvered and Gilt Tazza, enamelled with an African figure on a dragon in translucent colours—*by C. Lepec*, 1864"—is *La Fantaisie*. Lot 390 was a "Tazza and Cover, of enamelled and gilt metal, decorated with emblematic figures, arabesque foliage and other ornament, a figure of cupid on the lid; and a tazza on tripod foliage stem—*by C. Lepec*." The first part of this lot is the Fitzwilliam coupe, but the tazza on a tripod, the description resembling *La Fortune Conduite par l'Amour*,[99] has not been traced. Lot 391 was "A larger Tazza, similar, with Aphrodite and a border of arabesques and medallion heads; and a pair of plates, with groups of emblematic figures on gold ground—*by the same*"; these are *La Volupté* and the plates now in Amsterdam and Limoges.

It is fortunate that the same buyer, "Marcus," acquired all three lots. Although this purchaser has not been identified, these works were either handed down through his family or were sold to someone else who

fig. 14 Charles Lepec. Tazza and Cover, 1866. Enamel on copper, and gold, overall H. 9⅜ in. (23.8 cm); Diam. of foot 3⅛ in. (8 cm); Diam. of rim 5⅞ in. (15 cm); Diam. of cover 5¾ in. (14.5 cm). On one side of the cover, the border is broken by the mark *CHARLES LEPEC / - PARIS- / N 288.I.P.V.66* in gold below a coronet, and a dragon crest. On the tazza, the border is broken by the mark *CHARLES LEPEC / -PARIS- / N 287.I.P.V.1866.* Fitzwilliam Museum, Cambridge, England (M.5 and A-1994)

fig. 15 Interior of the tazza shown in fig. 14

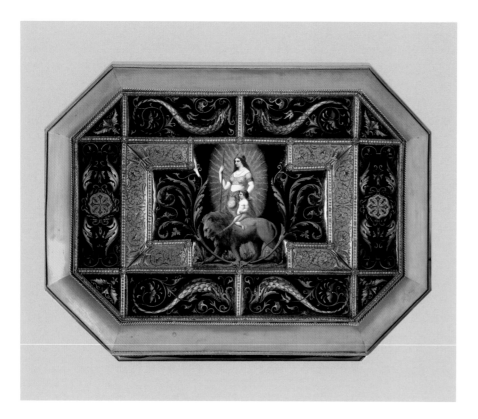

fig. 16 Charles Lepec. Top of a coffret, ca. 1870. Enamel on copper, silver gilt, and gilt bronze, 11¼ × 22 × 16¾ in. (28.5 × 56 × 42.5 cm). M & N Uzal, Brussels

retained the majority as a group. All but the tazza on a tripod were sold at Christie's South Kensington on September 20, 1994, lots 70–73. Lots 393–97 in the January 1899 sale, all untraced, were also by Lepec. It is possible that the circular plaques with busts of Laura and Marguerite (part of lot 393) are those lent by Morrison to the 1867 Paris Exposition Universelle (see Appendix).[100] The large coffer (lot 395), which has not been traced, does not correspond in size with the one dated here to about 1870 (fig. 16).

Among other pieces Lepec completed for Morrison between 1866 and 1867 are three substantial and equally significant but presently untraced works.[101] Fortunately, however, the original designs are in the collection of the Victoria and Albert Museum (figs. 17–19). The "Renaissance-inspired" vase design (fig. 17) is signed and dated "Charles Lepec 1866"; it is also inscribed *Mr. Morrison* against which is noted *£125*, but a price of *£200* is also mentioned on the sheet. The band of black, white, and gold masks, and the use of these colors in general, is reminiscent of sixteenth-century Limoges enamels by, for example, Pierre Reymond, and shows Lepec's response to such work more directly than has hitherto been apparent.[102] Once again, Lepec uses one of his much-favored profile portraits for the principal decorative motif.

Thus far, we have seen Lepec using pattern as the embellishment of borders, but on the design for the *cornet persan* (cornet-shaped vase with Persian decoration) (fig. 18) and the *coffret persan* (box with Persian ornament) (fig. 19), pattern is the main decoration. Although a precise source has not been identified, the

fig. 17 Charles Lepec. Design for "Renaissance-inspired" Vase, 1866. Pencil and watercolor, with gold highlights on paper, 12¼ × 8⅞ in. (31 × 22.5 cm). Signed and dated *Charles Lepec 1866*. Victoria and Albert Museum, London (D.409-1891)

fig. 18 Charles Lepec. Design for a Cornet Persan, 1866. Pencil and watercolor, with gold highlights on paper, 9⅛ × 12¼ in. (23.3 × 31.2 cm). Initialed and dated *Juil. 66 CLP*. Victoria and Albert Museum, London (D.411-1891)

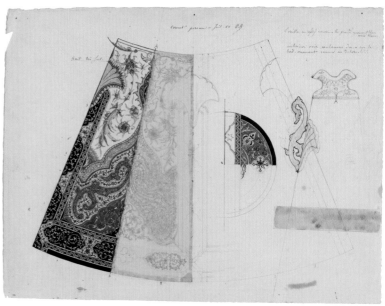

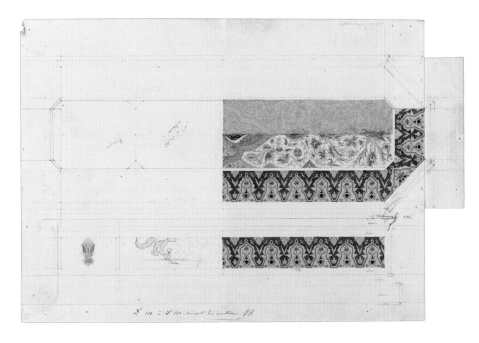

fig. 19 Charles Lepec. Design for a Coffret Persan, 1867. Pencil and watercolor, with gold highlights on paper, 9 × 13⅜ in. (22.8 × 34 cm). Signed and dated *Ch Lepec 1867*. Victoria and Albert Museum, London (D.412-1891)

fig. 20 Charles Lepec. Chimneypiece after a design by Owen Jones for Carlton House Terrace, ca. 1865. Enamel on alabaster

overall impression conveyed by both pieces is similar to that of a densely decorated Persian carpet or book cover.

Lepec was certainly aware of Owen Jones, who was working for Morrison at Fonthill House as mentioned, and at 16 Carlton House Terrace during the mid-1860s.[103] Jones published his influential *Grammar of Ornament* in 1856, and while the plates in this volume are highly stylized when compared with Lepec's more free-flowing designs, they are similar in spirit, and one can sense the influence. In the text to plate 48 in *The Grammar of Ornament* (Persian No. 5), Jones writes: "The ornament at the top . . . as well as the borders throughout, present that mixed character of pure ornament, arranged in conjunction with the ornamental rendering of natural forms, which we have considered as characteristic of the Persian style."[104] Another example of the perhaps not coincidental similarities between the ornamentation of Jones and Lepec can be seen, for example, in the ceilings at Carlton House Terrace.[105]

There is a single instance in which Lepec can be shown to have been working directly under the influence of Owen Jones: the enameled alabaster chimneypiece (fig. 20) that remains in situ at Carlton House Terrace. In 1879 the *Magazine of Art* published an engraving showing a detail of this work with "ornamentation . . . rendered in surface enamels—of opaque and translucent character . . . This work was executed by M. Le Pec, of Paris, and was carried out in accordance with the suggestions of Mr. Owen Jones. It is presumably a unique example of so costly an application of this kind of art-workmanship to a fireplace."[106]

The designs for the cornet persan (fig. 18) and the coffret persan (fig. 19) are different in decorative detail, but both respond to Asian influences. The cornet persan, with handles perhaps based on the mounts found on Chinese vases,[107] was exhibited at the 1867 Paris Exposition Universelle (see fig. 8, center right). There is a note on Lepec's monogrammed paper, probably from June 1867, recording that he had delivered to Madame Morrison the "cornet persan £100," and further down he writes that the mounting of the coffret persan will be complete within a month.[108]

The *Bouteille vénitienne*, now in the Metropolitan Museum (fig. 21), is reminiscent in form of early fifteenth-century Venetian flasks.[109] The decoration of this object, also lent by Morrison to the 1867 Paris Exposition Universelle (see fig. 8, center left), is inscribed around the portrait of its subject *BERNABO VISCONTI* and dated *MCCCLXXVIII* (1378). Perhaps significantly, this was the year that Chaucer traveled to

Lombardy on behalf of Richard II to meet Bernabò Visconti (1323–1385), the soldier-statesman who was ruler of Milan.[110] On January 10, 1867, Morrison received a receipt from Lepec for £250 in payment for "une bouteille venitienne [*sic*] et son plateau."[111] It is evident that the cost of Lepec's vases ranged between £100 and £200, and this puts into perspective the value he placed on the nef exhibited in 1867. On the same document in which Lepec records payment for the cornet persan, he notes, "Le vase d'or de £1000."[112]

By the time the *Bouteille vénitienne* was sold by the Morrison family, the name Lepec had been forgotten. On October 26, 1920, and in the following days, Waring & Gillow auctioned the contents of "Basildon Park, Pangbourne, Berks." Lot 1037 was: "A very fine European enamel rose-water vase of flat bottle-shape with quadruple lip on oval base, the whole richly enameled on silver, in claret, turquoise, white and gilt, etc., with a medallion portrait of a man, 12½-in. high." A photographic illustration shows this lot on a table with other works of art.[113]

fig. 21 Charles Lepec. *Bouteille vénitienne*, ca. 1867. Enamel on silver, partially gilt, 12½ × 10 × 7⅞ in. (31.9 × 25.4 × 20 cm). Inscribed: *BERNABO VISCONTI M.CCC.L.XXVIII.* The Metropolitan Museum of Art, Purchase, Friends of European Sculpture and Decorative Arts Gifts, 2004 (2004.452)

PARIS EXPOSITION UNIVERSELLE, 1867

By general acclaim, Lepec was a star exhibitor at the Paris 1867 Exposition Universelle, when his masterpiece (see fig. 1) was described as "a gold cup in the form of a *Nef*—a boat. It has been bought for a large sum (but not for more than its worth) by Mr. Alfred Morrison; and, indeed, nearly the whole of Lepec's productions have been purchased for England by Mr. Robert Phillips, who was the first in this country to appreciate the great artist, and who must rejoice to witness his accumulated fame."[114] The fabrication of the nef was another occasion on which Lepec collaborated with Duron.[115]

On August 23, 1867, the *Times* wrote at length in praise of Lepec:

> In the paintings of M. Lepec we see that he has at command a very wide scale of colours, and that he can associate them with a delicacy and a brilliance which is new to the art. Here and there in some of the specimens it may be that we shall find the colour a little hard; but in other pieces—as in the two miniatures of an English lady—we see that nothing can be more soft. Some of his processes of colour are known only to himself; many of his colours are hard enough to endure eight, ten, 12, even 15 fires; and, indeed, they attain their perfection only in a violent fire. It is no easy matter to get such beauty of colour—for, in the first place, it must be remembered that the artist does not *see* the colour which he desires to obtain. He paints with one colour in the expectation that after it has passed through the fire it will come out another. Again, his work has to pass through the fire so often that it runs continual risk of destruction.[116]

In addition to drawing particular attention to Lepec's technical prowess, the *Times* mentions, among other matters, "two miniatures of an English lady." As one of them was certainly of Mabel Morrison, surely she was depicted in both. In a letter to Alfred Morrison, dated December 13, 1866, Lepec reported that he had the previous day completed the portrait of Madame Morrison and that it was being forwarded that day via Phillips.[117] He worries at length over the resemblance and is anxious for Morrison's honest opinion. In the same letter Lepec refers to a smaller enamel for a Mr. Chermside with which he has struggled. He feels that the eye is not quite right, nor the mouth, and that the overall result perhaps makes the sitter look younger than she does in the larger work.[118] The second portrait was doubtless for Mabel Morrison's father, the Reverend Chermside.[119] By this date, as the letter shows, Lepec was in direct contact with the Morrisons and visiting them at Fonthill.

While we may never be able to form a complete picture of the items by Lepec that Morrison lent to the 1867 exhibition, we do know from a list in the Fonthill Estate Archive which pieces were sent over from England (see Appendix). The list includes the Metropolitan *Bouteille vénitienne*, the Fitzwilliam tazza and cover, the Rijksmuseum assiette, the Limoges assiette, the Saint Louis *Fantaisie*, the Karlsruhe nef, and the recently identified *Atalanta* and *Amazon*.[120]

Although by 1873 Lepec appears to have significantly reduced his production of enameling on metal, that year he reprised the form of the nef on a smaller scale and in a reduced form.[121] The original nef was also illustrated in 1873 by the largely technical *Practical Magazine* under the title "Enamels by M. Charles Lepec, Paris." In an article briefly recalling the history of painted enamels, there is a short description once more demonstrating the interest in the technical issues raised in such work. Lepec's nef is praised as:

> a complete specimen of the various kinds of enamelling. The painting, first, is indestructible, the opaque enamels re-touched, and the rich gamut of translucid enamels, directly applied to gold, in the ornaments; the enamels incrusted in the foot, which also throws up pretty medallions which are painted and set, completing an exquisite execution.[122]

As is clear from the letters in the Fonthill Estate Archive, Lepec made a practice of collaborating with his Parisian confrères. But he also acted as an intermediary on their behalf. In a letter dated December 21, 1863, he tells Phillips that he will be bringing to London a brooch by Duron for his inspection. The following year, on May 11, Lepec again writes to Phillips, this time about two inkstands, chandeliers, and a candlestick by Dotin, and in June 1867 he makes deliveries to Morrison on behalf of Dotin and Zuloaga. There are, in addition, two accounts to Morrison, signed by Lepec, but on the billheads of Dotin and Duron, both from 1866.[123]

THE 1870S

The carved and gilded ivory plaque (fig. 22)[124] demonstrates Lepec turning his considerable talents as a

fig. 22 Charles Lepec and Moreau-Vauthier (French, 1831–1893). Ivory Plaque, 1870. Ivory, parcel-gilt and painted, and ebony, glass, and velvet, 22¼ × 24¾ in. (56.5 × 62.7 cm). Signed on shield, proper right: *CH. LEPEC. INV. DEL. 70*, and on shield, proper left: *MOREAU, SCUT.* Gismondi, Paris

fig. 23a–d Charles Lepec. Four Designs for Masks, ca. mid-1860s. Pencil and watercolor on paper, 3½ × 3½ in. (9 × 9 cm). Each signed *Ch Lepec*. Victoria and Albert Museum, London (D.416-1891, D.420-1891, D.419-1891, D.417-1891)

draftsman to a new medium and again working in conjunction with another artist-craftsman. The shield at left is signed *CH. LEPEC. INV. DEL. 70* and the one on the right *MOREAU, SCUT.*[125] Yet again this was a commission for Morrison; it is monogrammed at the top with interlaced *M*s for Mabel Morrison. The first reference to someone named Moreau in the Fonthill Estate Archive, presumably in connection with Morrison himself, is a letter from Lepec to Phillips dated May 11, 1864, in which he reports that the day after Phillips departed Paris he inquired about the price of Moreau's *Oedipus*, but that it had been sold.[126] On August 4, 1869, Morrison records in his address-notebook: "Moreau 57 Rue Tiquetonne carved the ivory bust of Henry IV original by Germain Pilon ami de Jean Goujon—designer of the mausoleums of Francis I^st & Henri II a St Denis."[127]

The grotesque at the bottom of the plaque relates to a group of six such designs for masks by Lepec in the Victoria and Albert Museum's set of drawings acquired from Phillips (see figs. 23a–d, for example).[128] The Lepec/Moreau-Vauthier work was sold at Christie's on February 23, 1899, as lot 138: "A SCROLL-SHAPED IVORY PLAQUE, carved in relief with an emblematic group 'Omnia vincit Amor' and Cupids, gryphons, arabesques and other ornaments—*by Moreau, designed by Ch. Lepec*, 1870—in glazed ebonized frame." The buyer's name is hard to read but might be "Gibbes." It has not been ascertained what happened to this piece between 1899 and its recent reappearance in Paris. As we shall see, Lepec himself would later turn his own hand to carving—but in boxwood.

The ivory surely confirms the attribution of an apparently unsigned and unprovenanced coffret, embellished with a series of enamel panels (see fig. 16), that should perhaps now be dated about 1870. This large work first appeared at auction and was subsequently included in an exhibition mounted by Roxane Rodriguez.[129] The central group on the lid, with the surrounding scrolling borders as well as the scaly fish, for example, can be compared to details on the ivory.[130] It is conceivable that the two profile portrait plaques of Laure and Marguerite lent by Morrison in 1867 may have been similar in design to two of those on the coffret; the profile plaques on the coffret represent Laure, Julia, Bianca, and Margareta and are also similar to the profile on the front of the Limoges coffret (see fig. 9).

The record in the *Art-Journal* of Lepec's participation in the 1871 London International Exhibition is significant in its praise for his jewelry, a hitherto largely neglected aspect of his work, noted in passing in connection with the Morrison loan to the Paris Exposition Universelle, 1867:

> The *cloisonnés* enamels, by Lepec, are the most perfect examples of the Art, consisting of necklaces, pendants, brooches, ear-rings, lockets, &c., with central fields of lozenge-shape, or other forms, of the most delicate colours, serving as backgrounds for small painted figures, modifications and copied originals from the Greek, Pompeian, and Etruscan.[131]

Lepec's last appearance at a world's fair was at the London International Exhibition, 1872, where he exhibited three works, all lent by "Mrs. A. Morrison."[132] Number 2736 was an "Enamelled Coffer," which has not been identified; it may have been the unprovenanced coffret (see fig. 16) or, equally possible, the coffret persan (see fig. 19). Also unidentified is the "Small Enamelled Jewel Box" (number 2738); could this be the one now at Limoges (see fig. 9)?

The third exhibited piece was an "Enamelled Mirror." Although this too has yet to come to light, it may be the one for which three undated designs survive at the Victoria and Albert Museum (figs. 24, 25).[133] The colored and more finished design (fig. 25) includes details relating to colors and the manufacturing process, providing firsthand insights into Lepec's production

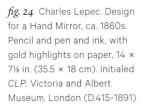

fig. 24 Charles Lepec. Design for a Hand Mirror, ca. 1860s. Pencil and pen and ink, with gold highlights on paper, 14 × 7⅛ in. (35.5 × 18 cm). Initialed *CLP*. Victoria and Albert Museum, London (D.415-1891)

fig. 25 Charles Lepec. Design for a Hand Mirror, ca. late 1860s. Pencil and pen and ink, with watercolor, and gold highlights on paper, 14⅝ × 8⅛ in. (37.3 × 20.5 cm). Initialed *CLP*. Victoria and Albert Museum, London (D.414-1891)

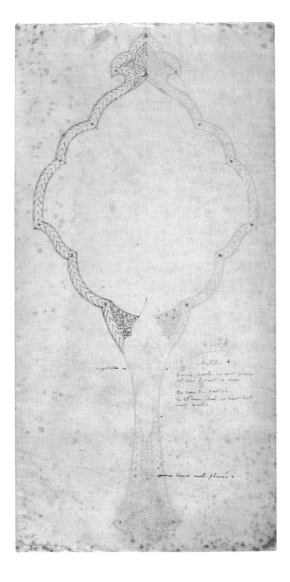

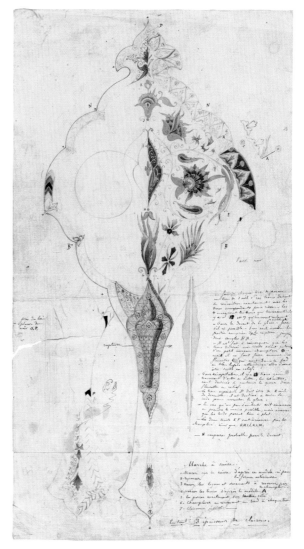

methods: "procedure—draw onto copper the design below . . . make divisions for the champlevé enamel . . . pierce holes on both sides, make divisions for champlevé, and apply three levels of cloisonné enamel."[134]

Press coverage for the less ambitious 1872 exhibition was not as extensive as had been the case in 1867. The *Birmingham Daily Post*, however, in an article titled "The Jewellery," noted Lepec's participation.[135] And the *Times*, under the heading "International Exhibition of 1872," reported that the "*Journal Officiel* of January 19, 1872, contains the following decree relative to the representation of French productions at that Exhibition." It is a sign of the respect in which he was by then held that Lepec was listed as a member of the committee responsible for selecting exhibits in "Class 7.—Reproductions from the Antique and from Works of the Middle Ages."[136]

Throughout his career Lepec created small-scale portraits and miniatures for significant members of society. In 1862 he made miniature portraits (present location unknown) of Napoleon III and Empress Eugénie.[137] Then, in 1864, he agreed to make portraits of the king and queen of Portugal, also untraced.[138] There are also three miniatures in the British Royal Collection. The second and third examples show Lepec's use of photography, while the first is based on another artist's work.[139]

It seems plausible that other such portrait miniatures await discovery. In a letter to Robert Phillips dated June 25, 1864, Lepec says that he has to return quickly to Paris because he has to make a miniature of Prince Napoleon for his mother.[140] Lepec requests, in the same letter, photographs of Princess Alexandra (1844–1925), the Danish consort of the Prince of Wales. In his quiet

fig. 28 Charles Lepec. Carved Panel, with a Portrait of Mabel Morrison, 1886/87. Boxwood, gilt metal, and painted ivory, mounted on gold velvet in a wooden metal-mounted frame, panel 9⅛ × 4⅝ in. (23.2 × 11.7 cm); frame 18½ × 14¼ × 2¼ in. (47 × 36.2 × 5.7 cm). The panel is signed Charles Lepec inv. scvlp., and the miniature is signed and dated Ch. Lepec 1886. Inscribed in detail on the reverse of portrait. The Metropolitan Museum of Art, Purchase, The James Parker Charitable Foundation Gift, 2010 (2010.33)

moments, Lepec intends to make an enamel portrait.[141] The references in the Fonthill Estate Archive to Lepec's work as a miniaturist suggest that there is considerably more to be discovered about the artist's activities in this genre.

THE 1880S

Toward the end of his life Lepec created one final major work for the Morrisons, *Carved Panel, with a Portrait of Mabel Morrison* (fig. 28). This remarkable object, now in the collection of the Metropolitan Museum, encloses a gilt-metal-bordered miniature on ivory of Mabel Morrison, supported by a flamboyantly carved box-wood figure of a winged beast, that leitmotif of Lepec's oeuvre, here holding up Cupid resting on a sphere. The panel bears the legend *CESAR IMP.*[142] and is signed *CHARLES LEPEC INV. SCVLP.*; the ivory, inscribed *MABEL*, is signed and dated: *CH. LEPEC 1886*. Behind the miniature, on the wooden back, there is a further, detailed inscription:

> *Ce buis / a été composé, dessiné / et sculpté, ainsi que la portrait / en miniature sur ivoire de / Mme Mabel Morrison par / Charles Le Pecq de Tourville[143] / habituellement nommé— / Charles Lepec, dans sa maison / de la Croix de Fer[144], à Reux / arrt de Pont l'Evêque, Dept / du Calvados et terminé / dans la 1ere semaine de / Février / de l'an 1887.[145]*

The panel itself is inscribed in ink on reverse: *Trous / de / Fixage pour / l'exécution / Le Pec.*

The drawings by Lepec in the Victoria and Albert Museum include three sheets relating to this work. The first drawing, dated 1884 (fig. 26), appears to be an initial sketch but the second (fig. 27), more fully worked, is signed by Lepec and inscribed *grandeur d'éxécution du buis*.[146] It is in its present form that this work was sold by the Morrison family in 1920 from Basildon Park. Lot 1306 in the sale conducted by Waring & Gillow was: "A miniature portrait of a lady on ivory in exquisitely carved cedar [*sic*] setting in design of a dragon and cupid (miniature and carving by LEPEC), in glazed frame."[147] The preceding lot in the Basildon Park sale was: "A very richly carved boxwood frame in cupids, dragons, etc 19-in. by 16 in., by CHARLES LEPEC"; this has not been traced.

A further, two-part drawing in the Victoria and Albert Museum, however, suggests that this piece may have been intended as a work on a grander scale (figs. 29a, b). The red "velvet" and gilt metal-mounted

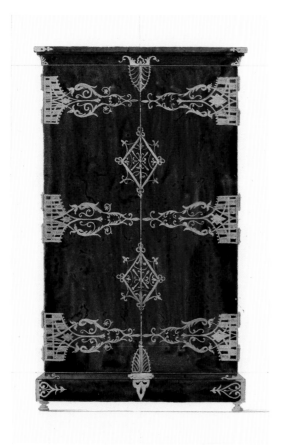

fig. 29a Charles Lepec. Design for "Morrison Tabernacle," 1886. Watercolor, with gold highlights on paper, 7⅛ × 4½ in. (18.1 × 11.4 cm). Victoria and Albert Museum, London (D.406-1891)

fig. 29b Charles Lepec. Design for "Morrison Family Triptych," 1886. Pencil, pen and ink, and watercolor, with gold highlights, on prepared paper, 7⅛ × 4½ in. (18.1 × 11.4 cm). Signed and dated *Charles Lepec 1886*. Victoria and Albert Museum, London (D.406-1891)

tabernacle (fig. 29a) seems to have been designed as a shrine. We know that the central portrait in the "Family Triptych" (fig. 29b) is of Mabel Morrison but can only speculate about the subjects of the other four portraits. We can deduce, however, that there are two male and two female figures. Alfred and Mabel had five children, the first of whom died when ten months old. Perhaps the four figures on the "wings" are the four surviving children, Hugh, Katherine, James, and Dorothy.[148] This drawing is signed and dated "Charles Lepec 1886." The grotesque from which the top miniature is suspended relates to the group of designs for "Masks" (see figs. 23a–d).

Lepec worked right up to the end of his life, and if his productivity was diminished, his ability appears to have remained intact. An undated drawing titled *Mabel Morrison* is inscribed *MM*, for Mabel Morrison, and signed *CHARLES LEPEC INV. DEL. SCULP.* (fig. 30).[149] This drawing, when compared to another in the Musée d'Orsay, demonstrates a consistency in his later work and may be part of a series. Based on the inscription on *Mabel Morrison*, it would appear that both drawings were designs for sculpture. The drawing in the Musée d'Orsay is signed and dated *Charles Lepec 1888* and inscribed with the initials *CHS* and *Constance Maria Josepha*.[150]

CONCLUSION

Charles Lepec was born into a relatively prosperous and educated milieu. His career, following a formal academic education, began with painting but flourished with the production of enamels. As Alcouffe notes, what distinguishes painted enamel of the Second Empire (1852–70) from its production in the Renaissance is that it tended to be practiced by artists who were painters by training rather than by those who were merely copying engravings.[151] Later in life Lepec returned, relatively seamlessly, to painting, drawing, designing, and carving. He was also, by his own account, an architect. Although probably independently financially stable, he seems to have run a professional atelier and had assistants or pupils, one of whom he married in 1882, when he was fifty-two.[152]

The 1860s were the most productive years of Lepec's career, and his greatest successes were works in enamel. These, it seems, can be divided into three broad categories: the elaborate creations that he exhibited, many of which ended up with Alfred Morrison; the exquisite and proficient portrait miniatures (invariably based on photographic images); and enamels for jewelry, which may represent a more overtly commercial aspect of his production. The 1867 Paris Exposition Universelle was clearly the highlight of Lepec's professional career, and his output, particularly after 1870, appears not to have been prodigious.[153]

The earliest Lepec enamel to have been identified dates from 1860.[154] From this it is evident that Lepec's style of decoration emerged fully formed out of his training as a painter and did not evolve noticeably over the following decade. The works he created for display started with simple dish shapes and progressed with various, increasingly ambitious vessels, such as vases, caskets, and tazzas, culminating with the elaborate nef that was the centerpiece of his display at the Paris Exposition. His miniatures and jewelry, which will be addressed in a later article, are no less proficient—but are less ambitious. During the last two decades of his life, Lepec reverted to painting, and produced designs and carvings. Morrison's relationship with Lepec continued after the artist appears to have ceased production of his famed enamels, and Morrison owned work in all the media in which Lepec remained active, seemingly with the exception of paintings in oil.

Whether in painting, enamel, design, carving, or portraiture, Lepec's work displays his technical ability and intellectual capacity, as well as the benefits derived from exposure to contemporary cultural luminaries. His production consistently shows an awareness of current trends in painting and an interest in the value of photography.[155] The evidence from Lepec's correspondence with both Phillips and Morrison shows a man at ease socially, and the way in which he interacted on behalf of his confrères, beyond professional cooperation, demonstrates that he was a valued and trusted intermediary.

Many manufacturers' careers benefited from the support of Alfred Morrison, the quintessential discerning patron. But in that company Charles Lepec's work stands out for its refined design and exquisite workmanship. The evident affection that Morrison felt for Lepec was such that he named Lepec's Room at Fonthill House after the artist.[156]

ACKNOWLEDGMENTS

Particular thanks are due to Charlotte Gere and Daniëlle Kisluk-Grosheide for their helpful comments on drafts of this article. We also express gratitude for their help in various ways to Reinier Baarsen, Marc Bascou, Rhoda Bucknill, Julia Clarke, David Conradsen, Caroline Dakers, John D'arcy, Max Donnelly, Julie Deslondes, Jean Dutacq, Suzanne Higgott, the late Robert Holden, Roisin Inglesby, Alette Kinébanian, Patricia Levy, Vicky Macaskie, Jeff Pilkington, Tamara Préaud, Katherine Purcell, Judy Rudoe, Katharina Siefert, Sara Sowerby, Erika Speel, Luke Syson, Dora Thornton, and Charlotte Walker.

OLIVIER HURSTEL
Independent Scholar, Paris
MARTIN LEVY
Antiques Dealer and Scholar, London

fig. 30 Charles Lepec. *Mabel Morrison*, ca. 1888. Pencil and white highlights on prepared paper, 18½ × 15⅜ in. (47 × 39 cm). Signed *CHARLES LEPEC INV. DEL. SCULP.* Private collection

APPENDIX

*Works by Charles Lepec lent by Alfred Morrison
to the Paris Exposition Universelle, 1867*[157]

Excluded from this list were "1 portrait de Madame
Morrison [and] 1 médaillon César," neither of which
has been traced.[158]

1   Deux profils de femmes: Laure [untraced]
2   Marguerite [untraced][159]
3   Boucles d'oreilles transparantes à jour [untraced]
4   Une petite Vénus [private collection][160]

Coffret de la Chasse:
5   La Chasse [untraced]
6   Attalante [art market][161]
7   Diane, coffret de la chasse [art market]
8   Lion [untraced]
9   Chevreuil [untraced]

10   Coupe Volupté [location unknown]
11   Coupe Fantaisie [Saint Louis Art Museum]
12   [no number 12]
13   Bouteille venitienne [The Metropolitan Museum
     of Art]
14   et son plateau
15   assiette sujet [Musée des Beaux-Arts de Limoges,
     Palais de l'Evêché]
16   assiette sujet [Rijksmuseum, Amsterdam]
17   une assiette indienne [untraced]
18   une assiette persane [untraced]
19   Bonbonière indienne [untraced][162]

NOTES

1   For the catalogue, see Victoria and Albert Museum 1952.

2   The Musée d'Orsay project led to a renewed interest in nineteenth-century French decorative arts, and gave rise to several major exhibitions. In addition to "The Second Empire, 1852–1870: Art in France under Napoleon III" (Philadelphia, Detroit, and Paris, 1978–79), others included "Le Japonisme" (Paris and Tokyo, 1988) and "Un Age d'or des arts décoratifs, 1814–48" (Paris, 1991). Another important exhibition, presenting an overview of nineteenth-century European decorative arts, was "Der Traum vom Glück: Die Kunst des Historismus in Europa" (Vienna, 1996).

3   Jean-Marie Moulin, "The Second Empire: Art and Society," in Philadelphia Museum of Art 1978, p. 11. See also Loyer 1992.

4   Just as the term "Regency," when applied to works of art, extends beyond the years 1810–20, when the Prince of Wales was regent before becoming George IV, so the description "Second Empire" is generally seen to cover a greater date range than the historical period when Napoleon III was emperor of France.

5   See, for example, Barbedienne's pair of candelabra, MMA 2008.267.1, .2; Diehl's cabinet, MMA 1989.197; Deck's bowl, MMA 1993.313; and Christofle et Cie's jardinière, MMA 1991.88a, b.

6   See Levy 2012.

7   See, for example, a display cabinet by Grohé Frères in the Royal Collection (RCIN 79769).

8   Dudley's important acquisitions included a clock by Gustave Baugrand (private collection), a version of which is in the collection of the Walters Art Museum, Baltimore, 58.230; a mirror designed by Carrier-Belleuse and manufactured by Barbedienne (Bowes Museum, 1992.1567432), and the "boite à whist," or "Card-Box," enameled by Lepec, manufactured by Falize, and exhibited by Boucheron (untraced); Purcell 1999, pp. 54–55, and *Art-Journal* 1867b, p. 314. One of the Baugrand clocks and the other two works were exhibited at the Paris Exposition Universelle, 1867.

9   A significant factor for Franco-British trade was the Cobden-Chevalier Treaty, 1860, which eased trade tariffs between France and Great Britain. At the same time, spurred on by British successes at the Great Exhibition, 1851, the French invested new energy in their own production of decorative arts.

10   This is how Lepec was described when he was awarded the Legion of Honor on June 30, 1867.

11   Christie's sale 1971, lot 98.

12   See *Jahrbuch der Staatlichen Kunstsammlungen in Baden-Württemberg* 14 (1977), pp. 213–15. At the time of writing, the Badisches Landesmuseum was closed for renovation, and so it was not possible to reexamine the nef. The authors are grateful to Katharina Siefert for her help (emails to Martin Levy, January 7–8, 2014). See also Fillitz et al. 1996, ill. p. 591.

13   Alcouffe 1980.

14   Miniature enamel painting began in France about 1630 and over the following two centuries, while considerably diminished, never entirely died out. See also, for the revival of enamel techniques under the Second Empire, Alcouffe 1978.

15   Lepec was alone in exhibiting under two categories: "oeuvres d'art" and "orfèvrerie."

16   See, for example, Meyer's *Allegory of the French Republic*, MMA 1993.178.1.

17 See, for example, Alcouffe 1980, figs. 1, 2, 12. See also, for Duron's prototypes, Alcouffe 2001 and Gabet 2007.

18 Alcouffe 1980, figs. 3, 5, 6. *Clémence Isaure* (1865–66) was sold by Christie, Manson & Woods, June 18, 1892, lot 172, purchased by Friedlander for 110 gns. It later reappeared at Christie's (New York), sale, November 16, 1979, lot 38; for further details see www.musee-orsay.fr/en/collections/index-of-works/notice.html?no_cache=1&nnumid=1401. Another work titled *Clémence Isaure, fondatrice des jeux floraux* was exhibited at the Paris Salon of 1861, but the present work is the *Clémence Isaure* shown at the 1866 Salon; see Sanchez 2005, vol. 2, pp. 918–19. This perceptive acquisition was driven by Marc Bascou, with the support of Daniel Alcouffe, when the new Musée d'Orsay was still being developed. For more on Bolckow, see Boase 2004.

19 Purcell 1999 and Gere and Rudoe 2010.

20 The authors are completing for publication a detailed analysis of Lepec's life, milieu, development, technical innovations, iconography, and work for other patrons and manufacturers, as well as discussing documents relating to the Paris Exposition Universelle, 1867. The article is provisionally titled "Charles Lepec: Peintre-Emailleur." Hereafter, it will be referred to as Hurstel and Levy n.d. (forthcoming).

21 See, for example, Wainwright 1995, pp. 13–18.

22 For Beckford, see Ostergard 2001; for Hope, see Watkin and Hewat-Jaboor 2008.

23 See, for example, Castellani's paper knife, MMA 1993.66; Brocard's mosque lamp, MMA 1976.311; and Falize's clock, MMA 1991.113a–f.

24 There are, in the collection of the Metropolitan Museum (according to the online catalogue), twenty-two engravings and etchings with an "Alfred Morrison" provenance. These include sixteen by Jacques Callot (1592–1635), MMA 57.650.400(1–16). On the autographs, see Dakers 2011, p. 302n134.

25 For Chinese examples, see Christie's sale 2004; and for Japanese examples, see Christie's sale 1899a, lots 145–222.

26 Dion-Tenenbaum 2005, pp. 145–64.

27 For the Morrison family, see Dakers 2011.

28 Reux is a tiny hamlet perched on a hillside above Pont l'Evêque, Calvados, France.

29 Might Lepec's untraced "Portrait de Mme la baronne T . . . ," exhibited at the Paris Salon, 1865, no. 2616 (Sanchez 2005, vol. 2, p. 919), depict the baronne de Tourville?

30 For example, *Recueil général des lois, décrets, ordonnances, etc. depuis le mois de juin 1789 jusqu'au mois d'août 1830* (Paris, 1839), the first volume in a long series that codified the rights of the French following the overthrow of the monarchy and before the inauguration of the Republic.

31 This explains why the younger Lepec was described as "a French gentleman, of Spanish origin" in *Art-Journal* 1867a, p. 154.

32 Founded in 1836 on the model of English private clubs, it closed in 1874. Le Cercle des Arts, which was at 22, rue de Choiseul, was limited to six hundred members. Over time, those who belonged included the artists Eugène Delacroix, Paul Delaroche, David d'Angers, Horace Vernet, and François Rude; the writers Charles Baudelaire, Prosper Mérimée, and Victor Hugo; and financiers such as James and Anthony de Rothschild.

33 "Heureux qui peut entrer dans les arts par la porte noble des lettres et des sciences!" Luchet in Mesnard 1869, p. 90.

34 Bellier de La Chavignerie and Auvray 1882–85, vol. 1, p. 1010.

35 Paris Salon, 1857, no. 1720 (*Portrait de Mme C . . .*), and Paris Salon, 1859, no. 1950 (*Cortège d'un roi Fainéant*); see Sanchez 2005, vol. 2, pp. 918–19.

36 The earliest enamel so far located is *Audaces Fortuna Juvat*, which is dated 1860; see Blairman & Sons 2011, no. 6, where this work is misidentified as *La Fortune Conduite par l'Amour*, a work exhibited at the Paris Salon (1861, no. 1950); Sanchez 2005, vol. 2, p. 918. The classical and mythological subjects favored by Lepec in many of his enamels reveal a debt to his formative years as a Salon painter.

37 Today, there is little trace in Reux of the Lepec family. Their house was on a property marked by a sign reading "Lieu Lepec." On the adjacent property, the "Lieu du Presbytère," there are, however, buildings abutting the Lieu Lepec. At the time of writing the precise status of the two properties and their existing buildings has not been established. In the graveyard outside the fifteenth-century church at Reux, there is a double grave purchased in 1853, according to a record kept in the town hall at Reux, by a member of the "Lepecq" family (the historic name by which the Lepec family was sometimes known). It has not been established whether this unmarked grave, restored very recently by the commune, contains the remains of Charles Lepec. Perhaps the best-known resident of Reux during the Lepec family's residence there was the banker Maurice Ephrussi (1849–1916), who married Béatrice de Rothschild. Their property today belongs to David de Rothschild. Martin Levy is grateful to the mayor of Reux, Jean Dutacq, for his courteous welcome, August 14, 2014. Full details of Lepec's life will be documented in Hurstel and Levy n.d. (forthcoming).

38 The formidable critic, and at the time *conservateur* at the Louvre, Alfred Darcel (1818–1893) commented that although Lepec's work displayed in London, in the category of miniatures, showed a great deal of taste, the manufacture left something to be desired; see Darcel 1862, p. 544. Darcel was, of course, more interested in Renaissance enamel. For the significance of the world's fairs, see Busch and Futter 2012.

39 In Morrison's address-notebook (Fonthill Estate Archive), Phillips's address is recorded sometime after December 26, 1861, so either at the time of the exhibition, or possibly just before. For Phillips, see Culme 1987, vol. 1, pp. 364–65. See also Gere and Rudoe 2010.

40 For more on Alfred Morrison, see Dakers 2011, pp. 225–47.

41 The Morrison archive of the Fonthill Estate Archive, Wiltshire, contains forty-seven letters, bills, and receipts covering the years 1862–69 relating to Lepec and his relationship with Phillips and Morrison. These include twelve letters from Lepec to Phillips, four from Phillips to Morrison, one from Lepec to Morrison, bills and receipts from Lepec (and others) for Morrison, and bills to Morrison from Phillips. The letters and documents in the Fonthill Estate Archive have been sorted by John D'arcy but are not yet formally catalogued, so it is impossible to give precise references. The authors are grateful to Lord Margadale (b. 1958) for granting access to the archive and for permission to quote from these documents.

42 This assertion is based on the handwriting on accounts from Phillips in the Fonthill Estate Archive.

43 See Darcel 1862, pp. 538–47.

44 An ebony and ivory toilet mirror, stamped "G. B. Gatti" and inscribed in ink *Roma 1862*, belongs to one of Morrison's descendants; it was presumably acquired from the London International Exhibition.

45 Account from Phillips Brothers to Alfred Morrison, 1863; the document itself is numbered fol. 490; Fonthill Estate Archive.

46 Sotheby's Belgravia sale 1975, lot 54.

47 Alcouffe 1980, p. 105; Falize 1893, part 5, p. 484 ("une étude de femme nue, Vénus ou Psyché, dans une gamme tendre et vaporeuse"). On July 26, 1865, Phillips Brothers invoiced Alfred Morrison for "Mounting an Enamel Plaque in Frame, Venus / a morocco & Velvet case." Account from Phillips Brothers to Alfred Morrison, September 29, 1865; Fonthill Estate Archive. The frame and the [silver-gilt?] border around the Venus (fig. 5) are by the same hand as that around *Atalanta*, lent by Morrison to the Paris Exposition Universelle, 1867 (see note 161 below).

48 Darcel 1868, p. 81, quoted by Julia Clarke in Sotheby's Belgravia sale 1975, under lot 54. In 1837 Godefroy Engelmann was granted a patent for chromolithography.

49 Hurstel and Levy, forthcoming.

50 Phillips fulfilled a similar role for Harriet Bolckow (the wife of Henry Bolckow), for whom he sourced secondhand goods. R & S Garrard, the Crown Jewellers, acted in a like vein for the Victorian royal family, and this was probably a common practice among luxury suppliers. The authors are grateful to Charlotte Gere for these observations.

51 For a List of Morrison's loans, see the Appendix.

52 "Fine Arts: Messrs. Phillips's Collection of Works of Art and Vertu," *Morning Post* (London), January 7, 1864, p. 5.

53 Christie's South Kensington sale 1994, lot 71: "An enamel tazza, the plateau polychrome painted with a figure of Venus drawn by Nereids, the circular foot and urn-shaped stem decorated with busts and masks, infant caryatids and scrolls, signed CHARLES LEPEC." On January 15, 1864, Phillips Brothers charged Alfred Morrison for "An Enamel Cup 'Lepec,' Birth of Venus / [£]300 / Mounting D° as agreed / [£]15." Account from Phillips Brothers to Alfred Morrison, receipt of February 5, 1864. Fonthill Estate Archive.

54 "j'ai heureusement terminé le pied de la coupe: cela a été bien long, car je n'ai pas cessé une heure de travailler depuis votre passage à Paris. Cela fait plus de trois mois pour le pied seulement."

55 "tellement augmenté les dessins de la coupe qu'il faut encore au moins quatre mois de travail sans interruption pour la terminer."

56 "J'ai terminé hier la coupe . . . un objet de cette importance . . . qu'elle nous fera honneur à tous les deux." A letter from Phillips to Morrison dated December 21, 1863, encloses Lepec's letter. Assuming that this was standard practice, it explains how letters from Lepec to Phillips have ended up in the Fonthill Estate Archive.

57 "J'ai fait faire la monture de la coupe par Mʳ Duron. C'est très bien exécuté, comme tout ce qu'il fait . . ."; Lepec to Phillips, December 21, 1863. For more on Duron, see Gabet 2007. Lepec's relationship with Duron and other contemporary craftsmen is discussed below.

58 See "Site of Nos. 25–34, Cockspur Street," in *Survey of London* vol. 16, *St Martin-in-The-Fields I: Charing Cross*, ed. G. H. Gater and E. P. Wheeler (London: London County Council, 1935), pp. 146–49, reproduced by British History Online, accessed August 5, 2014, www.british-history.ac.uk/report .aspx?compid=68126.

59 Paris Salon, 1864, no. 2306, *deux émaux*; see Sanchez 2005, vol. 2, pp. 918–19.

60 "[L]e succès des deux coupes ne laisse rien à désirer: j'ai plusieurs demandes et je dois dire que c'est surtout pour la dernière: c'est celle qui plaît le plus aux artistes et je sais que c'est surtout à cause d'elle que j'ai eu ma médaille." Fonthill Estate Archive.

61 Fonthill Estate Archive. The two coupes were also the subject of a glowing review by the sculptor and critic Louis Auvray (1810–1890); see Auvray 1863, pp. 81–82: "Les deux émaux, *la Volupté* et *la Fantaisie*, de M. Lepec, sont deux petits chefs-d'oeuvre; nous ne connaissons en ce genre rien de plus parfait, et lorsqu'on les compare aux autres émaux, on ne peut comprendre comment M. Lepec est parvenu à obtenir cette exactitude. . . . Non-seulement l'exécution industrielle est admirable, mais la partie artistique ne l'est pas moins."

62 "une femme sauvage de la tribu des Peaux-Rouges chevauchant une chimère, nous aimions mieux ses portraits de l'an dernier." In the same article, Darcel describes *La Volupté* as "deux sirènes de Paris, attelées de front à la conque où se tient debout une Vénus d'opéra. . . ." Darcel 1864, p. 84. *La Fantaisie* was sold at Christie's South Kensington, September 20, 1994, lot 72.

63 Fonthill Estate Archive.

64 "Je termine le coffret qui resemble, comme effet, à un travail d'orfèvrerie." Lepec to Phillips, letter dated June 25, 1864; Fonthill Estate Archive.

65 This coffret combines painted and *plique-à-jour* enamels. See http://www.museebal.fr/en/node/66. See also Notin 1995a.

66 Lepec's use of profile portraits echoes work he might have observed at the Musée du Louvre, such as the art of Jacques I Laudin (about 1627–1695), acquired in 1828; see Baratte 2000, pp. 401–2.

67 Sanchez 2005, vol. 2, pp. 918–19.

68 An architect named M. H. Durand was given responsibility about 1838 for making architectural drawings for a statistical survey in Rheims; see the *Foreign Quarterly Review* 1838–39, p. 23. A further speculation is that M. H. Durand might have had a connection to the silversmith François Durand (1792–1874); see Dion-Tenenbaum 2011, p. 277, for a biography of François Durand.

69 "Avant projet d'un bouclier en émail translucide sur argent. Le Bouclier sera trois fois plus grand que ce modèle et aura environs 3 pieds anglais. Le sujet du milieu sera en argent émaillé bleu translucide, les personnages seront en camaïeu d'or de différentes nuances dont il n'y a qu'un seul spécimen au Louvre. L'entourage composé de grands ornements d'un effet décoratif sera sur un fond sombre et tous les ornements serons en couleurs vives et translucides donnant l'effet des Jean Courtois: seulement ou bien d'être sur paillons ils seront directement émaillés sur argent de telle sorte qu'ils auront un éclat très grand. Une partie du fond sera ornée d'or pour composer un effet différent. Je pense que pareille chose n'a jamais été tentée dans de telles proportions." For Courtois, see Cocheris 1860. According to Alcouffe (1980, p. 104), *Roger et Angélique* was exhibited for a second time at the Paris Exposition Universelle, 1867.

70 "[J]e ne le vendrai pas sans vous prévenir." Fonthill Estate Archive.

71 *Orlando Furioso* 10.78–95, cited in Hall 2008, p. 18, s.v. "Angelica."

72 *Roger Délivrant Angélique* (Musée du Louvre); a smaller version—*Angelica Saved by Ruggerio*—is at the National Gallery, London (NG3292). Although no substantial evidence has been found to support the assertion, the *Art-Journal* (1867a, p. 154), records that Lepec was "a pupil of the lamented Ingres and of Flandrin, men who will always be illustrious among the artists of France."

73 "rare perfection calligraphique" but with a "violet désagréable, et d'ailleurs le caractère décoratif, si important ici, manque absolument à son oeuvre." Mantz 1865, p. 32.

74 "exécution éblouissante. . . . Rien n'est plus beau que cette chaire rose et transparente et ces membres souples et

gracieux reposant sur cette cuirasse d'acier; la main de Roger, heureusement placée sur l'épaule de la jeune fille . . . Ce groupe ravissant nage dans un ciel d'azur et au milieu de nuages tout parsemés de poudre d'or." Jahyer 1865, p. 256. The report also praises Lepec's untraced "portrait de *Mme la baronne de T*"; see Sanchez 2005, vol. 2, p. 919, and note 29 above.

75 As described in the list of loans to the Paris Exposition Universelle, 1867 (see Appendix).

76 Notin 1995b, p. 91, no. 34. The numbering and other marks on Lepec's enamels will be discussed in Hurstel and Levy n.d. (forthcoming).

77 Private collection; see Blairman & Sons 2011, no. 6. See note 36 above.

78 Baarsen 2013, pp. 539–41, no. 131.

79 Similar motifs can be seen on Lepec's nef and *La Fantaisie*. Lepec's *Tarasque* (exhibited at the Paris Salon, 1874, no. 1182), painted in oil on canvas, depicts a female figure riding on the back of a similar beast; sold Sotheby's (Olympia), March 9, 2005, lot 124.

80 "Je vous prie de dire de ma part à Mr Morrison que malgré la grande richesse des ornements et même malgré que je le voudrais, ces deux nouvelles assiettes ne pourront jamais atteindre le prix des deux premières . . ." Fonthill Estate Archive.

81 Fonthill Estate Archive.

82 Department of Prints and Drawings, Box M.39, D.406-1891–421-1891. Following the authors' inquiry, in May 2013, these have now appeared in the Victoria and Albert Museum's online catalogue (http://collections.vam.ac.uk). The authors are grateful to Erika Speel, who alerted them to the existence of this cache of designs.

83 Victoria and Albert Museum, MA/1/P1180. The drawings were entered on June 4, 1891. The authors are grateful to Roisin Inglesby for checking this reference (email to Martin Levy, May 10, 2013).

84 See, for example, figs. 17–19.

85 The overall scheme of decoration on Lepec's heavily annotated *Design for a Charger*, 1865 (Victoria and Albert Museum, [D.406-1891]), can be compared to the interior of the Fitzwilliam Tazza and Cover (figs. 14, 15) and has something in common with the two plates (figs. 11, 12). In Lepec's careful hand he reveals great attention to the proportion of the decorative elements, as well as to the different bands of color, partly filled in. Lepec notes that the thick branches must be thinner and that care should be taken in making insertions into the main body of the tree ("la branche mere").

86 Sanchez 2005, vol. 2, p. 919.

87 Gold ring, 746-1890; http://collections.vam.ac.uk/item /O118152/ring-lepec-charles/.

88 Lepec's atelier will be discussed in Hurstel and Levy n.d. (forthcoming).

89 "Depuis plus d'un an je travaille avec l'aide de mes deux plus habiles élèves à une oeuvre, d'émail, d'une proportion inconnue jusqu'à ce jour. La hauteur est de 71 pouces anglais et la largeur de 45.

Je dois vous avouer franchement que la majeure partie de ces plaques qui composent une arabesque très compliquée sont assez bien réussies pour ne craindre aucune comparaison. dans quelques jours elles seront enfin terminées. Mais le morceau du milieu qui a 21 pouces anglais de diamètre a été brisé entièrement au feu ce matin et mon plus grand et plus vif chagrin c'est que cette oeuvre énorme et si capitale par son importance ne pourra figurer dans l'Exposition de 1866, car il

faut déposer les ouvrages le 20 Mars. . . ." Letter from Lepec to Phillips, February 1, 1866; Fonthill Estate Archive.

90 Bascou, Massé, and Thiébaut 1988, p. 160.

91 "Je l'ai déjà manqué une autre fois. De même j'ai une fois fondu et une fois brisé le grand émail sur argent qui devait former le milieu du bouclier. Si par un bonheur extrême je parviens à terminer le travail interrompu aujourd'hui par cet accident, j'ose dire que jamais je n'entreprendrai des émaux qui ont 21 et 23 pouces de large. Je vous écrirai dans 4 ou 5 semaines pour vous dire si la fortune m'a été plus favorable. . . ." Letter from Lepec to Phillips, February 1, 1866; Fonthill Estate Archive.

92 Fonthill Estate Archive.

93 Letter from Lepec to Popelin, thanking him for a publication and for the author's personal handwritten dedication. This letter formed part of a cache of letters to Popelin sold by Chenu, Scrive et Bérard, Hôtel des Ventes, Lyon, April 9, 2008, lot 174. Private collection, London. An enamel portrait of Katherine Morrison (1869–1949), inscribed KATHARINA MDCCCLXXX, has been attributed to Popelin; its apparently silver frame bears the initial "BF" in a tablet at the top, for Bapst & Falize (partnership 1880–92); the portrait belongs to a descendant of Alfred Morrison.

94 Alcouffe 1980, pp. 104, 117n38, citing Falize 1893, part 4, p. 437: "jamais on n'avait tenté, hors de Sèvres, de passer au feu une plaque de semblable dimension. Dotin, qui cuit les émaux de l'artiste, a dû construire un four tout exprès et n'a pas osé l'établir dans son atelier de la rue Montorgueil. . . ." Charles Dotin (active 1844–89) worked in the enamel workshop at Sèvres, which operated 1845–72. He specialized in the Limoges grisaille technique, inspired by the work of sixteenth-century enamelers. It is of particular significance for the production of *Clémence Isaure* that Dotin operated a very large kiln.

95 "elle restera l'une des plus grandes pièces d'émail produites en ce temps-ci . . ." and Falize adds "le mérite en est à celui-ci plus qu'à l'artiste, et Dotin doit être nommé comme Gagneré, le cuiseur de Claudius Popelin, ce furent des praticiens de premier ordre." Falize 1893, part 5, p. 478.

96 *Art-Journal* 1867a, p. 154. The article continues: "After having been for a considerable time in the establishment of Mr. Phillips, in Cockspur Street, this enamel has been purchased by one of our great iron-masters, Mr. Bolckow. . . . We heartily congratulate that gentleman on thus having made so splendid an addition to his collections; and yet, at the same time, we are constrained to record our deep regret, that a work of such pre-eminent value as a teacher should not have been secured, as secured it might have been under very advantageous conditions, for the South Kensington Museum. . . ."

97 See http://webapps.fitzmuseum.cam.ac.uk/explorer/index .php?qu=lepec&oid=156465.

98 For more on Zuloaga and Morrison, see Lavin 1997, pp. 53–54, 57, and passim. Other French manufacturers named in the Christie's 1899a sale were "Brocart [*sic*]" (lots 322–25), Thesmar (lots 396 and 397), and Charlet (lot 402).

99 See Baarsen 2013, p. 541n3.

100 Christie's sale 1899a, lot 393 "A PAIR OF SMALLER DITTO [enamel plaques], with 'Le Saut d'Amour' and 'Les Lutteurs d'Amour'—*by the same*; and a pair of circular ditto, with busts of Laure and Marguerite—in ebonised frames." £9. 19s. 6d. to Giuliano (perhaps a member of the family of jewelers).

Lot 394 "AN OBLONG PLAQUE, with Cupids sacrificing to Venus; and a pair of small upright plaques, with Venus Anadyomene and Cupid—*by the same*—three in one frame." £9. 19s. 6d. to Marcus.

Lot 394A "A PAIR OF PLAQUES with 'Elixir' and 'Equilibre d'Amour'; a pair, with heads of Marguerite and Imperia; and a pair, with sporting trophies—*by the same*—in three ebonised frames" £8. 8*s.* to Heigham [?]

Lot 395 "A LARGE OBLONG ~~SILVER~~ GILT CASKET, with chased borders and arabesques in appliqué work, enamelled in brilliant translucent colours—18 *in.* by 12 *in.* by 8½ *in.* high—by CHARLES LEPEC—on ebonised stand, with glass shade." £22 to D. Duncan.

On June 10, 1902, Christie's offered "Valuable Lace from the collection of Mrs Alfred Morrison, and among other items 'Objects of vertu . . . from Numerous Sources.'" Perhaps coincidentally, a vendor named Gwinner entered two enamels by Lepec, lot 137, with a reserve of 40 guineas: "A PAIR OF CUPS AND SAUCERS, of gold enamelled in translucent dark crimson, and painted with Cupids sporting with dolphin, vines, flowers and doves grisaille and delicate tints, on a powdered gold ground, by Lepec, the handles chased with terminal winged female busts—*gross weight, 14 oz.*"; these were unsold and remain untraced.

101 The authors are grateful to Lord Margadale for confirming that he does not know the whereabouts of these pieces (email from Vicky Macaskie to Martin Levy, January 2, 2014).

102 For enamels by Reymond at the Louvre, see Baratte 2000, pp. 187–273.

103 For more on Owen Jones and his work for Morrison, see Flores 2006, pp. 175–77, 179, and 191 (Fonthill House) and 176–77, 181, 191–93 and 212 (Carlton House Terrace).

104 Jones 1856, p. 76.

105 Flores 2006, figs. 4.44 and 4.45.

106 *Magazine of Art* 1879, pp. 140 (fig. 1) and 144 (quote). The design of Lepec's chimneypiece can be compared with a wooden example, also in situ, reproduced in Flores 2006, p. 193, fig. 4.41.

107 See, for example, the handles on a Quianlong porcelain vase formerly in Morrison's collection, Christie's sale 2004, lot 55.

108 "Le coffret persan sera terminé dans un mois pour la monture." Fonthill Estate Archive.

109 Lepec might, for instance, have been familiar with the early fifteenth-century Venetian flask given in 1856 to the Louvre (OA 1013).

110 Pratt 1939, p. 191.

111 Receipt to Morrison, on Fonthill House notepaper; Fonthill Estate Archive.

112 At the lower end of Lepec's pricing were two items acquired in 1868, neither of which has been traced. On December 17 Phillips Brothers invoiced Alfred Morrison for an "Enamelled Cloisonné Locket by Chas Lepec / [£]13. 0" and two days later for "D⁰ Ring [by Lepec] / [£]7." Account from Phillips Brothers to Alfred Morrison, 1868; the document itself is numbered fol. 575; Fonthill Estate Archive.

113 Waring & Gillow sale 1920, illustration facing p. 105. The *Bouteille vénitienne* was offered as a "Viennese Enamel Rosewater Bottle on Stand" at Doyle, New York, February 25, 2004, lot 364; it was subsequently published in Blairman & Sons 2004, no. 11.

114 *Art-Journal* 1867b, p. 169. See also *Jahrbuch der Staatlichen Kunstsammlungen in Baden-Württemberg* 14 (1977), p. 213.

115 "nef d'or qu'avait exécutée Duron, mais que Lepec avait dessinée et émaillée." Falize 1893, part 5, p. 484.

116 *Times* (London) 1867.

117 On January 10, 1867, Lepec wrote a receipt to Morrison, on Fonthill House notepaper, for £100 "pour le portrait de Madame Morrison." Fonthill Estate Archive.

118 ". . . destiné à Mr Chermside: il m'a donné de grandes difficultés et n'est pas tout à fait semblable au grand: l'oeil est un peu trop grand et la bouche a quelque chose que je ne puis définir: cependant il a l'air plus jeune que le grand." Fonthill Estate Archive.

119 For more on the Chermside family, see Dakers 2011, pp. 236–39.

120 Art market, 2014.

121 Blairman & Sons 2009, no. 13.

122 *Practical Magazine* 1873, p. 262, ill. p. 263.

123 The letters and accounts are in the Fonthill Estate Archive.

124 Since 2014, with Gismondi, Paris.

125 J. L. Moreau or, more likely, his son Augustin-Jean Moreau, "dit Moreau-Vauthier (1831–1893) qui fit une assez brillante carrière de sculpteur, en particulier sur ivoire"; see Hauviller 1997. For a clock by Moreau père, see Malgouyres 2011.

126 "Le lendemain de votre départ j'ai écrit à Mr Moreau pour connaître le prix de l'Oedipus—il était vendu." Fonthill Estate Archive. This may be a reference to Gustave Moreau (1826–1898), whose *Oedipus and the Sphinx* (1864) is now in the collection of the Metropolitan Museum (21.134.1). For more on this major work, a sensation when exhibited at the Paris Salon in 1864, see Cooke 2014, pp. 49–51. In light of works by Lepec such as *La Fantaisie* (fig. 8), also exhibited at the Paris Salon in 1864, it is evident that the Moreau would have appealed to Morrison. Moreau, like a number of painters at the time, was interested in enamel.

127 Fonthill Estate Archive.

128 D.416.1891–421.1891; http://collections.vam.ac.uk.

129 Christie's (London), May 25, 2000, lot 228; the lot was incorrectly catalogued as "Viennese, about 1890." For the exhibition, see Galerie Roxane Rodriguez 2003, n.p.: "Magnifique coffret de marriage."

130 One can also compare the crowned female figure in *L'Amour triomphant* (Galerie Roxane Rodriguez 2003, n.p.).

131 *Art-Journal*, n.s., 10 (1871), p. 30. The subject of Lepec's jewelry will be addressed in Hurstel and Levy n.d. (forthcoming). See also Gere and Rudoe 2010, p. 101, fig. 63.

132 International Exhibition, London 1872, p. 94. Lepec also exhibited enamel crosses at this exhibition, lent by Mabel Morrison; see Lacroix 1873, p. 37.

133 D.413-1891 (inscribed *Modèle B*), D.414-1891, and D.415-1891. The latter drawing shows the mirrored side and is inscribed *Modèle A*. A possible candidate for this missing mirror might be "A French gilt brass and enamel decorated hand mirror, the reverse decorated in Persian style with stylized flowers and leaves, 35 cm long," sold Phillips, Bath, October 31, 1994, lot 55. The authors would be most grateful to learn of this object's whereabouts. The vendor George Sassoon was the son of the poet Siegfried Sassoon and Hester Gatty, a granddaughter of Alfred Morrison.

134 "Marche à suivre:

1 tracer sur le cuivre d'après ce modèle-ci pour / la forme intérieure

2 repercer

3 tracer les lignes et ornements à réserver pour le champlevé

4 percer les trous d'après le modèle A

5 les percer exactement sur l'autre côté

6 champlever en réservant un bord à chaque trou

7 cloisonner émailler

Entout 3 épaisseurs de cloisons"

Lepec's techniques and innovations will be discussed in detail in Hurstel and Levy n.d. (forthcoming).

135 "The International Exhibition: The Jewellery," *Birmingham Daily Post*, June 12, 1872.

136 Lefranc 1872. Others on the committee included Paul Christofle (1805–1863), of the famous Parisian manufacturer Christofle et Cie; the collector and art historian Eugène Dutuit (1807–1886); the ceramic collector and historian Albert Jacquemart (1808–1875); the collector Comte d'Armaillé (about 1822–1882); and Baron Alphonse de Rothschild (1827–1905).

137 Alcouffe 1980, pp. 104, 116n33.

138 "on m'a fait demander aujourd'hui même si je voudrais faire les portraits du roi et de la reine de Portugal. comme j'ai répondu affirmativement . . . ." Lepec to Phillips, May 11, 1864. Fonthill Estate Archive.

139 The Lepec miniature portraits are of Princess Helena (RCIN 421906), Princess Louise (RCIN 421907), and Prince Louis of Hesse (RCIN 422105); see Remington 2010, nos. 598, 599, 597, and www.royalcollection.org.uk/collection/search#/page/1. Another great enamel artist of the period, Claudius Popelin, was also using photography for portraits at about this time; see Bascou 1996, p. 236. Photography was also used during this period in the production of cameos; see Gere and Rudoe 2010, p. 479.

140 "Je reviendrai bien vite à Paris car je dois faire pour l'Impératrice un petit portrait de son fils." Fonthill Estate Archive.

141 "Je vous serai obligé de me procurer les meilleurs photographies de la princesse Alexandra: j'ai l'intention, dans mes moments perdus, d'en faire un bel émail." Fonthill Estate Archive. Phillips was, incidentally, commissioned by the Prince of Wales to make "Egyptian" jewelry for Princess Alexandra on the occasion of their marriage in 1863. See Gere and Rudoe 2010, p. 380.

142 The authors are unable to explain the presence of this inscription, which is presumably allegorical; "1 médaillon César" also appears on a receipt for objects lent to the Paris Exposition Universelle, 1867 (see Appendix).

143 Lepec is here making reference to his family's lineage.

144 At the bottom of the lane leading to the "Lieu Lepec" in Reux there is a nineteenth-century iron cross (croix de fer).

145 "This boxwood / was designed, drawn / and carved, as was the portrait / miniature on ivory of / Mrs Mabel Morrison by / Charles Le Pecq de Tourville / usually called / Charles Lepec, at his home / by the Iron Cross in Reux / area Pont l'Evêque, in the region / of Calvados and finished / during the first week of / February / in the year 1887." Another comparably inscribed boxwood carving, for a London patron named Aston, is in an English private collection; it will be discussed and illustrated in Hurstel and Levy n.d. (forthcoming).

146 "size of the boxwood carving."

147 Waring & Gillow sale 1920, lot 1306. This subsequently reappeared at Shapes Auctioneers, Edinburgh, October 4, 2008, before being reoffered at Christie's (London), September 24, 2009, lot 20; [art market]; purchased by the Metropolitan Museum. The carving and miniature is reproduced in a biography of Mabel Morrison in Olivier 1945, facing p. 53.

148 Dakers 2011, p. 240, and index, pp. 321–22.

149 The authors are grateful to Caroline Dakers for drawing this work to their attention; it belongs to a descendant of Alfred Morrison.

150 See Gabet 2006, no. 36.

151 "L'émail peint du Second Empire offre sur ses antécédents limousins de la Renaissance la supériorité d'être pratiqué par des artistes qui, peintres de formation, ne se bornent pas à s'inspirer de gravures, mais le plus souvent exécutent en émail des compositions originales." Alcouffe 1980, p. 102.

152 For details of Lepec's professional and personal life, see Hurstel and Levy n.d. (forthcoming).

153 Ibid.

154 Blairman 2011, no. 6; see note 36 above.

155 Hurstel and Levy n.d. (forthcoming).

156 "Estate of the Late Alfred Morrison . . . Inventory of Heirlooms," p. 73; Fonthill Estate Archive.

157 Undated list in Lepec's hand, probably June 1867, based on internal evidence; Fonthill Estate Archive.

158 Part of a receipt for objects received from Alfred Morrison, signed by Lepec and dated January 10, 1867; Fonthill Estate Archive.

159 On December 18, 1863, Phillips charged Morrison for "Mounting Two Enamels 'Laura and Margarette' / Silver Gilt pieced mounts fitted on to a velvet ground / Framed and glazed / 15. 7. 6." Account from Phillips Brothers to Alfred Morrison dated Christmas 1863, fol. 491, on document itself; Fonthill Estate Archive. See also Christie's sale 1899a, lot 393, perhaps for the same works: "a pair of circular ditto [plaques], with busts of Laura and Marguerite—in ebonised frames." This lot, which included two other plaques, was purchased by Giuliano for 6 gns.

160 Almost certainly fig. 5.

161 *Atalante* was sold at Christie's, February 23, 1899, in lot 392: "A PAIR OF [Three, written by hand] OBLONG ENAMEL PLAQUES, painted with an Amazon, and busts of Atalanta [and Diana, written by hand] in borders of arabesque ornament in brilliant colours on gold and silver ground—5 *in.* by 8 *in.*—by *Charles Lepec*—in glazed ebonised frames." £7. 7s to Roberts. *Atalanta* and *Diana* (alternatively called *Amazon*) emerged at Plymouth Auction Rooms, November 5, 2014, lots 291 and 292. The vendor was the great-granddaughter of Evan Roberts (1836–1918), presumably the buyer at Christie's. Roberts was a Manchester-born watchmaker and later collector (see Dictionary of Welsh Biography, http://wbo.llgc.org.uk/en/s7-ROBE-EVA-1836.html). These works, numbered 194 and 195, are dated 1864. Luchet describes and illustrates (in Mesnard 1869, p. 95) "une femme indienne tirant de l'arc . . . le couvercle d'un coffret don't l'ensemble doit symboliser la chasse." This is certainly what was described by Christie's in 1899 as an "Amazon." Although this second plaque is not named as such on the list of items sent by Morrison to Paris, it was included. Luchet continues: "Aux deux grands côtés, les profils d'Atalante et de la Diane antique; aux deux petits, des attributs de vénerie que surmontent une tête de chevreuil et une tête de lion. Cette belle Hécate indienne aux couleurs acajou se détache d'un disque en platine, sorte de lune nageant dans un fond d'or vermiculé." See Luchet in Mesnard 1869, p. 95. On removal of the back, June 7, 2015, the backboard to *Amazon* was found to be incised "La Chasse" (presumably referring to the coffret of which it was intended to be a part). The mahogany surround supporting the enamel plaque itself is marked in pencil "Diane Sauvage."

162 Further loans listed include works seemingly by other manufacturers, but the "Deux Diadèmes cuivre et email" may also be the work of Lepec.

REFERENCES

Alcouffe, Daniel
1978 "La Renaissance des différentes techniques de l'émail sous le Second Empire." *Métiers d'art*, nos. 4–5 (July), pp. 40–47.
1980 "Les Emailleurs français à l'Exposition Universelle de 1867." *Antologia di Belle Arti* (Rome), anno 4, no. 13–14, pp. 102–21.
2001 *Les Gemmes de la Couronne.* Exh. cat., Musée du Louvre, Paris. Paris: Réunion des Musées Nationaux.

Art-Journal
1867a "The Enamels of Charles Lepec." *Art-Journal* (London), n.s., 6, p. 154.
1867b *The Illustrated Catalogue of the Universal Exhibition Published with the Art-Journal* [1867, part 2]. London: Virtue and Co.

Auvray, Louis
1863 *Exposition des Beaux-Arts. Salon de 1864.* Paris: A. Lévy Fils.

Baarsen, Reinier
2013 *Paris, 1650–1900: Decorative Arts in the Rijksmuseum:* New Haven and London: Yale University Press, in association with the Rijksmuseum, Amsterdam.

Baratte, Sophie
2000 *Les Emaux peints de Limoges.* Paris: Editions de la Réunion des Musées Nationaux.

Bascou, Marc
1996 "Popelin, Claudius(-Marcel)." In *Grove Dictionary of Art*, edited by Jane Turner, vol. 25, pp. 236–37. New York: Grove's Dictionaries.

Bascou, Marc, Marie-Madeleine Massé, and Philippe Thiébaut
1988 *Musée d'Orsay: Catalogue sommaire illustré des arts décoratifs.* Paris: Editions de la Réunion des Musées Nationaux.

Bellier de la Chavignerie, Emile, and Louis Auvray
1882–85 *Dictionnaire général des artistes de l'école française depuis l'origine des arts du dessin jusqu'à nos jours.* 2 vols. Paris: Librairie Renouard.

Blairman, H., & Sons
2004 *Furniture and Works of Art.* London: H. Blairman & Sons.
2009 *Furniture and Works of Art.* London: H. Blairman & Sons.
2011 *Furniture and Works of Art.* London: H. Blairman & Sons.

Boase, G. C.
2004 "Bolckow, Henry William Ferdinand (1806–1878)," revised by J. K. Almond. In *Oxford Dictionary of National Biography*, www.oxforddnb.com. Oxford: Oxford University Press.

Busch, Jason T., and Catherine L. Futter
2012 *Inventing the Modern World: Decorative Arts at the World's Fairs, 1851–1939.* Contributions by Regina Lee Blaszczyk et al. Pittsburgh: Carnegie Museum of Art; Kansas City: Nelson-Atkins Museum of Art; New York: Skira Rizzoli.

Christie's sales
1892 *Catalogue of Modern Pictures . . . Including the Final Portion of the Collection Formed by H. W. F. Bolckow, Esq., M.P., Deceased.* Sale cat., Christie, Manson & Woods, London, June 18.
1899a *Catalogue of a Collection of Objects of Oriental and European Art, Including . . . Vases, Caskets, Plaques, Dishes, &c. of Silver and Gilt Metal, Beautifully Damascened and Enamelled by C. Lepec and P. Zuloaga . . . The Property of a Lady. . . .* Sale cat., Christie, Manson & Woods, London, January 25–27.
1899b *Catalogue of Indian, Persian, Turkish, and Other Embroideries, . . . and a Few Pieces of Decorative Furniture from the Collection of Alfred Morrison. . . .* Sale cat., Christie, Manson & Woods, London, February 23.
1902 *Catalogue of Valuable Lace, Old and Modern from the Collection of Mrs. Alfred Morrison, and among Other Items, Objects of Vertu . . . from Numerous Sources.* Sale cat., Christie, Manson & Woods, London, June 10.
1971 "The Property of the Rt. Hon. the Lord Margadale of Islay, T.D., from the Collection Formed by His Grandfather the Late Alfred Morrison, Esq., Removed from Fonthill House." In *Fine Gold Boxes and Works of Art*, pp. 34–40, lots 98–111. Sale cat., Christie, Manson & Woods, London, November 30.
2004 *Chinese Porcelains and Enamels from the Alfred Morrison Collection, Fonthill House, Sold by Order of the Lord Margadale of Islay, D.L.* Sale cat., Christie's, London, November 9.

Christie's South Kensington sale
1994 *Objects of Vertu and Miniatures.* Sale cat., Christie's South Kensington, London, September 20.

Cocheris, Hippolyte, ed.
1860 *Le Blason des couleurs en armes, livrées et devises par Sicille, Herault d'Alphonse V, Roi d'Aragon* [by Jean Courtois, 1414]. Paris: Auguste Aubry.

Cooke, Peter
2014 *Gustave Moreau: History, Painting, Spirituality, and Symbolism.* New Haven and London: Yale University Press.

Culme, John
1987 *The Directory of Gold & Silversmiths: Jewellers & Allied Traders, 1838–1914.* 2 vols. Woodbridge: Antique Collectors' Club.

Dakers, Caroline
2011 *A Genius for Money: Business, Art, and the Morrisons.* New Haven and London: Yale University Press.

Darcel, Alfred
1862 "Les Arts industriels à l'exposition de Londres." *Gazette des Beaux-Arts* 13 (December), pp. 538–55.
1864 "La Peinture vitrifiée et l'architecture au Salon de 1864." *Gazette des Beaux-Arts* 18 (July), pp. 80–94.
1868 "L'Emaillerie moderne." *Gazette des Beaux-Arts* 24 (January), pp. 75–84.

Dion-Tenenbaum, Anne
2005 "La Renaissance de l'émail sous la Monarchie de Juillet." *Bibliothèque de l'Ecole des Chartes* 163, pp. 145–64.
2011 *Orfèvrerie française du XIXᵉ siècle: La Collection du Musée du Louvre.* Paris: Somogy.

Falize, Lucien
1893 "Claudius Popelin et la renaissance des émaux peints," parts 1–5. *Gazette des Beaux-Arts*, ser. 3, 9 (May), pp. 418–35; 9 (June), pp. 502–18; 10 (July), pp. 60–76; 10 (November), pp. 426–37; 10 (December), pp. 478–89.

Fillitz, Hermann, et al.
1996 *Der Traum vom Glück: Die Kunst des Historismus in Europa.* 2 vols. Exh. cat., Künstlerhaus Wien, Akademie der Bildenden Künste in Wien, Vienna. Vienna and Munich: Christian Brandstätter Verlag.

Flores, Carol A. Hrvol
2006 *Owen Jones: Design, Ornament, Architecture, and Theory in an Age of Transition.* New York: Rizzoli.

Foreign Quarterly Review
1838–39 "Restoration of the Fine Arts of the Middle Ages." *The Foreign Quarterly Review* (London) 22, pp. 1–34.

Gabet, Olivier
2006 *L'Objet et son double: Dessins d'arts décoratifs des collections du Musée d'Orsay.* Exh. cat., Musée d'Orsay, Paris. Milan: 5 Continents Editions.

ILLUSTRATION CREDITS

Three Paintings by El Greco: *A View of Toledo, Cardinal Fernando Niño de Guevara, and The Vision of Saint John (The Opening of the Fifth Seal)*: figs. 2–3, 9, 18a,b: Album/Art Resource, NY; fig. 4: from Braun and Hogenberg 1966, vol. 1, part 1, p. 3; fig. 5: from Braun and Hogenberg 1966, vol. 3, part 5, p. 15; fig. 10: © DeA Picture Library/Art Resource; fig. 11: Scala/Ministero per i Beni e le Attività culturali/Art Resource, NY; fig. 12: Photo Les arts Décoratifs, Paris/Jean Tholance; fig. 13: bpk, Berlin /Alte Pinakothek/Art Resource, NY; fig. 14: Erich Lessing/Art Resource, NY; fig. 16: from Marías 2007, pp. 122–23; fig. 17: Scala/Art Resource, NY

A Rare Mechanical Figure from Ancient Egypt: figs. 1, 3–4, 7a, 13: Bruce Schwarz, The Photograph Studio, MMA; figs. 2, 6, 7b,c, 11: drawings by Sara Chen, Department of Egyptian Art, MMA; fig. 5: X-radiograph by Ann Heywood, Department of Objects Conservation, MMA; fig. 7b: drawing based on Hornemann 1966, pl. 989; fig. 7c: drawing based on Hornemann 1966, pl. 847; fig. 8a: bpk, Berlin/Aegyptisches Museum und Papyrussamlung/Sandra Steiss/Art Resource, NY; fig. 8b: Courtesy of the owner and Young Museum of Ancient Cultural Arts; fig. 9: from Gardiner 1931, pl. 4; fig. 12: Courtesy of the owner and www.bild-art.de/artefact/; fig. 14: © RMN-Grand Palais/Art Resource, NY; fig. 15: The New York Public Library/Art Resource, NY; fig. 16: Scala/Art Resource, NY; figs. 19, 22d: © The Trustees of the British Museum; fig. 20: Marion Wenzel; fig. 21: © National Museums Scotland; fig. 22d: from Loeben 2011; fig. 23: from Jantzen 1972, pl. 14; fig. 25: © Christie's Images Limited 2008; fig. 26: from Matthews 1916, unnumbered plate between pp. 290 and 291

Vases with Faces: Isolated Heads in South Italian Vase Painting: figs. 2, 4a,b, 9, 12, 13, 21, 23a,b, 26a–c, 27: Paul Lachenauer, The Photograph Studio, MMA; fig. 3a,b: Joseph Coscia Jr., The Photograph Studio, MMA; figs. 5a,b: © The National Museum of Denmark, Collection of Classical and Near Eastern Antiquities (photograph by Arnold Mikkelsen); figs. 6, 25: Renate Kühling; figs. 7a, 34a,b: © The Trustees of the British Museum; fig. 15: © Royal Museums of Art and History, Brussels; fig. 16: Peter Zeray, The Photograph Studio, MMA; fig. 18: © The Field Museum; fig. 22: Provincia di Bari, Servizio Beni, Attività Culturali, Biblioteca, Orchestra, Sport e Turismo; fig. 24: Juan Trujillo, The Photograph Studio, MMA; fig. 29: Ministero per i Beni e la Attività Culturali, Direzione Regionale per i Beni Culturali e Paesaggistici della Basilicata, Soprintendenza per i Beni Archeologici della Basilicata; fig. 30: Assessorato ai Beni Culturali e dell'Identità Siciliana della Regione Siciliana, Palermo; fig. 31: Ministero per i Beni Culturali, Soprintendenza per i Beni Archeologici della Puglia, Archivo fotografico, Taranto

A Bronze Hellenistic Dwarf in the Metropolitan Museum: figs. 1 a–c: Paul Lachenauer, The Photograph Studio, MMA; fig. 2a,b: © RMN-Grand Palais/Art Resource, NY, Hervé Lewandowski; fig. 3: © 2015 Museum of Fine Arts, Boston; fig. 4: The Trustees of the British Museum/Art Resource, NY; fig. 9: © Vanni Archive/Art Resource, NY

Ennion, Master of Roman Glass: Further Thoughts: fig. 1: © The Trustees of The British Museum; figs. 2, 4: Bruce Schwarz, The Photograph Studio, MMA; figs. 6, 7, 10: Paul Lachenauer, The Photograph Studio, MMA; figs. 8, 11, 14: Ardon Bar-Hama; fig. 13: © Eretz Israel Museum, Tel Aviv

The Kizil Paintings in the Metropolitan Museum: fig. 1: Deng Jie and Chen Lei; fig. 2: drawing by Pamlyn Smith, after Grünwedel 1912, fig. 395a; figs. 3, 13, 16, 18: Oi-Cheong Lee, The Photograph Studio, MMA; figs. 4, 11: © Staatliche Museen zu Berlin, Museum für Asiatische Kunst/Jürgen Liepe; figs. 6, 10: © Staatliche Museen zu Berlin, Museum für Asiatische Kunst/Archiv (Albert von Le Coq); fig. 7: from Zhongguo bihua quanji bianji weiyuanhui 1995, vol. 1, pl. 71; fig. 12: from Zhongguo bihua quanji bianji weiyuanhui 1995, vol. 3, pl. 120; fig. 15: from Xinjiang Qiuci shiku yanjiu suo 2008, pl. 139; figs. 17a,b, 19–22: Bruce Schwarz, The Photograph Studio, MMA

Giovanni Battista Lodi da Cremona and the *Story of Mercury and Herse* **Tapestry Series:** fig. 3: Fitzwilliam Museum, Cambridge/Art Resource, NY; fig. 4: © Trustees of the British Museum; fig. 5: Mark Morosse, The Photograph Studio, MMA

Collecting Sixteenth-Century Tapestries in Twentieth-Century America: The Blumenthals and Jacques Seligmann: fig. 1: Kathy Dahab, The Photograph Studio, MMA

Vincenzo de' Rossi as Architect: A Newly Discovered Drawing and Project for the Pantheon in Rome: fig. 1: © Cooper Hewitt, National Design Museum, Smithsonian Institution/Art Resource, NY; fig. 2: from Colnaghi 1983, no. 2; figs. 3, 7–9: Hyla Skopitz, The Photograph Studio, MMA; fig. 5: Musée du Louvre © RMN-Grand Palais/Michel Urtado/Art Resource, NY; fig. 6: © RMN-Grand Palais/Suzanne Nagy/Art Resource, NY; fig. 11: Courtesy of Gabinetto Disegni e Stampe degli Uffizi, Florence; fig. 14: Centrum voor Kunsthistorische Documentatie, Radboud Universiteit Nijmegen

The Pont Neuf: A Paris View by Johan Barthold Jongkind Reconsidered: fig. 1: Juan Trujillo, The Photograph Studio, MMA; figs. 2, 4, 5, 9, 10, 16, 17: © RMN-Grand Palais/Art Resource, NY; fig. 6a: From sale catalogue, Galerie Georges Petit, Paris, May 11–12, 1931, no. 21; overlays by Sophie Scully; figs. 6b, 8, 11, 12, 21: photographs and overlays by Sophie Scully, 2013–14; fig. 14: Courtesy Sotheby's New York; fig. 20: From *The Connoisseur* 119 (June 1947), p. 11

Charles Lepec and the Patronage of Alfred Morrison: fig. 1: Thomas Goldschmidt; fig. 2: Musée d'Orsay/RMN; fig. 3: Bibliothèque Nationale de France; figs. 4, 10, 13: by kind permission of Lord Margadale and the Fonthill Estate; fig. 6: courtesy of Saint Louis Art Museum; fig. 8: Martin Levy; fig. 9: © Musée des Beaux-Arts de Limoges/F. Magnoux; fig. 11: © Musée des Beaux-Arts de Limoges/V. Schrive; fig. 14: © Fitzwilliam Museum, Cambridge, England; fig. 16: Olivier Hurstel; figs. 17–19, 23a–d, 24–27, 29a,b: © Victoria and Albert Museum, London; fig. 20: from *Country Life*, May 18, 1989, p. 247, fig. 5; fig. 22: Olivier Hurstel; fig. 28: Joseph Coscia Jr., The Photograph Studio, MMA

2007 "Kunstkammer Objects in the Age of the World Fairs: Charles Duron in 1867." *Burlington Magazine* 149, no. 1251 (June), pp. 393–99.

Galerie Roxane Rodriguez

2003 *Emaux.* Exh. cat. Paris: Galerie Roxane Rodriguez.

Gere, Charlotte, and Judy Rudoe

2010 *Jewellery in the Age of Queen Victoria: A Mirror to the World.* London: British Museum.

Hall, James

2008 *Dictionary of Subjects and Symbols in Art.* 2nd ed. Boulder, Colo.: Westview Press.

Hauviller, Bernard

1997 "Jean-Louis Moreau et Augustin-Jean Moreau-Vauthier ivoiriers." *Les Amis de Bourron-Marlotte, Bulletin,* no. 38 (Autumn–Winter), pp. 30–31.

Hurstel, Olivier, and Martin Levy

n.d. "Charles Lepec: Peintre-Emailleur." Forthcoming.

International Exhibition, London

1872 *London International Exhibition of 1872. Official Catalogue: Fine Arts Department.* London: J. M. Johnson & Sons.

Jahyer, Félix

1865 *Salon de 1865. Etude sur les Beaux-Arts.* Paris: E. Dentu.

Jones, Owen

1856 *The Grammar of Ornament.* London: Day and Son.

Lacroix, Octave

1873 *Beaux-Arts et beaux-arts appliqués à l'industrie. Expositions Internationales: Londres 1872.* Paris: Imprimerie Nationale.

Lavin, James D.

1997 *The Art and Tradition of the Zuloagas: Spanish Damascene from the Khalili Collection.* Exh. cat., Victoria and Albert Museum, London. London: The Khalili Family Trust.

Lefranc, Victor

1872 "International Exhibition of 1872." *Times* (London), January 30, p. 4.

Levy, Martin P.

2012 "Manufacturers at the World's Fairs: The Model of 1851." In Busch and Futter 2012, pp. 35–49.

Loyer, François

1992 "Le XIXe siècle est-il à la mode?" *Quarante-huit/Quatorze: La Revue du Musée d'Orsay,* no. 4, pp. 4–6.

Magazine of Art

1879 "Treasure-Houses of Art. I." *Magazine of Art: Illustrated* (London) 2, pp. 140–44.

Malgouyres, Philippe

2011 "Une Pendule en ivoire par Moreau à Châlons-en-Champagne." In *Barocke Kunststückh: Festschrift für Christian Theuerkauff / Sculpture Studies in Honour of Christian Theuerkauff,* pp. 202–7. Munich: Hirmer.

Mantz, Paul

1865 "Salon de 1865," part 2. *Gazette des Beaux-Arts* 19 (July), pp. 5–42.

Mesnard, Jules, ed.

1869 *Les Merveilles de l'art et de l'industrie: Antiquité, Moyen-Age, Renaissance, Temps modernes.* Paris: Librairie des Arts Industriels.

Notin, Véronique

1995a "Acquisitions. Limoges, Musée Municipal de l'Evêché: Charles Lepec, *Coffret mauresque à la joueuse de mandoline.*" *Revue du Louvre; La Revue des Musées de France,* no. 1 (February), p. 84, no. 21.

1995b "Acquisitions. Limoges, Musée Municipal de l'Evêché: Charles Lepec, *Assiette.*" *Revue du Louvre; La Revue des Musées de France,* no. 4 (October), p. 91, no. 34.

Olivier, Edith

1945 *Four Victorian Ladies of Wiltshire, with an Essay on Those Leisured Ladies.* London: Faber & Faber.

Ostergard, Derek, ed.

2001 *William Beckford, 1760–1844: An Eye for the Magnificent.* New Haven and London: Yale University Press.

Philadelphia Museum of Art

1978 *The Second Empire, 1852–1870: Art in France under Napoleon III.* Exh. cat., Philadelphia Museum of Art; Detroit Institute of Arts; Galeries Nationales du Grand Palais, Paris. Philadelphia: Philadelphia Museum of Art.

Phillips sale

1994 *The Remaining Contents of Heytesbury House, Warminster, Wilts.* Sale cat., Phillips, Bath, October 31.

Popelin, Claudius

1866 *L'Email des peintres.* Paris: A. Lévy.

Practical Magazine

1873 "Enamels by M. Charles Lepec, Paris." *Practical Magazine* 1, no. 4, pp. 261–63.

Pratt, Robert

1939 "Chaucer and the Visconti Libraries." *ELH: English Literary History* 6, no. 3, pp. 191–99.

Purcell, Katherine

1999 *Falize: A Dynasty of Jewelers.* London: Thames & Hudson.

Remington, Vanessa

2010 *Victorian Miniatures in the Collection of Her Majesty the Queen.* 2 vols. London: Royal Collection Enterprises.

Sanchez, Pierre

2005 *Dictionnaire des céramistes, peintres sur porcelaine, verre et émail, verriers et émailleurs, exposants dans les salons, expositions universelles, industrielles, d'art décoratif, et des manufactures nationales, 1700–1920.* 3 vols. Dijon: L'Echelle de Jacob.

Sotheby's Belgravia sale

1975 *English and Foreign Silver and Plated Wares and Objects of Vertu, 1825–1970.* Sale cat., Sotheby's Belgravia, London, July 10.

Times

1867 "The Great French Exhibition (From Our Special Correspondent)." *Times* (London), August 23, 1867, p. 8.

Victoria and Albert Museum

1952 *Exhibition of Victorian & Edwardian Decorative Arts: Catalogue.* Exh. cat., Victoria and Albert Museum, London. London: Her Majesty's Stationery Office.

Wainwright, Clive

1995 "Alfred Morrison: A Forgotten Patron and Collector." In *The Grosvenor House Art and Antiques Fair: 15th–24th June 1995; Handbook.* London: Grosvenor House.

Waring & Gillow sale

1920 *Antique and Modern English and Continental Furniture.* Sale cat., Waring & Gillow, London, October 26–December 3. Sale held at Basildon Park, Pangbourne, Berkshire.

Watkin, David, and Philip Hewat-Jaboor, eds.

2008 *Thomas Hope: Regency Designer.* Exh. cat., Bard Graduate Center for Studies in the Decorative Arts, Design, and Culture, New York. New Haven and London: Yale University Press.